THE DEFEAT OF THE SPANISH ARMADA

Queen Elizabeth I. The 'Armada' portrait by George Gower, from Woburn Abbey.

GARRETT MATTINGLY

THE DEFEAT
OF THE
SPANISH ARMADA

HOUGHTON MIFFLIN COMPANY BOSTON

By the same author

CATHERINE OF ARAGON
RENAISSANCE DIPLOMACY

First published 1959
Second American edition 1984
Copyright © 1959 by Garrett Mattingly

Library of Congress number: 83-82187
ISBN: 0-395-35237-1

10 9 8 7 6 5 4 3 2 1

Printed in Great Britain

CONTENTS

CONTENTS

To
Ruth and Edward Mack

ABOUT THE CALENDAR

THE dates in this book are all, unless otherwise specified, New Style — that is, according to the Gregorian calendar which everybody uses now and which, although it had only been proclaimed by Pope Gregory XIII in 1582, most of western Europe was already using by 1587. England, of course, was not. With sturdy conservatism the English resisted the innovation, and their vernal equinox continued for more than another century to occur on March 11th instead of on March 21st as it did across the Channel. Consequently English historians always say that the first day's battle between the English and the Spanish fleets took place on July 21st, 1588, while the Spanish always date it on the thirty-first of the month.

This puts any historian who is writing partly about English and partly about Continental events in a quandary. Some historians escape by writing $\frac{21}{31}$ July, but most people find dates repulsive enough without encountering them disguised as fractions. Consequently, since in the following narrative the sequence of events in England and on the Continent is often important, and to go back and forth between two calendars would become too confusing, I had to choose between Old Style and New Style. I chose New Style because it corresponds to the actual season, and at some seasons ten days do make a difference in how much daylight there is and what kind of weather one may expect. Readers who are disturbed by finding events in England dated by the Continental system can recover the traditional date by subtracting ten days. Days of the week, of course, remained the same. Sunday was still Sunday, in Rome as in London.

'A Thankfull Remembrance'. Popish plots and treasons from the beginning of the reign of Queen Elizabeth.

PREFACE

THE idea of writing a book about the defeat of the Spanish Armada first came to me, as it must have come to others, in June 1940, when the eyes of the world were again turned to the shores of England and their surrounding seas. If the idea attracted me, in spite of all that had already been written on the subject, it was because it seemed there might be some interest in replacing the narrative of the naval campaign in the broader European context in which it had once been viewed but from which, in the peaceful years before 1914, it had become more and more detached. To minds formed by A. T. Mahan and the theorists of empire the issue in 1588 seemed to be the command of the ocean seas and the opportunity to exploit the newly discovered routes to Asia and the Americas. To such minds it was rational and right to fight for economic interests, but absurd and rather shocking to fight about the relative validity of conflicting systems of ideas.

The men of 1588 did not think so. To them the clash of the English and Spanish fleets in the Channel was the beginning of Armageddon, of a final struggle to the death between the forces of light and the forces of darkness. Which side was which depended, of course, on where one stood, but all across Europe the lines were drawn, and though most of the nations were technically non-combatants there were no real neutrals. All Europe watched the battle in the Channel with breathless suspense because upon its outcome was felt to hang not just the fates of England and Scotland, France and the Netherlands, but of all Christendom. Ideological wars are revolutionary wars, easily transcending national boundaries, and always, at least in intention and in the imaginations of the men involved in them, total wars. It was easier in 1940 to appreciate this point of view than it had been in, say, 1890.

In 1940 I contemplated a short book based on the standard accounts and mainly devoted to pointing out the various issues which depended, or were felt to depend, on the success of the Spanish attempt to invade England, the first of those efforts by Continental military powers to

11

establish a European hegemony which have provided a recurrent pattern in modern history. Before I could get very far with my notion other matters intervened. Before I could get back to it I had acquired some acquaintance — no more than a nodding acquaintance certainly, but more than I would have supposed likely to befall a sedentary middle-aged historian — with some aspects of naval and amphibious operations, and with some of the waters through which the Armada had sailed.

When I had time to think about the Armada again, although it no longer seemed urgent to finish a book about it right away, the idea still appealed to me of doing one which would present the campaign not just as a naval duel between Spain and England but as the focus of the first great international crisis in modern history. Since there was no hurry I decided to start again, working this time from the original sources, in the archives and in print, and visiting or revisiting as many as possible of the places I would want to talk about, not because I had any conviction of the higher purity of such procedures, or even because I expected to make any startling discoveries, but because that is the way I enjoy working. Besides, Professor Michael Lewis's brilliant series of articles in *The Mariner's Mirror*, 'Armada Guns' (vols. XXVIII–IX, 1942–3), had shown me that a fresh eye and a few fresh documents could make evidence long in the public domain yield a fresh and significant interpretation, and my friend Bernard DeVoto's *The Year of Decision* (1943) and *Across the Wide Missouri*, the manuscript of which I began to read not long after I got out of uniform, made me wonder whether it might not be possible, with luck, to re-create for the late sixteenth century a series of connected historical scenes perhaps half as alive as those DeVoto evoked from the history of the Rocky Mountain West.

In the end I found no startling fresh interpretation, but excavations among the unpublished documents and re-examination of the published ones did yield scraps of new evidence weakening certain accepted views and strengthening others. And the same spade-work did turn up, now and then, a communicative and resonant phrase or a concrete visual image to freshen a familiar tale. So, although this account agrees in the main with currently accepted scholarship, I hope it may prove to have enough shifts of emphasis and unfamiliar details to keep it from seeming completely trite.

Since this book is addressed not to specialists but to the general reader interested in history there are no footnotes. But on the chance that some student of the period, turning these pages, might feel a bit of curiosity about the grounds for some judgment or assertion, I have appended a general account of the documents and printed books most relied on, followed by short notes on the chief sources for each chapter with special reference to the evidence for any views which depart from those generally accepted.

My exploration of the archives was assisted by a Fulbright research fellowship and two grants from the John Simon Guggenheim Foundation. The many librarians, curators and archivists in England, on the Continent and in the United States, whose helpfulness I have shamelessly exploited will forgive me if I do not here thank them all by name. I cannot forgo a special word of thanks to Dr Ricardo Magdaleno and his staff at the Archivo General de Simancas for many kindnesses to myself and to my students, and to Dr Louis B. Wright and his staff at the Folger Shakespeare Library, Washington, D.C. for their sympathetic co-operation. The cordial interest and encouragement of Lieutenant-Admiral J. T. Furstner, and the unstinting generosity with which Professor T. H. Milo of the University of Leiden placed at my disposal his expert knowledge of Dutch naval history and its archival sources, made my all too brief stay in Holland far more fruitful than it could otherwise have been. My friends Ida and Leo Gershoy read most of the manuscript and made very helpful suggestions, and Edward Mack went painstakingly over every line of it, as he has done with almost everything I have written for the past thirty years. Mr Charles H. Carter also curry-combed the entire manuscript and helped prepare the Index. I am indebted to the Tides and Currents Division of the U.S. Coast and Geodetic Survey for a tide-table, to my colleague Professor Jan Schilt of Columbia University's Department of Astronomy for advice about celestial phenomena, and to Dr Hugh S. Rice of the Hayden Planetarium for additional help with puzzles involving the heavens and the tides and tidal currents in the Channel. In every stage of research and writing I have taken my wife's full participation so much for granted that this seems to me, as usual, as much her book as mine.

A sketch of the trial of Mary Stuart, Queen of Scots, preserved among the papers of Robert Beale (1541–1601), the clerk to Elizabeth I's Council.

I

CURTAIN-RAISER

FOTHERINGHAY, FEBRUARY 18TH, 1587

MR BEALE had not brought the warrant until Sunday evening, but by Wednesday morning, before dawn outlined its high windows, the great hall at Fotheringhay was ready. Though the Earl of Shrewsbury had returned only the day before nobody wanted any more delay. Nobody knew what messenger might be riding on the London road. Nobody knew which of the others might not weaken if they waited another day.

The hall had been cleared of all its ordinary furniture. Half-way along its length a huge fire of logs blazing in the chimney battled against the creeping chill. Towards the upper end of the hall they had set up a small platform like a miniature stage for travelling actors, jutting twelve feet into the hall, eight or nine feet wide and less than three feet high. At one side a pair of stairs led up to it, and the fresh wood of the scaffolding had everywhere been decently covered in black velvet. On the platform in line with the stairs stood a single high-backed chair, also draped in black, and three or four feet in front of it a black cushion. Next to the cushion and rising above it something like a little low bench showed where the velvet imperfectly concealed an ordinary wooden chopping-block. By seven in the morning the stage managers were satisfied, the sheriff's men trying to look soldierly in morion and breastplate and to hold their halberds stiffly had taken their places, and the chosen audience, two hundred or more knights and gentlemen of the neighbourhood peremptorily summoned for that early hour, had filed into the lower end of the hall.

The star kept them waiting more than three hours. In the almost thirty years since she had wedded a future king of France in the glittering, devious Court beside the Loire she had failed repeatedly to learn some of the more important lessons of politics, but she had learned how to dominate a scene. She entered through a little door at the side, and before they saw her was already in the great hall, walking towards the dais, six of her own people two by two behind her, oblivious of the stir and rustle as her audience craned forward, oblivious apparently of the officer on whose sleeve her hand rested — walking as quietly, thought one pious soul, as if she were going to her prayers. Only for a moment, as she mounted the steps and before she sank back into the black-draped chair, did she seem to need the supporting arm, and if her hands trembled before she locked them in her lap no one saw. Then, as if acknowledging the plaudits of a multitude (though the hall was very still), she turned for the first time to face her audience and, some thought, she smiled.

Against the black velvet of the chair and dais her figure, clad in black velvet, was almost lost. The grey winter daylight dulled the gleam of white hands, the glint of yellow gold in her kerchief and of red gold in the piled masses of auburn hair beneath. But the audience could see clearly enough the delicate frill of white lace at her throat, and above it, a white heart-shaped petal against the blackness, the face with its great dark eyes and tiny wistful mouth. This was she for whom Rizzio had died; and Darnley, the young fool; and Huntly, and Norfolk, and Babington and a thousand nameless men on the moors and gallows of the north. This was she whose legend had hung over England like a sword ever since she had hastened across its borders with her subjects in pursuit. This was the last captive princess of romance, the Dowager Queen of France, the exiled Queen of Scotland, the heir to the English throne and (there must have been some among the silent witnesses who thought so) at this very moment, if she had her rights, England's lawful queen. This was Mary Stuart, Queen of Scots. For a moment she held all their eyes, then she sank back into the darkness of her chair and turned her grave inattention to her judges. She was satisfied that her audience would look at no one else.

The earls of Kent and Shrewsbury who had entered with her, almost unobserved, had seated themselves opposite, and Mr Beale was standing clearing his throat and crackling the parchment of the warrant he had to read. He need not have been nervous. One doubts whether anyone was listening. 'Stubborn disobedience ... incitement to insurrection ... against the life and person of her sacred Majesty ... high treason ... death.' Nothing in the phrases could have mattered to Mary Stuart or to any person in the hall. Everyone knew that this was not the sentence for a crime. This was another stroke in a political duel which had been going on as long as most of them could remember, which had begun, indeed, before either of the enemy queens was born. Sixty years ago the parties had begun to form, the party of the old religion, the party of the new, and always by some trick of Fate one party or the other, and usually both, had been rallied and led by a woman. Catherine of Aragon against Anne Boleyn,

Mary Tudor against Elizabeth Tudor, Elizabeth Tudor against Mary of Lorraine, and now, for nearly thirty years, Elizabeth Tudor against Mary Stuart, the prisoner on the scaffold. The shrewdest politicians might wonder how for almost two decades England had managed to contain both these predestinate enemies and keep them both alive.

Whatever Elizabeth had done, Mary Stuart had, of course, sought by every means in her power to destroy her cousin and bring her low. In a duel to the death like theirs there were no foul strokes. When the arms of strength had fallen from her hands she had used whatever weapons weakness could grasp: lies, tears, evasions, threats and pleadings, and the hands and lives of whatever men her crowns, her beauty or her faith could win to her cause. They had proved two-edged weapons at last; but if they cut her now she had dealt wounds with them, and kept her cousin's realm in greater turmoil from her English prison than ever she had been able to do from her Scottish throne. And she meant to strike one blow more. She turned a bored chin on Mr Beale's concluding phrases.

The Dean of Peterborough was even more nervous than Mr Beale. She let him repeat his stumbling exordium three times before she cut him contemptuously short. 'Mr Dean,' she told him, 'I shall die as I have lived, in the true and holy Catholic faith. All you can say to me on that score is but vain, and all your prayers, I think, can avail me but little.'

This, she was sure, was the one weapon which would not turn in her hand. She had been closely watched at Fotheringhay, but not so closely that she could have no word from the daring subtle men who slipped in and out of the Channel ports in disguise. The north was Catholic, they said, and the west; and even here in the heretic's own strongholds, even in the Midlands, even in London, more and more turned daily to the ancient faith. While the heir to the throne was a Catholic, likely to succeed without a struggle on her heretic cousin's death, those thousands had been quiet; but now should the heretic slay her orthodox successor surely they would rise in their wrath to sweep away all this iniquity. And there were Catholic kings beyond the seas who would be more eager to avenge the Queen of Scots dead than ever they had been to keep her alive.

That Mary herself was a devout Catholic is one of the few things about her not open to dispute, but it was not enough for her simply to die in her faith. The duel would go on. All men must know that she had died not only in her faith but for it. Perhaps she had not always been its steadiest pillar. Perhaps her dubious intrigues had sometimes harmed her cause more than her devotion had helped it. Now the glittering sweep of the axe would cut off for ever the burden of old mistakes, silence the whispered slanders, and her blood would cry out for vengeance on her enemies more unmistakably than her living voice could ever have done again. For years she had favoured an ambiguous motto: 'My end is my beginning.' Martyrdom might make good both the promise and the threat. She had only to play this last scene well.

So she held the crucifix high, visible all down the long hall, as she flung defiance at her judges, and her voice rose with a kind of triumph above the voice of the Dean of Peterborough, always higher and clearer than his rising tones, arching over the vehement English prayers the mysterious dominating invocations of the ancient faith. The Queen's voice held on for a minute after the clergyman had finished. Her words were in English now; she was praying for the people of England and for the soul of her royal cousin Elizabeth; she was forgiving all her enemies. Then for a moment her ladies were busy about her. The black velvet gown fell below her knees revealing underbodice and petticoat of crimson silk, and she stepped forward suddenly, shockingly, in the colour of martyrdom, blood red from top to toe, against the sombre background. Quietly she knelt and bowed herself low over the little chopping-block. 'In manus tuas, domine ... ' and they heard twice the dull chunk of the axe.

There was one more ceremony to accomplish. The executioner must exhibit the head and speak the customary words. The masked black figure stooped and rose, crying in a loud voice: 'Long live the Queen!' But all he held in his hand that had belonged to the rival queen of hearts was a kerchief, and pinned to it an elaborate auburn wig. Rolled nearer the edge of the platform, shrunken and withered and grey, with a sparse silver stubble on the small shiny skull was the head of the martyr. Mary Stuart had always known how to embarrass her enemies.

A sketch of the execution of Mary Stuart, from the papers of Robert Beale, who carried the death-warrant to Fotheringay.

The execution of Mary Stuart, Queen of Scots, in 1587.

Den VIII february werde onthalst Maria
Stuart Schots Coninginne s'leuende Roomsch Catho-
lyck Hebbende gefocht veel onrust en ghy te richten Haer selven
mee ter te maecken van Engelant t'welck Haer van der Raet
ofte parlement solemnelyck werde vertoont, Anno 1587.

Metreu XIII. fol. XIII. en XIIII. b.

II

SIMPLICITY OF A CITY

LONDON, FEBRUARY 19TH, 1587

IN the wake of the rider from Fotheringhay bonfires blazed, and when London heard his news the citizens rang joy-bells, fired salvos and illuminated every street. An intolerable cloud had been lifted; a great dread was gone for ever. The continued life of Mary Stuart had become a threat to the life of every Londoner, a threat to everything England had become since the accession of Elizabeth. In the past year the public demand for Mary's death had risen to a continuous clamour. While Mary lived nothing was safe.

In the first place Queen Elizabeth's last birthday had been her fifty-third. Even if the 'best match in her parish' still had suitors — and there had been no suitors since Anjou — no one could pretend any longer that Elizabeth would ever have a child. She was the last of the Tudors, and her heir Mary Stuart ten years her junior and 'in health metely good'. Politicians might canvass for ever the other possibilities for the crown but they could agree on none of them and were not likely to. As long as Mary lived the chances were that she would follow her cousin on the throne. Even Mary's bitterest enemies on the Queen's Council — Leicester and Burghley, Hatton and Walsingham — had tried to keep open a line of retreat into Mary's camp in case the Queen of Scots survived their mistress. And when the most outspoken political leaders of the Protestant party thought it prudent to assure Mary of the reversion of their loyalty it was only natural that lesser men should try to carry water on both shoulders, and that the discontented lords and gentry of the north should hope through Mary to triumph over their enemies and with her to restore the old religion and the old times. Ever since Elizabeth ascended the throne there had smouldered in England a party of Catholic reaction, bedded on the embers of feudal prerogative and local conservatism, fanned fitfully by Spanish intriguers and mission priests. The bloodshed with which the government had put down the rising in the north had dampened the fire, not quenched it; it sucked a secret draught of hope from the fact that the heir apparent was a Catholic. While Mary lived the

Catholic party, as a potential political faction in the State, would never die.

Even to such Londoners as had cheerfully gone to mass in old Queen Mary's time, choking down whatever disgust they felt at the reek of the fires in Smithfield, even to such as would go again without obvious reluctance if that were the best way to secure their business and their families, even to such yeomen and country gentry as in spite of their prosperity under the new dispensation cherished a kind of affection for the old, the continued life of the Catholic party presented a dreadful menace. Scotland had shown the impossibility of a Catholic sovereign at the head of a Protestant State, even when the whole ordinance of religion did not depend, as in England it did, directly upon the Crown. And whatever had been true a generation ago when Catherine of Aragon's daughter had brought back the Church to Rome, whatever might be true now of the outlying parts of the realm in this twenty-ninth year of the reign of Elizabeth, the heart and strength of England, the southern and eastern counties, the flourishing seaport towns, and the great city of London itself were Protestant. Too many lords and gentlemen had committed their political fortunes to the new religion; too many merchants and tradesmen made their livings in ways which a change in church government would surely disrupt; too many yeomen and artisans had listened in whitewashed churches to preachers in Geneva bands. A whole generation had grown up, nurtured on the English Bible and Cranmer's *Book of Common Prayer* and Foxe's *Book of Martyrs*; a whole generation had grown up to hate and fear the papists and the Spaniards and foreign domination. If Mary Stuart came to the throne and tried, as considering her own history and the character of those who would be about her she surely would, to restore the Roman Catholic Church, there would be not such local flare-ups as Wyatt's brief rebellion but widespread, bitter religious war.

No one needed to tell Londoners what civil war would be like. For a hundred years England had been haunted by the fear that a failure in the Tudor line would toss the crown back into the arena to be fought for by contending factions, a recurrence of the generation of anarchy which we call the Wars of the Roses. But the worst of those struggles of the barons about the throne, of York and Lancaster's long jars, the chronicles of which in verse and prose were enjoying a kind of anxious popularity at the booksellers' and on the stage, would, men knew, prove mere armed riots beside the horrors of a civil war embittered by religion. The stories of Haarlem and Antwerp were commonplace, and there were plenty of merchants and plenty of refugees to tell the Londoners what Flanders and Brabant had been like twenty years ago and what they were like now. Men, now bearded, had been frightened when children by the tale of St Bartholomew's, and it was not only children who were frightened. The blood-brimmed gutters of Paris, the corpses floating in the Loire, the smoking desolation in Normandy, were not old wives' tales. If some of the beggars whose whines drew pennies from kind-hearted citizens had never been nearer the prisons of the Inquisition than Ipswich gaol, some of the stumps and scars told less than the plain truth. So when parsons reminded their parishioners that a land where men denied the authority of their rightful rulers and drew their swords on one another was a land accursed there were tightened lips and grim nods among the congregation, and when the people bent their heads to pray for the life of Our Gracious Sovereign Queen Elizabeth there was desperate sincerity in their voices.

The deepest longing of the troubled and divided sixteenth century was for unity and peace, and the only effective symbol men could find for the social order they craved was the person of a monarch. So the life of even the wickedest prince, most preachers taught, was sacred, and the duty of obedience was explicit no matter what the character of the ruler. Gradually that ultimate allegiance once given to the universal Church was being transferred to secular sovereigns, in preparation for its further transference to an abstraction called the National State when men should think of it. The blasphemous doctrine of the divinity of kings was beginning to be in the air, in England as everywhere in Europe. The sixteenth century belonged to the monarchs.

But in England the general doctrine of the divine right of kings was obscured for the moment by a purely personal equation. England's Elizabeth was, Englishmen agreed, a phoenix, singular in her kind, incommensurable by any general standard. In that they were more right than they knew. There has never been anything in history like the forty-five-year-long love affair between Elizabeth Tudor and the people of England. It is hard, now, to say just how it began, or to analyse all the elements that went into it, but it rose in those years to a fervour the intense sincerity of which we cannot doubt, however stilted and rhetorical we may find its expression.

On both sides, no doubt, one may discern vanity and calculation and selfishness; probably those are necessary elements in any love affair. If Elizabeth Tudor was to rule England at all — and she had all a Tudor's determination to rule — she had to win the love of her people because there was nothing else she could depend on. She had mounted a throne already tottering. The treasury was empty, the currency debased, the people impoverished and dismayed and divided against themselves. The kingdom had just lost its last foothold on the Continent — Calais, the last relic of Plantagenet glory — and could not pretend that it had not been beaten by the French. All the symptoms of disintegration and despair which in a few years were to send the neighbouring kingdom of France sliding down into anarchy seemed to be present in England in more acute form; less serious foreign humiliations and internal stresses had heralded, a century before, the Wars of the Roses. England had not a friend or ally in Europe, only a ring of watchful enemies waiting to pounce at the first sign of weakness, restrained only by their distrust of one another. And Elizabeth came to this tottering throne with a less certain right to it than almost any of her predecessors, to try the unheard of experiment of ruling alone, an unmarried queen. She had to fend off foreign dangers and dominate a greedy ambitious nobility, and a people notoriously the most tumultuous and unruly in Europe, with no resources save her woman's wit.

In a day when the successful monarchies were being fashioned into efficient centralized despotisms, when the weakest of the Valois could flout and bilk his Estates General at the moment of his greatest weakness, she had to govern, all her life, through a constitution which the political theorists of the Continent would have described, had they known the words, as an absurd feudal anachronism. All her life her sovereign power was doubtful and circumscribed, and her normal revenue less than that which Philip II was supposed to draw from his single duchy of Milan. She never had any standing army except a handful of ornamental guards, or any police beyond what was furnished by her practically independent local magistrates; and though in the years of her greatest danger her Secretary Sir Francis Walsingham built up for her protection what some historians have described with awe as 'an omnipresent network of spies', this impressive system of counter-espionage in England dwindles on inspection to a few underpaid agents of varying ability whose efforts were supplemented by casual informers and correlated by a single clerk who also handled much of Walsingham's ordinary correspondence — a system hardly larger or more efficient, except for the intelligence of its direction and the zeal of its volunteer aids, than that which every first-rate ambassador was expected to maintain for his own information, one which the governments of Florence or Venice would have smiled at as inadequate for the police of a single city. There was no way Elizabeth Tudor could govern the English by force. She ruled them by the arts by which a clever woman rules a lover.

From the first she courted them, posed for them, cajoled them. It was for them she made herself beautiful and a little remote, and surrounded by a glittering Court; for them she made herself suddenly affable and familiar and beguiling, jolting annually hundreds of weary miles over atrocious roads so that more of them might see her, sitting annually through dozens of jumbled Latin orations and stupid pageants, dancing gracefully in scores of manor houses, and always finding the right word, the right smile to warm their hearts. With sure instinct she composed herself into a picture of what they wanted her to be, as a lover must. She was proud and imperious often (a queen should be like a queen), and she did not forget sometimes to make them jealous and uneasy. She varied her caresses with slaps, and at times she could receive their well-meant advice with shrill scorn, warning them not to meddle with the affairs of princes, boasting that she could do without them but they could not do without her, and producing all the sudden tempest of a lover's quarrel to follow it with sunshine equally overwhelming. In a word, she was careful never to bore them but equally careful to assure them, often enough so they never forgot, that she loved them better than anything else. How much art there was in her conduct, and how much nature, a mere historian cannot be expected to say when King Solomon confessed himself baffled by a simpler problem.

If not all Elizabeth's courtship of her people was spontaneous, if she had her own urgent reasons for needing to win and hold their love, knowing that her throne rested on nothing else, her people on their side could find for their loyal affection, as the years went by, an increasingly solid basis of self-interest. In the midst of a Europe torn by foreign and civil war they remained placidly at peace. No royal tax-gatherers took from their pockets the fruits of their industry. Prices were high, business was good, money was plentiful; and the profits could be confidently ploughed back into land and shipping and the growing production of textiles, and of metals in which for the first time England was beginning to take a notable place in the world. No soldiers clanked through the streets except those home from fighting in foreign quarrels, and a sudden knock on the door at night would be only a neighbour or a carter. A man might drink his beer in peace and hold what opinions he liked, within reason of course, secure in the knowledge that an occasional attendance at the parish church was all the conformity the Queen expected. All in all Elizabeth's rule was the mildest and the most benign that Englishmen could remember, and England's prosperity was emphasized by the darkness and disorder of the surrounding world. But though men may suffer a government which taxes them lightly and lets them pretty much alone they do not develop a passionate devotion to it on that account.

Coquetry, of course, is a game that two can play at. In part, the protestations of devotion with which her subjects responded to Elizabeth's advances were just the extravagant convention of the time, and some of them like as not were meant to sugar a request for some personal advantage. But on both sides there was more than just a game, unless it is possible to misread all the records of the age. To Englishmen who never saw Her Majesty except over the shoulders of a crowd as she passed along a highway she was still Gloriana, a faery queen who cast over her island and over them all a golden spell; she was the living palladium of England, the incarnation of something they had dreamed. Her mystically guarded virginity was not only their pledge of independence from foreign princes, of security amidst the ills that troubled less happy lands; it made her somehow belong to all of them.

Nor to Elizabeth, either, can it have been all a game. She had never had a husband; she would never have a child. How much, one wonders, did the passion she gave to her people and the adoration they repaid her make up to her for what she had missed? And how much did they love her, the perfumed courtiers, the country squires, the yeomen and artisans and hard-handed seamen and rustic labourers, because she kept England peaceful and prosperous; and how much simply because when she told them at the beginning of her reign that nothing — no worldly thing under the sun — was so dear to her as their love, when she told them near the end of it, 'though you have had and may have many mightier and wiser princes, yet you never have had nor shall have any that will love you better', they heard something that made them believe it? The relation between Elizabeth and her people, like all great love affairs, keeps its final secret.

If Mary Stuart's life had merely menaced the English with the threat of civil war after the Queen's death it is likely that they would have gone on vaguely worrying about it, shaking their heads and doing nothing. But every year after the Queen of Scots crossed the border made it increasingly clear that the very existence of the Catholic heir was a daily threat to the life of their Queen. Some madman, some fanatic, some hired desperado had only to get near enough to use a knife or pistol — and Elizabeth was notoriously careless of her safety, notoriously went about unguarded — and the whole structure of the government would come crashing down: there would be no Council, no magistrates, no royal officials anywhere (their commissions would all expire on the Queen's death), no authority to punish the assassins, and indeed no certain authority at all until Mary Stuart had succeeded to her cousin's throne. It would not matter that most of the Catholics of the realm would be as horrified as anyone else by such an act of violence. It would not even matter whether Mary herself had approved the act. One desperate man, tempted by the enormous stakes, could change the history of England.

Ever since the rising in the north there had been plots and rumours of plots, and in recent years they had come thick and fast. Perhaps the city heard of more than there ever were, and perhaps the Puritan party in the government made them all seem more formidable in the telling than they could have proved in the acting, but the danger was real enough. A half-crazed youth who had boasted he would kill the Queen was taken, pistol in hand, within a hundred yards of her. Then the papers found on Francis Throckmorton revealed a widespread Catholic plot for a rising, the liberation of Mary, the assassination of the Queen and the invasion of the realm by Guisard troops. Then came William Parry's cold-blooded revelation that he had been promised plenary absolution from Rome for the murder of the Queen, besides substantial earthly benefits, and had come to England expressly for that purpose. England was still shuddering at that danger avoided when news came from Delft that a Burgundian serving man — one Gérard, secretly a Catholic — had succeeded where others had spectacularly failed and shot down in his own house the Prince of Orange, the second champion of the Protestant cause. Men remembered again the murder of Admiral Coligny, twelve years before, once the third in a triumvirate of Protestant leaders. Now only Elizabeth was left. And from all the attempts on Elizabeth's life one person stood to profit — Mary Stuart. All over England that autumn the nobles and principal gentlemen of the several counties bound themselves by a solemn Bond of Association to support and save the Queen from any plots in furtherance of a pretended title to her crown, and to proceed by their own forces against all persons that shall act or counsel anything tending to the harm of Her Majesty's person, to the utter extermination of them, their counsellors, aiders and abetters. Murder would be answered, if necessary, by murder and — their fear of civil war doubled by their fear for the life of

Elizabeth — the English were determined that next time Mary should not escape.

For the next time, Anthony Babington's unlucky conspiracy, they had had to wait a little less than two years. That Anthony Babington and his friends really meant to assassinate the Queen, and that they hoped thereby to secure the succession to the Queen of Scots, no one doubted at the time, and there can be little doubt now. That Mary herself was as deep in the plot as men then believed there may be some reasonable doubt, but even had she been wholly without knowledge of it her innocence would not have mattered much to the Londoners. It was, it could only be, in her interest as all the other plots had been, and as long as she lived the life of Queen Elizabeth would be in danger. Therefore, at the news of Mary's execution, the Londoners rang bells and lit bonfires and went about the streets with pipe and tabor, 'as if', said a contemporary witness, 'they believed a new era had begun in which all men would live in peace'.

III

PERPLEXITY OF A QUEEN

GREENWICH, FEBRUARY 19TH – 22ND, 1587

THE issue which seemed so simple to the Londoners did not seem simple at all to their queen. Elizabeth was still at Greenwich, that pleasantest of her palaces, whose lawns ran down to Thameside and whose many windows watched the tall ships going up and down the chief road of her kingdom. Only a week ago at Greenwich she had finally signed the warrant for Mary's execution, a paper which her new Secretary, Mr William Davison, had been keeping by him until the anxiety of her people and the arguments of her Council should wear down her resistance. When she had signed it she reminded Davison that there were more seemly ways for a queen to die than at the hands of the public executioner. But a public execution was exactly what her councillors were bent on, and without another word to the Queen they gave Mr Beale the necessary letters. Elizabeth heard no more about it, but if she really believed that the men who, ever since early November, had been besieging her collectively and severally with all the arts and arguments at their command for her signature to that warrant would not act upon it, now that they had it in their hands, she was guilty of one of her rare mistakes about her advisers. With her born instinct for politics and her seasoned knowledge of the game she must have known what news would soon be on the road from Fotheringhay.

When the Earl of Shrewsbury's son, having taken less than twenty-four hours to travel the long muddy road, pulled up his blown horse in the courtyard at Greenwich the Queen was just mounting for the hunt, and in the confusion did not see him. So the messenger carried to Burghley news which Burghley was glad enough to hear, but, with the wise passiveness which years of dealing with Elizabeth had taught him, quite content to let someone else pass on to the Queen. So apparently were all her councillors. London rang with the news and the corridors of Greenwich buzzed with it before Elizabeth returned to her palace, and the moment for telling her could be postponed no longer.

We have two accounts of how she took the news, two contradictory

28

accounts — just as one learns to expect where Elizabeth is concerned. A nameless informant told Mr Secretary Davison, as he mournfully sets down in the record of his tribulations, that when told of the execution of the Queen of Scots Her Grace's customary demeanour was unchanged and she showed no sign of any emotion. But Mary's son, King James VI of Scotland, heard that when the Queen of England learned of the tragedy of Fotheringhay she was utterly astonished and fell into such deep grief of mind, accompanied by unfeigned weeping, as the like had never been seen in her for any accident in her life.

Both accounts this time may be partly true. To guard her thoughts and her emotions was a lesson Elizabeth had learned in her sister's reign. If she felt any surprise on hearing that her warrant had done its work (and whatever surprise she felt cannot have been overwhelming), her first instinct would have been not to betray it among the motley press of courtiers and onlookers who thronged the more public parts of the palace. If Elizabeth wept while her people rejoiced, she did not do so where they could see her.

No doubt she wept afterwards, before a more appropriate audience. She had need to summon tears. Of all the dangers which the execution of the Queen of Scots entailed the most obvious and immediate was from Scotland. His Majesty James VI had been reared largely by his mother's enemies. His principal tutor in the formative years of his youth had ornamented his tutorial function by publishing a book about that God-abandoned woman Mary Stuart in language which any translator would do well to leave in the indecent obscurity of a learned tongue, a book the point of which was that among other notorious crimes Mary had been guilty of murdering the father of her child. Even after he escaped from Buchanan's tutelage James had shown no excessive enthusiasm for his mother's cause, his principal anxiety about her having been that the English should keep her safe in prison. His purest feeling on hearing of his mother's death was probably relief.

It is awkward, however, for a king to have his mother the victim of a public executioner, and not least awkward for a king of Scots whose turbulent people did not relish seeing their ancient privilege of exterminating their own kings usurped by the hereditary enemy across the border. There would be plenty of warlike Scottish lords to encourage James to avenge his mother's death upon the English with fire and sword in the old fashion, and plenty of encouragement from abroad for such a foray. Mary was a Catholic heroine, the former Queen of France and

29

sister-in-law to the king now ruling; she was also the cousin and political ally of the powerful Duke of Guise. More powers than Scotland would be offended by Mary's execution, and all would be eager to push Mary's son into the front rank of the avengers. In Scotland, Elizabeth heard, the anti-English party grew daily stronger, daily more insistent that Mary's death at the hands of her gaolers would be immediate cause for war. If James were to evade the perilous prominence which honour seemed to thrust upon him he would need all the help Elizabeth's tergiversation could afford. Later, Mr Secretary Walsingham, who would have scorned to shed one tear for Mary Stuart, was to urge Elizabeth to award the King of Scots a tremendous pension by way of bribe and blackmail, to open her purse wider to other purchasable Scots, and to take stronger measures to arm the northern borders. Honest Walsingham was frantic at his mistress's indifference to the threat that an invasion from the north would be added to England's other dangers. But Elizabeth had found tears cheaper than blood or gold. She would not pay more for Scotland's neutrality than James's lowest price.

Tears, however, were only the first instalment of the payment. On Friday Christopher Hatton, her old friend and new Lord Chancellor, found the Queen dark as a thundercloud and blaming chiefly Davison for having been so rash as to let the warrant out of his hands without her express permission. On Saturday she poured out on the full assembly of her Privy Council the unstoppered vials of her wrath. One would give a good deal for an unexpurgated transcript of the royal eloquence that crisped the beards of Elizabethan councillors, and reduced toughened courtiers like the Lord Admiral and Lord Buckhurst and even the great Burghley himself, to tears and incoherence. We have the word of those who served her that the full spate of the Queen's wrath was awful to behold and terrible to suffer, but this outburst was something special. In all her reign, one councillor said afterwards, he had never seen Her Grace so much moved. The gist of it was that though the dignified councillors, cringing like whipped schoolboys, might escape with no more than a dreadful tongue lashing, one victim she would have. Although her councillors went on their knees to dissuade her, order was taken for the arrest of Mr Secretary Davison and his immediate conveyance to the Tower. That was drastic action. When a Tudor councillor of Davison's station went through Traitor's Gate he rarely emerged in one piece. Elizabeth seemed to be anticipating the cynicism of one of her Scottish friends who, in pointing out that if Davison were sacrificed Scotland might be appeased, found occasion to observe that often 'necesse est unum mori pro populo'.

In the end the payment did not go as far as Davison's head. The lords who tried the unlucky man found him guilty as accused, sentenced him to a fine of ten thousand marks and to confinement in the Tower at the pleasure of the Queen, and with that the Scots were sulkily satisfied. Confinement in the Tower might be extremely disagreeable, or it might be as light as that Elizabeth herself had once incurred. It seems unlikely that Davison's was harsh, and eighteen months later, when the noise of greater events had diverted attention from him, he was quietly released. The heavy fine levied against him was all remitted, and he went on drawing his salary as Secretary. The beggary of which he later complained was beggary only in a very relative sense.

It is impossible not to be sorry for the man as he disappears so abruptly from history, but it is possible to be too sorry. Almost his only noteworthy duties in his new post of Secretary were those which drew on his ruin, but there was a stiffness about William Davison which makes one wonder how long he would have lasted in any case in an environment in which flexibility, even a certain sinuosity, was one of the first requisites of survival. Once the warrant was signed Elizabeth had approached him, obliquely at first, as to whether there was not some way in which Mary could be removed less opprobrious than a public execution. Davison would not understand her, and when he did would not pretend not to be shocked. When she made her meaning unmistakable he sulkily undertook to write at her direction to Sir Amias Paulet in the matter, and later returned Paulet's indignant refusal to shed Mary's blood without law or warrant with, one suspects, just the air of righteous approval calculated to evoke Elizabeth's scornful outburst against the precise and dainty Puritans who served her nowadays. Nor would her new Secretary have been exempt from her scorn. Historians insensitive to the shifting moral accents of the centuries have applauded Davison's attitude and condemned Elizabeth's — forgetting that Mary's life was equally forfeit in either case, that the custom of the day regarded the assassination of royalties with a tolerance it could not extend to their legal execution, forgetting that both Davison and Paulet had taken the Bond of the Association to perform, in only slightly different circumstances, the act they now refused. The fact was that the grim-faced lords about her, their nerves tautened too long by complex anxieties, had sunk their differences in a common conspiracy to drive Elizabeth into an irrevocable act, and

Elizabeth knew it. She had given Davison a chance to elude the noose contracting about them both; he had only drawn it tighter.

She had warned him at least once. She told him when the warrant was in his hands, but before it had been sent to Fotheringhay, that she had dreamed the Queen of Scots was dead by his act, unknown to her, and that she had been so full of grief and so angry with him that had he been at hand she would have done him a mischief. Davison only replied he was glad he was not at hand. Had she warned him earlier? When he left her to get the Great Seal for the death warrant from the Lord Chancellor she directed him to stop at the London house where for some weeks Sir Francis Walsingham had been suffering an illness providentially prolonged, and to show the signed warrant to the Senior Secretary, adding: 'The grief thereof will go near to kill him outright.' Did she only mean a somewhat heartless joke upon Walsingham's notorious implacable hatred of the Queen of Scots? Elizabeth's ironies were often more devious than that. Perhaps she meant to make Davison wonder whether, if the mere sight of the warrant were intended for a tonic, the news of Mary's death would not cure his colleague altogether. Poor rigid Davison was not the man to take that sort of hint. But it is hard not to feel a sympathy for Camden's view that Davison was a chosen scapegoat, and that the jealous factions who had eased his sudden rise to his great post had foreseen that disaster for at least one of their number would follow from Mary's ruin. Certainly, when Davison was suddenly swept from the board, his room was welcome to the players who remained.

Elizabeth's attitude towards Davison was not for Scottish consumption only. It was for all Europe. To Mary's former brother-in-law, the King of France, she wrote an elaborate account of her astonishment, her rage and her sorrow which the diplomats at Paris spread broadcast. The Venetian ambassador told the Signory that the Queen of England bitterly regretted that, having signed the warrant and given it to Davison only because she hoped by doing so to satisfy the demands of her subjects, her officer had been so rash as to overstep his commission. She had ordered Davison to be arrested and deprived of his office; she meant to do all she could to make manifest her grief. Other Governments heard similar stories, and in London the Queen's most intimate councillors seem to have been genuinely alarmed by the consequences of their act, genuinely concerned by its effect on her. Even Mendoza, her bitterest enemy, longing in Paris for his return to London behind the pikes of his old comrades in Flanders, wrote to Philip II that the Queen of England was so grief-stricken at

Sir Francis Walsingham (1530–90). Painting after John de Critz the Elder (?).

Mary's death that she had taken to her bed. Elizabeth, at need, was a remarkable actress, but if this was acting she had never given a more convincing performance.

We need not be too sure that it was all acting. About a character so complex as Elizabeth's it is safer never to be too sure of anything. One may doubt that Elizabeth had quite succeeded in hiding from herself the most probable consequence of her giving Davison the signed warrant, that her surprise at the turn of events was quite unfeigned. And one may discount the sincerity of her affection for her sister of Scotland. She had no ties with Mary except those of enmity, and had the deadliest threat to her life and her kingdom been terminated in some other fashion one suspects that Elizabeth could have mastered her grief. But neither personal sorrow nor personal remorse need have had any part in what Elizabeth regretted. In the event that had overtaken her there was ample cause for tears. Better perhaps than anyone else in England Elizabeth could see how completely that falling axe at Fotheringhay had sheared through the chief link that bound England to the past.

At fifty-three it is not easy to forsake a past in which one has been brilliantly successful, and face a world of new and untried conditions. From the beginning of her reign, after a brief disastrous experiment in France — an experiment which had taught her the uncertain chances of war and its certain costs — Elizabeth had avoided, whenever possible, every irrevocable commitment. Her foreign policy was to have no foreign policy not alterable by the lightest touch on the helm. Her consistency was in being always inconsistent. 'To enjoy the benefits of time' was one of the chief maxims of the statecraft of the age. Time untied so many knots, cancelled the necessity for so many desperate decisions, revealed so many unexpected shifts of pattern in a kaleidoscopic world, that the shrewdest statesmen were glad to take refuge in a wise passivity, a cautious opportunism. But Elizabeth did more than merely profit by time: she baffled it; she seemed sometimes to annul it altogether. If she was always the same it was because she was always different. While all Europe moved by inexorable steps, day by day, year by year, down the steep path to economic ruin and fratricidal strife, Elizabeth seemed by mere capriciousness and indecision to cast a spell of timelessness over her favoured island. No diplomat in England would ever be sure that today's facts made tomorrow's in any way inevitable when by the mere operation of her whim the Queen might bring everything back to the state of yesterday or, with no more apparent effort, to that of the year before last.

Europe found her as changeable as the moon her courtiers called her, tricksy as Puck, elusive as quicksilver. Merely to watch the intricate convolutions of her diplomacy, her airy balancing on the lip of one precipice after another, made sober statesmen dizzy. To imitate her would have over-tried the strongest masculine nerves in Europe. But if evidence means anything, Elizabeth enjoyed herself.

Her problem had been to rule one of the most unruly realms in Christendom to preserve her independent will and judgment among a crowd of burly courtiers all eager to assert their male superiority, never to place herself in a position where any man could say to her: 'You must do so and so.' Her means were feminine wit and feminine guile, a deliberate refusal of the obvious, an instinctive preference for enigma and ambiguity, an uncanny skill in mystification. The object was to arrange the courtiers and councillors around her, the diplomats and envoys, the kings and powers of the Continent in an elaborate interlocked design so cunningly and delicately balanced that each part should counteract another and she herself should always be free. For years Elizabeth had been the prima ballerina in a spectacle of her own designing. As long as she could call the tune she felt confident of leading the measure.

But no dance, however charged with magic, achieves more than the illusion of escaping time. While for over a quarter of a century Elizabeth had warded from her island the threatening march of history, substituting therefor the circular entertainment of her peculiar ballet, the eventless progress of the years had brought its own event. Elizabeth was not the mistress but the mother of the temper we call Elizabethan, and she was as little able as most mothers to estimate her offspring. To the daring they had from her they added a determination of their own, a flaming imagination which was none of hers, and a thrust of ambition it would tax her to control. It delighted Elizabeth to see her subjects sailing impudently in oceans claimed for Spain, but it would be hard to prove that she ever grasped the significance of those voyages. It amused Elizabeth to keep the ground on which her cousin Philip stood in the Low Countries so shifting and precarious that it would never do for a springboard to her island, but she could sympathize as little with the temper which yearned to crusade against the Catholics because they were Catholics as she could with Cousin Philip's determination to burn Protestants because they were Protestants. To her cool, sceptical, disenchanted mind the enthusiasms of her own people were becoming almost as unintelligible as the dark passions of Spain. But more and more the thrust of those enthusiasms disturbed the delicate balance of forces which preserved her own freedom of action. Some lust or idealism the *Golden Hind* had stirred when it floated triumphantly on the Thames sent more and more of her subjects to trail pikes beside the Dutch or wake West Indian echoes with their guns. More and more of a people who had been grateful for peace now itched for war. And subtly but inevitably the balance of forces in her own Council had shifted. Where once there had been an intricate pairing of old families against new men, conservatives in religion against Puritans, now she confronted a Council whose strength and weight were thrown towards forcing her into an irrevocable step, into a road which would have to be followed to the end.

Actually, of course, history was doing the forcing: the clash of irreconcilables could not be postponed for ever by any magic. Every step which the leaden-footed Spanish colossus took across Europe brought collision that much nearer. There was no balance in Europe any more: only a fatal dichotomy to be resolved by violence. Burghley had bowed to the fact. Elizabeth had acknowledged it. She had sent Drake raiding to the Indies with a squadron of her ships of war; she had sent Leicester to the Netherlands with English troops, and taken up reluctantly the leadership of Protestant Europe cast at her feet by William the Silent's assassin. But she did not have to like it. Drake's voyage to Cartagena had humiliated Spain and exacerbated Spanish feelings, but it had dealt no serious blow to Spanish power and had not even paid a decent dividend. Leicester in the Low Countries had been a continuous annoyance and little short of a continuous disaster. The money she conscientiously dribbled into Dutch coffers (nobody else seemed to realize how little money there really was!) vanished in the quicksand of incompetent financing and dishonest paymasters, leaving her troops as hungry and as ragged as if it had never been sent, and the Dutch more suspicious of her motives and more exacting in their demands with every unsatisfactory month. In two years the war cost her more than two hundred and fifty thousand pounds and the lives of some thousands of sturdy yeomen and gallant gentlemen, among them her favourite Philip Sidney, and all its effort barely seemed to slow the inexorable Spanish advance. In the previous July Walsingham had written to the Earl of Leicester: 'These two things being so contrary to Her Majesty's disposition, the one that it breedeth the doubt of a perpetual war, the other for that it ever requireth an increase of charges, do marvellously distract her and make her repent that ever she entered into the action.' Matters had not improved since. Within the fortnight

Elizabeth had learned that two English traitors, Sir William Stanley and Rowland York, had sold Deventer and the Sconce of Zutphen to the Spaniards, undoing all the meagre gains of the year, and the very day before the news from Fotheringhay Elizabeth had ended a stormy interview with the latest set of Dutch envoys by flatly refusing their requests for another loan and increased reinforcements, and bluntly imparting to them her low opinion of the Dutch Estates. All her fears of an interminable ruinous involvement beyond the strength of her throne to support seemed to be realizing themselves before her eyes. Burghley and Leicester, Walsingham and Davison, her whole Council seemed packed against her, forcing her to one fatal decision after another.

Their assault on the Queen of Scots was of a piece with the rest. So far the war with Spain had been a limited war, neither declared nor directly prosecuted. Ever since William the Silent's death Elizabeth had struggled to keep it in that ambiguous phase, hedging her captains about with warnings and prohibitions, fighting to preserve the illusion that the chasm might still be bridged, that a way of retreat still lay open. In that devious game the Queen of Scots was an important piece; had been a key piece for more than twenty years. As long as Elizabeth's ruin meant the triumph of Mary Stuart, cousin Philip might think twice before throwing his full strength against the Queen of England. Mary was French to her fingertips and France was, after all and in spite of her temporary eclipse, the hereditary foe of the Spanish-Habsburg power. Mary would lean on France if she could, and on the Guises no matter what she owed to Spain, and in the end Philip might find a pro-French Catholic queen on the throne of England more dangerous to his loosened hold on the Low Countries and to his growing hegemony of Europe than any heretic. Philip's sage father, the emperor, had all his life made it the chief point of his policy to keep France and England apart, had accepted a good many slights and rebuffs from the English rather than risk throwing the island kingdom into the arms of France. Philip had shown in the past that he was in that respect of the same mind as his father. Elizabeth had hoped that he might remain so, and that as long as Mary lived Philip's outraged orthodoxy and injured majesty would continue to be so nicely balanced by his dynastic interests that he would be as reluctant as she to risk the final trial by battle.

Neither the shrewdest of her diplomatic adversaries nor her own intimate councillors ever succeeded in reading the mind of Elizabeth Tudor. No one can pretend to now. She was complete mistress of the politician's art of using words to conceal meaning. On public questions and on personal relations she covered sheet after sheet with her vigorous scrawl, winding her sentences like an intricate coil of serpents about her secret conclusions, hinting, alluding, promising, denying, and at last gliding away from the subject with no more said than served her purpose. In council and in public negotiation she permitted herself at times the frankest outbursts, the most vehement outpourings of personal emotion, apparently unrestrained, and those who knew her best were the least certain that they had netted from the torrent of her words the smallest fragment of her real intentions.

But if we can be sure of anything about Elizabeth it is that she hated war. Because it was the one point of the arts of a ruler at which a woman could not pretend to be as good as a man? Because its uncouth violence offended her complicated sense of order? Simply because it cost money? Or because it was by nature unpredictable and uncontrollable, and thus thwarted what after her insecure youth had become the chief passion of her life — always to be in control of every situation, always to be the mistress of herself? For whatever reason, she hated it. She had been forced into war with Spain against her will. She still hoped for a way out. She had hoped that Mary Stuart's life might keep one important exit open. That to prolong Mary's life had been to risk her own, probably counted with her very little. Whatever Elizabeth Tudor was careful of, it was not her own life. Her desperate resistance to the mounting clamour for Mary's execution had certainly been sincere. Now that another door had closed for ever, now as she lay in her darkened bedchamber at Greenwich looking ahead down the narrow corridor of interminable war from which henceforward there would be less and less chance of escape, we need not doubt the sincerity of her tears.

IV

THE END OF A GAY SEASON

PARIS, FEBRUARY 28TH–MARCH 31ST, 1587

THE news from Fotheringhay took ten days to reach Paris. Even with storms in the Channel and the roads one bog after another such news should not have taken so long. But a suspicion that the French ambassador was involved in the plot around Mary had interrupted normal diplomatic communications and stopped cross-Channel traffic. No embassy courier had come from London for more than a fortnight, and the King of France was still hoping that his special ambassador had found some word to stay his sister-in-law's execution when the English resident in France was reading that the axe had fallen.

It was characteristic of the situation in Paris that winter that the first person outside the English embassy to hear the news was Don Bernardino de Mendoza, the Spanish resident ambassador. Very little that went on at the French Court escaped Don Bernardino — for that matter, not much in France that interested him. The Queen Mother, Catherine de Medici, made occasions to gossip with him intimately, mixing pleas for sympathy and advice with calculated indiscretions. Wisely he believed almost nothing she said. The King's ministers treated him with anxious deference, replying affably and circumstantially to queries which coming from any other embassy than Spain's would have been snubbed as impertinent. Even Henry III himself sometimes favoured Mendoza with fluent and eloquent expositions of policy, thickets of verbiage through which the ambassador flattered himself he could catch furtive glimpses of the King's real meaning.

On such informants Mendoza relied very little. He had the usual embassy spies, but they brought him only odd scraps. He was incomparably the best-informed diplomat in Paris because he represented the champion of Catholic orthodoxy and acted for his king as the paymaster of the ultra-Catholic, anti-royalist conspiracy known as the Holy League. The League's powerful chieftains, Henry, Duke of Guise and his brothers (who used most of the Spanish money as personal pensions), gave much information in return. So, without so much inducement, did some lesser personages who were coming reluctantly to prefer loyalty to their religion to

39

loyalty to their king. And Mendoza was in touch, in some covert fashion, with the Paris Committee of Sixteen who were moulding the city mob into a revolutionary force. Exiled Catholic Scots and Irishmen and Englishmen brought their rumours, their fears and their schemes regularly to the ambassador of the champion of their faith. And Mendoza drew confidently on the resident agents and travelling emissaries of that disciplined and devoted company whose strategic deployment stiffened the ranks of Catholicism on every battle-front from Poland to Galway. Unless contemporary observers were mistaken and circumstantial evidence misleads, Bernardino de Mendoza by 1587 had struck an alliance with the Jesuits closer than he ever told his king. Recently another source of information had been added in which Mendoza was beginning to feel confidence. An inconspicuous visitor had several times assured him that the English ambassador in Paris, Sir Edward Stafford, was anxious to serve the King of Spain in any way 'not against the interests of his mistress the Queen'. In the early morning hours of February 18th this go-between brought to the Spanish embassy the first news that, ten days before at Fotheringhay, the Queen of Scots had been beheaded.

Soon all Paris knew, with various and growing additions, some story of the execution. Before Sir Edward Stafford had finally succeeded in conveying to the Royal Council the official English version, the propagandists of the League had already agreed upon theirs. The judicial murder of her orthodox rival was the latest and blackest crime of the English Jezebel. And to that murder Henry of Valois, King of France, was a passive accessory if not an active accomplice. The Queen of England would never have dared to go so far without assurance that any resentment displayed by the French king would be for form's sake only. Jealousy of the Guises and the double tongues of atheistical politicians had persuaded the King to prefer the alliance of heretics like the Queen of England and the King of Navarre to the friendship of Spain and the safety of Mother Church. And for the slack in faith, no less than for outright infidels, God was preparing a swift and terrible judgment.

That winter most of the pulpits of Paris rang with eloquence which skirted close to treason. Fanatical friars and demagogic priests vied with one another in calumny, innuendo and the spreading of horrendous rumours. Such and such a person close to the throne was a secret Protestant. Such and such another had sold his soul to the devil. No one knew how far the poisons of heresy and witchcraft had eaten into the inner circles of the Court. Ten thousand secret Huguenots lurked, armed, in the cellars and by-ways of Paris, ready to issue in the dead of night and cut the throats of all the Catholics. (Perhaps memories of St Bartholomew's made the population of Paris, which had initiated that form of religious argument, particularly susceptible to rumours that it might be turned against them.) One could only guess why the King took no steps to guard his faithful subjects against these ravening heretics.

Even a hint of the kind of near-treason that was commonplace in Paris pulpits would have cost one of Queen Elizabeth's subjects his ears. The English Privy Council would have made short work of the kind of libels that fluttered from the Paris presses, and dealt faithfully with the authors and the printers. Licence of speech and writing was always notoriously greater at Paris, within the precincts of the Sorbonne at least, than anywhere in Tudor England, but never — not at least since the riotous quarrels of Orleans and Burgundy more than a century and a half before — had controversialists grown so noisy and unruly without some check by the Crown. Henry III seemed not to hear them. The little balustrade which he had set up to fend off his courtiers while he took his meals might have been the symbol of the wall which yearly grew higher between the King's spirit and the outer world.

It was little more than thirteen years since Henry of Valois, the elected King of Poland, from his youth famous as the victor of Jarnac and Montcontour, the scourge of the Huguenots, the paladin of the Faith, had returned to take the crown of France. Since then nothing had gone right. There were no more thrilling victories, no more exciting midnight butcheries even, only indecisive manœuvres, dull colloquies, compromises, evasions, mean shifts, stalemates and defeats. The great plans for the reorganization of the kingdom remained only plans on paper. The royal debts grew always higher and harder to meet. The royal purse grew leaner. And the reality of royal power went on crumbling, even faster than it had done when his mother was regent, one great province after another slipping away into the control of Huguenots or Leaguers or selfish noble governors, and only the patrols of private armies or the co-operation of citizens for self-defence making little islands of relative order in the endemic anarchy of brigandage and civil war.

Those thirteen years had sufficed to turn the buoyant self-confident young man into a flaccid hesitant old one. The hands, the beautiful slender hands, were as restless as ever, for ever shaping elaborate arabesques of meaning to accompany the fluent melodious voice; for ever, when the King was silent, toying with something — with a marmoset, a sweetmeat, a lap-dog, a muff, or the hair and ears of a handsome young man. But although defiantly painted into a red and white mask of health, like some triumph of the embalmer's art, the face had a shrunken stillness. The eyes, peering out from sockets yearly deeper and more corpse-like, were sick, sullen, distrustful. The last of the Valois looked like a man secretly at grips with death.

Openly, the King chose to ignore his inner enemy as he chose to ignore the overt enemies in his kingdom. He still gave audience with royal pomp and the gracious solemnity of which he was a master. He listened gravely to his councillors and lectured them with wisdom and subtlety on the arts of government. He corrected edicts just as if he expected them to be obeyed, and drafted elaborate reforms just as if he thought he was capable of carrying them out. He spoke to foreign ambassadors and wrote to his own as if France were still the great and united power it had been in his father's time. And he pursued his royal duties and his religious devotions as if the King were not only above all criticism, but somehow exempt from all observation, as if the little balustrade about his table were really an impenetrable wall which he could close about himself whenever he liked.

That carnival season of 1587 was feverishly gay. Secretary Brûlart was worried about money (he generally was), but ball followed extravagant ball. At intervals the merrymakers would froth out from the light and music of the Louvre to cut capers in the public streets while His Most Christian Majesty in one odd disguise or another, but most often in that of a maid of honour, whooped and giggled in the centre of a knot of those handsome young courtiers the Parisians called his mignons. The Court never seemed to go to bed, and sober citizens grew accustomed to encountering the revellers, and avoiding the more rowdy of them, at any hour. The only interruption of the gaiety was when the King would suddenly hurry away, change his carnival finery for a penitent's coarse gown and be off to his favourite convent of Capuchins in the faubourg St Honoré where he was said to spend whole days on his knees, fasting and scourging himself, weeping and praying. There was no hypocrisy in these devotional excesses. They were not meant to conciliate public opinion — nor, in fact, did they. In the anguished contrition of the convent as in the hysterical follies of the carnival Henry indulged his passion for self-abasement without much regard for the spectators. One may guess that the tears and floggings gave a sharper zest to the amusements that were sure in a day or two to follow.

Anxiety about Mary Stuart's life had cast no perceptible shadow on the King's diversions, but the news of her death cut them off abruptly. Not, probably, because of any personal grief. When Mary Stuart had been the toast of the Valois Court her brother-in-law was scarcely out of the nursery. When she sailed to meet her dark fate in Scotland, Henry was barely ten. And in the years since he had been king, Mary Stuart had meant largely a stream of pleas for money he could ill afford and actions he could not afford at all, unpleasant complications in his relations with England, and occasions for the bullying and blustering of her kinsmen the Guises. Henry was certainly guiltless of the conduct imputed to him by the Spanish-Jesuit-League party. He had honourably instructed his special ambassador to take every lawful step in his power to save Mary's life, and the ambassador had diligently carried out those instructions. But now that every step had failed, now that the unlucky queen had been swept from the board, Henry may well have reflected that all these years she had been a piece in the game of his rivals the Guises, and that their loss was his gain. He may have hoped that now the chief disturbing element was removed his relations with England, at least, might take a turn for the better.

Nevertheless, honour and policy and respect for the opinion of his subjects all obliged the King to put the Court into full mourning. Mary had been his brother's wife and Queen of France. She was the cousin of the popular and powerful Guises. She had been a staunch Catholic who had died at the hands of heretics, for the sake — so people thought — of her faith. And the memory of her charm still cast its spell upon many at Henry's Court, even among the Guises' enemies. If the grief and anger of the King were merely politic some about him felt such emotions genuinely enough.

Outside in the streets of Paris grief and anger were unfeigned and almost unbounded. The Guises had always seen to it that Mary's adventures, amatory and political, had been presented to the Parisians in the most favourable light. She had long been the favourite heroine of tens of thousands who can scarcely have remembered her as Henry II's daughter-in-law or as Francis II's queen. Now her picture, draped in black, hung in windows; and ballads, celebrating her constancy in martyrdom and calling down perdition on her persecutors, were sung about the streets. Mary's sad story was the theme of most of the pulpits of Paris that next week, and from one of them a particularly eloquent orator aroused such a storm of weeping in his audience that he had to descend, leaving his sermon unfinished. Crowds paraded outside the Louvre, bellowing for vengeance on the English, and King Henry felt obliged to send a message to Sir Edward Stafford, begging him for the sake of his personal safety not to leave the shelter of the embassy.

We can only speculate now on how much of this Parisian storm of rage and grief was genuine and how much whipped up by propaganda. In the people of Paris, as elsewhere in France, fears and anxieties had been bred by an era of rapid, puzzling change. Money was not worth a quarter as much as it had been in Henry II's time, and though prices were so high the pressure of taxes and the uncertainty of the times made the earnings of merchants and craftsmen narrow and precarious. Meanwhile ancient landmarks in Church and State had been swept away, ancient values challenged, ancient loyalties shaken, and life and property in many parts of the kingdom had become as unsafe as in the bad old days of the Hundred Years War. It gave a shape to vague terrors and an outlet for uneasiness to blame all the evils of France on the Huguenots, and to make a desperate minority, fighting for its existence, into a menacing conspiracy about to overwhelm the kingdom. It was reassuring to the insecure to hear themselves clamouring for the blood of the heretics, as if one more act of aimless violence could cure a world whose malady was aimless violence. Overtones such as these gave an edge of hysteria to the emotional debauch of the Parisians over the death of Mary Queen of Scots.

But whenever loyalties are uprooted and people are swept back and forth in blind storms of emotion there is likely to be some political clique or party seeking to ride the storm to its own advantage. If the people of Paris and the other Catholic towns of France responded irrationally to emotional stimuli, there was nothing irrational about the manipulations of popular emotion by the leaders of the Holy League. This is not to say that strong and ill-understood emotions were absent from the drives and interests which united its ill-assorted elements. But the objectives of the League, its real objectives, were clear and definite, and its techniques were appropriate. Most simply the League existed to serve the religious interests of the papacy and the ultramontane wing of the clergy against Huguenots and Gallicans alike, the dynastic interests of the Guises against the ruling Valois and the Bourbon succession, and, because Spain was the paymaster, the international interests of Spain. The enemy could thus be represented as the heretics, the enemy of all good Catholic Frenchmen, and the declared aim of the League could be simply to preserve France for the orthodox faith.

From the beginning of the movement its preachers had found the persecution of Catholics in England one of their surest themes, one to which the King's government could not possibly object while at the same time it stressed unmistakably the shape of the future should France once fall, as England had fallen, under the sway of a heretic prince. The sufferings of the Roman Catholic mission priests in England in those days were real and terrible, as real and terrible as the sufferings of Englishmen, Dutchmen and Spaniards at the hands of the Spanish Inquisition. But it would be too hard to say now which set of martyrdoms was the more exaggerated and distorted. The propagandists of the militant Puritans and the propagandists of the League found the same utility in the pains of their co-religionists.

For this kind of propaganda the execution of the Queen of Scots was made to order. For almost a fortnight the pulpits of Paris rang with the innocent virtues of the martyred queen, the wickedness of her enemies and the treachery of her false friends; then came the climax of the Queen's solemn obsequies at Nôtre-Dame. For the event the League put up that formidable orator, the Bishop of Bourges. Bourges made the customary eulogy of the dead a bridge to a eulogy not of the royal house as custom dictated but of the house of Lorraine, and especially of the dukes of Guise and Mayenne, the Scipios of France, the thunderbolts of war, poised to avenge their martyred kinswoman, the strong props of Holy Church, the hopes and joys of God's afflicted people. The bishop's eloquence was unchecked by the sight of Henry III and his queen, conspicuously incognito in a special pew in the transept. And the last Valois may have reflected that he might have been listening to his own obsequies and the praise of his successor, except that had he been the corpse instead of the chief mourner in rank and sib, his name could scarcely have been passed over in such pointed silence. If nothing had gone well with him in the past thirteen years, he had at least tested the capacity of a tough institution like the French monarchy to survive a great deal of misfortune; and if the Queen of Scots' death eased the pressure of the Guises and let France draw closer, after the appropriate diplomatic sulks were over, to England, its only possible ally against the King of Spain, then Henry could endure with equanimity another blast of pulpit wind.

The ambassadors who attended the obsequies for Mary Stuart at Nôtre-Dame on March 13th took various views of the probable effects of Mary's death. Sir Edward Stafford was, or professed to be, so much alarmed by the fury it aroused in Court and city that finally Walsingham ordered him testily to leave off writing about the subject since his letters only increased

Elizabeth's vexation with her Council. The Italian observers, on the other hand, although they reported to Rome and Venice and Florence the popular outcry for vengeance, all agreed that on the whole Mary's execution improved the English position. It not only eliminated the natural head of any domestic rebellion but it removed any rational motive for a French intervention in English affairs and opened the way to one of the alternatives of sixteenth-century high politics, an Anglo-French alliance. Since no Italian not thoroughly committed to Spain could avoid feeling a pleasant anticipatory tingle at the idea that Spanish power might be checked, and few Italian politicians did not secretly yearn for a time when the incommensurable passions of religious controversy might be stilled and Europeans brought back to the calculable game of power politics, it may be that the Italian diplomats in being cynically realistic about the effects of Mary's death were indulging in a kind of wish fulfilment. But most sophisticated politicians in Paris that March seem to have agreed with them.

Don Bernardino de Mendoza saw deeper. Like his Jesuit allies the Spanish ambassador had already discounted the Queen of Scots. Without the promise of foreign intervention, he had reasoned, there would be no major rising of the English Catholics; at the first serious threat of such intervention Mary's life would be forfeit. Although she still seemed enormously important to observers hypnotized by the glamour of the past, Mary Stuart was in Mendoza's eyes a piece already sacrificed and only waiting to be taken from the board. He had half expected his opponents to remove her two years ago. That they had done so now instead of waiting until that last possible moment when the Enterprise of England should be launched (was it to be six months off? A year? Two years?) just simplified one aspect of a complicated game. Mendoza had already discounted, too, the Anglo-French alliance. The only power in France he even half-way trusted was that of the Holy League and its chieftain, the Duke of Guise. When the moment of the Enterprise came, not Henry of Valois, Mendoza hoped, but Henry of Guise would be master of France. Towards that goal the death of Mary Stuart gave another thrust, provided another lever to prise at the structure of royal power. To Madrid and to Rome Mendoza wrote plainly what a thousand Leaguer pulpits were openly hinting: Pomponne de Bellièvre's special mission to Queen Elizabeth had been a sham; instead of trying to prevent the execution of the Queen of Scots the French ambassador's charge had been to stiffen the will to murder. In Madrid and Rome, in Brussels and Prague, friends of the League and Jesuit fathers gave independent confirmation to the lie. For the sake of the triumph of the faith it was necessary that the French king's position be weakened not only in respect to the allegiance of his subjects but in the eyes of Europe.

But it was not about France that Mendoza was mainly thinking. His gaze was fixed on England. More than two years before, his embassy to England had ended in expulsion. He had been unceremoniously set aboard a ship and returned to the custody of his master because his plots 'disturbed the realm of England'. 'Tell your mistress,' he said at the last, to the councillors who saw him aboard, 'that Bernardino de Mendoza was born not to disturb kingdoms but to conquer them.'

Ever since, plans for the great Enterprise which would mean his personal vengeance and the triumph of his faith had obsessed Mendoza. Long before his expulsion he had been one of the undertaking's chief advocates, assuring King Philip of the strength of the Catholic party in England and in Scotland, of the slackness and corruptibility of Elizabeth's captains, and the contemptible weakness of the raw English militia. He knew, therefore — no man better — that one of the chief obstacles to the Enterprise was the leaden slowness, the incurable caution of him whom his subjects called not unjustly the Prudent King. And the chief use he meant to make of Mary's death was to spur his master. No sooner had he got the news than he sat down to summarize for Philip what he knew the reaction in England, in France, in Christendom would be. He did not need to remind the King that now there was no longer the slightest danger that a Spanish conquest of England would end by setting a French queen on the throne. Nor did he mention a certain important document signed by the Queen of Scots which he had himself forwarded to Spain not long before. Piety, honour and simple self-defence all combined to counsel the punishment of the English for this last atrocity. 'Therefore,' he concluded, 'I pray that Your Majesty will hasten the Enterprise of England to the earliest possible date, for it would seem to be God's obvious design to bestow upon Your Majesty the crowns of these two kingdoms.'

V

PLANS OF OPERATIONS

BRUSSELS, MARCH 1ST – 22ND, 1587

On the same day he wrote to Philip, Bernardino de Mendoza also advised Philip's Governor General in the Netherlands — Alexander Farnese, Duke of Parma — of Mary's death. But Parma, in his winter quarters at Brussels, had already heard the news, was already reassessing the European situation which was part of the complex military problem of the Dutch revolt. From the variables in that problem one exasperating x could now be struck out. Mary Stuart was ferried across the border and into the custody of the English Queen in the same year that the discontented Netherlands had first risen in arms against the King of Spain. Ever since, the effort of King Philip to reduce his rebellious subjects to obedience (including, of course, obedience to the Roman Church) had been draining Spain of gold and blood, and wrecking the lives and reputations of a series of Philip's captains and bureaucrats. Periodically the problem had been complicated by the existence of Mary Stuart. Pressure to use the army in the Netherlands to liberate the Queen of Scots distracted Philip's commanders, and fears of this kind of Spanish intervention worsened relations with England.

When Alexander Farnese had joined his uncle, Don Juan of Austria, in the Netherlands in December 1577, that adventurous paladin was obsessed with the idea of a dash across the narrow seas to rescue the Queen of Scots, and a triumphal march on London to dethrone Elizabeth and reestablish the ancient faith. For such a feat there was only one obvious reward, and after Darnley and Bothwell there was little reason why Mary Stuart should balk at marrying the hero of Lepanto. Don Juan's assigned task was to pacify the rebellious Netherlands, and in the last months of his life that goal seemed as far off as ever; but though Spain held only a few scattered towns, though its ill-paid army seemed on the point of breaking up and its commander lay dying, the wheels of the conspiracy to combine Scotland and the English Catholics, the Pope, the Guises and the King of Spain in support of Queen Mary and King Juan ground creakily on. 'Everyone believes', Don Juan had written to Philip before he had even

48

taken up his government, 'that the only remedy for the disorders of the Netherlands is that England should be ruled by someone devoted to Your Majesty. If the contrary case prevails it will mean the ruin of these countries and their loss to your crown.' That seems to have been his view to the end.

There was more force to the argument in March of 1587 than there had been a decade earlier. English troops paid by the Queen were now in the Netherlands, and English support was now, in the view of most European politicians and according to the frequent (though not invariable) statement of the rebels themselves, the chief prop of Dutch independence. For under Alexander of Parma the Spanish cause in the Netherlands had at last begun to prosper.

In politics and diplomacy Parma had proved himself a match for his greatest adversary, the Prince of Orange. In war he was easily the first captain of his age. Of his soldiership his contemporaries noted chiefly his dash, his courage, his physical toughness, his readiness to share danger and hardship with his men. Less often they mention the speed and sense of timing which dismayed his enemies, and the patience and tenacity with which he hung on to an objective once he had decided it was worth the cost. Scarcely ever do they hint at the powers of intellectual analysis and organization which lifted the art of war to a level which the sixteenth century saw but rarely. Parma had an unrivalled sense of terrain, and if his soldiers grumbled that they did more work with shovels than with pikes Parma knew just when a stream diverted, a dike broken, a new canal dug might yield the result he wanted more surely than a bloody victory. Spread out in Parma's mind was a strategic map of the Netherlands and all the intricate network of its communications by land and water, so that while previous commanders, even the great Alba, even William the Silent, seem to have blundered about the Low Countries like belligerent boys in a strange thicket each of Parma's moves was calculated and controlled by a workable, orderly plan.

Meanwhile, in Parma's hands the heterogeneous collection of mercenaries which went by the name of the Spanish army developed new potentialities and a new coherence. Pioneers and siege-trains became serious professional units, not unreliable civilian auxiliaries. Formations of different equipment, different organization, different tactics, different tongues and military traditions, Spaniards, Italians, Germans, Walloons, were welded together into a single instrument which was almost a tool of precision. The Spanish infantry had been feared and famous before Parma

Alexander Farnese, Duke of Parma, from a portrait by Otto van Veen.

was born — before, indeed, his grandfather Charles V had first smelled powder. But the irresistible Spanish army, irresistible because professional, owes much of its legend and much of its subsequent fame to the Prince of Parma.

With that army Parma began the systematic conquest of an adequate base in the south. One after another the chief towns of Flanders and Brabant yielded to his pressure, until he was ready to close his grip on the great port of Antwerp, the commercial metropolis of northern Europe. After a siege marked by desperate fighting, heroic endurance and unparalleled feats of engineering on both sides, Antwerp surrendered in August 1585. A year earlier, in July 1584, a fanatical assassin had shot down the Prince of Orange on the stairway of his house at Delft. The death of William the Silent was a greater blow to the Dutch cause than the loss of Antwerp. Parma was ready to begin the reconquest of Holland and Zeeland. In Spain the best informed of the King's ministers assured a subordinate that the last phase of the war could not take long.

But the murder of the Prince of Orange and the fall of Antwerp had finally drawn England into the Dutch war. England had already given the Dutch enough aid in money and volunteers to provide the Spanish with justifiable grounds for resentment, and Elizabeth's councillors had finally been able to persuade her that a completely triumphant Spanish army just across the North Sea would be too great a risk. She made an ambiguous treaty with the Dutch and got in return the right to put English garrisons into Brill and Flushing, the likeliest invasion ports if Philip should try to throw Parma's army into England. Before the campaign of 1586 opened she sent to the Netherlands five thousand foot and a thousand horse under the most conspicuous nobleman of her Court, Robert Dudley, Earl of Leicester.

About the merits of the English army (Leicester's levies, not the veteran mercenaries under Black John Norris) there were several opinions. Their own countrymen were apt to describe them as a set of miserable rogues and vagabonds, untrained, ill-armed and half naked. (It is true that one contingent of them was armed chiefly with bows and arrows, and that of another its captain wrote that there were not three whole shirts in the company.) The Dutch remarked of them chiefly that for thieving and brawling they had no equals. But Parma, after he had tasted their quality, never underrated them. The first of their infantry to be blooded stood for the best part of two hours on the slippery mud by the Meuse at push of pike with picked Spanish veterans, and it was not the raw English levies that gave way. The hot fight at Warnsfeld which we remember for the death of Philip Sidney was remembered by soldiers in the Netherlands as a demonstration that armoured men on heavy horses charging home with lance at rest could break through, bowl over or brush aside many times their number of light horsemen and pistoleers. Thereafter Parma was wary of English heavy cavalry, and his habit of noting in his estimates of the strength of fortified places that among the garrison there are so many English shows that he was not contemptuous of their other arms.

Partly because of the English reinforcements, partly because of English money and partly because of the stimulus to Dutch morale, Parma's campaign in 1586 was less triumphant than everyone had anticipated. He managed to keep his lines of supply open and to hang on to Zutphen, but the balance in the northern provinces was unchanged when winter set in, and only by speed and daring and sheer intellectual superiority had Parma been able to retain the initiative against forces strong enough, if properly handled, to have penned him into Brabant to starve. English intervention had moved the assault on the major centres of Holland and Zeeland farther enough away on Parma's timetable so that it would have been natural for him to echo Don Juan's judgment that the place to conquer the Netherlands was in England.

If he did so without enthusiasm, it was partly because he was less confident than his uncle had been of conquering England and partly because he was more interested in conquering the Netherlands. The papers of Alexander Farnese are rich in detailed analyses of political and military situations, not only of the concrete factors of geography and economics, finance and logistics and supply, numbers and discipline and arms, but of the psychological factors, the ambitions and jealousies, the fears and hatreds and loyalties of individuals and groups in his camp and in the enemy's. The only motives he never analysed on paper, not even in his letters to his mother, are his own. But it would not be surprising if the Netherlands, the whole of them, engaged in him something like a primary loyalty. His mother had ruled over them; so had his illustrious grandfather. He had by now spent more years of his life in them than he had in any other country, and for almost a decade they had absorbed him completely.

He was the chief architect (as the future would reveal) of modern Belgium. The reconquest of the southern ten of the seventeen provinces was the work of his hand and brain. But it was a work still incomplete. What had been the fattest land in Europe faced starvation. The fields, trampled by too many armies, were going back to weeds and brambles.

MECHE LEN.

Als Bergen ingenommen war, Die der Prinß ingenommen hatt. Das da khein ordnung wart gehalten all ir gutt dem Alba geben
Khumpt der von Alba mitt seiner schar Zu plundern auff allsolche weiß Dan zu gleich junge vnd die alten Anno Dni. M.D.LXXII. I. oro.
Vor Mechlen eine Schone Statt Er gibt sei seinen knechten preiß In großtem elend musten leben

Spanish troops plundering a town.

The Siege of Antwerp, 1585.

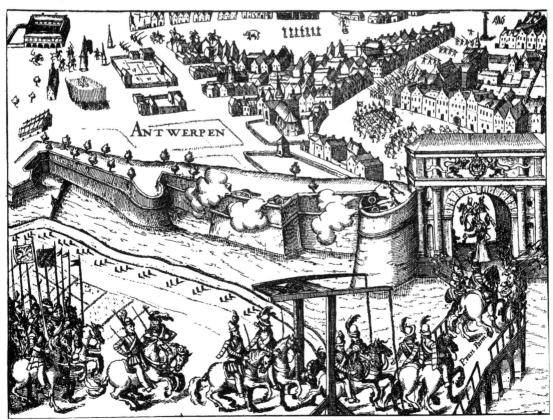

ANTWERPEN

The industrial towns were listless and half empty. In the Antwerp bourse, under the inscription which still proudly proclaimed it to be 'for the use of all merchants of whatever land or language' and where almost every land and language had once been represented, a few bill-shavers still lingered to prey on the necessities of out-at-elbow captains. In the great port of the metropolis the last cargo hulks rotted idly at the docks, would go on rotting there as long as a Dutch squadron blocked the entrance to the Scheldt. Not only the renewed wealth and greatness of the recovered provinces but, it seemed, their survival depended on reopening the ways to the sea, and so on the ending of the Dutch revolt. This, so far as we can read his motives behind the careful veil of his language, was Parma's great objective.

When Philip had first consulted him about the Enterprise of England, Parma had warned him that by grasping at an uncertain gain he might incur heavy loss and urged him to wait. There was the danger that if the army of the Netherlands was engaged in England the French might be tempted to march into the undefended southern provinces as they had tried to do so many times before. To a professional like Parma the thought that his reserves might be wiped out and his base overrun while he was in the midst of a difficult campaign on the other side of the North Sea was a nightmare. Even if he could trust the Duke of Guise and the Holy League to cover his flank and rear there was the problem of combining operations with the fleet to come from Spain.

Parma had once played with the idea of a sudden raid across the Channel entirely by his own troops in barges under cover of darkness, landing in England before anyone discovered that they had left Flanders. But the chance for such a surprise was long past. His troops could get to England now only under cover of a fleet. On blue water, or for that matter on any inland waterway too wide to be barred by chains and commanded by shore batteries, the Dutch were masters. The covering fleet could only come from Spain. And having come, where could it go? Until he could take Brill or Flushing, Parma did not hold a single deep-water port where seagoing ships could ride in safety, no port for his escort fleet before the crossing, nowhere the Spaniards could run to if they were pounded too heavily by the storms of the Channel or the English guns. While an increasing number of people were urging on Philip that he would never be able to subdue his Dutch rebels until he had conquered England, the Duke of Parma was more and more of the opinion that a successful invasion of England required a reunited Netherlands.

Nor was Parma certain that the English intervention was going to increase his difficulties as much in the future as it had in 1586. However modest his abilities in the field, at the council table the Earl of Leicester had shown a positive genius for dividing, antagonizing and infuriating his friends. He regarded his rank as more than offsetting his military inexperience. Sir John Norris, the grim English veteran, who had fought with distinction under William of Orange and should have been the earl's right-hand man, had been relieved of his command and gone back to England growling that he would never serve under Leicester again. The other able field commander in the Dutch service, Count Hohenlo, a brutal roistering mercenary equally formidable in a desperate battle or a drinking bout, had been Leicester's boisterous champion when the earl had first come to Holland. Now, for months past, Hohenlo's friends had feared that if he met Leicester again it would come to bloodshed, and at the moment Hohenlo was busy cashiering Leicester's officers, ousting his garrisons and chivying out of the service every Englishman or Dutchman of Leicester's party. For the Earl of Leicester had gone home. His affairs in England were almost as parlous as his affairs in the Low Countries, and if in conference with his sovereign it was unlikely that he would find a remedy for the state to which he had reduced his own fortunes and his country's hopes abroad, he might at least be able to appease the wrath of the one person in the world he really feared. After him went an embassy from the Estates of Holland to complain that, in his efforts to browbeat the Dutch burghers into fighting their war his way, Leicester had stirred up factional differences among them almost to the point of civil war.

Parma knew all this. He had his informants in every Dutch city, in London and even at the Queen's Court. Part of his success was due to accurate intelligence, and he had reason to hope that English intervention would slacken. But he had a more solid reason for discounting the English. Before he had left for England in November Leicester had placed two of his captains, both known Catholics, in command of two of the most important posts in the Dutch line of defence — the recently captured city of Deventer and the Sconce of Zutphen, the fortress built to observe and beleaguer the Spanish garrison in Zutphen itself. The Dutch had protested vigorously. They might tolerate Roman Catholics in the exercise of their religion, a laxity which shocked the earl's political puritanism, but they stopped short of trusting Catholics in independent military commands at vital spots. Leicester only replied haughtily that he would stake his life on the loyalty of his officers. It was fortunate for him he did not have to. On

January 28th, 1587, Sir William Stanley opened the gates of Deventer to a Spanish force and went over with the twelve hundred wild Irish kerns of his command to the service of Spain. On the same day Rowland York betrayed the Sconce of Zutphen.

From what we know of York, profit may have weighed with him as much as religion. But Sir William Stanley was no bought traitor. He came of an old and illustrious family whose fortunes had been linked with the Tudors since before Bosworth. He had served the Queen well. He had Leicester's trust and affection, and had been talked of both as the earl's successor in the Netherlands and as the Queen's Lord Deputy in Ireland. There was nothing the Spanish could offer him worth what his defection would sacrifice, and Parma assured Philip that in their negotiations there had been no word of pay. Stanley had acted for conscience sake. Like other men in that troubled century in which the clash of rival religions cut across national lines Sir William Stanley had been torn between his loyalty to his country and his allegiance to his faith, and long before the surrender of Deventer he had known that he would have to choose and what his choice would be. Some weeks after the surrender of Deventer he offered an English captain a lucrative post in the Spanish service, and when the captain indignantly replied that he would rather be a loyal beggar than a rich traitor at odds with his conscience Stanley had commended his choice. 'This,' he said, 'is the very principle of my own enlargement [of his escape, he meant, from an intolerable dilemma]. Before I served the devil; now I serve God.'

English Catholic refugees in the Low Countries had frequently assured Parma that many of their fellow countrymen shared Stanley's faith, and between those who thought the service of Spain was the service of God and those who were willing to serve the devil if the pay was high enough the duke did not despair of making an even better market in the next year than he had made in the last. 'The Zutphen fort ... and Deventer which was the real objective of last summer's campaign and is the key to Groningen and all these provinces [of the inland north],' Parma had written Philip, 'are thus Your Majesty's at a trifling cost. But what is better, the effect of this treason must be to sow great suspicion between the English and the rebels, so that hereafter no one will know whom to trust.'

On the whole the best general in Europe had never seen more favourable omens for finishing his long task. With half the men Philip said he was collecting in Spain, and half the money Parma guessed he must be spending, the duke felt confident of mopping up the inland enclaves of

Mary Tudor and Philip II of Spain, by an unknown artist, 1557.

Above, 'The Dream of Philip II', by El Greco, 1580. Philip appears among the saints before the jaws of Hell.

Opposite, Palace of El Escorial just after the completion of the building. By an anonymous painter.

Opposite below, 'Cow of The Netherlands'; an allegorical representation of the political situation in The Netherlands in 1580. The Low Countries are represented as a cow: fed by Elizabeth, ridden by Philip and milked by William of Orange.

1591

SIC PARVIS MAGNA

Sir Francis Drake, in a portrait by Marc Gheeraedts.

resistance and cutting off the burghers of the coastal towns from their river communications. That would be the time, if the rebels still would not see reason, for a final drive against Holland and Zeeland. There would be tough nuts to crack, but hardly tougher than Antwerp, and he had cracked Antwerp. Then, with the North Sea ports in his hands and the shipping of Holland added to his strength, if the King of Spain still wanted to conquer England the odds would be heavily in his favour. It seemed to Parma a better gamble than an immediate attempt at invasion.

Nevertheless, when he learned of the execution of Mary Queen of Scots, he wrote Philip as if this new offence against Spanish honour and the Catholic faith made the Enterprise the inevitable next step. Perhaps Parma really believed that since Philip had been unable to rescue Mary he would feel obliged to avenge her. Perhaps he merely guessed how much less awkward vengeance would be for Philip than a rescue. Whatever his reasons, Parma not only wrote but acted as if the death of the Queen of Scots had made a decisive change in his plan of operations. After the fall of Deventer he had been looking northward — north-east to the clearing of the Yssel and the way to Groningen, north-west to Utrecht and so to Amsterdam itself. But from the beginning of March the maps in his study were all of the mouths of the Scheldt, and the first orders had been written for the south-west shift of his battalions and the movement of munitions towards Flanders. If there was to be a rendezvous with the fleet from Spain the army, lacking the ideal deep-water port of Flushing, would need at least a concentration point for his barges, with access to the sea — Bergen-op-Zoom perhaps — sheltered behind Bevenland on the eastern Scheldt, or better still a port in western Flanders like Ostend or Sluys.

Meanwhile he would try to arrange some sort of peace conference with the English. The Queen preferred talking to fighting, and the more eagerly the Spanish negotiated the less ready the English might be when the great stroke was delivered. That it would be delivered, and soon, Parma seems from the time he heard of Mary Stuart's death to have had no doubt.

VI

THE BITTER BREAD

ROME, MARCH 24TH – 30TH, 1587

BEFORE he slept, on the day he heard of Mary Stuart's death, Bernardino de Mendoza had dictated three dispatches. The first was to his master, Philip of Spain. The second was to Parma, brief because he and Parma were in frequent touch. The third was to Enrique de Guzman, Count of Olivarez, the Spanish ambassador at Rome. Madrid, Brussels, Rome: the three corners of the wedge Mendoza hoped to drive into the heart of England. At Madrid the final word must be spoken if navies were to be launched and armies march. At Brussels was based the invading army, the army Mendoza himself had served in and still thought of with fierce pride as the finest in the world. And Rome. Little as Mendoza relished mixing priests and politics, he had long realized that in this enterprise priests were indispensable.

Count Olivarez, in Mendoza's view, knew how to handle priests. He talked to cardinals like an equal, as a Guzman (or a Mendoza) should. He had been firm with the last Pope, Gregory XIII, and he was firm with the present one, Sixtus V, as scarcely anyone else in Rome now dared to be. Olivarez shared Mendoza's impatience with their master's slowness and, though without Mendoza's personal animosity, his eagerness to finish with the English. Certainly in the present situation Olivarez could be trusted to do everything needful.

And yet with the news of Mary Stuart's death Mendoza heard a bell strike. He had a sense, stronger than he could have explained, of crisis, of a turning point. This time it was essential that nothing which Spanish diplomacy could do at Rome should be neglected, that every point should be clear and explicit no matter how many times each had been stressed before.

One by one Mendoza passed them firmly in review. To begin with, the Queen of Scots had died a martyr; she had been murdered because she was a Catholic and the main hope of the English Catholics. His Holiness should be perfectly clear about that. Moreover she had, at her death and for months before, utterly rejected her heretic son and bequeathed her

claim to the throne and her care for the people of England to his Most
Catholic Majesty the King of Spain. Mendoza had a copy of the letter in
which she said so. Another was in Spain and still another in Rome. His
Holiness should be made to realize, too, the slipperiness of the King of
France. His pretence that he had sent a special embassy to try to save
Mary's life was an obvious fraud. Actually the French ambassador probably had urged Elizabeth to hasten Mary's death. Mendoza was as positive
of this as if he had listened to the conversation. Now, unless Henry III
was badly frightened, he would strike hands with the heretics for the sake
of injuring Spain. His Holiness should be reminded that the Church could
rely in France only on the Duke of Guise and the house of Lorraine.
Meanwhile, now that the Enterprise was so close, His Holiness should
have an especial care for the English Catholics. They could be useful once
the Duke of Parma's army had landed, but they needed a leader. Dr
William Allen should be made a cardinal at once so that he could accompany the army as papal legate. All the English Catholics, open and
secret, would trust and obey Dr Allen. So, his dry voice keeping pace
with the scratch of his secretary's quill and his purblind eyes staring into
the dead embers on his hearth, the ambassador dictated the last dispatch of
a long day, and the solid sentences wheeled past like companies of Spanish
pikemen who finally see the enemy, not quickening their step but knit
close by a new tension. It was a long letter.

No couriers in any service rode harder than Mendoza's. But, at this
season, on the shortest route from Paris to Rome the ways were foul and
snow still lay in the passes, while farther south there was constant danger
of marauding Huguenots. It was not until the morning of March 24th,
therefore, that Mendoza's man clattered across the Ponte Sisto and along
the Via Giulia into the courtyard of the Spanish embassy. He was well
ahead of any other bearer of his tidings.

Olivarez swung into action at once. He saw Cardinal Caraffa, the papal
Secretary of State, that afternoon, and made Mendoza's points together
with a couple of his own. One of these was a suggestion, almost a demand,
that the Pope celebrate a requiem mass for Queen Mary in St Peter's. The
other was the proposal that now that prompt vengeance on the heretic
queen was more pressing than ever His Holiness ought to advance to
Spain a loan sufficient to make up for the delay of the silver from America.
The loan could be secured against the Pope's own pledge of a million gold
ducats to be paid when Spanish soldiers first set foot on English soil. For
more than a year Olivarez had been trying to get some part of that promise

anticipated in cash. Between him and Caraffa it was an old topic. Caraffa was sufficiently impressed by the news about the Queen of Scots to promise to discuss Olivarez's proposals with the Pope at once. Sometime that evening Sixtus V learned of the execution at Fotheringhay. We do not know what he said.

It might not enlighten us if we did. Now, as in his lifetime, the character and policies of Sixtus V lie hidden under a foam of words. In part, of other people's words. Throughout his papacy Rome buzzed with stories about Felice Peretti — some malicious, some terrifying, some amusing, some awestruck, some simply outrageous and incredible. He fascinated the Romans, and for five years the rhyming statues, Pasquino and Marforio, and their interlocutors, seem to have had almost no other topic of conversation. Sixtus fascinated the diplomatic corps, too. All the embassies retailed anecdotes about him, usually in the greatest detail when he was being the most absurd and indiscreet, perhaps in revenge for his making them a little afraid of him. The chief source of the smother of language which concealed and still conceals the character of Felice Peretti, however, was the Pope himself. Words gushed from him in a torrent, spontaneous, uncalculated, recklessly emotional, apparently utterly revealing. And yet, revealing almost nothing. Not, one guesses, usually from any intent to deceive but rather because this spate of language gave relief to all those surface impulses which his stern inner concentration prevented from finding an outlet in action. What is hard to find in his recorded words, or in the gossip about him, is any clue to the great ruler who brought peace and order to the papal states and water to Rome. To know Sixtus V one must look at what he did, not what he said.

For instance, he often spoke of Elizabeth of England with admiration. What a woman she was! What a princess! Ruler of half of one small island she snapped her fingers at the two greatest kings in Christendom. What a gallant heart she had, and what ready wit! If only she were a Catholic, there was no one he would befriend more gladly! Of Philip of Spain Sixtus spoke often too, in a variety of tones ranging from humorous impatience to white-hot fury. Yet it would be hasty to conclude that Sixtus wished Elizabeth well or Philip ill. Philip was the partner to whom the Pope was permanently yoked, however the double harness might gall them both. It was their joint task to restore the unity of Christendom. Philip was the indispensable ally. Elizabeth was the enemy. Wherever heretics resisted their sovereigns there was, Sixtus knew, English intrigue and English gold. In France and the Netherlands still, as lately in Scotland,

Cardinal Allen, d. 1594, engraved by J. Cochran, from the original in the possession of Browne Mostyn Esq.

Pope Sixtus V, from a portrait in the Pinacoteca Vaticana.

the Protestant revolution depended on English support. And the Protestant princes of Germany and Scandinavia looked to England to keep the readvancing armies of Catholicism at a safe distance from their borders. Sixtus might jeer at Philip and urge him for his own sake to finish with the English, but Sixtus knew that the issue was as large as Christendom, and no Pope of the great post-Tridentine line was more single-mindedly devoted to the recovery of all the provinces lost since Luther to the faith. Sixtus might be loud in his admiration for the Queen of England, but he was eager to assist in her overthrow by whatever means might offer. Whatever Sixtus may have felt or said about the death of the Queen of Scots, only one question was really important to him. Would it spur the laggard King of Spain? In the weeks that followed Sixtus acted as if he thought it might.

By the night of the 24th, Olivarez's news by one means or another had percolated to the chief embassies — the French, the Venetian, the Florentine — and to a number of the cardinals, and Sixtus's question was being asked with varieties of emphasis under many roofs in Rome. Nowhere was it asked more anxiously than in a little sparsely furnished house shoved in next to the English college, not far from the Spanish embassy. By whatever means he let the news leak out to the other embassies Olivarez had sent to that modest address one of his own servants with a few lines in his own hand, apparently before he had even talked to Caraffa. In that house lodged the subject of Mendoza's earnest recommendation to Olivarez — the founder and president of the English College at Douai, and co-founder of the English College at Rome, Dr William Allen.

The English College at Rome still stands on the Via di Monserrato, much as it was in Allen's time, but the little house next door has vanished. Here and there in old letters we catch a glimpse of it. A door opened directly on to the street, and beside it a narrow alley, perhaps only a covered passage, led to a dark courtyard. Through the street door one entered a sort of hall where Dr Allen's visitors waited, and servants slept at night and laughed and quarrelled all day. It must have been at the back of this room that the cooking was done. Dr Allen's own rooms were on the piano nobile at the top of a double flight of stairs at the front of the house. There a study held a large table, some stools and benches, a massive chest (a gift from His Holiness), and a hanging shelf for books; beyond, a low round arch showed a cell-like alcove just big enough for a bare bedstead with a crucifix above it and some pegs for clothes.

The bareness was only partly the result of poverty. Dr Allen's income was small and the demands upon him many, but he could have afforded some hangings and a chair or two. Even years later, when he had been for some time a cardinal, he still had not done so. Yet the omission was certainly not ostentatious self-denial; nothing could have been more unlike William Allen. It must have been rather that, although he had been some two years in residence here, it just did not seem worth while to settle down in this latest wayside station. One has seen the same look of temporary tenancy in the dwellings of more recent exiles. It was twenty-two years since William Allen had seen England. For twenty-two years he had not seen Oxford where, at an early age, he had made himself an honourable place, sacrificed before he was thirty for conscience sake. He had not seen his father's house, Rossall in Lancashire, for longer than that, though when he was young and ill his mind had turned so steadily thither that his Belgian doctor had told him he must go home or die. Since he had left England William Allen had thoroughly learned, as another exile had learned before him, how steep the stairs are going up and down in strangers' houses, how bitter-salt the bread that exiles eat.

In all the years of exile Allen had never given up working and scheming and hoping that some day he could go home again. In 1561 when he had resigned his principalship at St Mary's Hall, Oxford, it may have seemed to him, as it did to most English Catholics then refugees, that it would not be for long. A few exiles already pinned their hopes to the young Dowager Queen of France who had sailed that summer to Scotland. A few had begun to talk about a papal bull of deposition to be executed by France or Spain or both. But most relied on less violent courses. Either God would remove Anne Boleyn's daughter or he would soften her heart. To optimists among them, and even to some experienced politicians, this last seemed the most probable event. A woman could not long rule alone over a turbulent country like England, and all her likeliest suitors were Catholics. Once she had married she could escape the dominance of Puritans, and England could be reconciled once more to Rome. For some years the refugees clung to this hope.

Later, expectations darkened. Allen himself was shocked when he returned to England in 1562 to see the drift away from the old faith, and how many individuals who thought of themselves as Catholics were attending Anglican services with the consent or even the encouragement of their pastors. By '65, when he quitted England for what was to prove the last time, Allen was convinced that when his country returned to the fold a freshly trained priesthood would be necessary. That was the inspiration for the English college which he helped to found at Douai.

Then came the Rising of the North and after its failure a fresh wave of refugees, more bitter and desperate. They had seen the first blood of the reign shed for religion's sake, and as the hangings and confiscations went forward in the north they became more embittered still. Though most of them remained in the Netherlands, others spilled over to Paris, to Madrid, to Rome, clamouring for a chance at vengeance. Only Rome listened. King Philip had other cares: the restless Netherlands, the revolt of the Moors, the Turkish navy daring him in his own seas. He had had serious provocation from the English, but he wanted peace with them at almost any price. If the French could end their religious civil war they seemed more likely to attack England than Spain was. But although no one was listening except the English the saintly Pius V on February 25th, 1570, issued the bull 'Regnans in excelsis', declaring Queen Elizabeth a heretic and persecutor of true religion and cut off by excommunication. Furthermore, invoking a right which the Holy See had more frequently claimed than exercised, the Pope deprived Elizabeth of 'her pretended right to the throne', released her people from their allegiance, and commanded all of them on pain of anathema never henceforward to obey her laws and orders.

The bull merely sharpened an issue already critical. 'I ought rather to believe the doctrine of the Church than an Act of Parliament,' was the mild way one Catholic refugee put the case to Lord Burghley. But that meant, for Catholics as for Protestants, choosing to obey an international authority rather than the laws of one's own state. The governments thus defied, Philip's government in the Netherlands, the Valois government in France, the Tudor government in England, called such men traitors and rebels and dealt with them accordingly. But there were many in the sixteenth century, Catholics and Protestants alike, who for conscience sake were ready to defend their beliefs by any means, including secret conspiracy or armed rebellion. The bull of Pius V seemed to call the English Catholics to such courses.

The bull must have had weight with William Allen from the first. Just when he concluded that it pointed the only way of salvation for what in his letters he often called his 'lost fatherland' we do not know. By 1575 he was already deep in a plot to rescue Mary Queen of Scots by force of arms and turn out the woman whom he had come to regard as a tyrant and a usurper. When, in 1577, his friend Nicholas Sander wrote him that 'The state of Christendom dependeth upon the stout assailing of England', we can be sure he agreed. Certainly, after Sander went to raise in Ireland the revolt in which he found his death, it was Allen who became the chief voice of the English refugees in their clamour for foreign intervention against Elizabeth.

In the decade since he had taken up Sander's task Allen had known many disappointments. Promising conspiracies, promised crusades, one after another had come to nothing. 'If this time the Enterprise is not begun,' he had written in 1582, 'my life will be for ever bitter to me.' A few months later that elaborate plan had collapsed, and in a few months more he was patiently building another. When that failed in turn he was ready to abandon politics in despair, but in the very letter in which he said so he announced the launching of a new scheme. All the while he was arguing, writing, solving the problems and directing the administration of two colleges, arranging for the printing of books and their clandestine distribution, and running an active underground to convey priests and students, couriers and refugees in and out of England. An infuriated government searched out his books and burned them. But more than twenty thousand copies of some dozen titles were, he estimated, passing from hand to hand in England. Royal agents chivvied his priests about the countryside, tortured them horribly, executed some with all the obsolete medieval obscenities of hanging, drawing and quartering, and shipped others out of the country. But more than three hundred, Allen was confident, were still living in 1587 in the households of noblemen and principal gentlemen throughout the realm, keeping the minds and hearts of the faithful ready for the day of liberation.

These were but minor victories, however. The main campaign was still unlaunched; the old sorrow still unassuaged. Allen had phrased it for laymen and priests alike, when he had written: 'Thou knowest, good Lord, how often we have lamented together, that for our sins we should be constrained to spend either all, or most, of our serviceable years out of our natural country, to which they are most due, and to which in all ages past they should have been most grateful; and that our offices should be acceptable, and our lives and services agreeable, to strangers, and not to our dearest at home.' While they clung to their faith Allen and his fellows would never find their services agreeable in England until there was a Catholic on the throne.

There was another anxiety, another reason for haste, which all the

English exiles felt, but which Allen felt most because he had had a main hand in heightening it. From the first the seminarists whom Allen sent to England were charged to exhort their flocks to separate themselves from the heretics, and so avoid as a deadly sin attendance at Anglican services. Only so, Allen felt, could the ranks of the faithful be kept unbroken. This meant that really zealous Catholics had to declare themselves openly, and this in years just after the Northern Rising, Pope Pius V's bull, the Ridolfi Plot and the massacre of St Bartholomew had excited Protestant opinion.

The government replied by more drastic persecution. In 1580 Gregory XIII was persuaded to issue an explanation of his predecessor's bull which made matters rather worse. He said that while Elizabeth and her heretic abetters were to remain excommunicate and accursed, Catholics could obey her and take her for queen without fear of anathema, *rebus sic stantibus*, while things stood as they were. Until, that is, the public execution of the bull should summon all good Catholics to the duty of rebellion. In effect, Catholics were permitted to protest their undying loyalty to the Queen 'in all civil matters' as long as they bore in mind their duty to overthrow her at the first convenient opportunity. Lord Burghley was frightened into inventing new treasons, laws which aimed no longer at overt words and deeds, but at 'the secret treasons of the mind and heart'. The persecution of Catholics was again intensified.

Allen was not afraid that English priests ready to face rack and scaffold would be lacking. But the Protestants had a weapon more potent than hanging. In 1559 non-attendance at church cost twelve pence a Sunday. By the 1580s the fine had risen to twenty pounds a month, and since only a handful of rich men could afford such a sum month after month an Act of Parliament authorized seizing the land and chattels of those behind in their payments. In all his plans for the restoration of the faith in England Allen had counted most on the Catholic landed aristocracy. But no landed class could preserve their leadership indefinitely against the grinding attrition of such fines. The longer the execution of the papal bull was delayed the graver the danger that the hard core of avowed Catholics would be reduced to poverty and impotence, at the same time the greater the danger of defection by the 'Schismatics', the Englishmen who attended Anglican services but sympathized with the old faith. Allen counted heavily on them too, but he knew that with the passing of every year since he had deliberately cut them apart from the professing Catholics their ties with Rome and with the avowed followers of Rome in England had grown weaker. If the day of divine chastisement was delayed much longer the Catholic party in England might be too weak to help, and without their support, Allen felt sure, a foreign invasion would fail.

So for ten years Allen had been urging haste with the Enterprise. Yet now, as always whenever the ghost of a chance appeared, he felt there was still time. The old arguments marshalled themselves in his brain. The old dream stirred behind his eyes. England was an open land. The harbours were many and safe. It abounded with cattle and all sorts of provisions to be had for the taking. Its cities were ungarrisoned and practically unfortified. Not one could stand a three-day siege. Its people were unaccustomed to war, no match for the Spanish veterans. But more important still, two-thirds of them were Catholics or secret sympathizers with the Catholic cause. The professed Catholics would join a Catholic army at once. They knew now that they owed the Queen no duty and only obeyed her through fear. Some of the schismatic magnates (Allen had their letters) could also be counted on to join, for conscience sake or for ambition or for hatred of the Queen and the men around her. Most of the others would hold aloof, waiting to see how things came out. Only the climbers and adventurers who had flourished by the Queen's favour would stand in her defence, they and a vile sect called Puritans, but these men (all of the southern and eastern counties) were rotten with soft living and the greed of gain. They were no match for the hardy Catholics of the north and west who lived on simple country fare and still knew the use of arms. Allen could see them now — the Nevilles and their kin welcoming returning Westmorland, Dacres riding again at the head of his friends and tenantry, Northumberland's sons raising the Percy country to avenge their murdered father, Montague and Morley and Lovell and Storton rallying to the cause, all names of power; and others even more powerful and more unlikely — Oxford and Derby, Cumberland and Southampton and, perhaps, if a swift dash at the Tower could succeed, Arundel galloping off to add the Howard banner to the rebel clump. Among all these noblemen, with his old friends and kinfolk pressing admiringly behind him, and peers deferential at his bridle hand, would ride a man in a cardinal's habit — the papal legate. William Allen would have reproved himself and turned away from dreams before he quite saw the legate's face.

It would be odd if that evening William Allen had not been joined in his bleak study by a priest from the college next door, Father Robert Parsons, s.j. In the past few years the name of Parsons the Jesuit had become almost as famous in England as that of William Allen. Parsons had been in England with Edmund Campion on that mission which could scarcely have caused more alarm if the two Jesuits had been an invading army, and he had proved himself since a formidable pamphleteer. But, while even his enemies were eager to speak well of Allen, Parson's fame had already acquired a sinister tinge, due partly perhaps to his membership in a mysterious order. That Jesuits were men of dark secrets and devious ways was well known by most people who knew nothing else whatever about them.

In appearance and temperament the two men were as different as they were in reputation. Allen looked the north-country gentleman, tall, straight-limbed, graceful and dignified in bearing. His hair and beard which had been butter yellow were turning white, and his face was beginning to be lined with care and with the pain of the disease he had suffered for three years and was to suffer seven more, but it was still a countenance 'full of sweetness and benignity', forehead high and rather narrow, nose long and delicately chiselled, eyes the colour of Morecambe Bay on a clear day with the north wind blowing. He spoke slowly and gently, but without hesitation and with an air of calm authority, using few gestures. His patience was phenomenal; he was almost never angry. Most men liked and trusted him at sight, many were devoted to him. There is no sign of a quick or remarkable intellect, but he was a natural leader, 'born and apt for great affairs'.

Parsons was fourteen years younger than Allen, a convert who was said for a time to have been almost a Puritan, a man of another class and another corner of England. Such stocky bodies, swarthy complexions, coarse hair and liquid brown eyes, might be found anywhere in England, but more often in the south-west. Among other Englishmen such men had a flavour of the Celtic fringe, but their breed was old in the island before the first Celts came, as old as Stonehenge or Robin Goodfellow or the Quantock Hills. Parsons was born in Nether Stowey, where his father was said to have been a blacksmith. His big hands and feet, thick shoulders and barrel chest suggested that he might have thrived as a blacksmith himself had he not become a scholar. His head was big too, and the features all large and coarsely modelled, seeming in repose unfinished and almost brutal. But men seldom saw them in repose. They were animated and lighted from within by the constant play of intelligence and humour and passion, so that with his vivid sweeping gestures and mellow flexible voice he had an orator's presence to match his eloquent prose. Those who had heard Parsons speak did not easily forget him, but they easily forgot that at first sight they had found him clumsy and loutish. The discipline of his novitiate had enabled Parsons to cover his feverish questing spirit with at least an appearance of patience, and given him a hard-won if sometimes precarious self-control. He had further depths. He could turn from writing his angry jeering pamphlets to composing one of the simplest, sweetest, soundest books of devotion in the English tongue.

On the surface there can scarcely have been a less likely pair of collaborators than Parsons and Allen, yet for six years the younger man had been Allen's right hand, serving as a special envoy on one occasion to the King of Spain, on another to the Pope, and deeper in the maze of intrigues and negotiations about the Enterprise than anyone except Allen himself. That among available aides Parsons had the readiest tongue and pen, the nimblest wit and the most fertile brain, only partly explains their closeness. That no one, not even Allen himself, believed more passionately in the urgent need for a foreign intervention than Parsons did, may have helped Allen to decide on him. And they had in common, too, that they were among the least reconcilable of the exiles, that each in his way yearned with a special fervour for the martyrdom that had so far evaded him, and perhaps even more for the mere touch of English soil. But there was something even deeper than that. Their qualities were complementary, so that the sum of their strengths seemed more than mere addition could make it. It was as if each recognized in the other something of home that he had lacked and missed, as if together they made a microcosm of that sturdy society that had been medieval England.

We know in any case that they worked together in perfect harmony for at least ten years, and that from the time they met until a time long after the Armada survivors had struggled back to port, when Allen was dying in Rome and Parsons eating his heart out in Spain, no one who knew them hinted at any division between them.

In the autumn of 1585 they had travelled together to Rome and since that time they had worked shoulder to shoulder. Recently, for instance, they had collaborated on an elaborate genealogical study, demonstrating that, by his descent from Edward III, Philip II had after Mary Stuart the nearest claim on the throne of England of any orthodox prince. They had sent off the document for Philip to study. Since then they had begun work on a pamphlet in English, a defence of Sir William Stanley's surrender of Deventer to the Prince of Parma. They may have been at work on it when Olivarez's message arrived, since they had had the news of Deventer only about three weeks before, and the book was ready for the printer three weeks later.

It was a short book, but a tricky one to write. Its avowed purpose was to resolve the scruples of a Catholic gentleman of Stanley's regiment about his present position and that of his commander. Was it right for Stanley to deliver over to the Spaniards a Dutch city entrusted to him to defend? And what about the soldiers who had taken an oath to serve the Queen and now found themselves in the camp of her enemies? But the real scope of the book was larger. It was aimed not just at English Catholics serving in the Netherlands but at all the Catholics, secret and professed, in England, and it undertook to say explicitly, with all the proper citations from the Bible and the canon law, what hitherto Allen had only hinted: 'That, as all acts of justice within the realm done by the queen's authority ever since she was, by public sentence of the Church and See Apostolic, declared a heretic and an enemy of God's Church and ... by name excommunicated and deposed ... [are] void by the law of God and man, so, likewise, no war can lawfully be waged by her. That no man, by law, can serve or give aid [to a heretic prince] but he falleth into excommunication ... [for] those that break with God cannot claim any bond of oath or fidelity of them that were their subjects.' And so Allen can wish his country no better than that all Englishmen in any war at home or abroad waged about religion, should imitate Stanley's regiment, and 'in the service of the Almighty, and of the greatest and justest monarch in all the world [Philip, of course] and under a general so peerless [Parma] ... be notable helpers ... to reduce our people to the obedience of Christ's Church, and deliver our Catholic friends and brethren from the damnable and intolerable yoke of heresy.' If Mary Stuart's death meant that a time of decision had come at last, and Allen hoped that it might, then it was more important than ever to get this manuscript finished promptly, printed and into the channels of clandestine distribution in England.

About other matters Allen and Parsons had only immediate courses of action to decide. They had been over the big question so often; they had considered every possible contingency from every possible angle. In day-to-day politics they were realists. They had discounted Mary Stuart ever since her straighter imprisonment made her rescue unlikely. The Guises and the French they had written off even before that, and they had long assumed that unless a surprise raid could reach her the Queen of Scots would be dead before an invading army had been many hours on English soil, more likely before the attacking fleet had sailed.

That night they decided that next morning they would go to the Spanish embassy with a request for advice and instruction on specific lines of action which needed co-ordination with the ambassador's. Parsons probably drafted the list of gently leading questions which the ambassador passed on to Spain. For some time past Allen and Parsons had found this the simplest method of handling Olivarez. It gave him a high opinion of their prudence and sagacity, as well as of their Christian humility.

Parsons also undertook the immediate business with the Curia. He would sound the three or four cardinals on whom he most relied. Sixtus ought to make the most vigorous pronouncement about Mary's death that could be got out of him. It would be well for him to hear from several sources that about Mary the French had been negligent or worse. There was a new project for converting Mary's son, James VI, to Catholicism. It could not have been more inopportune. It must be handled delicately if King Philip's suspicions were not to be aroused by too much show of enthusiasm, and the Pope not angered by too obvious coldness. And it was time to give another shove to the campaign for Allen's promotion to the cardinalate. That had always been in Parson's special charge.

As for Allen, he would write to the English refugees with Parma and send what word was needed at the moment to England via Rheims, and to Scotland where he was in indirect touch with the Catholic Lords. But first of all he must write to Philip. It would be a respectful but manly summons to punish this crowning iniquity of the English Jezebel. There would be no reference in it to the English troops in the Netherlands or to Drake's recent raid on the West Indies. Allen knew his man better than that. There would only be something about the pitiful state of the English Catholics who could now look to no one but Philip for relief, a reference to the King's duty to God and the Christian republic, and an assurance that victory could not fail the champion of the faith. For years Allen had addressed Mary of Scotland as 'Most dread Sovereign Lady' in token of the transference of his allegiance from Elizabeth to her. In Latin the customary address to a great king is necessarily more ambiguous, but Allen made his position explicit in his close. He signed: 'your devoted servant and subject, William Allen.' With the death of Mary Stuart he was prepared to take Philip of Spain for his lawful king.

VII

GOD'S OBVIOUS DESIGN

SAN LORENZO DE ESCORIAL, MARCH 24TH–31ST, 1587

ENDOZA'S dispatches for Spain may have arrived as soon as
those for Rome. The Venetian ambassador finally heard that the
news of Mary Stuart's death had reached the Escurial on the night
of March 23rd. It should have. From Paris the route to Madrid was
rougher than to Rome, more dangerous in Gascony, bleaker and steeper
in Old Castile but rather shorter. The courier for Spain had started first —
he would have had the best mounts in the ambassador's stable — and as
soon as he reached the border his pouch would have been sped southward
by the royal post. But we cannot be sure. Although he tried, Philip II
could not repair with his own pen every error and omission of his under-
lings. This dispatch lacks a date of receipt. The diplomatic corps knew
nothing of Mary's death until March 31st, but they were shivering in
Madrid, nearly thirty miles by road from the Escurial; and even when these
miles were not foul and slippery with rain and snow, court gossip was
often a week stale before any ambassador heard it. They could only
wonder meanwhile what the King was doing up there on his mountain.

Whenever the news came, up to March 31st Philip was doing nothing.
For that there could be more than one reason. When a diplomatic pouch
reached the Escurial its contents, however urgent, were receipted by the
appropriate official, deciphered by the appropriate clerk, and placed
along with the originals on the appropriate corner of the long table in the
cheerless little room in which the King now spent most of his waking
hours. All sorts of official papers lay piled on that long table. It held the
correspondence of ambassadors, the reports of viceroys and governors, of
customs and treasury and municipal officials; it held petitions and memorials and the findings of judicial investigations, the accounts of dockyards
and mints and mines, and of the royal household. Every day the papers
came in from all the kingdoms of Castile and of the crowns of Aragon;
from Portugal now, too, and from Philip's other dominions; from Naples
and Sicily and Milan, from Franche Comté and the Belgian provinces,
from Mexico and Peru and Brazil, from golden Goa and African Sofala

and the islands of the eastern and the western seas. Nobody since the beginning of history had ever ruled so much of the earth's surface as Philip II of Spain. Nobody had ever owned so many titles of kingdoms, dukedoms, counties, principalities and lordships of all sorts. And nobody, surely, had ever had so many papers to read. Sooner or later Philip read, if not all, at least a very great many of them, leaving in his spidery scrawl in their margins shrewd statesmanlike comments and trivial corrections of spelling and grammar, each annotation a witness to posterity of his appalling, his stupefying industry. Naturally, he sometimes got a little behind. If the message that Mendoza sent off with such haste had remained unread for days and even weeks on the King's desk it would not have been the first dispatch, or the last, to be treated so.

Usually, however, the more important dispatches got fairly prompt attention. Usually, if Philip delayed action, it was because he made a habit of second thought. He liked to review methodically all the arguments for and against a given step, preferably outlined in writing and supported by relevant files. Among his councillors he listened, but rarely spoke. Afterwards in silence, entrenched behind comforting stacks of paper while candles flickered and an under-secretary yawned in a corner, slowly and stubbornly Philip made up his mind alone.

For this trait of the royal character, as for others, the monastery of San Lorenzo de Escorial provides a symbol and a revelation. Philip had dreamed of San Lorenzo while he was still fighting his father's wars in the Netherlands. Even in those first dreams the monastery-palace had always been in Spain. He had begun to search for its site almost as soon as he returned to his kingdom. He had paced the bare hillsides above the wretched village of Escorial before a peg had been driven or a trench dug, had drunk from the mountain springs, sniffed the keen air, felt the wind and rain on his cheek. Once decided he had hurried an army of workmen to the chosen spot, and a somewhat confused and irritated convent of Hieronymite monks along with them. Thereafter Philip could not keep himself away. He preferred this pastoral austerity to stately Toledo or soft delicious Aranjuez, the parish priest's spare bedroom or an improvised cell in a makeshift wooden monastery to his pleasantest palaces. During the twenty years San Lorenzo was being built he constantly pored over the plans with the architect, scrambled about scaffolds with the master builder, and encouraged the workmen with more interest and affability than he ever showed to his grandees. The main outlines of the building and many of its details were intimately his.

Early he had planned for the centre of the structure a noble church where his father's bones and his own might lie, and where masses could be said for their souls — many masses daily — until the end of time. From then on Philip seemed obsessed with the fear that he might not live to see his tomb. He pressed the work so urgently that his councillors grumbled about a king who spent as much time on one monastery as he did on all his kingdoms. Now, although the decoration of the interior would never be finished as long as the King's agents could find another painting in Venice, another tapestry in Flanders or another piece of classical sculpture in Naples or Rome, the last stone had been placed and the last tile laid for more than two years. Philip had begun to live inside his dream. The vast stone pile which he had drawn about him like a garment spoke of his peculiar self as no other building in Europe had ever echoed the spirit of a single man.

The building is seated on the knees of the mountains, the saw-toothed rock ridge of the Guadarramas rising steeply behind it and the rolling piedmont falling swiftly away before. It stands like a monument held out on a pedestal for the admiration of the Spanish plain. In its elevation, its distant prospects, its savage backdrop to the north, and the light and air and silence all around it, there is an overpowering sense of solitude, of isolation. The massive unornamented walls, built of the local granite, might almost have grown up out of the mountain. Their meagre, deeply recessed windows might be the mouths of caves or the embrasures of cannon.

At the centre of the building rises the dome of the monastery church. Its shape suggests St Peter's, a resemblance which did not escape contemporaries, which probably was meant not to escape them. Whoever might be emperor by the choice of the German electors, Philip felt that he was emperor by God's election and so a sacred personage, the equal of the Pope. The church which says so is smaller than its Roman rival, but there was no group of buildings in sixteenth-century Europe which compared in size with the Escurial except the complex of St Peter's and the Vatican. Both combined, conspicuously, a palace and a church. Both were, for Europe in the 1580s, modern buildings in the latest architectural fashion. Both breathed the spirit of the Counter-Reformation. But here the resemblance ceased. The church of San Lorenzo in Philip's time had none of St Peter's gaiety and lavish popular magnificence within. It has never had St Peter's air of open, all-embracing welcome without. Philip's San Lorenzo is shut away at the centre of the massive walled monastery like

the innermost citadel of a fortress, like a sacred standard in the middle of
a phalanx. St Peter's stands for the spiritual counter-offensive of Rome,
the confident, magniloquent advertisement of a catholic faith. The church
of San Lorenzo stands for the embattled defence of orthodoxy by the
temporal sword.

The great monastery actually seemed to Philip a defiance and a threat
to the heretics of Europe which those wicked revolutionaries would risk
anything to spoil. He often said so, attributing every accident or delay to
the machinations of heretic spies, and a building thought of in those terms
could hardly fail to resemble a fortress. That the church at the centre
should be at the same time a tomb where, according to plans which affected
the whole complex structure, masses in overpowering numbers were to
be said for the soul of Philip and his relatives, tells us less of the King's
spiritual views than it does of his sense of the unique position which he
and his family occupied in Christendom — just as the site he selected is
eloquent of his elevation above even the greatest of his subjects. But the
Escurial reveals more than Philip's public image of his public self. At the
secret heart of the great building, right next to the monastery church, a
meagre suite of rooms is hidden. The most important pieces are a sort of
study or workroom decently lighted but somehow meanly proportioned,
and off it an alcove bedroom which has a shuttered little window opening into the church near the high altar. Monastery, palace and tomb
prove only so many masks concealing a retreat, a refuge, almost a
hiding-place.

It was not enough that the site Philip had chosen for the Escurial insured isolation. On the bare rocky slope where he had built it there was
no decent human habitation except San Lorenzo itself, and the use of the
land around left no room for any. Moreover, vast as the building was, the
King's plans had so filled it with activities — a school, a library, a work-
shop, a hospital — that it would barely hold the enlarged congregation of
Hieronymite monks and a reduced royal household. There was no room
for the swarms of courtiers, of suppliants and projectors who closed in on
the King as soon as Court moved to Madrid or Valladolid. His overpowering courtesy-cousins, the grandees, and the watchful, importunate
envoys of his clients and allies could neither impose on his hospitality
here nor set up their households at his doorstep.

Yet inside the isolated pile Philip had managed a further isolation. The
unkingly little huddle of rooms where Philip now spent a longer time
each year had been designed to keep people out. The chambers were too

small, the corridors too narrow for any crowd. The approaches were easily controlled; the eye could sweep each room at a glance; there was no chance of an unexpected encounter. Philip was an affectionate family man, but his family lodged elsewhere. Philip loved and trusted his monks, but his way into their choir was by a hidden door and a secret stairway. Even the public entrance to his apartments had something closed and secretive about it. Once inside it Philip could enjoy real privacy. In the sixteenth century, as throughout the Middle Ages, privacy had been the unenvied prerogative of hermits. The greater a man was the larger the crowd in the midst of which he was expected to pass most of his waking life. It was probably his increasing passion for privacy rather than his conventional piety which led people to feel, as he grew older, that there was something monkish about Philip.

In a sense there was. There was true asceticism in the way he toiled, eyes red-rimmed, bones aching, fingers stiff, at his self-imposed task of chief clerk of the Spanish Empire. Increasingly, as he grew older, he gave up for it not only the hunting, dancing and feasting which were the conventional diversions of kings, but the things he really loved — flowers and pictures, country excursions and the company of his children. And there may have been true religious meditation in the agony of doubt with which he confronted every major decision of his reign. We know that he believed God expected more of kings than of other men, and far more of the King of Spain than of any other king. He was conscious of bearing a terrible, a unique burden. Perhaps the solitude of that cell-like cabinet, within sound of the chanting of the Hours, was as necessary to him as he wrestled with the problem of what God wanted him to do as it might have been to the lonely wrestling of any other monk.

There in his cell-like cabinet Philip sat for a week, as far as we know, without writing a line touching England, or consulting anyone, except his confessor about a funeral service for the Queen. Not that there was anyone further to consult. If English firebrands had been urging the Enterprise on Philip for nearly twenty years, Philip had been seriously considering it for about four. In his mind and in his voluminous files it had begun to take a definite shape, preparations for it were going forward in Spain, and the officials most concerned had already been told as much of the King's plans as they needed at this stage to know. When, if ever, the next stage would be reached, when the cumbrous administrative machine would move into a higher gear, only the King could say.

Early in the 1580s, sometime after the King had returned from his

Philip II of Spain (1527–98), consort of Mary I. Painting by an unknown artist, *c.* 1580.

military promenade into Portugal and not long before the last tile was laid on the roof of the Escurial, the Enterprise of England began to be a definite plan. The acquisition of Portugal meant a great increase in Spanish strength in the Atlantic. The Portuguese had been the pioneers of the Ocean. In the Indian Ocean they had used the guns of their sailing-ships to smash the war galleys of the Egyptians and the Turks and win an empire based on command of the sea. In African and Brazilian waters their galleons had been equally successful against French and English and Spanish interlopers. And in the last phase of the Spanish conquest of Portugal, the reduction of the Azores, a Spanish admiral commanding Portuguese galleons had won two brilliant victories against squadrons the Portuguese pretender had recruited in French ports. These were combats between sailing-ships in the Atlantic style, and in the second action the Spanish thought they had beaten English ships as well as French ones. In the exhilaration of that victory the admiral, Don Alvaro de Bazán, Marquis of Santa Cruz, a grizzled veteran of Lepanto, offered to take on the whole English navy at a word from his king.

In reply Philip asked for an estimate of the naval forces needed for the Enterprise of England. The King's matter-of-fact request was sobering, and the admiral's final estimate showed no undue depreciation of English naval strength. Santa Cruz wanted one hundred and fifty great ships, including all the galleons (the battleships of the time) available, and the rest, merchantmen as large and as heavily armed as possible, forty *urcas* for stores and provisions (large freighters, one might say), and some three hundred and twenty auxiliary craft of all kinds, dispatch boats, picket boats, fast armed cruisers for scouting and pursuit (zabras and fregatas), a total of five hundred and ten sail, besides forty galleys and six galleasses, the whole to be manned by thirty thousand mariners and to carry sixty-four thousand soldiers, a force far greater than any Europe had ever seen at sea. Don Alvaro calculated that with the naval ordnance he wanted, the arquebuses, the corslets, the pikes, the powder and ball, the ropes, the anchors, the biscuits, the rice, the oil, the salt fish and everything else the expedition would need for an eight months' campaign, the whole thing could be done for only about 3,800,000 ducats. Not nearly enough, if one may judge by what Philip's money bought in the way of ships and stores in the years following, but the admiral might as well have said 38,000,000. Either sum, in addition to all the other demands on him, and the mounting pressure of his debts, was almost equally out of Philip's reach. And even the larger sum could not have conjured together the whole tale of ships without years of delay. To assemble the five-hundred-odd sail the admiral asked for would strip the harbours of Spain and Italy almost bare of shipping. In terms of the mission to be undertaken the admiral's estimate was reasonable; in terms of economic realities it was absurd.

Philip had another estimate on hand, one from his greatest army leader to balance the one from his best admiral. Santa Cruz wanted the whole force to sail from Spain, a unified naval expedition with himself in command. Alexander of Parma was willing, given favourable conditions, to dispense with the navy altogether. Thirty thousand infantry and four thousand cavalry, he thought, might be enough to do the job with the help of the English Catholics. With favouring winds and tides he would undertake to put such a force across in barges from Nieuport and Dunkirk in a single night. The same idea occurred later on to Napoleon Bonaparte and to Adolph Hitler. Parma, at least, stipulated that the essential condition for the success of his scheme was complete surprise. How the English were to be kept from noticing that thirty-four thousand men and seven or eight hundred barges were assembling on the Flanders coast, Parma nowhere said. Perhaps he reasoned that if when the time came the English fleet turned out to be in the way, the reinforcements he asked for would come in handy in the Netherlands. Philip noticed the catch. At the point in Parma's plan where the need for complete surprise was stressed the King's pen scrawled: 'Hardly possible!'

Out of the plans of his two ablest commanders Philip made a plan of his own. Parma should be reinforced by land from Italy, though not perhaps to the strength he asked for. As the time approached he was to poise, with his army and his barges, on the Flemish coast. Meanwhile Santa Cruz was to collect a fighting fleet at Lisbon, an armada meant to cope with the English navy and to carry or escort a strong force of Spanish infantry. The armada would steer for England and advance up the Channel. Parma would embark his army, and the Spanish fleet would rendezvous with his barges and escort them to a chosen invasion point somewhere near the mouth of the Thames. Once he had shepherded Parma's barges to safety and landed the infantry from Spain, Don Alvaro would stand by to secure Parma's communications by sea. If the English fleet forced a battle, or if a favourable occasion should offer, Don Alvaro would engage and seek to destroy the enemy, but the main function of the armada was to convoy a landing-force. Whether Don Alvaro understood this plan fully we do not know, but Parma did, as Don Bernardino de

Lisbon in 1582, from Braun, *Civitas Orbis*.

A Spanish galleass in action. The Spanish ships were powered by oars, whereas the English relied on a favourable wind. Detail from a contemporary painting, 'The Spanish Armada'.

Mendoza understood all that concerned his own role half a year at least before the Queen of Scots died.

In some ways it was a good plan. It did not rely too much on the English Catholics, as Parma did, though without some division of English strength the invasion force would scarcely be big enough to conquer the whole island. It was economical to use Parma's veterans, encamped just across the Channel, instead of bringing the whole invading army all the way from Spain. (As if Philip could have raised the army Don Alvaro asked for, or found the ships to transport it!) And it was highly desirable to use Parma's matchless skill in land warfare. At the same time it did not leave Parma without communications or means of retreat, committed to the desperate gamble of conquering England or losing his whole army. And by reducing and simplifying the role of the fleet it might be hoped that what naval forces could be scraped together would suffice. Of course it was a complicated and rather rigid plan, without much allowance for mistakes or accidents. But Philip relied on the skill and obedience of his commanders; no better plan seemed possible.

Nevertheless there was, so far, a tentative hesitant air about all the Spanish preparations. Contracts were being let for considerable quantities of biscuit and dried fish, sailcloth and tackle. New companies of infantry were being raised, and old ones brought up to full strength. In Germany and Italy the King's agents were looking for naval ordnance, big guns for choice, cannons and culverins, but anything brass or iron that a ship could carry, down to the little bases and mosquetes that were scarcely more than small arms. In Andalusian and Biscayan ports there were huddled clusters of miscellaneous shipping — Ragusans, Neapolitans, Genoese, Frenchmen, Danskers, ships of the Hansa towns, chartered or pressed for some eventual service. And at Lisbon masts had been stepped in new galleons and repairs completed on old ones, though most of them so far had neither guns nor crews. The bustle up and down the coast was enough to show that something was afoot, but was scarcely as yet so urgent as a life and death struggle with England would call for. The Italian ambassadors at Madrid that spring, a Venetian, a Genoese, a Florentine, a Mantuan and two representatives of the Pope, could not make up their minds whether the preparations were intended against the English or not.

Perhaps Philip had not made up his mind either. The English had given him provocation enough: Drake's impudent raid down the Spanish coast and across to the West Indies, Leicester's army in the Netherlands, the worsening fate of the English Catholics for whom, ever since his marriage in England, Philip had felt a special responsibility. The Pope exhorted him to act, the English exiles begged him to hurry, and among his counsellors the war party was in the ascendant. It may be that Philip was only making haste slowly because, as he had once written, in so great a matter it was better to walk with leaden feet.

On the other hand many things about the Enterprise repelled Philip. For one thing, its cost. All the silver of Mexico and Peru had not kept him from sinking deeper into debt every year, mortgaging every year another slice of his revenues, and paying higher and higher rates of interest for the ready money drained away into the bottomless bog of the Netherlands. Portugal, legendary monopolist of all the wealth of Ormuz and of Ind, had turned out to be as near bankruptcy as Spain, or nearer, and Philip had learned that navies were even more expensive than armies.

Even worse than the expense was the uncertainty. Any war was risky, abhorrent to a prudent man. Philip liked to think that he had never sought war, never fought except in defence, never used his strength to rob or oppress his neighbours. 'He fears war', Father Parsons wrote of him contemptuously, 'as a burned child dreads the fire.' He feared war with England especially. He knew something of the country of which he had been king, enough to know that his plan, or any plan for the Enterprise, involved a desperate gamble. More than once his pen had scrawled a curt 'disparo' (nonsense!) in the margin of some paper telling him how easy it would be to conquer England. In the days when he had been Mary Tudor's husband he had once written: 'The kingdom of England is and must always remain strong at sea, since on this the safety of the realm depends.' Strong at sea, so his most experienced captains told him, England had remained, a strength not to be challenged without risk.

And in the Enterprise there had seemed to be in victory a risk even greater than in defeat. If Mary Stuart was alive when his armies overthrew the English she would have to be Queen of England. She was a Catholic, at least. She had courted him of late and she might prove grateful. But her heart was French, and Philip had learned from his father that the gravest danger to their dynasty lay in a union of France and England. It would be a bitter irony if Spanish blood and Spanish treasure were to be spent only to make the King of France again the greatest king of Europe. Could God ask so much, even to restore England to the faith?

Now that risk at least was cancelled. We cannot be sure how much that mattered to Philip, any more than we can know what thoughts he had as he brooded over Mendoza's letter. We only know that, after days when his pen hardly touched paper and his secretaries stood idle, suddenly on the evening of March 31st the secret heart of the Escurial pulsed with action. There was a volley of curt missives. Santa Cruz must try to be ready to sail before spring was over. The ships and stores at Cartagena and Malaga must hurry to Lisbon. The Biscayan shipwrights should have the 25,000 *escudos* advance they asked for, only let them make haste! The arsenal of the galleys at Barcelona was to review its ordnance and stores and release everything it could spare to equip the Atlantic armada. A similar order to Naples. An emphatic query as to what was delaying the saltpetre expected from Genoa. A brief veiled note to Parma: the plans already agreed on would be carried out with increased speed in view of recent events. One almost equally curt to Mendoza. He was to condole with the Scots ambassador in Paris over the Queen's death. In other matters there were no fresh instructions, and the ambassador might take it that his advice was approved.

The same night saw the drafting of a fatter bundle of letters, in more explicit language, to be sent to Rome. Philip never forgot that his letters to Parma and Mendoza might be intercepted by the Huguenots to whom no seal was sacred and no cipher long secure. The pouch for Rome ran no such risk. So, besides a cordial greeting to Cardinal Caraffa and a detailed set of instructions to William Allen, assuming the obedience offered in the letter Philip had not yet seen, there was a whole set of letters and papers for Olivarez. He was to try again for an immediate loan. He was to remind the Pope that the King of France was not to be trusted. And he was to show the Pope all the documents supporting Philip's claim to the English Crown and ask him for a secret brief conferring the investiture on him. Philip, of course, would hand it on to his daughter. He had no want of further kingdoms. But the cruel death of the Queen of Scots made him more eager than ever to push on with the Enterprise.

There was another letter, apparently meant to be shown at the Curia. 'I am grieved,' [at Mary's death] Philip wrote, 'since she would have been the most suitable instrument for leading those countries [England and Scotland] back to the Catholic faith. But since God in His wisdom has ordained otherwise, He will raise up other instruments for the triumph of His cause.' That, we may take it, was the final fruit of Philip's lonely meditations. It strengthened him through all the trials to come, so that whoever else might blench Philip walked straight forward, like a man led by a vision, like a somnambulist. Perhaps as he set down his conclusion his eye rested again on a passage in Mendoza's letter: 'So it would seem to be God's obvious design to bestow upon Your Majesty the crowns of these two kingdoms.'

VIII

'THE WIND COMMANDS ME AWAY'

LONDON AND PLYMOUTH, MARCH 25TH–APRIL 12TH, 1587

WHILE in the recesses of the Escurial Philip II pondered the consequences of Mary Stuart's death, chafing on the fringes of the Court at Greenwich was a sailor-man who had fewer doubts than Philip about what God meant him to do in the world, and had known long before Philip did that God's plan was for war between the two of them. Like the King of Spain Francis Drake had learned the rudiments of his mission in the world from his father, and though that father was a Devonshire hedge-parson Drake cherished his words as Philip did those of the Holy Roman Emperor. In spite of all their temperamental differences King Philip and Sir Francis Drake were much alike in the unquestioning filial piety with which they held their basic convictions.

From Edmund Drake the lay preacher Francis learned a simple Puritan faith. Everything that happened, happened by God's will. One thing God certainly willed was the ultimate destruction of the Bishop of Rome and all his works. Therefore steadfast hostility to the Church of Rome and all its adherents was a sure sign that a man was on God's side, was one of his elect. Consequently Francis Drake was never shaken in his confidence that as he waged his private war against the King of Spain he was spoiling the idolaters, like an Old Testament hero, under the highest auspices.

Drake's private war with Spain, however, was not itself an inheritance, and arose from nothing so abstract as a sense of public or religious duty. It sprang, like Samson's private war with the Philistines, from a deep personal grievance. Young Francis Drake had been in the harbour of San Juan de Ulua with John Hawkins when the armed ships of that prosperous merchant were treacherously set upon and overwhelmed by the Armada of New Spain. Drake had got home to Plymouth in a leaky little bark with, for all he knew, the sole survivors of the venture. When Hawkins also limped home with the only other ship to escape he said only of the aftermath of the battle, that 'the bark *Judith*, the same night, forsook us in our great misery'. He laid no charge against his junior, but perhaps Drake thought men would say he had forsaken his admiral for fear of the

Spaniards, and that he was touched in his honour. Certainly he was touched in his purse. What modest capital he could gather had been invested in the voyage, and all was lost.

The very next year Francis Drake had set about recouping his money and his reputation. In the eighteen years since his inglorious return to Plymouth he had had some glorious homecomings. The first was on that Sunday in August '73 when, with a handful of Devonshire lads and a captured Spanish frigate, he had brought home the gold from the gates of Nombre de Dios. The most triumphant was that day in the autumn of 1580 when the *Golden Hind* rounded Rame Head with the circumnavigation of the globe behind her and the spoil of the virgin Pacific in her hold, bullion and jewels, spices and silks enough to yield a dividend of 4700 per cent for all the shareholders in the voyage and something over for the captain and Her Majesty. Just recently he had returned with a powerful squadron which had dared the King of Spain in the harbours of the peninsula and beaten up the commerce of his Indies, an expedition which the London merchants regarded as a failure because they lost five shillings in the pound on it, but from which the Spanish took slight comfort. No silver from Peru or Mexico had crossed the Atlantic in 1586, some great merchants of Seville were all but ruined, and there had been a minor panic among King Philip's bankers.

Though she lent Queen's ships to his later ventures and took a royal share of the profits Elizabeth I was always quick to deny any knowledge of Drake's plans or any responsibility for his behaviour. In the Spanish view that made Francis Drake a pirate. But Drake regarded himself as at war with the King of Spain. On more than one occasion he had sent King Philip his personal defiance. For him the war between them had begun with the attack at San Juan de Ulua, and he meant it to go on until one of them was dead, or until the King of Spain was brought as low as Francis Drake had been when the beaten little *Judith* with her crew of sick and wounded men had crawled back into Plymouth Harbour.

The notion that a private person, a simple knight, could be at war with the greatest king in Christendom belonged in a romance of chivalry. In the actual society of the sixteenth century one would expect it to be entertained only by someone as mad as Don Quixote. That Drake himself could believe it seems just possible, for though he was certainly no madman a part of his genius was a devastating self-confidence which transcended ordinary sanity. The surprising thing is that all Europe was beginning to take Drake's view. Newsmongers, pamphleteers, even capable politicians and diplomats, were coming to speak of the naval war between Spain and England as if it were a personal duel between King Philip and Francis Drake. As early as 1580 the Protestant princes of Germany and Scandinavia, the Huguenot lords and other enemies of Spain, had begun to send for copies of Drake's portrait, until soon the stocky broad-shouldered figure, the bristling aggressive brown beard, the ruddy merry countenance, the wide bright blue unblinking stare, were as familiar as they have remained ever since. Later, when the navies of England and Spain were at grips in the Channel, Germans and Frenchmen, Spaniards and Italians wrote as if the English fleet were merely an extension of Drake's person. 'On Sunday Drake was sighted,' they wrote. 'Drake has sunk so many ships ... Drake has lost so many ... Drake is off the Isle of Wight ... Drake has appeared before Calais ... Drake is defeated ... Drake is victorious.' Just as if the Queen's fleet had no other admiral, and indeed as if it were not the Queen's at all. Already spies and letter-writers were saying: 'Drake is gathering his forces ... Drake plans to waylay the plate fleet ... Drake will descend on Brazil', as if the movements of the Queen's ships depended on this strange pirate's whim.

As he went back and forth from London to Greenwich, from Greenwich to Gravesend and so to London again, Francis Drake must have wished heartily that the popular belief were true. He gathered from sailormen, he smelled on every wind from the south, and he heard in impressive detail from his friend and patron the Queen's Secretary, Sir Francis Walsingham, that great preparations were afoot in Spain. Drake felt that he knew how to hinder those preparations by such sudden thrusts as his campaigns in the Caribbean had taught him. This time his private war would be all England's war, and if only he could strike hard enough and quickly enough the King of Spain's great enterprise might be ruined before his armada could set sail. But, however often the men about her might regret it, England was ruled by a woman, and the Queen's ships did not sail without a queen's word. As March wore on Drake had been waiting months for that word. Once the Queen had admitted him to her presence nine times in one day. Now weeks went by without his seeing her at all.

Drake's biographers explain that Elizabeth was vexed with their hero because the Indies voyage had lost, not made, money. No doubt she was disappointed. There were so many unusual demands on her purse that winter of 1586 that probably she had hoped for the profits of a raid into the Caribbean which with luck might have bagged the treasure fleet. At the time the Queen's courtiers inclined rather to the explanation that she

Sir Philip Sidney (1544–86). Painting by an unknown artist.

Sir Francis Drake, from the Hilliard miniature (1581).

Sir John Hawkins, *c.* 1581.

Sir Walter Raleigh (1552–1618). Painting attributed to the monogrammist 'H'.

was so concerned about the fate of the Queen of Scots and then so distraught with sorrow and anger at the execution that lesser matters had gone by the board.

Probably there was a certain measure of truth in both explanations. A month after Mary's death Elizabeth was still in deep mourning, still sullen and snappish with her councillors, still neglecting her customary amusements. By that time the Scots were calmer, and the Queen's display of grief was beginning to make an impression on the French. It was worth Elizabeth's best efforts to prevent a possible alliance of Spain and France, or Spain and Scotland. Meanwhile, perhaps a Spanish attack could be at least postponed. Throughout late February and March the Queen was not too grief-stricken to follow up, through appropriately devious channels, proposals which in January she had commissioned a Spanish prisoner of Walter Raleigh's to make directly to the King of Spain. At the same time, with the knowledge of how many of her Council we cannot be sure, Elizabeth continued her cautious negotiations with the Duke of Parma. If things could be brought back to the precarious balance of the day before the axe fell at Fotheringhay, Elizabeth would do her best to restore the old uncertainty.

Meanwhile the more likely chance could not be neglected. Spain threatened England on three fronts. In the first place, in the Netherlands. With Parma's army poised on the Flemish coast Elizabeth needed the Dutch as much as they needed her. The ruling faction in Holland had, Elizabeth considered, been insolent and niggardly. The English expeditionary force had been, so far, a military and financial catastrophe. But somehow more money must be found for the starving English troops, the Dutch must be reassured and the working alliance re-established. In spite of her sulks Elizabeth found time during the month after Mary's death to set these matters in train.

She found time, too, to consider the second danger spot, France. King Henry III had achieved, in the midst of his miserable failures, one diplomatic triumph. Nobody took him for granted. Everybody thought him thoroughly unreliable. If Mendoza and Philip II believed him likely to choose the day the Armada sailed to strike hands with England and Navarre, Stafford and Walsingham and perhaps Elizabeth herself were afraid that at any moment he might join Spain and the Guises. On one thing English and Spanish statesmen were agreed. The way to deal with the King of France was by force. The Spanish counted on the Holy League. The war party on Elizabeth's Council favoured using German

Protestant troops to strengthen the Huguenots. Elizabeth suggested wistfully that perhaps the German princes might be persuaded this time to fight for religion's sake instead of just for pay, but she cannot have been serious. With a sigh she agreed to find them a subsidy of fifty thousand pounds, and she flinched but did not draw back when the price rose to a hundred thousand. At the same time she contrived to squeeze out some more money for the penniless King of Navarre. For the Queen such bitter pills were not sweetened by anything like Walsingham's enthusiasm for the common cause of Protestants everywhere. But she recognized that in the present danger it was worth something to keep the French busy at home.

That left the major threat, the threat of a Spanish attack by sea, still to be parried. England was not unprepared by sea. Nobody in the sixteenth century kept a fighting fleet mobilized between campaigns, but thanks to John Hawkins Elizabeth's was more nearly ready than any other, and had better ships, all built and kept in repair at the lowest possible cost. Her sea-dogs were confident of beating the Spaniards wherever they found them, but a pitched naval battle whether off the Spanish coast or in the Channel would be a terribly risky and expensive business. Francis Drake thought he knew of a cheaper way, and swore he could stop the Spaniards in their harbours by a raid down their coast. Elizabeth hesitated to offer her royal brother any further provocation or to spend a penny more than was absolutely necessary, and she knew that a firebrand like Drake might embroil her past hope of retreat. Still, if the Armada could be delayed even for a year, who knew what the unanticipated fruits of time might be? And perhaps the expedition could be financed like a private venture and so need not compromise her peace negotiations fatally, nor commit her beyond the point of no return.

The resulting plan bears all the signs of Elizabeth's personal intervention. Drake was to have six of the Queen's ships, four first-rate galleons and two pinnaces. He was authorized to agree with London merchants for as many ships as would join him. The Lord Admiral offered to send his own galleon and a pinnace, and Drake had outfitted at Plymouth four ships of his own. The squadron was to cruise for prizes, dividing the profits, so that from one point of view the voyage had some of the aspects of a private commercial venture. But Drake's instructions read, 'to impeach the purpose of the Spanish fleet and stop their meeting at Lisbon', the means being left to his discretion, even to 'distressing their ships within their havens'. For this he held the Queen's commission. At last his private war with the King of Spain was becoming England's own.

It would be odd if Drake had not discussed with Francis Walsingham the chance that there might be more chopping and changing in the Council if he delayed. His commission was dated, he said, March 15th (Old Style, March 25th, by the new Roman calendar), but some days earlier than that Mendoza's spies heard that Drake was recruiting the Queen's ships up to their full war complement. Three days later Drake had signed his agreement with the London merchants and the Queen's ships were weighing anchor at Gravesend. Drake did not sail with them. Perhaps he stayed for an interview at Greenwich. If so it was a secret interview. Then he and his wife hurried down to Dover where a pinnace put them aboard his flagship. Ten days after the date of his commission he led his squadron into Plymouth Sound.

He stayed there only a week, working furiously. He had the final readiness of his own four ships to see to, and the provisioning of the Queen's ships to finish — a task his haste must have led him to scamp, for it turned out later that the Plymouth contingent and the royal ships were much less well supplied than the Londoners. And he had other troubles. Perhaps it was at Plymouth that the word spread, as the word will sometimes spread even in the silent service, that the target was not the Indies and the Spanish main, with market towns and fat plantations to be plundered and a chance at the plate-fleet and enough silver pesos to make the humblest sailor rich, not the ill-guarded Brazilian coast, not even the Azores, but the ports of Cadiz and Lisbon, covered by forts and full — so people thought — of armed ships, where there was little to be got but hard knocks. We know at least that the first word that Drake's destination was probably Cadiz reached Mendoza just about the time Drake's mariners began to desert, starting from him in such numbers that Drake, as he was somewhat too prone to do, suspected traitor's work. This time he was in too much haste to do more than warn the local authorities to lay the deserters by the heels, and to write to the Lord Admiral that a matter so dangerous to the Queen's service called for severe punishments. Meanwhile he filled up his watch bills with soldiers, and when *The Royal Merchant* and four other ships, the last of the London contingent, hove in sight on April 1st (O.S.) he was ready to be off.

The next morning he wrote a farewell letter to his friend Walsingham from the cabin of his flagship, the *Elizabeth Bonaventure*, in his customary shaky syntax and with more than his customary enthusiasm. Of his company he wrote: ' ... we all persuade ourselves there was never more likely in any fleet of a more loving agreement than we hope the one of the other. I thank God I find no man but as all members of one body to stand for our gracious Queen and our country against Antichrist and his members. I thank God those gentlemen of great place, as Captain Borough, Captain Fenner and Captain Bellingham, which are partakers with me in this service, I find very discreet, honest and most efficient. If your honour did now see the fleet under sail and knew with what resolution men's minds do enter into this action, as your honour could rejoice to see them, so you would judge a small force would not divide them.

' ... I assure your honour here hath been no time lost ... ' Then comes a dark allusion to the chance that there might be some 'ill-affected, as there hath not wanted in other actions ... ' and the complaint that 'it is a hard measure to be reported ill by those which will either keep their finger out of the fire or too well affect to the alteration of our government which I hope in God they shall never live to see.' At the moment of writing one gathers that Drake could not have identified among his present companions any of those shadowy treacherous enemies who somehow haunted his career. Later he was to be very sure that Captain Borough, his vice-admiral, was one of them.

As he wrote he was probably thinking of the peace party on the Queen's Council, his enemies and Walsingham's, as were all those (except Gloriana herself) who did not want war with Spain. Had Walsingham warned him that the Queen might change her mind and restrict the freedom of his commission? His emphasis on the haste he had made sounds as if he might have been urged to hasten. Certainly Walsingham knew that Elizabeth's negotiations with Parma had recently taken another cautious step forward, and that the Queen would not endanger those negotiations for the sake of a blow at the Spanish coast. But no change in Drake's instructions could catch up with him now. 'The wind commands me away', he finished triumphantly. 'Our ships are under sail. God grant we may so live in His fear as the enemy may have cause to say that God doth fight for Her Majesty as well abroad as at home. Haste! From aboard Her Majesty's good ship the Elizabeth Bonaventure, this 2nd April, 1587.'

The Queen did change her mind. A courier did come galloping down to Plymouth with changed instructions whereof the gist ran that Her Majesty, hearing that the King of Spain was desirous that their late jars and unkindness might be compounded, and loath to exasperate matters further, hath commanded Drake to 'forbear to enter forcibly into any of the said King's ports or havens, or to offer violence to any of his towns or shipping within harbouring, or to do any act of hostility upon the land. And yet, notwithstanding this direction, her pleasure is that both you and such of her subjects as serve there under you should do your best endeavour (avoiding as much as may lie in you the effusion of Christian blood) to get into your possession such shipping of the said King or his subjects as you shall find at sea.' Whatever might be true of Sir Francis Drake or others of her bellicose subjects, Elizabeth wanted to make it clear that she was not at war with the King of Spain.

Had Drake received these instructions and obeyed them his campaign would have been very different, of course. But his failure to receive them was not such a near thing as some of his biographers, in the interest of dramatic narrative, have implied. There are several drafts of the countermanding order, but the first one, signed by the privy councillors, a copy of which would have been sent down to Plymouth, was dated April 9th. On that very day (April 19th, N.S.) Mendoza had heard in Paris that Drake had put to sea. It seems odd that no word of his sailing had affected the deliberations at Greenwich. When a pinnace put out to follow him with the Council's orders Drake had been gone nine days. He rarely needed that much time to elude any pursuer. The flaw which blew the pinnace back into the Channel must have been the last of the tempest which had scattered Drake's squadron off Finisterre some days before. Even so, the fact that the pinnace cruised about the Channel until it picked up a fat Portuguese merchantman suggests that its captain may have been allowed to guess that his mission was not so urgent after all.

A distinguished historian remarked of the countermanding order that it was 'highly characteristic of Elizabeth as a War Minister'. He meant no more, of course, than to express his disapproval of letting a woman interfere with men's work. A good many of Elizabeth's councillors felt the same way. And yet the more one looks at the affair of the countermanding order, the more one comes to feel that it is indeed characteristic of the way of Elizabeth I in war as in peace. In the first place it is veiled in mystery, part of which would seem to be deliberate mystification. The very language is elusive and ambiguous; only about financial arrangements, with special reference to insuring the Queen's full share in any loot, is it blunt and to the point. Elizabeth might almost have written it herself. And finally the outcome of the affair (whether it was intended that way or not, though one gets the feeling that it was intended) was to make the best of two contradictory lines of policy, simultaneously pursued. Walsingham could write to Stafford (did he know that Stafford

93

would pass it on to Mendoza?) that the Queen had forbidden Drake to enter any Spanish harbour; and Burghley might protest to Parma's representative, De Loo, on his honour and with his hand on his heart, that Her Majesty had sent expressly to forbid Drake to show any act of hostility to the King of Spain and would have punished severely the captain who failed to deliver the message, had he not been able to clear himself on his oath. All this could be confirmed by public evidence, so that the fiction that England and Spain were not at war could be maintained, and the negotiations in the Netherlands could go on. At the same time Drake was left absolutely free to impede the gathering of the Spanish fleet by any means that appealed to him. Elizabeth may have felt that Drake knew as much about that end of the business as anybody.

The *Golden Hinde* captures the *Cacafuego*, Spain's richest treasure ship, 1579.

A BEARD IS SINGED

CADIZ BAY, APRIL 29TH–MAY 1ST, 1587

O n Wednesday, the 29th of April, at four in the afternoon, it would
have been pleasant in the gardens of Charles V's old hunting-lodge
at Aranjuez. In all the high plateau of New Castile there is no place like
Aranjuez for flowers, and there is no season at Aranjuez like the beginning
of May. Usually Philip passed the month there. Only when he was making
himself King of Portugal had he missed spending May at Aranjuez. Then
he had written wistfully of the flowers and the nightingales in its gardens.
This year he had hurried thither as soon as he could decently leave
Madrid. In springtime the late afternoon sun was kindest to his gout, and
this was the time of day Philip visited his flowers. While he lingered
among them a dispatch came from Paris. Don Bernardino de Mendoza
wrote that on April 12th Drake had sailed from Plymouth with some
thirty ships. His mission was almost certainly to hinder the assembling of
the Spanish fleet, and his first target would probably be Cadiz. Perhaps
the King stayed longer than usual that day in his garden; perhaps his gout
sent him earlier than usual to bed. Whatever the reason he did not read
Mendoza's alarming dispatch until the next morning. It was too late,
anyway.

On Wednesday, the 29th of April, at four in the afternoon Captain William
Borough clambered aboard Drake's flagship, the *Elizabeth Bonaventure*.
Borough, a sailor of the old school, was the Lord Admiral of England's
Vice-Admiral for the Sea, serving now as Drake's vice-admiral and commander of the *Golden Lion*, one of the Queen's new galleons. Whether he
had come aboard in response to his admiral's signal he left unsaid, and
time has blurred most of the faces he saw on Drake's quarter-deck. It was
some sort of Council of War, though not a full one, for the most laggard
ships were still almost hull down on the horizon, and not at all the kind of
council William Borough was accustomed to.

The occasion was plain. On its low, humpbacked promontory the town
of Cadiz would soon be taking shape and a fair south-west wind filled the
squadron's sails. Behind the admiral was spread out much the same force

he had led from Plymouth eighteen days before. In spite of the tempest that had scattered them off Finisterre the voyage had been, on the whole, quick and prosperous. One pinnace had been lost in the storm but several prizes had been picked up, one a handy Portuguese caravel, so that the squadron which rendezvoused off the Rock of Lisbon must have numbered about twenty-six sail. There were four Queen's ships, the *Elizabeth Bonaventure*, the *Golden Lion*, the *Dreadnought* and the *Rainbow*, fine stout galleons rated at four to five hundred tons apiece, bristling with ship-smashing guns; and three tall ships of the Levant Company of London, almost as large as the Queen's galleons and, because of the hazards of the Levant trade, almost as heavily armed, though with more iron and fewer brazen guns. For a second line there were seven more men-of-war of roughly a hundred and fifty to a little over two hundred tons; and for scouting, picket duty, dispatch service and inshore work some eleven or twelve lighter craft, 'frigates' and 'pinnaces', ranging in size from almost a hundred tons down to a mere twenty-five, but all capable of keeping the high seas. Except for galleys it is doubtful whether the Spaniards had anything like as many fighting-ships in commission and fit for duty that spring in all the waters around Spain.

At the Rock of Lisbon it was decided, if it had not been decided before, that Cadiz was the first objective. Two intercepted Dutch merchantmen reported a great concentration of shipping there, meant for the armada gathering at Lisbon. Now, on his quarter-deck, Drake asked Borough whether they should go in that afternoon or wait till morning.

Something might be said for waiting, Borough answered, yet the wind might fail before morning and it ought to be possible to hold a council, work out a plan, and still anchor in the outer bay by about eight, at the shutting of the evening.

'That is my opinion,' said Drake, 'though there are some would have us stay till morning. We shall not stay at all.'

In spite of Borough's expostulations, that was all the council there was. When the vice-admiral got back to the *Golden Lion* he could see his commander still standing in towards Cadiz Harbour, and the rest of the fleet scrambling to close up behind him in such confused order, Borough noted gloomily, as was never heard of in such an action. But as long as the fleet followed him Drake did not much care in what order. He knew the advantage of surprise; he had it, and he meant to keep it.

At four o'clock in the afternoon of Wednesday the 29th of April the town of Cadiz could not have been more relaxed. Most of the principal gentlemen and citizens were watching some strolling players perform a comedy. In the great square a larger audience admired the skill of a tumbler bold enough to pit the rhythms of trained muscles against the acrobatics of verse. Since sailors of a dozen nations thronged the streets one may assume that the wine-shops had their share of custom. Among this cheerful crowd the word that a line of great ships was standing in for the harbour spread but slowly. By the time much attention had been drawn from the tumbler and the comedians the leading ship was almost off the monument called 'the Pillar of Hercules' at the entrance to the harbour. Juan Martínez de Recalde and his brave Biscayans, said some, approving the order of the approaching ships. No, said others, these are too many. Enemies then; Frenchmen or Englishmen, perhaps even the terrible Drake.

Fortunately for them, as the townsfolk of Cadiz afterwards agreed, the harbour was not unguarded. Eight galleys and a galliot under Don Pedro de Acuña had come in from Gibraltar a few days ago on a leisurely patrol that should take them as far as Cape St Vincent and a rendezvous with Recalde. Two of the galleys had gone off on some errand to Puerto Real in the upper bay, but the rest of the squadron lay in the harbour, close under the old castle. The galleys must have been in a good state of readiness, for Don Pedro was able to draw them out in a businesslike line across the entrance to the lower bay, and to detach one galley to challenge the strangers while they were still in the channel. The challenger dashed ahead, oar blades flashing, arquebusiers and pikemen in steady ranks on the forecastle, bronze ram gleaming and the banner of Spain fluttering at the mast-head. It meant to hail, but before it got within distance cannon balls began skipping about it. The *Elizabeth* and perhaps some of the other leading ships had opened fire. If he followed his usual custom it was then that Drake broke out English banners and trumpets brayed from his quarter-deck.

In the town something like a panic ensued. The corregidor, expecting that the English would try to sack the town and anticipating fighting in the streets, ordered the women and children, the aged and the halt to take refuge in the old castle. The captain of that fortress, not wanting to be hampered in his defence by a crowd of non-combatant civilians, shut his gates. The narrow street without, scarcely more than a passageway, was blocked at its far end by the closed gate while all its approaches were filling up with an inward pressing throng, fleeing from they scarcely knew what. In the packed space hysteria mounted while the weight of the crowds behind pressed the trapped vanguard closer and closer together. Before the captain of the fortress came to his senses, or the citizens mustering in the open streets and squares below realized what was happening, some twenty-five women and children were trampled to death.

Meanwhile, companies were hastily being formed, issued whatever arms there were and marched off to critical points. A scratch troop of cavalry emerged warily from the south gate and began to patrol the Puental, the rocky waste without the wall marked by a point which divided the lower from the upper bay. Here, the corregidor thought, the English would be most likely to try to land. He sent his best company of infantry to support the mounted patrol and another to man the fortified gate. All this to the sound of cannonading from the bay.

There the heavier English ships were engaged first with Don Pedro de Acuña's galleys in a fight the outcome of which can never have been very doubtful to either side. It is tempting to talk of the beginning of a new era of naval warfare in Cadiz Bay, of the unexpected triumph of the Atlantic over the Mediterranean, and the end of the two-thousand-year rule of the seas by the galley. It is tempting, but it is misleading. The galleys looked formidable fighting-machines, long and lean with wicked bronze rams, their forecastles crowded with soldiers and cannon, each ship manœuvring with a speed and grace and precision which took no account (at least in smooth water) of the wind, and wheeling and circling together like a water ballet. They were formidable, but only to other galleys. Their bronze rams were terrible weapons in a galley fight, capable of shearing off a whole bank of oars or dealing an enemy caught on the flank a mortal wound, but no galley captain in his right mind would have attempted to ram a heavy sailing-ship. Their brass guns could rain death on the crowded decks of other galleys and were quite big enough to cow the little merchantmen who carried the bulk of Mediterranean trade, but of their usual armament of five brass pieces four were only man-killers, and the fifth, the bow-chaser, was generally only a four- or six-pounder. Any one of Drake's seven heaviest ships could throw more metal in a single broadside than all Don Pedro's galleys put together, and throw it a good deal farther.

Galleys were not meant to fight against sailing-ships armed with heavy batteries and had never beaten them, even by boarding, except when in overwhelming force. Galleys were too low in the water, too fragile, too vulnerable to gunfire, and carried too few guns. The Portuguese had demonstrated the combat superiority of the sailing-ship in the series of victories of their armed merchantmen over the war galleys of the Turks

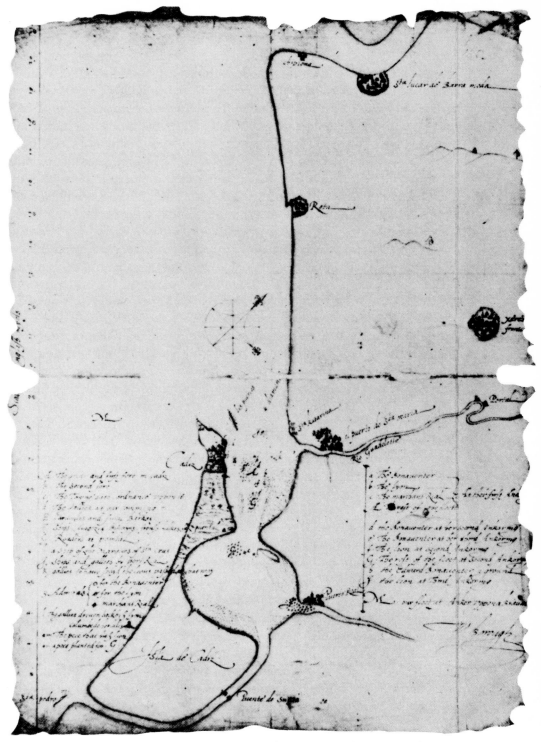

The chart used by Francis Drake in 1587 when he raided the harbour of Cadiz, destroying over thirty Spanish ships which were being prepared for the sailing of the Armada.

and Egyptians in the early decades of the century. Less than a year ago Englishmen had seen another demonstration. Five tall ships of the Levant Company returning from Near Eastern ports had been halted off Pantellaria by ten Spanish galleys of the Sicilian guard, and after an inconclusive parley had fought a set battle against the Spaniards, each ship against two galleys, until the beaten galleys drew off and let the unscathed merchantmen pass free. Three of those same ships followed Drake into Cadiz Bay. Had the Spanish galleys numbered twelve as Drake reported, or twenty for that matter, it would not have made much difference. Though they could almost always escape from sailing-ships by dodging behind shoals, or rowing away into the eye of the wind, galleys were for fighting other galleys.

If Don Pedro was not sure of it to begin with, he soon learned how hopelessly outgunned he was. He opened the battle gallantly enough, but as the English ships swung their broadsides towards him he was caught in a hail of round shot before his own bow guns were in range. He wheeled off away from the town and the anchorage, then wheeled back and tried again, perhaps for the smaller ships. But again the tall galleons gave him their broadsides and again he turned away. He was fighting a delaying action, as he was bound to do, to give ships in the anchorage a chance to get away into the comparative safety of the upper bay. Perhaps he hoped to lure some of the English galleons on to the treacherous shoals with which the eastern shoreward side of the lower bay was strewn. But the English were content simply to drive the galleys off, and Don Pedro, with wounded stretched on his fore-decks and two of his ships hurt so badly that Drake thought he had sunk them, limped away at last into St Mary's Port, a haven sheltered behind shoals more than four miles northeast of Cadiz on the opposite side of the lower bay.

In Cadiz anchorage there was something of the same panic that had seized the town. The roadstead was crowded with a medley of shipping, perhaps sixty sail. Some of them, of course, were for the Armada at Lisbon, including five *urcas*, round tublike freighters fully loaded with wine and biscuit, and a number of Dutch hulks, confiscated by the Spanish for eventual service with the invasion fleet and meanwhile stripped of their sails. But Cadiz was a busy port. There were ships from the Mediterranean, bound for French, Dutch and Baltic ports, waiting for a fair wind for Cape St Vincent. There were ships from the Atlantic bound east and pausing for one reason or another before making for the Straits of Gibraltar. There were, as there usually were at appropriate times of the year, ships waiting to join the fleet for the Americas. There was even a stray Portuguese bark taking on cargo for Brazil. And because Cadiz is the port of Xerez there were ships of several countries loading the noble wines to which English drinkers were to remain loyal throughout the long war with Spain.

Out of this confused mob of shipping those who could struggled to escape. The little fellows scrambled in against the sea-wall of the old fort where the galleys had been moored. Others who knew the channel or whose draught was light enough to risk the shoals ran for the shelter of the upper bay. But many of the larger ships were without enough crew to make sail or without sails to hoist, or were simply paralysed by surprise into inaction or blocked by the inaction of their neighbours. These swung helplessly at their anchors, huddled together like sheep who scent the wolf.

Or all did but one. At the outer edge of the anchorage lay a great ship of seven hundred tons, built and armed for the Levant trade. She may have hailed originally from Ragusa, for the English, judging by her lines, called her an 'argosy', their name for Ragusan ships, but she was owned or chartered at Genoa and her captain was a Genoese. She was on her return voyage now, loaded with a full cargo of cochineal and logwood, hides and wool for Italy, and she must have been waiting only for a turn of the tide and a puff of land breeze to clear the harbour and steer homeward past Gibraltar, for all her crew were aboard. We shall never know what made her captain decide to fight, but when Drake and the heavy ships left the galleys and bore down on the anchorage it was to find the 'argosy' blazing away from every gun-port at the smaller English ships, and hindering their business with the anchored merchantmen.

A seven-hundred-ton Levanter is a serious opponent. The Queen's galleons chose their positions (there was little room for manœuvre in the narrow gut of the anchorage) and methodically pounded the stubborn Genoese to pieces. The Englishmen spoke wistfully later of those forty fine brass cannon gone to the bottom of the bay, but there had been no way to get them. The 'argosy' was still firing when she began to sink. We do not know whether any of her crew got ashore, but Drake's ships cannot have picked up any of them since they never learned the nationality of their adversary. We do not even know the Genoese captain's name or what became of him. Had he been a Spaniard, the commander of one of King Philip's galleons, who thus deliberately took on the whole English fleet and fought his ship until it sank beneath him, his gallantry would have been properly celebrated. But one doubts whether his Genoese owners appreciated it. If he got back to Genoa at all it was probably to hear that Genoa was not at war with England, and to ponder on the beach the axiom that it is easier to get a neutral ship out of a prize-court than off the bottom of a bay.

The sinking of the argosy ended the resistance of the ships in the harbour. Drake was able to anchor his squadron among them and set to work, sorting out the prizes he wanted and the cargoes worth shifting, and marking for destruction ships cleared or empty. As night fell the first hulks were towed free, fired and set adrift on the flood-tide. Soon the blazing ships lighted up the bay and cast a glow on the white walls of Cadiz.

The work did not go on without opposition. From time to time the old fort loosed off such guns as it had, and as the working parties edged farther up the anchorage a second battery on the harbour side of the lower town also opened fire. But both batteries had been meant rather to repel Moorish landing parties than to command the harbour, and the English squadron gave them only the edge of its attention. The galleys were more distracting. Before night fell the two from Puerto Real poked their noses cautiously out past Puental and began taking pot-shots at whatever targets offered. Several times the Londoners who were covering that flank of the operation drove them off and they always scuttled away quickly enough from the heavier guns, but after a while they would be back again, tossing their little round shot at the nearest English pinnace. The galleys from St Mary's Port played the same game, coming out two at a time to take long shots with their bow guns from the comparative safety of the shallows, and on this flank they had their one small victory.

Just as night fell an advancing pair of galleys came upon the captured Portuguese caravel far out beyond the rearward wing of the English squadron, laggard perhaps, or careless, or bent on some private adventure. The galleys cut her off before anyone at the anchorage noticed what was happening. She scorned the summons to surrender and banged away with her little popguns as if she were a galleon, but ships like this were the galley's meat. They swept the caravel's deck with a storm of fire so deadly that when they boarded five wounded men were all that were left alive of the prize crew. These prisoners and the recaptured prize the galleys brought into Cadiz.

Except for this one incident neither the forts nor the galleys did any harm we know of that night. By dawn on Thursday the work of destruction was all but finished, and Drake led the bulk of his squadron to a new anchorage off Puental at the entrance to the upper bay. He had seen ships fleeing through that passage the evening before. From captured mariners he had learned that close inside lay a magnificent galleon, the property of the Marquis of Santa Cruz. She had just come down to Cadiz from the Biscay shipyards to take aboard her guns and some companies of soldiers. Probably she was meant to be the flagship of the invasion fleet. Her destruction would be the crowning blow of the Cadiz raid.

Drake left the *Elizabeth Bonaventure* at anchor opposite Puental, got into his barge, formed a force of pinnaces and frigates with the *Merchant Royal*, the largest London ship, to act in support, and worked his way into the upper bay. Drake himself saw to the burning of the great galleon, some of the pinnaces burnt the small craft which had got no farther the evening before than the lee side of Puental, and others went off to reconnoitre the upper end of the bay where about forty sail lay at anchor behind the shoals and batteries that guarded Puerto Real or in the narrow strait called Río de Santi Petri across which a wooden bridge connected Cadiz with the mainland.

All these movements in the upper bay were watched by the defenders of the town with strained attention. They had spent a night of anxious vigilance, more concerned about a possible landing than about the ships burning in the harbour. All these movements of small boats, they felt sure, were the precursors of a landing. When English pinnaces approached the mouth of the *río* they thought Drake's first step would be to burn the bridge across which their reinforcements must come, and they blessed the two galleys that drove the pinnaces away.

Already the situation was not quite so bad. One company of infantry had come in at dawn, having marched through the night from Xerez. Another, with some horsemen, arrived about two hours later, and all around the bay there was a bustle of martial activity, dust rising from marching columns, far-off trumpets calling, moving lance points glinting against the dark foliage of orange trees. The great Duke of Medina Sidonia was coming to the rescue with all the forces he could rally. The town might be saved yet.

Hope stirred the townsmen to a burst of activity. On either side of the Puental gate were mounted two huge old bronze culverins, their great barrels nearly eighteen feet long, weighing, each of them, several tons. Such guns could throw eighteen-pound iron cannon balls more than two miles. If there had been guns like them in the harbour batteries things might have gone differently. Now the enthusiastic militiamen manhandled one of the bronze monsters out across the rough waste of Puental to a little rocky eminence overlooking the upper end of the lower bay. Across the bay rode the great ships of the English squadron — the nearest, the *Golden Lion*, only a little over a mile off.

The captain of the *Golden Lion*, William Borough, vice-admiral of the squadron, was not aboard. He was uneasy about many things, the distribution of wine and biscuit from the captured stores, the exposed position of the fleet lying in a narrow gut between shoals open to attack by galleys or fire-ships, the unexplained activity of pinnaces and ships' boats up yonder at the head of the lower bay, but most of all he was uneasy because there had been no council held. For Drake to have gone plunging headlong into a strange harbour full of unknown perils, with his fleet trailing higgledy-piggledy after, without inquiry as to channel or forts, without advice taken or formal orders issued, was to Borough's mind inviting disaster. So far things had gone reasonably well, he was obliged to admit, but what more was there to do now except finish shifting stores and get out to sea? All this fighting and so little talking, no conferences over charts and orders, no weighing of various courses, no deference to the opinion of senior officers, seemed most irregular. Borough was not trying to remind people that he had commanded a fleet and won a pitched battle in the Baltic before Drake had ever commanded anything larger than the *Judith*. He was not standing on his dignity as England's Vice-Admiral of the Sea. But he did want to know what was going on. He had himself rowed over to the *Elizabeth Bonaventure* to find out.

On the flagship they told him that Drake had gone into the upper bay with the pinnaces and the *Merchant Royal*. That was all anybody knew. If Borough's comments were not insubordinate his expression may have been. He took his barge up past Puental where Santa Cruz's galleon was burning towards the water-line and inquired aboard the *Merchant Royal*. They told him the admiral had gone back to the lower bay. Finally Borough found his chief aboard the *Elizabeth*, but found him briskly uncommunicative. Borough returned to his own ship, his temper unimproved.

While he was away the gunner on the opposite headland had found the range of the *Golden Lion*. At anything over seven hundred yards or so even a culverin had to shoot, as Elizabethan gunners not inappropriately put it, 'at random', but lately the Spaniard was coming too close for comfort. One shot had pierced the *Lion* at the water-line and struck off the leg of her master gunner. When Borough came aboard, the *Lion's* master had already laid out an anchor and was preparing to warp the ship down towards St Mary's Port out of range. Borough approved. It was bad enough to be hulled, but another unlucky shot might strike down a mast or even hit the magazine.

Seeing the *Golden Lion* warping down alone, well separated from the rest of the English, the galleys made another sortie. There was always the chance that six galleys might do a single galleon not under sail a serious mischief, particularly if some of them could get under her stern. They advanced now with mincing precision in two files of three, well spread out to offer a minimal target, the leading pair firing all their guns together, then wheeling away from each other like squadrons of cavalry so that the next two could fire. Borough managed to swing round and give them a broadside. For a while the *Golden Lion* kept the six deadly dancers in play, and then, though nobody says so, the wind must have freshened from the south, for Drake who had seen his vice-admiral's danger was able to send the galleon *Rainbow*, six merchantmen and his own pinnace to support the *Lion*. With wind in his sails and reinforcements behind him Borough took the offensive, led his line farther into the outer bay, cut the galleys off from St Mary's Port, sent them scuttling behind the shelter of Las Puercas reef at the edge of the outer channel, and came to anchor with his squadron about half-way between the old fort of Cadiz and the battery which guarded St Mary's Port. Though it was held against him later, at the time nobody criticized Borough's manoeuvre. In fact the position was skilfully chosen. It neatly immobilized the galleys which could not come out from behind the reef to pester either division of the fleet without the risk of being cut off by the other as long as there was wind.

The wind, rather than Borough's position, was what concerned Drake at the moment. It had been a morning of fitful airs, and now, at a little past noon when all was done that could be done and the fleet was ready for sea, the breeze that had carried Borough into the mouth of the lower bay was dying. The sails of the division still off Puental were shaken out, the admiral's flagship glided to the head of the column, banners were displayed and trumpets and kettle-drums brayed their derision at the vain cannonading from the town. Then, before the flagship had come abreast of the *Golden Lion's* morning anchorage, the sails flapped idly and the English squadron drifted without steerage way on the flat oily water.

For twelve hours thereafter there was no wind. In one sense it was an embarrassing and pathetic anticlimax to the brilliantly successful raid. In another sense it was the most triumphant possible conclusion. By noon the Duke of Medina Sidonia had entered Cadiz with reinforcements total-ling more than three hundred cavalry and about three thousand foot. The townsfolk burned to avenge their night of helplessness and terror by doing at least some harm to the English fleet. Some of the guns of the two harbour forts at maximum range would carry as far as the English ships, and these blazed away industriously. The gunner of the culverin on the headland resumed his practice, this time taking the *Elizabeth Bonaventure* for his target. Under the inspiration of the duke's presence the garrison of the Puental gate wrestled their other culverin down to the foreshore with-in long range of the *Dreadnought* and the *Merchant Royal*. The galleys, the only ships that could move on the windless waters, began their circling ballet. On the waterfront citizens and sailors stuffed some of the smaller ships huddled under the old fort with combustibles, set them ablaze and let them drift out on the tide towards the English. The galleys co-operated by towing the fire-ships into more favourable positions and trying to cover them with their guns. The enthusiasm of the Spanish for this form of attack grew as darkness closed in, and the bay of Cadiz was almost as brightly lit by burning ships as it had been the night before.

It was all in vain. Though the English fleet was defending itself under the most adverse conditions, immobile in a confined space amidst un-known shoals and shallows, neither the shore guns nor the galleys nor the fire-ships did the slightest harm. Not a ship nor a man was hurt. The culverin on the headland failed to repeat its lucky hit of the morning. The culverin on the foreshore merely raised splashes round its targets, and the town batteries were less effective still. Let us remember, in extenuation of Cadiz gunnery, that in the sixteenth century gunpowder was expensive, so that peace-time target practice was not encouraged. Also the quality of the powder was undependable, and not only were no two cannons ever quite alike but the cannon balls supplied any given piece were unlikely to be all the same size, so that the 'windage', the difference between the diameter of the shot and that of the bore, usually considerable, was also variable. As a result it was only in the textbooks that a piece of a given bore and length loaded in a given fashion would hurl a ball of a given size a given distance. In fact, even the most experienced gunner might hesitate to predict whether when next he fired it his gun would send its shot directly to the target, drop it with a sort of discouraged burp a few hundred feet ahead, or blow up at the breach, probably killing him and his crew. At long ranges the chances of effective execution were slight.

If the English fleet owed its escape from the shore guns to the enemy's poor weapons and poor marksmanship, it owed its preservation from the galleys and fire-ships to its own seamanship and alertness. No matter how they dodged and circled the galleys were always driven off before they could close the range. (Properly laid out anchors and crews that haul in and pay out smartly can swing a sailing-ship through a wide arc in a short time.) As for the worst menace, the fire-ships, skilfully handled boats towed or fended them off to drift away and burn out in the shallows. Meanwhile the admiral's joke that tonight the Spaniards are doing our work for us and burning their own ships was bawled from one end of the fleet to the other. The English got as little sleep in Cadiz Bay on Thursday night as they had the night before, but they seemed to have ended by enjoying themselves. After those twelve hours none of them would ever be much afraid of shore batteries or galleys, or even fire-ships, again.

At last, a little after midnight, enough land breeze blew to get the fleet through the channel. Don Pedro's galleys followed, all eight of them, with the galliot and another oared vessel of some kind, perhaps the 'frigate' which the Duke of Medina Sidonia had told off to shadow Drake's fleet. At dawn the galleys opened fire, whereupon Drake anchored to invite combat. Don Pedro, who could have hoped at most to cut off a straggler, was careful not to accept the challenge. Instead he sent the English admiral a complimentary message, along with a present of wine and sweetmeats, and after an exchange of courtesies worthy of two knights in a romance of chivalry the two commanders began to consider an exchange of prisoners. As their boats went back and forth over the calm sea a fresh breeze sprang up, and Drake with a gesture of farewell bore away in the direction of Cape St Vincent.

Drake estimated that he had sunk, burned or captured thirty-seven vessels in Cadiz Harbour. Robert Leng, a gentleman volunteer with the expedition thought 'about thirty'; an anonymous Italian observer in the town named the same figure; and the official Spanish estimate, prepared not for propaganda purposes but for King Philip's eyes, listed twenty-four, valued at a hundred and seventy-two thousand ducats. Probably the figures depend on how many of the small craft one counts, and whether one adds in the unsuccessful Spanish fire-ships. 'The loss,' said Philip after he had studied the news, 'was not very great, but the daring of the attempt was very great indeed.'

Nor was the material loss inconsiderable. If some of the merchant ships were neutrals, and many had cargoes not intended for Lisbon, a quantity of the supplies were on their way to Santa Cruz, the *urcas* and the Dutch ships were certainly meant for transport and supply duty with the Armada, and the marquis's great galleon would have been one of his most formidable fighting-ships. Drake's countrymen did not consider his boast vain when he said that at Cadiz he had singed the King of Spain's beard. But he may have meant the phrase more modestly than it sounded. After the battle of Lepanto the sultan said: 'When the Venetians sunk my fleet they only singed my beard. It will grow again. But when I captured Cyprus I cut off one of their arms.' Drake knew that beards grow again. In the same letter in which he told Walsingham of the Cadiz raid, he wrote: 'I assure your honour the like preparation was never heard of nor known as the King of Spain hath and daily maketh to invade England ... which if they be not impeached before they join will be very perilous ... This service, which by God's sufferance we have done will breed some alterations ... [but] all possible preparations for defence are very expedient ... I dare not almost write of the great forces we hear the King of Spain hath. Prepare in England strongly and most by sea!' And then in an ominous afterthought: 'Look well to the coast of Sussex.' As he steered for Cape St Vincent, Drake knew his main work was yet to do.

Assembling the Armada at Cadiz.

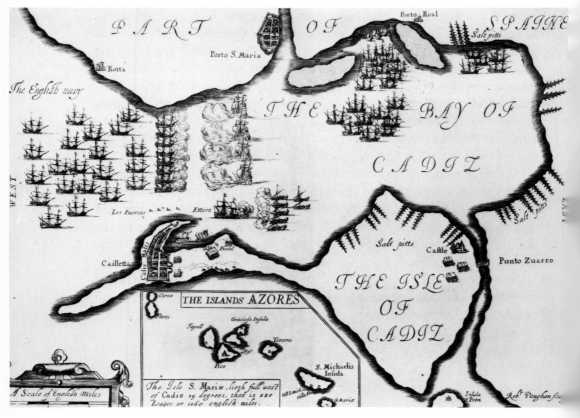

X

'NO MATTER OF SUBSTANCE'

THE PORTUGUESE COAST, MAY 2ND–20TH, 1587

DRAKE must have heard at Cadiz that Juan Martínez de Recalde, perhaps the most famous Spanish seaman after Santa Cruz himself, was supposed to be at sea somewhere off Cape St Vincent with a squadron about half the size of Drake's. When he steered west from Cadiz on May 2nd, Drake was probably looking for Recalde. The nearest he got was the capture of a dispatch boat also looking for Recalde with urgent orders from Philip to avoid the stronger English by retiring into Lisbon. Drake stood well out to sea, spread his wings wide and swung back again in a northward sweep. He was too late. Recalde had got word of Drake's strength and anticipated Philip's orders. As Drake was rounding the cape, Recalde's squadron, seven stout Biscayan ships and five pinnaces, was being borne on the flood-tide into the mouth of Tagus to drop its anchors in the shelter of the forts that guarded Lisbon.

On May 9th, satisfied that Recalde had got away, Drake broke off his search abruptly. When at his signal his captains came aboard for a council or, as more usually happened with Drake, for orders, he told them that they were heading back to Cape St Vincent where they would land and capture the castle of Sagres and the other strong places near by. He did not say why. 'Being moved ... in his prince's service with his courageous company to aggravate the honour of his fame', said Robert Leng, who had come on the expedition as a gentleman adventurer, perhaps with the hope of making literary capital out of the voyage. 'Born strategist that he was, he had grasped the conspicuous importance of that famous Cape', said the great Victorian naval historian who was Drake's most devoted admirer. Besides the judgment based on reading romances of chivalry and the judgment based on reading about Nelson's campaigns, we have the sour judgment of Drake's vice-admiral and reluctant companion-at-arms, William Borough. Borough, in a grimly disrespectful letter written to Drake on the night after he had heard his plan, rejected the idea that it was either the watering facilities at Sagres which tempted his commander, since 'there is no watering place nearer than half a mile which is but a pool to the which the way is bad', or the value of the brass ordnance in the castle. 'If you should achieve your purpose,' Borough wrote, 'what have you of it? No matter of substance, neither shall any man be bettered by it, but a satisfying of your mind that you may say, "Thus have I done upon the King of Spain's land." '

Borough had no doubts about the importance of the Cape St Vincent station, and he implied that it was sufficiently recognized so that it was precisely there that Drake had been ordered by the council. Drake's business, Borough told him, was to cruise off the cape and so disrupt Spanish preparations. The landing operation was risky and unnecessary, and the Lord Admiral had specifically warned against such attempts. Probably what exasperated Borough most was that again there had been no proper council and that he, the Vice-Admiral of the Fleet, had learned Drake's plans from the loud arguments of junior officers before he had heard them from Drake himself.

How far wrong Borough was in his judgment of Drake's motives is more than anyone can tell now. Borough seems to have believed that the fleet could cruise off Cape St Vincent long enough to accomplish its mission without seizing any anchorage, and certainly later English admirals often managed to keep similar stations for considerable periods without a near-by base. The Elizabethan man-of-war, however, had not the sea-keeping qualities of later ships, and if Drake meant to stay throughout the summer a safe anchorage not threatened by hostile guns, a place where ships could be careened and men refreshed ashore, would be a great convenience. In his Caribbean voyages Drake had always sought such bases. But there may have been also the old corsair's urge to look for booty, and the urge of Philip's sworn enemy to do some deed of note upon the King of Spain's land.

Weather delayed Drake's landing until May 14th, and then he struck not at Sagres but at Lagos, a comfortable port and harbour some fifteen miles east along the coast towards Cadiz. Lagos had once been a rich city, but of late years its trade was much decayed and Drake may have expected to find it lightly defended, though it is hard to see how he can have expected to hold it afterwards. He anchored his ships in the bay west of Lagos towards nightfall and landed his soldiers, unopposed, at dawn. Anthony Platt, Lieutenant-General for Land Service, formed them up on the beach, eleven hundred men in a single column, skirmishers ahead, then two ranks of arquebusiers in front, two files of arquebusiers on either flank and two more ranks in the rear, pikes in the centre — an array which the Portuguese found impressively professional. In this order the column moved off, choosing a route that would keep to flat open country, and marched on Lagos with a triumphant shrilling of fifes and thud of drums as if passing in review before the Lord Lieutenant of Devonshire.

The landing, though unopposed, had not gone unobserved. Presently the invaders were aware of bands of horsemen shadowing them on their flank, a rough unmilitary-looking lot, but well mounted and good riders. The horsemen kept out of long musket range, but as the column neared the town the number of mounted observers increased and there were signs of infantry movements on the high ground inland. The English column marched all along the landward walls of Lagos, finding the defences everywhere much stronger than had been reported, and drawing a rolling fire of great guns, wall-pieces, muskets and arquebuses. Then the column marched back, pausing to exchange unprofitable volleys with the walls, and so by the way it had come towards the bay. Dom Hernan Teller, Governor General of the Algarve, commanding the defence, was astonished and relieved. Dom Hernan knew how much less the real strength of the garrison was than the ensigns displayed along the walls proclaimed, and he was uncertain how long his peasants and fishermen would stand against men who marched like veterans. He counted none of his infantry fit for a sortie, but as he saw the backs of the English he led out the two hundred cavalry of his escort to join the horsemen already in the plain.

The column had a hot, uncomfortable two hours getting back to the boats. Musketeers shot at them from behind walls and olive trees. There were an increasing number of wounded to carry. And the irregular-looking cavalry wheeled threateningly around them, obliging them at intervals to halt and form squares to repel attack, and not leaving them until they reached the shore and the great guns on the ships opened fire.

William Borough was in no position to point out that events had confirmed his warning that landing operations were risky. Drake had brooded for forty-eight hours over his vice-admiral's letter. It was a tactless letter, but under the free and easy customs of Tudor armies and navies most people would not have called it insubordinate or even irregular. Being a genius Drake did not judge like most people. He remembered (perhaps not quite accurately) that Borough had wanted to stop him from going into Cadiz Harbour. He reflected (perhaps not altogether fairly) that Borough had been in a great hurry to get out before the shipping in the upper bay had been burned. He recalled, with how much bitterness we can only guess, that on account of Borough his own flagship the *Elizabeth* had lain for nearly twelve hours under the fire of that damned culverin on the headland, in a spot where, except for his flight, Borough ought to have been. He did not remember (perhaps no one had ever told him) that Borough was having trouble of his own that be-calmed evening, and he thought of Borough as so completely in safety that he converted the miles by which Borough was distant from him into leagues. Taking all this at its worst most irritable commanders would have diagnosed no more than stupidity or cowardice on Borough's part, but Drake saw deeper. He knew that there was a vast shadowy conspiracy in England, pro-Spanish, pro-papist, bent on the defeat and destruction of all honest Protestants devoted to the common cause. He knew that ever since he had shown himself the determined enemy of the King of Spain his rise in the world had been dogged by the agents of that con-spiracy, sometimes faceless and shapeless adversaries, slandering him to the Queen, inciting his seamen to desert, warning Spanish towns and Spanish ships of his impending pounce, sometimes villains unmasked by Drake's own astuteness like that black wizard Thomas Doughty whom Drake had had beheaded at St Julian's Bay before the *Golden Hind* entered the Pacific. Doughty's chief crime, or at least the only one that seems provable today, was that he had intimated that Drake had exceeded his instructions. Borough had done the same thing. Borough had also accused him of violating the customs of Her Majesty's service. Francis Drake had once had his ship's chaplain chained and padlocked to the deck after what he thought a disrespectful sermon, and summoning his crew around him, himself sitting 'cross-legged on a sea chest with a pair of pantouffles in his hand' had told the clergyman: 'Francis Fletcher, I do here excommunicate thee out of the Church of God and from all benefits and graces thereof, and I denounce thee to the devil and all his angels.' Such a man was not likely to accept meekly a lecture on naval etiquette from a subordinate, no matter how much his senior in years and service. When he had considered, Drake convened a sort of drumhead court-martial aboard the *Elizabeth*, read them at least some of Borough's letter and announced that he was sending Captain Marchant, the sergeant-major of the land forces, to the *Golden Lion* to take command of that vessel and confine Captain Borough to his cabin under arrest. There Borough re-mained during the attack on Lagos and for the next month in daily fear of his life.

Having confined him there, Drake probably forgot him. No sooner were the soldiers aboard from their fruitless parade before Lagos than Drake weighed anchor and stood out beyond sight of the coast, and then in again on the next long tack to Sagres. Dom Hernan Teller was still sending for reinforcements for Lagos when Drake's troops had climbed the winding cliff road up from the beach and swarmed out on the bare windy headland. The whole tone of the new operation was so different, so brisk, businesslike and determined, that one wonders whether the attack on Lagos was anything more than a feint.

A fortified manor house barred the road to Sagres Castle but it was undefended when the English reached it, and the landing force pushed straight on. The castle of those days crowned the jutting cliffs at the tip of Cape Sagres. East of its site lies the bay with a tiny town on its shore below the cliffs, southward the ocean stretches towards the far-off curve of Africa, and on the west the waves roll in from three thousand miles of open Atlantic. Just north of due west and not far away juts the promontory of Cape St Vincent, the south-west corner of the Iberian Peninsula and of Europe. On this headland of Sagres the monkish visionary prince, Henry called 'the Navigator', once sat, staring out at unknown seas. He built here on the roomy little plateau guarded by precipitous cliffs the oldest buildings that Drake found, his residence and the accommodations for his library, his astronomers and his seamen, the Vila do Infante. On this bare cliff-top were hatched the schemes that were to open for Europeans the sea-road to the fabulous east and to continents undreamed of. In a sense all Francis Drake's exploits in the world up to that moment were just one of the minor by-products of Prince Henry's dream.

Although Castle Sagres was now no royal residence, no centre of learning and high enterprise, just a third-class fort meant to guard a fishing village against Moorish raids, it had a strong wall on its northern side, the only approach accessible to any but sea-gulls. The wall was of stone, forty feet high, thick and properly parapeted with four round towers and a gatehouse, each provided with a large brass 'Portingale sling', a long swivel-mounted wall-gun which would fire a ball weighing about half a pound to kill a man at three hundred yards or more. Slings were breach-loaders and could be fired fairly rapidly. Even though held by only a handful of men such a castle was thought wellnigh impregnable against a force unprovided with siege guns.

Drake summoned the castle, and having received a courteous but resolute defiance ordered his musketeers and arquebusiers to keep up a constant fire to drive the garrison from their loopholes. Faggots soaked in pitch took the place of cannon or petards, and in the dangerous work of piling these against the main gate under fire from the walls Drake toiled amidst his men. After two hours of continuous assault the great gate was no more than a crumbling heap of embers, the fire of the English muske-teers was sweeping an arc of the inner defences, a number of the garrison were killed or wounded, and the captain who had been shot twice through the body was ready to surrender. Drake gave him generous terms. Soldiers and civilians within the fort were to be free to depart safely with all their personal property except weapons. By mid-afternoon the English held the castle, and the surprise and terror of their sudden success led the other strong places in the neighbourhood, a monastery and a small castle near Cape St Vincent, to surrender without firing a shot.

One doubts whether Drake knew that he had captured the castle of Henry the Navigator, the cradle of all Europe's colonial empires, past, present and to come. One wonders whether he would have cared. What mattered to him was that he had swept the neighbourhood of the Cape clear of enemy troops and taken the stronghold which overlooked his chosen anchorage. Perhaps, also, that he had done a victorious deed of war on the land of the King of Spain. As for Castle Sagres, he had no thought of occupying it — he only meant to make it uninhabitable and harmless. The eight brass pieces of the castle's armament, five slings from the north wall, and three big guns, a demi-cannon, a culverin and a demi-culverin commanding the harbour, he ordered to be tumbled down the cliff to the shore where they could be taken off to the ships. Before the last working party made their way back to the beach he had them set fire to all the buildings within the enclosure, leaving them blackened roofless shells, Prince Henry's hall and bower and library among the rest.

Five days later the English fleet was off Lisbon, or more exactly off Cascaes just out of range of the guns of the fort guarding the northern entrance to the Tagus. In Lisbon dwelt the Cardinal Archduke Albert of Austria, King Philip's nephew and his viceroy for the kingdom of Portugal. In Lisbon the old Marquis of Santa Cruz kept his headquarters, fuming at an emergency which found him with an enemy fleet at his door and his twelve galleons of Portugal without the new guns that had been promised them, with only skeleton crews and with neither gunners nor soldiers for an action. Word had come the day before that the English were standing northward, and after a hasty conference the viceroy and the marquis had agreed that Drake's target was probably the rich and open town of Sezimbra. They had hurriedly reinforced it, though troops were so scarce around Lisbon that they had to draft arquebusiers from Lisbon Castle and fighting-men from Recalde's ships. These the galleys of the harbour guard, the fastest ships available, had taken around Cape Espichel.

The English fleet, however, had not looked at Sezimbra but held on well out to sea, and the Lisbon galleys, seven of them under the command of Santa Cruz's brother Don Alonso de Bazán, had slipped back ahead of them to form in battle order under the guns of Castle St Julian.

That was the critical point. At that point a bar marked the mouth of Tagus, a bar which could be passed by two channels, both narrow and rather tricky, one at its northern, one at its southern end. The northern channel, the one usually used because it was deeper and safer, was commanded by the batteries of Castle St Julian; across the river a work known as the Old Tower guarded the narrower southern entrance. Once past there, although there was a second less formidable gauntlet to run at Belem, a fleet like Drake's could do deadly harm in Lisbon Harbour and perhaps sack the town as well. Santa Cruz knew that a resolute commander, if he had pilots who knew the approaches to Lisbon, could force either entrance. The southern channel was crooked and narrow but the guns in the Old Tower were few and feeble. The guns at St Julian's were more formidable but the channel was easier, and with a brisk west wind and a flood-tide a line of galleons might sail past with only minor damage, might even hope to sail back out again.

There was another danger which Santa Cruz, who knew something of Drake's methods, took even more seriously. On its sea side Castle St Julian was a menacing fortress. By land it had scarcely more than token defences. Beyond it to the west lay the shallow bay of Cascaes. At its western end, where the fishing village straggled, the beach was covered by the guns of Cascaes Castle, but between the two forts stretched a long curve of beach with only the gentlest surf on most days, no tricky rocks and a slow easy ascent, two miles of it equally out of range of Cascaes and St Julian. Just opposite this stretch of beach the English fleet dropped anchor.

The old marquis had come to Castle St Julian as soon as he heard that the English were rounding Cape Espichel. He had only one weapon to parry any of the thrusts open to Drake, his brother Don Alonso's seven galleys now lying under the guns of the castle. If the English tried a landing in Cascaes Bay the galleys could dash out through the shoal water, splintering and scattering the ships' boats long before they could be beached. If the English tried to force the northern entrance the galleys might delay them until the land batteries had sunk a couple of ships in the channel. If Drake knew the secret of the twisty southern approach and made for it the galleys could at least be flung across in a suicidal charge. They might accomplish something. Meanwhile the local gentry were martialling the Portuguese militia, stiffened by a few hundred Spanish arquebusiers, along the curve of Cascaes Bay, and the Cardinal Archduke was sending for reinforcements from as far as a day's march away.

In fact, Drake had no pilots for either channel and not enough men to be willing to risk a landing against either a prepared shore defence or galleys, let alone both. He had come to Lisbon just for a look at the state of things, a gambit which had more than once turned out well for him, and if no chance of profit offered at least to have the satisfaction of braving King Philip at his own front door. Finding no opportunity for surprise, and unable to tempt the galleys into open water to protect the small craft which he captured or chased ashore, Drake tried to negotiate an exchange of prisoners of war. Told that there were no English prisoners of war in Lisbon, probably an honest answer though Drake did not think so, he defied the marquis to come out and fight, as if he knew how bitterly the old sea-dog resented his helplessness to do so. As at Cadiz the wind broke off the vain exchange of messages. It freshened from the north and the English ran before it, back to the Cape. If it had served no other purpose the demonstration before Lisbon had broken the monotony of commerce-destroying and kept the enemy uneasy, irritated and off-balance, something Drake liked to do.

Spanish seaports in 1582 Artist unknown; from Braun, *Civitas Orbis*.

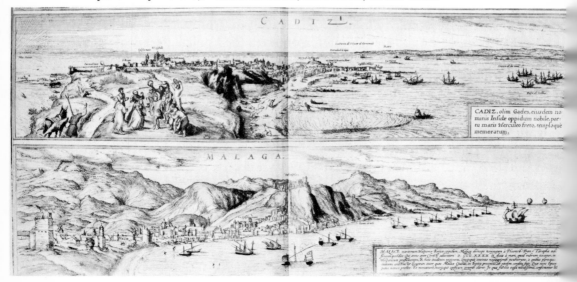

XI

BARREL STAVES AND TREASURE

CAPE ST VINCENT AND THE AZORES, MAY 21ST – JUNE 18TH, 1587

URING the next ten days at Sagres the ships of the fleet were cleaned, fumigated and rummaged, bilges pumped and ballast freshened. A galleon the size of the *Elizabeth Bonaventure*, crowded with two hundred and fifty men, could grow remarkably foul in the course of seven or eight weeks, and the smaller ships were no sweeter. Elizabethans knew that the fouler the ship the unhealthier the crew, and there were already too many sick men in the fleet. As many as possible were put ashore, the best remedy available, and preparations were set on foot to send the worst home in a couple of prizes. Meanwhile the ships at sea — particularly the pinnaces, handiest for this kind of task — swept methodically up and down the coast, ten or fifteen leagues north and back, then about the same distance east, sinking, burning or bringing back to Sagres everything that ventured in their way.

It was not exciting work, scarcely enlivened by the arrival at Lagos of a squadron of ten galleys which with commendable prudence refused to come out and fight, and the prizes taken were unspectacular. They were very numerous, many more than a hundred, counting those destroyed on the beaches around the Cape as well as those taken at sea, but only a very few were as large as sixty tons and none of them was going to bring a penny in prize money. They were of two general classes. Rather more than half belonged to the tuna fisheries of the Algarve and Andalusia, a flourishing industry at which Drake had struck a heavy blow, systematically destroying not only every fishing-boat he could find but the little shore-nested villages of the fishermen and even their nets, causing the people, Drake thought, 'to curse their governors to their faces'. They probably cursed somebody. The rest of the prizes were the little coastwise cargo boats, barks and caravels, which carried ordinary freight around the shores of Spain. Most of them turned out to be laden with cooper's stores, 'hoops and pipe staves and such like' and bound for Cadiz or the Straits. Drake knew the value of these apparently valueless prizes. 'The hoops and pipe staves were above 16 or 17 hundred ton in weight', he wrote to Walsingham, 'which cannot be less than 25 or 30 thousand ton if it had been made in cask, ready for liquor, all which I commanded to be consumed into smoke and ashes by fire, which will be unto the King no small waste of his provisions besides the want of his barks.' For the navies of the day casks were a prime necessity, not only for stowing water and wine but for salt meat, salt fish, biscuits and all sorts of provisions. For tight casks, well-seasoned barrel staves of the proper quality were essential. Of this commodity there was never much surplus and the outfitting of the Armada was already creating an extraordinary demand. If, when the Armada finally sailed, its water-butts proved to be leaky and foul, if much food spoiled because of green barrel staves and ill-made casks, the smoke which hung over Sagres was to blame. Burning those barrel staves was probably a graver blow to Spain than burning the ships in Cadiz Bay.

For the moment, however, the gravest blow was the presence of the English at Cape St Vincent. At Lisbon the Marquis of Santa Cruz was immobilized by a want of soldiers and seamen, of cannon and supplies. Coming in from the Mediterranean and hanging back at Malaga and Cartagena, hesitating at Gibraltar or at most venturing no farther than Cadiz, were ships with what Santa Cruz urgently needed — cannon and cannon balls, powder and biscuit, drafts of seamen from a dozen Mediterranean ports and the veterans of the Naples regiments — all escorted by the armed merchantmen who would make up the 'Levant' squadron and by the four great galleasses of Naples, besides some Sicilian galleys, a formidable addition to Santa Cruz's fighting strength. Almost daily, as he received the latest reports at Aranjuez, Philip showered the faithful Duke of Medina Sidonia with new orders. Ships in the river at Seville were to proceed at once to Lisbon. No one was to move while Drake was prowling off Cape St Vincent. Drake was gone from the Cape; let the galleys take aboard the artillery and the soldiers which were so urgently needed and make a dash for Lisbon. Drake was back at the Cape; the galleys were to be stayed and the soldiers were to march for Lisbon overland, followed by whatever artillery or provisions could be moved.

Meanwhile Drake and Captain Fenner, who was more or less Drake's Chief of Staff, were quite aware of the advantage of their position. Captain Fenner, after a clear account of the fleet's operations to date, and of what he knew of the disposition of the Spanish forces (what he knew was very close to the truth) concluded:

We hold this Cape so greatly to our benefit and so much to their disadvantage as a great blessing was the attaining thereof. For the rendezvous is at Lisbon where we understand of some 25 ships and seven galleys. The rest, we lie between home and them, so as the body is without the members; and they cannot come together by reason that they are unfurnished of their provisions in every degree ...

As there hath been a happy beginning, so we doubt not but God will have the sequel such as it shall appear ... that it is not the multitude that shall prevail where it pleases Him to stretch out His hand.

Drake wrote to Walsingham the same day. A cloudy Biblical-sounding paean of triumph over the enemies of Truth and upholders of Baal and Dagon's image changes abruptly to straightforward prose:

As long as it shall please God to give us provisions to eat and drink and that our ships and wind and weather will permit us, you shall surely hear of us near this Cape of St Vincent where we do and will expect daily what her Majesty and your honours will further command.

God make us all thankful that her Majesty sent out these few ships in time.

If there were 6 more of her Majesty's good ships of the second sort, we should be the better able to keep their forces from joining, [Drake had, apparently, already appealed for reinforcements] and haply take or impeach his fleets from all places in the next month or so after which is the chiefest times of their returns home, which I judge in my poor opinion will bring this great monarchy to those conditions which are meet.

There must be a beginning of any good matter, but the continuing to the end, until it be thoroughly finished yields the true glory ... God make us all thankful again and again, that we have, although it be little, made a beginning on the coast of Spain.

Both these letters were written on May 24th (N.S.) and Drake added a brief note on the 30th, suggesting that the Dunkirk ship which he had dispatched with his letters after the Cadiz raid be sent back to join him with the other reinforcements. Meanwhile the ships which were to carry the dispatches and the diseased or disabled home were being made ready, and on June 1st they weighed anchor. The whole fleet weighed anchor with them and escorted them west of the Cape. Then, when the homeward-bound vessels turned away northwards, the rest of the fleet held on, out into the open Atlantic towards the setting sun. It never came back again to Sagres Bay.

It was bound for the Azores. Mystery surrounds this sudden departure from Cape St Vincent. As far as we know the homeward-bound ships carried no hint that the admiral was leaving his station; indeed his dispatches insisted that he would be there for two months more and asked for reinforcements. When Drake wrote that 'continuing to the end yields the true glory', surely he did not know that he would continue only five days more. Was he arguing with himself? It cannot have been want of provisions or sickness in his crews that drove him so suddenly away. A man of his capacity for leadership and his stubbornness cannot have been yielding to pressure from his officers or his crews. And why leave so hastily that not all the ships in the squadron had finished taking on fresh water or shifting their invalids to the returning transports? Some mystery remains, even if we assume as we must that Drake had suddenly heard of a new target of prime importance.

The *San Felipe*, carrack, homeward bound from Goa with the annual cargo of spices and oriental goods which were the fruits of Portugal's eastern empire, had been reported to India House from Mozambique and later from São Tomé. King Philip was afraid that Drake would hear of her, since caravels in the Guinea trade would now be making for Lagos or past the Cape to Lisbon, and some of them would be sure to have sighted the great carrack. If she followed the usual track of Portuguese ships homeward bound from India the *San Felipe*, instead of beating up the African coast, would make one long tack across the northeast trades from the Cape Verdes to the Azores and then run before the westerlies for Lisbon. Once news of her reached Drake he had only to calculate her probable speed and choose where to cut her off. Sure enough, when on June 18th the *Elizabeth Bonaventure* raised São Miguel in the Azores, there between her and the island was the great carrack under all easy sail. No wonder the Spaniards thought Drake had a magic mirror in his cabin on which he could see the ships moving on all the seas of the world.

Before the *Elizabeth* sighted the *San Felipe* she had lost some of her company. On June 3rd a violent storm arose which did not blow itself out for forty-eight hours. When the squadron re-formed, all the Queen's galleons were present and the three private galleons, Drake's *Thomas*, the Lord Admiral's *White Lion* and Sir William Winter's *Minion*, with some pinnaces. But all the London ships had disappeared. It was learned later that they all got safely back to the Thames.

Then the next day a sail was sighted and *Golden Lion* and *Spy*, pinnace, were ordered in pursuit. Presently *Spy* was seen returning alone. On her was Captain Marchant. He reported that the sail had proved to be English (could it have been one of the London contingent?) but that the crew of the *Golden Lion*, instigated by their former captain, William Borough, had mutinously refused to rejoin the admiral and were now on their way home. Drake found his worst suspicions confirmed, assembled a court-martial, had Borough sentenced to death for treason, then dismissed him from his mind. [So may this history, except to note that nobody on the *Golden Lion* was punished for mutiny, that everybody including Borough drew pay and prize money, and that the documents of the court of inquiry held after Borough's accusers got home yield much information about the campaign available nowhere else.]

The disappearance of the Londoners and the desertion of the *Golden Lion* had reduced Drake's squadron to six galleons and some pinnaces, but a smaller force would have been ample to overcome the carrack. It is true that she towered over the tallest of the English galleons like a percheron over a pony and her tonnage surpassed that of the three largest of them put together, but like most Portuguese carracks on the homeward voyage her crew was weakened and depleted by disease, her main deck was too crammed with merchandise for her gun-ports to be used, and the brass pieces in her forecastle and after-deck, though quite adequate to beat off the pirates of the Indian Ocean or the Barbary coast, were never meant to argue with the heavy guns the English carried. Her captain fought his ship as long as honour required and then surrendered gracefully. He and his men were given a ship to carry them to São Miguel, or wherever they liked, and Drake steered for Plymouth with his tremendous prize, the first of its kind in history.

The carrack was stuffed with pepper, cinnamon and cloves, calicoes, silks and ivories, besides a satisfactory quantity of gold and silver and some caskets of jewels. The total value turned out to be nearly a hundred and fourteen thousand pounds. That was more than three times the value of all the ships and cargoes seized, sunk or burned in Cadiz Bay. All the barrel staves and all the fishing-boats in Spain could not have been sold for such a figure. Although the London merchants insisted on getting their share of the loot, without having done the work of taking it, Drake's share was still over seventeen thousand pounds and the Queen's more than forty thousand. Now a galleon the size of Drake's flagship could be built new for about two thousand six hundred pounds, or hired for about twenty-eight pounds a month. In the Queen's ships a seaman's cost for wages and victuals was fourteen shillings a month, and a full crew for the *Elizabeth Bonaventure* could be paid and fed a month for a hundred and seventy-five pounds or less. Seventeen thousand pounds was the worth of a noble-man's estate; forty thousand pounds would put an army in the field. Both for Drake and for his mistress the capture of the *San Felipe* 'made' the voyage as a commercial venture.

In view of the facts of life in the sixteenth century, Drake's modern biographers seem unnecessarily embarrassed by the *San Felipe* episode and driven to offer explanations for it which none of Drake's contemporaries found necessary. One is that 'hunger and disease drove Drake from his station'. It is true that the mutineers of the *Golden Lion* alleged that they had small store of victuals left, forty-six men ill (probably about a fifth of the crew), and all of them fallen into weakness and feebleness through spare and bad diet. It may be. The *Golden Lion* seems to have been the stepchild of the fleet almost from the first. But the Queen's ships were supposed to be provisioned for three months when they sailed, and the *Golden Lion* was back in a little over nine weeks. In the meantime the Queen's ships had had first rights to the masses of wine and biscuit and oil captured at Cadiz, besides other opportunities to provision themselves from captured vessels and shore raids. Neither Drake nor Fenner seem to have been worried about provisions right up to the end of May; and certainly the Londoners, who repeatedly asserted that they had been provisioned for nine months, could not have been short of victuals.

It is the behaviour of these Londoners that is the heart of the mystery. For the other excuse offered for Drake is that he was 'deserted' by the bulk of his fleet so that he could not return to Cape St Vincent. Now the Londoners, as we have said, were well provisioned and in staunch ships. There is no hint that they were in trouble after the storm. And if they may have been a little bored burning barrel staves they would scarcely have forsaken a treasure hunt. It was for them particularly that the voyage was a commercial venture, up to this time not very profitable. After the storm which had scattered the fleet off Finisterre on the out-voyage the Lon-doners, like the other ships, had had no difficulty rejoining. It seems odd that they apparently made no effort to rejoin this time. It rather looks as if

Drake had appointed no rendezvous — had perhaps not even revealed his destination or what he hoped to find there. Because he was in too much of a hurry to get away? Because he wanted the absolute secrecy so necessary to complete surprise? Or because for the moment the old corsair's instinct not to divide a rich booty among too many companions overcame him?

At any rate, we may be sure that no matter how many ships had been with him, Drake would not have returned to the Cape after taking the great carrack. For one thing he had already been gone eighteen days and even with favourable winds would have to count on another week to get back. If the Spaniards had been reasonably prompt Santa Cruz might already command a fighting-fleet which Drake's full strength could hardly match. But the chief point was that he could not risk losing the carrack. Sixteenth-century wars were fought with money, and should Philip recover his property it should be as good to him as five hundred thousand ducats. Francis Drake was not to know that the cargo of this carrack, like all the Portuguese cargoes that had come from India for years past, was completely mortgaged to the bankers who in return for a steep rate of interest continued to support the bankrupt wholesale grocery business, which was what the King of Portugal's oriental empire had somehow turned into. The loss of the *San Felipe* would aggravate Philip's financial difficulties, but its recovery could hardly have increased his liquid assets. This Drake did not know, but he did know what her share of the plunder would mean to his royal mistress and might mean to her navy. Even if he had not cared about his own share Drake would not have dared risk losing so great a prize.

In the excitement of counting the spoil of the *San Felipe*, nobody remembered those brave words: 'to continue to the end, until it be thoroughly finished, yields the true glory.' Nobody has remembered them against Drake to this day. And in fact he might not have done much good by staying longer at the Cape. If his crews were not depleted by illness after seven weeks they would have been after another seven. That was what happened to the overcrowded ships of all nations in that century. Drake had already so confused and disrupted Spanish plans that few supplies moved for a month after he was gone, and no Spanish Armada could sail that year for England, whether the English were still off Cape St Vincent or not.

An allegorical painting by Adriaen van der Venne, depicting Protestants and Catholics fishing for souls.

XII

AN ARM IS CUT OFF

SLUYS, JUNE 9TH – AUGUST 5TH, 1587

AMONG the losers by Drake's raid in Cadiz Bay was a respectable corn merchant, a North German by birth now a naturalized denizen of Dixmude in West Flanders. Jan (to give him the Flemish form of his name) Wychegerde seems to have been primarily a broker for Baltic wheat, but like any alert merchant of the day he turned a penny where he could. Now and then, as when he had unluckily invested in the cargo of the Dunkirker Drake had taken at Cadiz, Mynheer Wychegerde took a flyer in the Spanish or Mediterranean trade, sometimes going along as his own factor, for he was as fluent in Spanish as in Flemish. Sometimes he handled a consignment of unfinished English cloth for the Rhine towns, or a shipment of Burgundy wines for Amsterdam. And, on the side, shaving a bit off the usual outrageous sutler's rates out of admiration for the Prince of Parma or devotion to the King of Spain, he catered to the hungry Spanish army, finding them not only Baltic wheat for biscuit but supplies of butter and cheese and salt fish from Holland and Zeeland, a business in which he had much competition since the Dutch towns made a regular thing of provisioning the enemy, in order they said to get the money to keep up their end of the war. Besides his relations with Parma's commissariat, Jan Wychegerde had another side line. He was one of the toughest and cleverest of Sir Francis Walsingham's spies.

It took toughness just to stay in business as a merchant in Flanders at this stage of the war. At sea that June, under the guise at least of his lawful occasions, Wychegerde was unlucky enough to be captured by a Rochellais privateer. The Huguenot pirates, who, had they known, might have shown some mercy to an agent of Walsingham's, were blithe to plunder a papist merchant, and Wychegerde, robbed of his last sous and his personal luggage, was unceremoniously set ashore at Boulogne to make his way home in his shirt. On reaching Dixmude he was warned that he had better wait to join a wagon-train with armed escort if he wanted to get to Parma's army base at Bruges. The near-by hostilities had made all the roads unsafe. Deserters from one army or the other and peasants whose holdings had been laid waste, formed wandering bands who daily waylaid and murdered such wayfarers as they found travelling singly or in small groups.

Even the convoys offered only relative safety. The English garrison at Ostend scoured the countryside and lay in wait for the wagon-trains. In fact, the first convoy that Wychegerde planned to join was ambushed just outside Dixmude. Wychegerde reported to Walsingham that he had counted twenty-five Spanish dead and only one dead Englishman, noting that the English troops had made a commendably clean sweep of the wagons. The Ostend garrison was so feared, he added, that no one durst move except when guarded by two or three hundred soldiers, and this time two companies of Walloons had run at the first English shot. Wychegerde noted only one flaw in the technique of the ambush. Next time a detachment should be placed to cut off the head of the convoy. By neglecting this precaution the English had missed the corn merchants who, riding ahead, had managed to spur into Dixmude with between ten and fifteen thousand Flemish pounds in their purses. Wychegerde waited for the next convoy. He was in a hurry to get to Bruges, and so on if he could to Parma's camp before Sluys; but though haste might have been served by a dash on horseback across country, the Dixmude corn merchant could not afford to seem in more of a hurry than would be natural for an honest burgher scenting a profit.

The siege of which Walsingham wanted more accurate news was four weeks old when Wychegerde finally reported on it. Since the beginning of spring there had been rumours that Parma would strike at the last rebel strongholds in Flanders, but when in June he moved his head-quarters and about half his field army to Bruges the concentration was so swift that he achieved something like tactical surprise. Almost all the county of Flanders, once the soul of the revolt, was already in Parma's hands. The delegates of Flanders no longer sat in the States General. After the fall of Antwerp the merchant oligarchs of Holland and Zeeland began to think of the great towns of Flanders rather as rivals to be crushed than as sisters to be rescued. But in the north-west corner of the county two towns still held out, Ostend and Sluys, both of strategic importance and near enough to support each other — Ostend, strongly seated on its dunes beside the North Sea, and Sluys, once the greatest port in Flanders but beginning to be stranded now by the silting up of the Zwyn.

Ostend was defended by an English garrison, Sluys by its own burgher militia, strengthened by militant Calvinist exiles, Flemings and Walloons who were reluctant to move a mile farther than necessary from their homeland. Both garrisons had made a sport of harassing the Spanish posts around Bruges, but both were under the strength they needed to man the circuit of their walls and neither was provisioned for a siege. When they suddenly learned that Parma was in the neighbourhood with seven, fourteen, eighteen thousand men, both commandants appealed for help, for victuals, munitions and reinforcements, to the Dutch States General, to Lord Buckhurst at the Hague, to the English Governor of Flushing, to Walsingham, to Leicester, and, of course, to the Queen.

The States seemed inclined to let the Flemings see to their own defence, but the English were more concerned. Lord Buckhurst, her Majesty's representative at the Hague in the absence of the Earl of Leicester, immediately ordered reinforcements and provisions for the English garrison of Ostend, and asked for authority to do the like for Sluys. Before he could receive it, Lord William Russell the Governor of Flushing, with the enthusiastic co-operation of the burghers of that town, sent enough provisions into Sluys to last, he thought, for two or three months; and on his own authority, having learned that Parma's first movement on Ostend was only a feint and that he now threatened Sluys, ordered the veteran Sir Roger Williams with four companies of English foot to quit Ostend and try to get through to reinforce the threatened town. Meanwhile, in England her Majesty was granting Leicester almost as much in the way of money and men as he asked for. She still hoped something might come of her negotiations with Parma, but she knew better than to put too much trust in talk. Every mile of the Flemish coast that the Spaniards won was an added danger to England. She told Leicester that Sluys must be relieved.

Parma's movement against Ostend had not been a feint, but a reconnaissance in force. He had hoped to take the town by surprise. But when he got there opened dikes flooded the approaches, reinforcements were being put ashore, and an English squadron in the offing was a visible reminder that Ostend could never be starved out while the King of Spain's enemies remained masters of the sea. The fortifications looked too strong, and a Council of War voted for withdrawal.

Next day Parma set three columns moving northward and eastward — one to seize Blankenberghe, the small fort which protected the line of communications between Ostend and Sluys; one straight along the main road from Bruges; one, which he led himself, to loop round eastward of the town and throw a bridge across the Yzendijke Canal which entered the Zwyn north of Sluys.

When these first objectives were achieved Parma held another Council of War. His captains, poring over the maps and remembering what they had seen of the terrain, shook their heads. This was worse than Antwerp. Sluys stood amidst a jigsaw puzzle of islands separated from one another by a network of channels and sluices broader than ordinary canals, most of them brimming with water twice a day, then scoured by fierce tides, then twice a day stagnant lagoons or swampy gullies. The chief water-road through this tangle into the deep basin of Sluys where once, it was said, five hundred great ships had ridden at anchor, was the estuary of the Zwyn threaded by a tricky but negotiable channel. An old castle, strengthened by recent works and joined to the town by a causeway and wooden bridge, guarded the basin. Each approach to the town was divided from any other by water, and in this labyrinth of waterways any army that attempted to surround the town risked being cut up into isolated detachments. Parma's officers were unanimous that a siege would be long and costly beyond any possible advantage, and attended by a grave risk of losing the whole army. They again advised withdrawal.

This time Parma disagreed. He did not need to tell his captains that he would share every danger and hardship with them. He could not tell them that although he would have liked to take Ostend, if it could have been done quickly and easily, he had to take Sluys, less because it was the nearest thing to a deep-water port he could hope for than because it lay athwart the network of waterways between Bruges and East Flanders, which would be essential to the logistics of his invasion of England. Some of his old comrades must have known, however, that the labyrinth of canals around Sluys offered exactly the kind of problem in military geometry Parma delighted in. He knew how to make the peculiar Dutch defences serve his own style of attack. He had already seen what the Flemish commander at Sluys also knew, that the key position was the barren, sandy island of Cadzand.

On its western side Cadzand bordered the channel of the Zwyn, opposite and beyond the old castle of Sluys. On its eastern side it was separated from an island which Parma himself held by what was, when tides were running, a boiling strait, but at dead low hardly more than a marsh spattered with stagnant pools. On the morning of June 13th Parma led a picked force of Spaniards floundering across, holding their weapons above their heads to keep them dry, some of them breast high in mud and water, those unlucky enough to slip plastered with slime from head to foot, the duke himself as muddy as any.

For almost twenty-four hours thereafter the Spaniards huddled on the desolate dunes of Cadzand, without food except a few soggy biscuits, without shelter or fuel or any means of getting warm or dry, without even water to drink. The barges Parma expected were unaccountably delayed. Cadzand had neither tree nor hut. It was raining. The match for their firearms was wet; so was their gunpowder. The strait they had crossed cut them off from their comrades. Had they been attacked (they could have been attacked at any time from the sea), these weary, hungry, shivering men would have had to defend themselves with cold steel. They complained so bitterly that anyone who did not know them would have predicted a mutiny. But somehow in the midst of their grumbling they got their camp laid out and entrenchments dug to shelter musketeers, and the sight of the steady lines of pikes and gun barrels guarding the working parties sent reconnoitring Dutch barges rowing hastily out of range.

Then Parma's own barges, delayed by skirmishing along the Yzendijke Canal, began to arrive, though even the next day Cadzand was still not strong enough to prevent the English under Sir Roger Williams from reaching Sluys. The two small Zeeland men-of-war escorting Williams beat the Spanish musketeers from their trenches with a cannonade and the expedition sailed on into the basin, sinking or capturing a number of Parma's boats on the way. But the following day the tables were turned. During the night a battery of Parma's precious siege guns was planted to command the channel. When the ships of the relieving expedition started back for Flushing on the morning ebb they were unexpectedly cannonaded, and their captains, trying to steer as wide of the battery as possible, ran both ships firmly aground. The tide was still ebbing, the battery could still reach them, and captains and crews swam and waded off to the shallow-draught little hoys which, having squeezed by out of range, could carry them to Flushing. Parma added the two Zeeland men-of-war to the small flotilla he was arming, and anchored them in the deepest part of the channel off the Cadzand battery. The shallower stretch beyond was blocked with a kind of palisade of upright stakes, the buoys and landmarks along the estuary were removed or changed to lure ships on to the shoals, and the English Governor at Flushing was obliged to report that the passage to Sluys was closed.

This was about three weeks before Jan Wychegerde made his way from Bruges to Parma's camp. In that time the States General had done nothing, the English at Flushing had been able to do nothing, and Parma had gradually tightened his grip upon the town. But the Earl of Leicester was returning at last with money and men. His first task was the relief of Sluys, in the teeth of Parma's army.

Wychegerde's mission was to find out how formidable that army was. He went about it methodically, as if he were making a commissary's estimate. He found four quarters, each fortified for independent defence since they could support each other only with difficulty: one outside the Bruges gate, where the principal fighting had been so far; one with Parma's own headquarters, on the isle of Cadzand, out of range of the town; a third across the river from Cadzand on St Anne's Island towards the old castle; and a fourth astride a canal over against the Ghent gate. In all four quarters there were, Wychegerde judged — counting Spaniards and Italians, Germans and Walloons — between five and six thousand men, probably nearer five thousand. Reports so far to Walsingham and Leicester had sometimes doubled, sometimes trebled this figure, and if Walsingham passed Wychegerde's estimate on to Leicester, Leicester seems not to have believed it. But Parma's secret dispatches to Philip II confirm its surprising accuracy.

Wychegerde was quick to warn Walsingham that though fewer in numbers than had been previously reported these were first-rate fighting-men, Parma's finest — vigilant, wary, seasoned, not to be surprised or panicked, working steadily in half-flooded trenches with the enemy on the walls looking down their throats, accepting the deadly hail of musketry with the same sullen curses they used for the grumbling of their empty bellies and the pelting rain on their backs, never missing an advantage or taking an unnecessary risk. 'They maintain great order ... their chief strength lies in the carefulness of their watch and the prudence of their methods by day and by night.'

They were opposed by men as good as they were. Parma wrote to Philip II that never in his experience had he met more gallant or more cunning foes, and the common foot-soldiers, back from digging under fire in clay that spurted water at every spade-stroke, or from being driven by a night sortie out of a lately hard-won trench, or from some sudden blind man-to-man knife fight in the mines and countermines by the Bruges gate, affirmed the same to Wychegerde with blasphemous admiration. Parma's casualties had already been heavy. A number of officers, among them the veteran La Motte, perhaps Parma's ablest lieutenant, had been seriously wounded, and it looked as if the fifteen hundred hospital beds Parma had ordered to be prepared at Bruges would all be filled before the Spanish army made much progress.

Nevertheless Wychegerde felt sure that unless Sluys were relieved it would be obliged to surrender. Parma was keeping the garrison under a relentless pressure, and his resources of men and munitions were greater than theirs. Already, Wychegerde guessed shrewdly, judging by their rate of fire the defenders must be worried about their supply of powder. Sluys could still be relieved, Wychegerde was convinced, most easily by sea. Parma's little flotilla could not really close the channel against a determined attack, and the battery on Cadzand could not sink enough of a hurrying swarm of small craft to make much difference. But the attempt should be soon. There were rumours of a great wooden bridge being built in thirty sections at Bruges: for an assault on Sluys by water, the engineers said. But it sounded like the same sort of device, a covered bridge with musket-proof walls, floating on barges, which Parma had used to close the Scheldt three years before. That bridge had sealed the fate of Antwerp.

Wychegerde must have been at Bruges, finding out about the floating bridge when the fleet carrying the Earl of Leicester and three thousand English troops swept along the Flanders coast. From the walls of Sluys the naval parade could be watched all the way from the neighbourhood of Blankenberghe until it entered Flushing Harbour. The keen-eyed could make out the banners and heraldic devices, and the besieged acknowledged the appearance of their rescuers by loosing a storm of small arms and cannon-fire on the heads of their besiegers. The Spaniards replied, and as Leicester's ships entered the mouth of the western Scheldt he could hear the thunder of the guns and see the Spanish positions marked by clouds of smoke. That was on July 2nd, twenty-three days after Parma had taken Cadzand.

It was another twenty-three days before the garrison of Sluys saw their would-be rescuers again. What had happened in the meantime had been mostly bad. In desperate fighting they had beaten back the besiegers from the Bruges gate; a sortie of de Vere's company had broken up another assault, taken some prisoners and almost taken some siege guns; the 'great sconce', the old castle and its outworks, had been held against a series of attacks. But there had never been quite enough men to work and watch and fight along the circuit of the walls, and for those who fell there were no replacements. Then Parma's floating bridges had begun to arrive. Two sections assured communications between the troops before the Bruges gate and those at St Anne, over against the old castle. Two more sections closed a gap to the east. Then, towed out past Blankenberghe and floated down the Zwyn a great line of them were swung across from Cadzand to St Anne's. Not only was the channel blocked but the men and guns at Cadzand could now be turned against the old fort or against the town.

Parma's first move was to redouble his attack on the fort. By using every available man the commandant, Groenevelt, repulsed the first assaults, then just in time he saw the trap. The fort was joined to Sluys only by a long wooden bridge. Once the strength of the defence had been committed to the fort Parma had only to burn or blow up the bridge and shift his attack by his new lines of communication to the other side of the town. The garrison would be helpless. Silently at midnight the troops in the castle, all but about two hundred of the fighting-men in Sluys still able to stand, withdrew into the town, the rearguard burning the castle and then the bridge behind them.

Parma was disappointed but he pressed grimly on, probing for weak spots, moving his batteries closer to the walls. Time, he felt, was running out for him, too. Soon, surely, the Dutch and the English would move and even with his improved communications he could not risk a battle in this tangle of canals. If the relieving force was numerous and determined he would be lucky to save his siege-train and perhaps his army, for with their command of the sea and the Scheldt estuary the enemy could attack suddenly from any one of several directions. Parma knew how he himself would use so decisive an advantage.

So he pushed forward his batteries and concentrated his attack on the blood-soaked ground before the Bruges gate. On the morning of the feast of Santiago the siege-train opened what was meant for a final bombardment. By afternoon the gatehouse was an untenable pile of ruins, and gaps had opened in the curtain wall wide enough, some of them, for twenty men to mount the breach abreast. But behind the ruined wall Parma, limping forward to reconnoitre in person in spite of a wound only two days old, saw a half-moon of a fresh earthwork manned by the apparently indestructible garrison. A wild rush might carry the work. But judging by previous performance Parma knew how many of his people would be killed. Desperate as was his need for haste he could not afford so many. So his bugles blew a retreat, and the general went back to his headquarters to combine a bombardment just beyond the line of the demilune and a simulated escalade on the Ghent side to divide and confuse the defence.

That night the besiegers saw lights flickering from the belfry of Sluys — more lights and moving into more new patterns than they had ever

Robert Dudley, Earl of Leicester, K.G. (1531–88). Artist unknown.

seen before; and watchers from Cadzand reported answering clusters of lights winking across the water from Flushing. The beleaguered town was sending some message, perhaps a last cry for help, perhaps an exclamation of despair, and was receiving some reply.

That was the night of July 25th. The next morning the whole mouth of the western Scheldt between Sluys and Flushing was white with sails, warships and transports of Zeeland and Holland and England. Pinnaces skirmished and took soundings in the mouth of the Zwyn, and beyond them men could make out the flags of Justin of Nassau the Admiral of Zeeland, and of Charles Howard of Effingham the Admiral of England, of Prince Maurice the youthful head of the house of Orange, and of the Queen's great Captain-General the Earl of Leicester. As he digested this news Parma heard that an army of the States was threatening 's-Hertogenbosch, and so the whole extended right wing of his army in East Flanders. Swiftly but cautiously Parma began regrouping his forces. There could be no assault on Sluys until he saw what the Dutch and the English meant to do. If Parma kept cool it was because so often before he had found himself balanced on a knife-edge between triumph and catastrophe.

What the Dutch and English meant to do was more than they knew themselves. Leicester wanted to drive with the shallow-draught ships straight down the channel of the Zwyn, run the batteries, destroy the floating bridge and so force a way into Sluys. But such an operation needed Dutch boats and Dutch pilots. Justin of Nassau was reluctant to risk his warships, and the pilots shook their heads. Perhaps with a spring tide and a north-west wind, they said, the channel might be forced. In another week the tides would serve; as for the wind — Then Leicester proposed landing his English troops on Cadzand to capture the battery and destroy the bridge. But the only flat-bottomed barges available were the property of Holland and Zeeland and not expendable without the authority of the States. Justin was willing to write and request authority. Meanwhile he proposed that the English land at Ostend and march along the dunes to Blankenberghe to try to draw off Parma's army. If they succeeded the Dutch would try to force the channel. Reluctantly Leicester agreed, and though baffled at first by unfavourable winds finally landed the bulk of his forces, four thousand foot and four hundred horse under Sir William Pelham, at Ostend, just a week after the rescuing fleet appeared off Sluys.

The next day the English marched on Blankenberghe while Leicester and Howard's squadron followed along the coast. Only a couple of guns behind an earthwork defended Blankenberghe on the Ostend side, strengthened at the last moment by a hastily broken gap in the dike. The garrison was small and Parma was seriously alarmed. If Blankenberghe were taken his position before Sluys would be untenable, and a safe withdrawal might prove difficult. He hurried off a reinforcement of eight hundred men and prepared to follow with his whole army as soon as he could. But Pelham stopped to think over that gap in the dike and the cannon beyond, and from the deck of his galleon Leicester saw the gleam of Spanish breastplates coming up from the east, the vanguard of Parma's terrible veterans, who knew how many thousand strong, hurrying to encircle and devour his half-trained levies. Leicester sent a hasty message, and the English fell back in good order on Ostend where they re-embarked and presently rejoined their allies off Sluys. Parma did not have to finish his regrouping, and the Dutch fleet had not stirred.

The next evening everything was at last right for forcing the channel. There was a spring tide. The wind blew briskly, but not too briskly, out of the north-west. The warships formed in double line ahead with Justin of Nassau in the leading ship. They were to cover, as far as possible, the fleet of hoys and flyboats in which the reinforcements and supplies were loaded. The Earl of Leicester had himself rowed about in his barge, supervising the sounding and marking of the channel, careless of the skipping shot from the Spanish batteries. He meant to lead the rescue into the town himself. And the Dutch launched the fire-ship which was to burn through the floating bridge and open the way to the basin.

On the bridge, where a company of Walloons manned the musket-proof parapet, there must have been a tense moment as flames licked up out of the advancing ship's hold and lines of fire began to run up her rigging. Just so, a fire-ship had drifted with the tide against such a bridge at Antwerp two years ago. Bold Spanish pikemen had leaped aboard to extinguish what seemed but a sulky fire when the whole ship blew up. Her entrails had been lined with brick and stuffed with gunpowder, stones and scrap-iron, and more men were killed and wounded in that one explosion than in many a pitched battle. No one who had seen 'the hell-burner of Antwerp' would ever forget it. The Marquis of Renty in command of the floating bridge had seen it. But he had seen, too, how Parma had dealt with a second such attack. As the fire-ship bore down Renty ordered the sections of the bridge directly in her path to be uncoupled. They swung back, and the ship swept through and on to burn herself out harmlessly on the edge of the basin of Sluys. She had no gunpowder in her belly.

Had Leicester with the barges been right behind the fire-ship he might have forced the channel and perhaps destroyed the bridge. Instead he was more than a mile away, too far to see what was happening, having a furious wrangle with his Zeeland pilots. Before the row was over the bridge was back in place, the tide was slackening and the wind was veering round towards the south. The fleet that should have rescued Sluys ran ingloriously back into the haven of Flushing.

The chief effect of this fortnight of imbecile manœuvres was on the morale of the beleaguered garrison. We can read the story best in the letters of Sir Roger Williams, commanding the English battalion. Williams was a professional soldier who had spent most of the past fifteen years campaigning in the Netherlands. He was a Welshman, a bantam gamecock of a man who wore on his morion the longest plume in either army 'so that his friends and his foes might know where he was', a man so like Captain Fluellen in his level head and blazing temper, forthright tongue and indomitable heart, even in the quirks of military pedantry that adorned his speech, that one must believe that William Shakespeare either knew him personally or drew heavily on the reminiscences of someone who did. Early in the siege Williams summed up the position for the Queen with a grim jauntiness. 'Our ground is great and our men not so many,' he wrote, 'but we trust in God and our valour to defend it ... We mean to let out every acre for a thousand of their lives besides our own ... We doubt not your Majesty will succour us for our honest mind and plain dealing toward your royal person and dear country.' Later, as relief delayed, he could grumble to Walsingham that the military education of young Maurice of Nassau and his half-brother Justin looked like costing the States half the cities they still held, but his tone was still confident. 'Since I followed the wars', he wrote, 'I never saw valianter captains or willinger soldiers ... At eleven o'clock the enemy entered the ditch of our fort with trenches upon wheels [carts, these were, covered by musket-proof shields]. We sallied out, recovered their trenches ... repulsed them into their artillery, kept the ditch until yesternight, and will recover it, with God's help, this night or else pay dearly for it.'

The same day Williams was urging Leicester to enter the channel of Sluys boldly with galliots and flat-bottomed boats. 'If your mariners will do a quarter of their duty, as I saw them do divers times, the Spanish cannot stop them. Before you enter the channel we will come out with

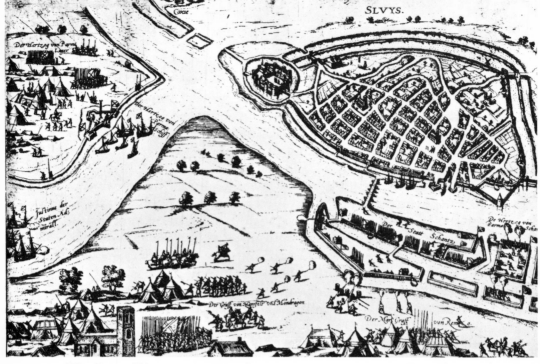

'The Siege of Sluys', an engraving from a contemporary series by Franz Hagenberg illustrating the history of France and The Netherlands.

Capture of 'Tormacum' in 1581; part of the revolt of The Netherlands against Spain.

our boats and fight with the enemy and show there is no such great danger. You may assure the world that here are [no traitors] but valiant captains and valiant soldiers such as had rather be buried in the place than be disgraced in any point that belongs to men of war.' Ten days later he wrote again to Leicester, outlining tactics for the relieving forces and adding in Captain Fluellen's own tone: 'You must consider that no wars may be made without danger. What you mean to do, we beseech you to do with expedition.'

Another week passed and at last the rescuing fleet could be seen from the walls of Sluys, could be seen for three days doing nothing. That was when he wrote: 'Since the first day we ... keep always in guard nine companies of the twelve, and for this eighteen days all, more than half continually with arms in their hands ... We are slain and spoiled ten captains, six lieutenants, eighteen sergeants, of soldiers in all almost six hundred. Never were brave soldiers thus lost for want of easy succours ... We have not now powder for three skirmishes. For myself, I wish myself dead for [leading] so many brave men to their ruin. The old saying is true, wit is never good until it be dearly bought, but I and the rest of my companions are like to pay too dear for it.'

And in a bitter postscript: 'Little doth Sir William Pelham and the rest consider the Duke of Parma his proceedings with fury and all manner of engines. They see in their card the town of Sluys, but do not see the works of both sides nor feel the pain of their poor friends.'

After this letter the town held out another eight days and paid for the time thus won with more than two hundred lives. Then, whilst the charred ribs of the fire-ship were still smoking, Groenevelt asked for a parley. Parma gave generous terms. The garrison, what was left of them — for, of seventeen hundred, eight hundred had been killed and two hundred were too sorely hurt to stand — was to march out with their arms and baggage and the full honours of war. Parma respected a valiant foe. He sought out Sir Roger Williams where he stood at the head of the remnant of his battalion, his arm in a sling and his great plume broken, praised his soldiership and offered to find a command worthy of it where he need never fight against his co-religionists or his fellow countrymen. Williams replied courteously that if he ever served any but his Queen in future, it would be in the army of that hard-pressed champion of the Protestant cause, the Huguenot hero King Henry of Navarre. But it cannot have soothed his spirit to know that his gallant enemy suspected and sympathized with the bitterness he felt at the useless sacrifice of his men. For the moment Williams wanted no more of any prince's service. On his way back to England, too poor even to find himself a horse, he ended a letter to the Secretary: 'I am weary of the wars. If I can devise how to live I will quit [soldiering] and follow my Lady Walsingham's counsel to marry a merchant's widow.' Of course he did nothing of the sort.

The Duke of Parma was almost as weary as Sir Roger. The siege had cost him nearly seven hundred killed and more wounded than he had provided for. 'Never since I came to the Netherlands', he wrote to Philip, 'has any operation given me such trouble and anxiety as this siege of Sluys.' But, looking towards the invasion of England, the objective had been worth the cost. Perhaps Parma told himself that he could repeat the sultan's boast. This arm of the enemy's he had cut off would more than make up for the singeing of a beard.

Caricature of Leicester's departure from The Netherlands, 1586/7.

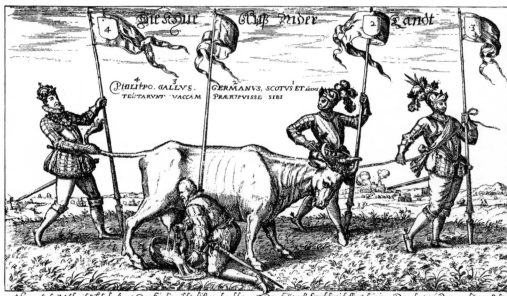

THE HAPPY DAY

COUTRAS, OCTOBER 20TH, 1587

THE King of Navarre and his army were trapped. The bulk of the Huguenot troops could not possibly escape the powerful Catholic host so suddenly come upon them. The only desperate chance to save them lay in committing the whole Huguenot force to unequal battle, and if that were risked the odds were that the whole little army and its princely Bourbon leaders would be wiped out — a blow to the Protestant cause, in France and throughout Europe, beside which the loss of Sluys would seem a very minor amputation, a victory for the Faith to achieve which Philip of Spain would have sacrificed half a dozen towns like Sluys.

With his customary boldness Navarre had been leading a picked force, the flower of the Huguenot army, away from the shores of Biscay where the Catholics hoped to pin him, right across the enemy's front towards Bergerac and the hills. The bulk of that picked force, and with them Navarre himself, his Bourbon cousins, Condé and Soissons, and many famous Huguenot captains, slept the night of October 19th in the little village of Coutras, between the rivers Dronne and Isle, on the road that ran from Tours and the north through Poitiers to Bordeaux. The Huguenot captains struggled awake in the grey dawn of the 20th to hear the distant popping of small-arms in the woods north of the village, and to learn that the powerful royal army under the Duke of Joyeuse, the army they were trying to evade, had stolen a night's march on them and was already in contact with their pickets. In an hour or so, perhaps less, Joyeuse would have them neatly shut into the fork between the Dronne, which they had crossed yesterday afternoon, and the Isle, which they expected to cross this morning.

It was a bad position to be caught in. The straggling, indefensible village where they were quartered ran down the middle of a narrow wedge between the two rivers, a cul-de-sac with the Duke of Joyeuse already closing its mouth. To make matters worse the rear guard, a squadron of cavalry and some arquebusiers, had not yet crossed the Dronne, while the advance guard, a troop of light horse, two skeleton regiments of foot and the three cannon which were all their artillery, were already crossing the Isle on their way to the friendly strongholds of the Dordogne. If he hurried, Navarre and his cousins and captains with most of the cavalry could still get away, following the vanguard across the deep narrow ford of the Isle. The bulk of the infantry would have to be left behind to buy with their lives time enough for the cavalry's escape. That way the leaders, at least, could be saved, though whether anybody would ever follow them afterwards was another question. On the other hand, if they stayed and fought and were beaten few of any rank were likely to survive. The rivers that flowed together behind them were too deep to ford and too swift to swim, the one bridge at the end of the village street was impossibly narrow and the Catholic army of M. de Joyeuse gave no quarter.

If the capture of Sluys had crippled Protestant resistance, the destruction of this Huguenot army and its leaders would almost paralyse it. Here and there isolated pockets of resistance might hold out, but the back of Protestant power in France would be broken, and the future would belong for some time to the house of Guise-Lorraine, to the radical fanatics of the Holy League, and to the paymaster of both, the King of Spain. That would be an evil day for the rebels in the Netherlands, and perhaps an even worse one for the reluctant Captain-General and paymaster of the Protestant coalition, Elizabeth of England. Once thoroughly in the power of the Duke of Guise and the League, as with the collapse of Huguenot opposition and the extinction of the Bourbon line Henry III was sure to be, not only would there be no more threat to Parma's flank but the French Channel ports would offer secure bases for the invasion of England and French ships and men would be available to reinforce the Spanish Armada. Towards some such end Spanish diplomacy had been working ever since the death of the last Valois heir, harnessing to its service the skill of the Jesuits, the eloquence of the preaching orders, the authority of Rome and all the forces of the renascent militant Catholicism of the Counter-Reformation. The Spanish diplomats were able to manipulate these forces the more easily because they themselves were penetrated and inspired by them, and were so certain that the power of Spain was the chosen instrument for bringing all Europe back to the faith that the interests of Spain and the interests of God's Church honestly seemed to them to be the same.

In France they had manipulated the forces of the Counter-Reformation so successfully that for more than two years now the Huguenots had been fighting — not as they had once fought, for the triumph of their faith and the establishment of God's kingdom, but for their lives. They were, as the King of Navarre's Secretary had recently written, perforce chief actors in a tragedy in which all Europe had a share. They had been thrust back upon the stage in July 1585. It was thirteen months since the death of the last Valois heir; a year since an assassin's bullet had struck down the Prince of Orange; seven months since the Guises and the adherents of the Holy League had been bound by the secret treaty of Joinville to supply the civil war Philip needed in France while he dealt with the heretics in Holland and, perhaps, in England. In July 1585, Henry III, cornered by the League, revoked the royal edicts of toleration and outlawed the Reformed Church. In September the new Pope, Sixtus V, issued a tremendous bull, denouncing Henry of Navarre as a relapsed heretic, depriving him of his estates, absolving his vassals from their allegiance and declaring him incapable of succeeding to the throne of France.

So began the 'War of the Three Henrys' — of Henry of Valois, King of France, the last surviving male of his line; against Henry of Bourbon, King of Navarre, by Salic law his heir; a war fought at the bidding of Henry, Duke of Guise, of the half-foreign house of Lorraine, the only one of the three Henrys who could profit. A genealogy of the house of Lorraine showed descent from Charlemagne, and there were people to say that so descended the Duke of Guise had a better right to the French crown than any descendant of Hugh Capet. Probably no one would have said so out loud in normal circumstances. But the heir to the French crown was a heretic, and the more or less acknowledged chieftain of the Huguenot party. Whipped on by their preachers, the Paris mob was ready to revolt rather than accept a Protestant king. Financed by Spain the magnates of the League were determined to make war to the death on the heretics, whether the King of France was for them or against them, since either way both their faith and their greed could be served. The mixture of powerful motives made the 'War of the Three Henrys' the bitterest since the aftermath of St Bartholomew's.

Henry of Navarre rallied his party to resist. He replied to the royal edict with an aggrieved protestation of his own loyalty and that of his co-religionists. He replied to the Pope's bull with a jaunty letter to 'M. Sixte' which some daring spirit managed to affix to Pasquino's statue, to the mingled wrath and amusement of His Holiness. And by an adroit campaign which combined guerrilla forays with the stubborn defence of selected strongpoints he slowed, at least, the advancing Catholic tide. But, as he used to say afterwards, that autumn his moustache turned white

143

from anxiety. Anxiety kept him constantly in the saddle as long as there was an enemy in the field, until his slight wiry frame was worn to the bone with weariness. He knew that he himself, his cause and his people were in deadly peril.

After Henry of Guise there was no Catholic in France more dangerous to the Huguenots than the commander of the royal army south of the Loire — Anne, duc de Joyeuse. That handsome young man had rocketed from obscurity to be, before he was half through his twenties, a duke, the husband of the Queen's sister and so brother-in-law to the King, lord of vast estates, governor of wide provinces and Admiral of France. Probably what helped most in this rapid rise was Henry III's weakness for handsome young men. But others among the mignons, the long-haired, scented darlings who minced and giggled around the King, were said to be equally handsome. Some, at least, showed equal physical courage. A few were almost equally quarrelsome and impudent. What distinguished Anne de Joyeuse was what has been called, in another royal favourite, the passion for command. He had a reckless effrontery, a sublime self-confidence, a kind of magnanimity which so imposed upon his contemporaries (not only on the King) that it is impossible now to say whether he had any other extraordinary qualities at all.

Into the cause of the League Joyeuse flung himself with the same headlong fury with which he had plunged into the quarrels and revels of the Court. He must have known that his patron and master was suspicious of the League, and had signed the edict outlawing the Huguenots with sorrowful reluctance. Perhaps Joyeuse had been suddenly converted from a conventional into an ardent Catholic. Perhaps his wife influenced him in favour of her cousins the Guises. Perhaps he simply wanted to assert his independence of the doting friend who had put France at his feet before he was twenty-five. Events seemed to justify his contemptuous confidence that he could carry the King along with him, even on a course of policy ruinous to the crown. The King made him his lieutenant in the principal theatre of war, and gave him a fine field army; then, when he had frittered most of it away, gave him another even stronger and more splendid. It was this second army which ever since midnight had been plunging southward down the Chalais road to trap Navarre at Coutras.

Henry had meant not to fight Joyeuse but to elude him. He had done that all summer, meanwhile helping the Catholic army towards disintegration by constant harassment. The Protestants scarcely ever won a pitched battle and for years had not risked one, but they were seasoned partisan

Henry III, from drawings attributed to François Clouet.

'Bal à l'occasion du mariage du Duc de Joyeuse'; French school, sixteenth century, from the Louvre.

troops, and that summer, as before, they were the usual victors in a hundred petty skirmishes. When Henry heard that Joyeuse had returned to the field with a new army he got together all the Huguenot troops who could be spared from the defence of La Rochelle and the lesser Protestant towns of Poitou and Saintonge, and prepared to slip across in front of the royal army to the Dordogne and the tumble of hills and valleys that ran southwards to Pau and his principality of Béarn. He could find reinforcements there and the security of a dozen loyal hill-top fortresses, and could either make life difficult for the duke's army or leave it to unprofitable sieges while he cut away northward to join the Swiss and German mercenaries (paid partly with Queen Elizabeth's money) which his friends and allies were already leading, so he thought, towards the sources of the Loire.

The Béarnais moved fast; it was one of his chief distinctions as a captain. But this time he was too slow. He had thought Joyeuse's main army a good twenty miles away when in fact it was scarcely more than ten, and he had not reckoned upon the willingness of dainty courtiers to ride half the night in order to force a battle in the morning. Now, as he listened to the crackle of small-arms which showed that his outposts were being driven in, he faced the unpleasant fact that although he himself could still get away he would have to leave most of his troops behind.

Nothing in the record suggests that Henry entertained for a moment the idea of escape. Rather, he gave his captains the impression that this was just the place he would have chosen for a battle. Probably the decision was automatic; Henry knew that he owed his leadership of the Huguenot party less to his place in the succession and his somewhat ungracefully reassumed Protestantism than to his willingness to risk his life in the forefront of every skirmish, and to bear himself in these long partisan campaigns less like a prince and a general than like an industrious captain of irregular light horse. If he shunned the perils now forced upon his companions he would not only lose an army, he might lose for ever the only support he could rely on in his progress towards the crown.

If Henry seemed delighted at the prospect of a fight he was less pleased at the disposition his captains were making. Coutras then, as now, was one long street of serried houses ranged along the Chalais–Libourne road. In those days, half-way along this street and flanking it on the east, where the road from the west having crossed the Dronne ran on to cross the

Isle, there stood a fortified château built some sixty years earlier and already fallen into partial ruin. In some fashion not clear in any of the accounts the Huguenots were beginning to align themselves along the east–west road, with arquebusiers in the houses of the village and their defensive position pivoting on the château. The field was cramped and broken by the line of the village street, and Henry would have none of it. Although the rattle of small-arms was now at the edge of the wood, less than a mile away, Henry ordered a general advance to the open meadows at the north end of the village and there began to re-deploy his army, practically in the presence of the enemy.

As he did so his artillery, three bronze guns, one of them an eighteen-pounder, came hurrying back at his orders from the crossing of the Isle and were sent to take up their position on a sandy hillock on the left of the new front, a modest elevation but commanding the whole little field. Before they could reach this mound, and while part of the Huguenot infantry was still coming up in column on the right and the Huguenot horse were either still in the narrow street or just wheeling into position, the vanguard of Joyeuse's army began to debouch from the wood into the amphitheatre of open meadow.

'If at this juncture the king was in difficulties, the duke was not without them.' When Joyeuse learned that the Huguenots had reached Coutras and were planning to slip by in front of him it was nearly midnight and his army, roused in the scattered villages where they were quartered, had to converge on their objective by narrow roads and bridle-paths in pitch darkness and often in single file. In the wake of the cavalry which had driven in Henry's outposts a sluggish serpent of mixed horse and foot was now stretched out for miles along the Chalais road. So, each commander about equally embarrassed by the disorder in his own ranks and the presence of the enemy, and 'neither army knowing what the other meant to do', the two hosts deployed on opposite sides of the meadow, ignoring each other, as if by mutual consent, until their formations were unsnarled and their ranks were dressed. The sun was just rising when the duke's light horse emerged from the forest on the spectacle of their deploying foes. It was two hours high before Navarre's artillery, later on the field than the duke's but earlier in position, opened the ball.

The King of Navarre had chosen the better position and his dispositions were the more skilful. On the right, behind a deep ditch which marked the edge of the warren attached to the park of the château, Henry stationed his four skeleton regiments of infantry. Their position was invulnerable to cavalry, and in the broken ground and rough thickets from which they would be firing it mattered less that they had not enough pikemen. On the left a much smaller force of infantry was somewhat drawn back and covered by a marshy brook. Across the centre the Huguenot heavy cavalry were stationed in four compact squadrons, six or more files deep. Picked detachments of arquebusiers were posted in the gaps between the squadrons with orders to hold their fire until the enemy were within twenty paces and then pour in a concentrated volley. Beyond the last squadron of men-at-arms La Tremoîlle's light horse, who had been skirmishing with the enemy since daybreak, closed the gap towards the warren where the bulk of the infantry were. These were cunning dispositions; the Huguenots were going to need whatever advantage they could win from them.

Opposite them Joyeuse had ranged a similar but simpler line of battle. On each wing he posted two regiments of royal infantry, those on his left at least as strong as the four regiments opposite him in the warren, those on his right much stronger than the scratch force beyond the brook. Across the centre stretched his cavalry, the light horse opposite Henry's light horse, and opposite the Huguenot cuirassiers the royal heavy cavalry, the famous gens d'armes d'ordonnance, not in squadron columns but 'en haye', one long unbroken double line. Joyeuse himself commanded the gens d'armes. With them he expected to break the back of the Huguenot cause in one overwhelming charge. Not one heretic, he promised his officers, not even the King of Navarre himself, should leave the battlefield alive.

Across the few hundred yards of open ground the opposing horsemen had time to eye each other. The Huguenots looked plain and battle-worn, in stained and greasy leather and dull grey steel. Their armour was only cuirass and morion, their arms mostly just broadsword and pistol. Legend was to depict Henry of Navarre as wearing into this battle a long white plume and romantic trappings, but Agrippa d'Aubigné, who rode not far from Navarre's bridle-hand that day, remembered the King as dressed and armed just like the old comrades around him. Quietly the Huguenots sat their horses, each compact squadron as still and steady as a rock.

Opposite it the line of the royalists rippled and shimmered. It billowed out here, shrank back there, as its components jostled each other and jockeyed for position like riders at the start of a race, curvetting their horses and now and then breaking ranks to exchange a greeting with a

SONET

Voyant en ce recueil ceste troupe diuine
Il me semble, THEVET, q'rauy hors de moy
Aux champs Elysiens ie me trouue auec toy,
Comme le Phrygien guidé par sa Deuine
Là tu vas remarquant en chacun plus insigne
Ce quil monstre de rare & memorable en soy:
Mais i'y voy entre tous l'image de mon ROY,
Qui du premier honneur seule se monstre digne.

Si tu voulois, THEVET, mettre deuant les yeux
Les exemples diuers des actes glorieux,
Le portrait de HENRY seul te pouuoit suffire.
Car toutes les vertuz que le hault Ciel depart,
Tout ce qui peut orner tous les autres à part
On le voit en luy seul heureusement reluyre.

P.R. Scevole de S.t Marthe
Tresorier general de France

Henry II, King of Navarre (1503–55).

friend or an insult with a foe. The flower of the Court had accompanied
M. de Joyeuse on his journey to Poitou. More than six-score lords and
gentlemen served as troopers in his first rank, most of them accompanied by their own armed servants. So the lances with which the duke
had insisted they be armed were gay with pennons and bannerets and with
knots of coloured ribbon in honour of noble ladies, and there was a
great display of armour, as much armour as anyone ever saw in combat
any more, even to cuisses and gorgets and visored casques, and every
conspicuous surface chased and inlaid with curious designs, so that
d'Aubigné wrote afterwards that never was an army seen in France so
bespangled and covered with gold leaf.

This glittering cavalry was still adjusting its alignment when Navarre's
three guns, ensconced on their hillock, opened fire. The round shot, fired
at an almost enfilading angle, tore holes in the Catholic ranks. Served by
veterans and commanded by a first-rate artilleryman the Huguenot guns
fired eighteen deadly rounds while Joyeuse's battery was managing six
harmless ones. 'We lose by waiting!' the duke's adjutant-general, Lavardin, cried, and the duke's trumpets signalled the attack.

Lavardin, on the Catholic left, was first off the mark. His charge struck
Tremoîlle's light horse and Turenne's squadron beyond them with irresistible force, bowled them over and drove them back on the village street.
Turenne rallied part of his force (eighteen recently joined Scotch volunteers made him a solid nucleus) but some of the light horse who had fought
so gallantly in the morning galloped off to spread the news of Navarre's
defeat over the countryside, and the Huguenot ranks heard Catholic cries
of 'Victory!' in the village behind them.

The band of infantry on the left, thinking they might as well die attacking as attacked, flung themselves in a headlong rush across the brook, and
before the royalist regiments grasped what was happening were in among
them, rolling under the pikes or dragging them aside with their hands and
closing in with sword and dagger. The startled royalists broke ranks, and
the whole of that side of the field dissolved into a confused hand-to-hand
mêlée. Meanwhile the infantry on the Huguenot right were briskly
engaged, though not so busy defending the warren as to be unable to
spare an occasional volley for Lavardin's horse.

But the battle was to be decided in the centre. The duke's trumpets
sounded, the shimmering line swayed forward, the long lances came down
to point at the foe, their pennons shadowing the ground before them. The
tempo of the drumming hooves rose to the thunder of a gallop. 'Too soon,'

the Huguenot veterans breathed to one another. When the duke's trumpets blew the chaplains of the Huguenot heavy cavalry had just finished prayer. Still quietly sitting their horses the men-at-arms raised the battle hymn of their party:

> La voici la heureuse journée
> Que Dieu a fait à plein désir
> Par nous soit joye démenée ...

It was a metrical version of Psalm 118 beginning with the verse: 'This is the day which the Lord hath made; we will rejoice and be glad in it.' Still singing the solid squadrons took up a slow trot. As the drone of the psalm reached the quickening advance some gilded darling, riding knee to knee with the duke, cried out gleefully: 'Ha, the cowards! They are trembling now. They're confessing themselves,' to be answered by a veteran on the duke's other hand: 'Monsieur, when the Huguenots make those noises, they are ready to fight hard.' It cannot have been a minute later that the arquebusiers fired their volley, and the massed columns of Huguenot horse, quickening their trot, crashed into the galloping line.

That blow decided the battle. Under the impact of the solid columns the Catholic front broke in pieces, and the Huguenots began rolling up the fragments by the flank. There was a minute or two of desperate, scrambling fighting. The Prince of Condé was unhorsed and his successful opponent, after a look no doubt at the field, dismounted and presented his gauntlet to the discomfited prince in token of surrender. The King of Navarre, having pistoled one adversary and taken a sharp rap on the head with a lance-butt from another, recognized the seigneur de Chasteau Renard, the standard-bearer of the enemy troop he had smashed, and seizing his old companion round the waist crowed joyfully: 'Yield thyself, Philistine.'

In another part of the field the Duke of Joyeuse was cut off by a clump of horsemen as he tried to escape. He flung down his sword and called out: 'My ransom is a hundred thousand crowns.' One of his captors put a bullet through his head. For the commander who had ordered the Huguenot wounded to be killed on the field, who had hanged prisoners by the hundred and butchered garrisons who had surrendered relying on the laws of honest war, there was not much chance of quarter. Indeed, until King Henry furiously intervened, little quarter was given to any of the royal army. Three thousand common soldiers were slaughtered, more than four hundred knights and gentlemen, and an impressive roll of dukes, marquises, counts and barons — more, d'Aubigné thought, than had fallen in any three battles of the century. The Catholic host was utterly destroyed; nothing was left of that glittering army. 'At least,' said Henry of Navarre at the day's end, 'nobody will be able to say after this that we Huguenots never win a battle.'

Battle of Coutras, from a contemporary series by Franz Hagenberg illustrating the history of France and The Netherlands.

XIV

THE USES OF VICTORY

FRANCE, OCTOBER 21ST – DECEMBER 16TH, 1587

WINNING a battle is one thing, using the victory another. Among the victorious Huguenots there were several opinions as to how the crowning mercy vouchsafed at Coutras might be used. The gentlemen of Poitou were all for recapturing their lost towns and castles and mopping up Catholic strongholds south of the Loire. So was the Prince of Condé, who could see himself carving out an almost independent domain in that region, something like the great apanaged dukedoms of the past. The Gascons pointed out, however, that there was still a Catholic army in the south-west, about four thousand men under Matignon actually marching northward for a rendezvous with Joyeuse. To wheel and fall upon Matignon before he could get back to Bordeaux would be to clear Guyenne of any Catholic field army for the first time for years. But the wisest heads in Navarre's councils saw that there was really only one course open. Somewhere approaching the sources of the Loire should be, at this moment, the great mercenary army for which Queen Elizabeth had spent so much money and promised more. Eight thousand German cavalry, the formidable 'reiters' under the Baron von Dohna, and about an equal number of landsknechts, German mercenary infantry, plus some eighteen thousand Swiss, recruited and led by the Duke of Bouillon, in all the most powerful foreign army seen in France for thirty years and already reinforced by from four to six thousand Huguenots. If Henry joined them at once and led them, further strengthened by his own troops, against Paris, the King of France must either yield or give battle and the long weary years of civil war might end in victory before the first snow fell. Staunch Huguenots like Maximilian de Bethune, later Duke of Sully, never really forgave Henry for letting slip so magnificent a chance.

Instead, Henry paused awhile at Coutras, dealing with such matters as wounded (mostly enemy wounded, his own casualties had been surprisingly light), ransoms and spoils. Then he suddenly mounted and spurred for Pau, slightly attended, to lay the captured banners of Joyeuse's army at the feet of his current mistress, la belle Corisande. The army was left to break up and go home. The grave champions of the Reformed Religion could only shake their heads in disappointment and sorrow. Everybody knew that Henry had a fatal weakness for the fair, that he was, not to put too fine a point on it, a notorious womanizer. But for a man in his mid-thirties, a prince, a veteran commander and the chief protector of God's churches in France to act like a moonstruck boy, tossing away the fruits of victory and leaving his campaign in confusion for the sake of tumbling a wench, was really too bad. It was sheer weakness in the King of Navarre, but, after all, for most of his followers it was a disarming even if an exasperating weakness.

That may have been all there was to it. But there are hints of a more complicated explanation. The romance with Corisande was fading. The banners of Coutras were practically a farewell present. And though Henry was generally a hard rider he made an unusually short stage in order to stay the night and talk with a literary gentleman whose château lay somewhat off his direct route. Much as some of us would give to have an evening's gossip with Michel Eyquem de Montaigne one doubts whether Navarre had gone out of his way just for the charm of his host's conversation. He knew that Montaigne, though a Catholic and a loyal subject, was a moderate man, an advocate of peace and toleration. He knew also that he could call him a friend.

What the two friends said that night by the fireside we shall never know, but if Navarre had chosen to expound the courses before him he might have said something like this: Much as the Prince of Condé and the Huguenot gentlemen of the province might want to press the campaign in Poitou it was not to the interest of the Crown to help Condé carve out a principality for himself, there or anywhere, and in this matter Henry of Navarre's interests were the interests of the Crown. Similarly, to defeat old Matignon, a staunch Catholic but a moderate man and a loyal servant of the King, would probably just lead to his replacement in Guyenne by some fanatical or ambitious Leaguer. There had been enough bloody sieges and savage cross raiding in south-west France. The more there were the more bitterness would be aroused and the harder it would become to keep the King's peace. Here, too, the interests of the Crown were the same as the interests of Henry of Navarre. As for the obvious course of action, joining Dohna's reiters and marching on Paris, what could that lead to except a pitched battle between the King of France and his heir apparent? And whose interests could be served by that except those of the greedy magnates, Leaguers or Huguenots or politiques, who hoped to use this troubled time to grab for themselves a slice of the kingdom and a share of the Crown's authority?

It is not hard to conjecture what further Navarre may have said. The interest of the Crown was domestic peace, and for this all that was needed was a return to the moderately tolerant terms of the Edict of Poitiers and a bridling of the power of the Guises, who had forced the King, against his will, to revoke it. Perhaps the campaign in the north had already diminished the prestige of Henry of Guise, and if further steps were needed, for that or for uniting the realm in a war against the old enemy Spain now the chief poisoner of domestic peace, Henry of Valois could rely on the devoted services of his cousin and sworn liegeman, Henry of Navarre.

Just after Coutras a captured courtier said to his captor: 'In winning this battle, you have really won nothing, for you will have angered the king.' 'Ha!' said the tough Protestant partisan, 'God send me the chance to anger him so once a week!' Henry of Navarre was rather of the courtier's opinion. On another occasion Navarre had said that rather than fight against the person of his sovereign, the King of France, he would flee from him to the ends of the earth — out of pure respect. Perhaps he repeated something of the sort to his friend Montaigne.

Whatever he said, not long after Navarre left the Château de Montaigne its lord ordered his saddle-bags packed and set off northwards. Perhaps a sedentary old gentleman of fifty-four, suffering from gout and kidney stone, undertook to traverse the length of France through roving bands of broken soldiers and cold autumn rains just to talk to his publishers about a new edition of his essays. Most of his modern biographers seem to believe so. That vigilant diplomat Bernardino de Mendoza did not. Although Mendoza had not heard of the recent conversation with Navarre and appears not to have known that Montaigne had served as a liaison between Navarre and the Catholics on at least one previous occasion, when the ambassador learned that a M. de Montaigne, a friend both of Matignon and of Navarre's current mistress, was being received at Court he instantly concluded that the man had come on some underhand political mission. Mendoza, of course, was apt to suspect the worst, particularly where Henry III was concerned.

We shall never know whether Montaigne brought the King of France any message from his heir apparent or, if so, what it was. Garrulous and all-confiding about the intimate details of his personal life, Michel de

Montaigne was as close-mouthed as a family lawyer about his excursions into politics. But if he brought any offer or any message it came too late. Once again, in the weeks after Coutras, events had twitched the guiding-reins out of the fingers of the Valois king.

It may be that Henry of Valois was not so angry after all about the outcome of Coutras. Courtiers whispered that the King's affections and confidence had already shifted to the Duke of Epernon, and that Henry found the presence and power of his former favourite an embarrassment. Ambassadors pointed out that since Joyeuse had gone over to the Leaguers any victory he won would only fasten the League's shackles tighter on the King of France. Sir Edward Stafford even reported the King as saying, some days before Coutras, that if Joyeuse should defeat Navarre it would be the ruin of the State. Whether he thought so or not, Henry III's plans certainly did not depend on Joyeuse's triumph and might have been better served by his defeat.

The King of France had planned the campaign of 1587 with some care. Though he never had as much to do with the famous victories of Jarnac and Moncontour as he now sincerely believed, in military matters as in most matters Henry III was no fool. It is not hard to guess his scenario for the campaign. Joyeuse would be kept busy south of the Loire, where Henry may have suspected that Navarre would moderate the favourite's pride. Meanwhile Dohna and the reiters would be invading France from the north-east. (Henry knew all about Queen Elizabeth's negotiations with the Count Palatine and all about Bouillon's negotiations with the Swiss. Justice and finance, internal administration, army and navy might all be breaking down, but the French diplomatic corps still functioned almost as well as ever.) The Germans would pass through Lorraine, might even stay there for some time, and, of course, Henry of Guise would go to protect his own domain and those of his family. His mission, in fact, would be to guard the northern frontier. Only he would not have enough men, scarcely more than those he could raise by his own resources. The promised reinforcements from France just would not arrive. Whether the Protestant army gobbled Guise up or brushed him aside, besieged him in one of his towns or sent him flying back to France with his tail between his legs, he could scarcely fail to be defeated and humiliated; with any luck he might be killed or captured.

The defeat of the Leaguers would be the King's cue. Between Etampes and La Charité during the summer he had concentrated a powerful reserve, estimated at the time as about forty thousand men. Part of it was

posted to defend every practicable crossing of the Loire. The rest, with
the Duke of Epernon commanding the van and the King himself the main
body, was ready to prevent any junction between Navarre and the Germans. Whether his lieutenants were wiped out or fell back to join him the
King was prepared when the time came to take the centre of the stage and
dispel the threatening storm. Henry felt confident of victory, and one
victory, following upon the defeat of Guise, would make him again King
of France.

The drastic conclusion of Coutras, though certainly not foreseen, could
still be fitted into the King's scenario. But before he got that news things
had begun to go badly wrong in the north. Bouillon and the Swiss
expected to stay some time in Lorraine, capturing Guisard towns and
thoroughly plundering the countryside. But Dohna and the reiters were
all for pushing on into France at once. Some such promise, Dohna insisted, had been made to the Queen of England through Sir Horatio
Pallavincino. Also, the Germans had some scruple about attacking Lorraine, which was, after all, a part of the Empire. And finally, the Duke of
Lorraine had gathered all his peasants into fortified towns with all the
food and goods they could carry, and taken measures for the systematic
destruction of supplies and forage. There would be more to eat in France
than in Lorraine, and fewer hard knocks. So Dohna's reiters and the rest
of the clumsy, almost leaderless army blundered on into France, ignoring
the Lorrainers. Guise was neither forced to give battle nor bottled up on
the one ground where this would have been easy to do.

The Swiss and Germans swung southward in a wide arc to clear the
crossings of the Marne and Seine, but refused after an argument to take
the upland road towards the sources of the Loire. They held instead to the
plain where, said a French chronicler, they found more beef and chickens
and eggs, whiter bread and better wine than they had ever seen in their
lives. It was the kind of campaign mercenary soldiers liked — slow, easy
marches, a well-stocked, open countryside to live on, lots of plunder and
very little fighting. There were only two drawbacks. Whether it was the
hot, late summer, or the strange food, or the strong red wines, there was
a steadily lengthening sick-list and since invalids left behind were likely
to be knocked on the head by the justifiably irritated peasantry the long
unsoldierly trains of wagons, loaded with plunder, were further burdened
with men unfit to march. The other drawback was that having chosen a
way through the fat plains, instead of the rugged mountain roads Navarre
had advised, the Protestant army as it approached the Loire found its

march blocked by the main army of the King of France. Epernon threw back their reconnaissance parties in a series of brisk well-handled skirmishes, and the Swiss, dismayed by the news that the King of France in person was in the field against them, positively refused to advance. Arrayed against them, under the King's command, were the regiments traditionally recruited for the French Crown in Catholic Switzerland, displaying the standards of the cantons which the invaders had sworn never to attack. When they enlisted, they said, they were promised that they would not have to, that they would be fighting against the Duke of Guise and his Lorraine relatives, never against the King of France. In any case, they had not been paid for months. Neither had the Germans for that matter. Every week the straggling, quarrelsome, undisciplined mercenaries behaved less like an army and more like a vast mob of brigands. Now it looked as if they would break up amidst mutual recriminations and go home.

This was exactly as Henry III had foreseen; perhaps exactly as he had arranged. What he had not foreseen was that Dohna's army of thirty-odd thousand men would not by this time have disposed of Guise's five or six thousand. Guise had circled warily around the Germans in their passage through Lorraine, slashing in to win a skirmish or two, enough to furnish prisoners and a standard for display in Paris, then dodging quickly out. When the Germans blundered on into France Guise accompanied them, keeping a careful five leagues or so from their right flank, just close enough to keep touch by patrols of light horse and to hamper the Germans foraging towards the west, just far enough away to be safe from any sudden rush. Dohna made no such rush. The threat of a force no bigger than Guise's was not serious enough to deflect his advance, and for the moment Paris was not a strategic objective. Dohna did not dare, as Henry III knew he would not dare, to involve himself in an assault on Paris while the King of France was in the field with a powerful army, and the route of attack bristled with well-garrisoned fortresses. But how were the Parisians to know this? Instead, they heard daily from a hundred pulpits the bulletins of the Duke of Guise. He had taken up such-and-such a position between the invaders and Paris. He would continue to guard her approaches; he would die sword in hand before the Germans should penetrate even her suburbs. The Parisian preachers added that the King of France, who ought to be guarding his capital, was skulking somewhere behind the Loire, no doubt conniving with heretics. If it were not for the brave Duke of Guise they would all be murdered by Protestant brigands.

The news of Coutras reached the Germans just in time to prevent the army's breaking up. Dohna was able to persuade his wrangling contingents to follow him away from the Loire and the royal army through the easy open country towards Chartres. The direction was certainly not well chosen for a rendezvous with Navarre, assuming any such rendezvous was still expected, nor had it any other discernible strategic value. But logistic value it had. The Beauce was a rich region. It had not been plundered or burned over for some years. So it would be attractive for a while as quarters, until money came from England, or Navarre or some other prince came from Guyenne, or a better offer came from the King of France.

By October 26th the leisurely, slovenly advance of the Germans had reached the neighbourhood of Montargis, and since that place was held for the King by a strong garrison and nobody had any intention of doing anything so strenuous as besieging a fortified town, the army sat down in a group of villages from three to six miles apart, and all a cautious five miles or so distant from Montargis. Dohna himself made his headquarters at a little hamlet called Vimory, on the extreme right flank. Guise heard of him there at once, and determined to attack him before dawn.

What followed is not altogether clear. Guise's little army marched through rain and darkness on Vimory and, somewhat to their astonishment, encountered not so much as a picket until they reached the first houses of the village. Thereupon the Leaguer infantry burst into the village street and began setting fire to houses, shooting or spearing the sleepy Germans as they emerged, and plundering the wagons with which the street was clogged. Evidently surprise was complete.

How the situation was reversed is not so evident. Dohna got himself into the saddle and somehow managed to rally several troops of reiters. He led them out through an alley at the other end of the town towards open fields, probably because a village street, cumbered with wagons and with half the houses blazing, is not the best place for cavalry. In the dark his troopers ran head on into half the Guisard horse, led by Guise's brother the Duke of Mayenne. The reiters seem, on the whole, to have had the best of the ensuing fracas, though what we know of it is what one would expect to know of an encounter in the dark between two equally surprised and disconcerted columns, a fight broken off less by any decision than by a violent thunderstorm. Whether at this point some fresh German reinforcements came up, which is what the French accounts say — but where would they have come from? — or whether the Duke of

Guise, assuming that all Dohna's reiters were entangled in the village, mistook for the arrival of more Germans all that uproar in the fields where his brother's column was engaged with Dohna, is anyone's guess. Probably Guise's bold determination to attack with six thousand men an army of perhaps thirty thousand had led to some sober second thoughts. At any rate he gave the order to retreat and by dawn his army was clamouring for admission at the gates of Montargis.

Both sides claimed victory — Dohna because he had beaten off a surprise attack by a greatly superior force, Guise because he had beaten up the headquarters of the invading army and got away with prisoners, horses and loot. It seems to be true that the Germans in Vimory were outnumbered by the French, and there is no real evidence that any other Germans were engaged. Shaking itself like a big dog snapped at by a small one Dohna's army lumbered off into the Beauce, ignoring the Duke of Guise. Guise, on the other hand, fell back from Montargis all the way to Montereau-Faut-Yonne, as if he felt sure Dohna was after him, and so lost touch with the Germans. But there was nobody except his own tough cynical mercenaries to be impressed by Dohna's claim, and they would scarcely have felt that the ignominy the general had incurred by being surprised in his own headquarters and losing his personal baggage had been wiped out simply by his chasing away the intruders. Guise, however, had carried off enough of the fruits of victory from Vimory to intoxicate the Parisians. He had some of the Germans' wagons and more of the Germans' horses. He led away prisoner some of the famous and terrible reiters to be exhibited in their black armour with their hands tied behind them to the delighted Paris mob. He had Dohna's own field tent, and Dohna's personal standard. And best of all he had two camels which Dohna had brought with him all the way across France as a present from Johan Casimir of the Palatinate to the King of Navarre. It was enough to make a small Roman triumph; more than enough to persuade the Parisians to accept the fantastic tales of slaughter inflicted on the Germans with which their preachers regaled them.

In the Beauce, where again the invaders spread themselves out carelessly in scattered cantonments, the disintegration of the army continued. There were more sick than ever. The vintage that autumn had been exceptionally abundant and exceptionally strong. Those well enough to bend an elbow were rarely sober. The Swiss resumed their negotiations with the King of France, haggling for the last sous of their nuisance value, but fully decided to go home. Dohna, who had got no more money from

Elizabeth of England and only ambiguous words from the King of Navarre, was ready to go home too. He told the Huguenots that he would lead his Germans eastwards to the sources of the Loire, the rendezvous at which he and Navarre had both failed two weeks before. He told his own officers that unless the King of Navarre was at the rendezvous with money and men they would continue eastward into Burgundy and so home, via Franche Comté. Nobody expected Navarre to be there. The campaign was practically over.

At this point Guise struck again. Like the rest of the participants he realized that the campaign was practically over. Nothing could be less to his advantage than to have it close as it was closing in a muted diminuendo of negotiations, with The Most Christian King quelling the tempest by the sheer majesty of his presence and the invaders retiring deferentially before him, thanking him for sparing their lives and for the royal pourboires which would ease their way home. Dohna, Guise learned, was quartered with a part of his troops in the little walled town of Auneau some ten miles east of Chartres. A French garrison still held the château for the King, and its Gascon captain had replied to Dohna's summons to surrender with rude remarks and musketry. Since the Germans were mainly interested, at this point, in having a dry place to sleep they had been content to barricade the streets leading to the château and to settle down out of musket range. The Gascon captain, chafed at being ignored, sent word to Guise that it would be easy to introduce a French force into the town through the château, and again the Leaguers marched by night.

Again surprise was complete, and this time there was no question who won the victory. Baron von Dohna cut his way out at the head of a handful of reiters; the rest of his force, trapped within the walls, perished in what was more like a massacre than a battle. Again there were wagonloads of captured loot to display to the people of Paris, and this time the butchery of the Germans bore in fact some proportion to the figures ecstatically proclaimed from Parisian pulpits.

Dohna tried to take the rest of his Germans back to Auneau where there was a good chance of finding the Guisards as unprepared as they had found him, but the Germans had no fight left in them. The Swiss had already taken the King's terms and marched quietly away. Five days later as Epernon caught up with them and Guise hovered hungrily on their flank the Germans followed suit. The King's terms were not harsh. In return for the surrender of their standards and their promise never to serve in arms against the King of France again he gave them safe conduct, and Epernon saw them to the borders of Franche Comté, less for fear of anything they might do than to protect them from Guise.

One may doubt whether Guise's famous victory at Auneau made the slightest difference to the result of the 'campaign of the reiters', or even shortened it by more than a day or two. The arrangements with the Swiss had already been completed, and without the Swiss Dohna's Germans and the Huguenot contingent under the Prince de Conti had little hope of defeating the royal army and almost less of escaping it. In the circumstances mercenary armies were accustomed to accept such terms as Henry III was prepared to offer, especially when their own pay was months overdue. Guise's attack on Dohna was less an aid to the success of Henry III's beautiful plan than an impertinent interference with it. Nor had Guise's subsequent actions, his pursuit and slaughter of some remnants of the Germans after they had reached what they thought was the safety of neutral Franche Comté, and his foray into Mompelgard where the Leaguers proved on a defenceless countryside that they could be as savage and rapacious as Germans, any military value for France.

But a victory may have other uses than military decision. In vain Henry III sent the Parisians a veracious account of his conduct of the campaign in which the great foreign army had been turned back at a minimum cost in money and blood. In vain he ordered Te Deums for his triumph. The Parisians gave all the credit to the Duke of Guise. Guise's picture was in every shop window; the pulpits rang with his praises. He alone had saved France from the heretics. 'Saul has slain his thousands but David his ten thousands', the Parisians sang triumphantly. And already they had found another appellation for their king more offensive than Saul. Some popular preacher had found in the letters of Henri de Valois' name what he thought a significant anagram, and from veiled witticisms and obscene scribblings the allusions to 'Vilain Herodes' in pamphlets aud pulpit oratory became more and more open, more and more charged with hatred and contempt. Then, just as the King was preparing to re-enter the Louvre to keep his Christmas there, the doctors and masters of the Sorbonne, feeling sure that in Henry III they had a king who might be threatened and insulted with impunity, met in a session which was secret only, as the French say, 'in principle' to declare that it was as lawful to depose a prince who failed in his duty as it was to remove a trustee suspected of malfeasance. The air of Paris was charged with revolution.

About that time Bernardino de Mendoza summed up for his master the results of the campaign. 'On the whole,' he wrote, 'in spite of the victory of the King of Navarre ... and the present eminence of the Duke of Epernon ... events here could hardly have gone more happily for Your Majesty's affairs. The people of Paris can be relied on at any time. They are more deeply than ever in obedience of the duke of Guise.' The Duke of Guise, Mendoza did not need to say, would prove obedient when the time came to his patron and paymaster the King of Spain.

The ... *thrust out of England.*

Mendoza, Spanish ambassador to England, expelled for his scheming against the Queen. He holds a catalogue of papist English noblemen and a list of English 'havens' in which the Spanish could land. From Carlteton, 'A Thankfull Remembrance', London 1630, p. 78.

XV

THE OMINOUS YEAR

WESTERN EUROPE, MIDWINTER, 1587–8

As the year 1587 drew to a close a shudder of apprehension ran across western Europe. In part it was perfectly rational apprehension. As the closing in of winter made it less and less likely that the fleet gathering at Lisbon would sail before the year's end it became increasingly certain that come spring it would sail — against England. In fact, although Philip still wrote to his ambassadors that the Armada's destination must remain a secret closely kept; although at Paris Mendoza maintained an enigmatic silence, meanwhile trying every security and counter-espionage device he could think of; although Parma attempted misdirection by putting it about that the obvious aim at England was only a blind for a sudden descent on Walcheren, the shape of Philip's plan was becoming unmistakable. Lisbon was always full of foreigners and the least experienced observer could tell that this vast mobilization of ships and seamen, soldiers and cannon was not meant just to protect the commerce of the Indies or stir up trouble in Ireland. Flanders was still a crossroads of trade, and among her own people there were many whose sympathies were with the rebels. Parma had to carry out his plans under their attentive eyes, and it was hard to persuade the Flemings that an amphibious invasion of Walcheren required five leagues of new canals linking Sluys and Nieuport. When the new canals were finished a barge could pass from the Scheldt above Antwerp to Dunkirk Haven without once venturing out into open water and, by Parma's estimate, a flotilla from Dunkirk with favourable weather could be off the North Foreland and nearing Margate between dusk and dawn of an April night.

By the end of November the master pattern, a cross-Channel operation by Parma's army convoyed and supported by a fleet from Spain, was clear to Buys and Oldenbarneveldt, Burghley and Walsingham, and Dutch and English naval dispositions were being made accordingly. For that matter the pattern was hardly less clear to bankers of Augsburg and merchants of Venice and argumentative idlers in Parisian wine-shops. All

Christendom came to attention to watch the contest between England, the traditional overlord of the narrow seas, and the new Spanish colossus, aspirant to the empire of the oceans.

To the majority of intelligent observers the issue seemed highly doubtful. There was no doubt that the English fleet was still, as it had usually been in the past, the most formidable fighting force in Atlantic waters. And experience had shown how difficult it was, as the sixteenth century practised war, to conquer a resolutely defended land. On the other hand there was the record of Parma's army. It had beaten, time and again, armies of veteran professional soldiers. Its commander was, by common consent, the greatest captain of the age. In contrast the English militia were green troops and their probable commander, the Earl of Leicester, without conspicuous military talent. No city in England had really modern fortifications and many people said that the English were too disunited for resolute resistance. Once ashore, the English exiles in Spain insisted, Parma would find England an easier conquest than Holland and Zeeland. Towards getting him ashore, everybody knew, Philip was making an unparalleled effort. He had all the maritime resources of the Mediterranean to draw on. He had added to his own marine the Portuguese navy, the second in strength of Atlantic fleets. Some of his captains were able deep-water seamen. Most important of all was the fact that Spain under Philip had moved from victory to victory. 'Fate', men called it in the sixteenth century, or 'Divine Providence', the irresistible will of God. Centuries later they were to talk about 'the wave of the future' or the triumph of objective historical forces, but all they meant really, at either time, was that one success or one failure seems to foreshadow another, because it is always easier to imagine things going on in the same way than to imagine a change. On those grounds chiefly even the cautious Venetians, who could not have hated the idea of another Spanish victory more if they had been Turks or heretics, were willing to lay modest odds on the success of King Philip's invasion.

However men might estimate the chances of a Spanish victory no one had much doubt about the fate of Europe if Spain won again. Once Philip had England in hand the days of the Dutch would be numbered. Mastery of England entailed almost as a matter of course mastery of the adjacent seas, and without command of their coastal waters the Dutch could not resist long — would be fools, most men thought, to resist at all. As for the divided French, an English defeat would doom the already desperate Huguenot cause, and the last of the Valois, deprived of his balance on the seesaw of the civil wars, would only have the bitter choice of surviving as the puppet of Spain or of being contemptuously swept aside. Henry of Guise would be king of whatever was left of France after Philip had recovered all that either branch of his family had lost, plus the provinces and strongpoints which prudence made desirable. The shadow of Spain, of the banners of the unending crusade, of the unitary State which was the armed aspect of the Church, lay long across Europe. Some optimists in Pau and Amsterdam, Heidelberg and Geneva, Venice and even Rome felt that if Philip's Armada should fail Europe might escape from the shadow. And there were tough fighting men, fidgeting through the winter months in Plymouth or Flushing or beside London River, who wanted nothing more than the sight of Spanish sails. But even they did not foresee an easy victory.

Another cloud lay over the coming year, more mysterious and terrifying than that of war. It had been discerned over a century before, perhaps many centuries before, and as 1588 approached the awful rumour of impending disaster spread throughout western Europe. Basically the prophecy of doom depended on the numerology of the Revelation of St John, clarified (if that is the right word) by hints in Daniel xii, and reinforced by a blood-curdling passage in Isaiah. To those who had sufficiently studied the question there seemed to be no doubt that all history since the first year of Our Lord was divided into a series of cycles, complicated permutations of multiples of ten and seven, each cycle terminated by some gigantic event, and the whole series closing with awful finality in 1588. Philip Melancthon observed that the penultimate cycle had ended in 1518 with Martin Luther's defiance of the Pope, and from that event there remained only a final cycle of ten times seven years, the length of the Babylonian captivity, until the seventh seal should be opened, anti-Christ be overthrown and the Last Judgment be at hand. In the midst of their afflictions zealous Protestants had for many years found a grim comfort in Melancthon's prediction, and jingles stating the gist of it in German, Dutch, French and English had long been current.

But the prophecy was much older than Melancthon. In the mid-fifteenth century Johan Muller of Königsberg, known as Regiomontanus, the great mathematician who provided Columbus and a whole generation of navigators with astronomical tables, had his curiosity aroused by it and was led to draw up a picture of the heavens for the fatal year. He found that it would be ushered in by an eclipse of the sun in February and marked by two total eclipses of the moon, one in March and one in August, while at the time of the first and for some time thereafter, Saturn, Jupiter and Mars would hang in ominous conjunction in the moon's own house. What all this seemed to mean Regiomontanus set down with due professional caution in resonant Latin verse:

Post mille exactos a partu virginis annos
Et post quingentos rursus ab orbe datos
Octavagesimus octavus mirabilis annus
Ingruet et secum tristitia satis trahet.
Si non hoc anno totus malus occidet orbis,
Si non in totum terra fretumque ruant,
Cuncta tamen mundi sursum ibunt atque decrescent
Imperia et luctus undique grandis erit.

A prosaic translation might be:

A thousand years after the virgin birth
and after five hundred more allowed the globe,
the wonderful eighty-eighth year begins and
brings with it woe enough. If, this year,
total catastrophe does not befall, if land
and sea do not collapse in total ruin, yet
will the whole world suffer upheavals, empires
will dwindle and from everywhere will
be great lamentation.

The best Regiomontanus could augur from the future heavens was none too cheerful, and subtle contentious Johan Stoffler, learned Leovitius and the eclectic polymath Guillaume Postel, when they came in turn to scrutinize his findings could only confirm his prognosis. When the most modern science and the profoundest esoteric learning chimed so exactly with scriptural numerology, what could anyone conclude except that 1588 was indeed a year of dire portent? It was even pointed out that the new star of 1572 (the first such appearance in the eternal and incorruptible heavens since a star had shown over Bethlehem) had blazed in men's sight for seventeen lunar months and then vanished twice seven years before the first lunar eclipse predicted for 1588, and one hundred and seventy lunar months plus one hundred and eleven days before the second. Little reflection was needed to grasp the significance of these apocalyptic numbers, and little science and less piety to appreciate that the strange star had come as a herald and a warning.

Spread from one end of Europe to the other, the prophecies about 1588 were differently received and differently interpreted according to the country. In Spain the King regarded all attempts to forecast the future as idle and impious, and the Holy Office looked with about equal disfavour on chiliastic speculations and astrological ingenuity. Officially the Court ignored the prophecy in all its forms, and if the printers did not, their almanacs, as happens so often with these flimsy leaflets, have not survived. Perhaps action by the King's officers helped make away with them.

For the authorities could not afford to ignore the prophecies altogether. Spain buzzed with them. In Lisbon desertions from the fleet increased alarmingly in December and one fortune-teller was arrested there for 'making false and discouraging predictions'. In the Basque ports recruiting lagged 'because of many strange and frightening portents that are rumoured', and at Madrid there were reports of monstrous births and excited visions in the provinces. No such superstitious rubbish could have affected Philip II, and there is no record that anyone tried to persuade him that 1588 was not a lucky year. But, perhaps in the interest of his subjects' morale, he took some action. After Christmas of 1587 there was an epidemic of sermons denouncing astrology, sorcery and all impious prognostications. It would be natural enough if some Spaniards found the verses of Regiomontanus disturbing. A ruinous confusion of land and sea is not exactly the setting one would wish for an amphibious operation, and if empires were to diminish what could be more clearly threatened than the world's greatest empire?

In Italy, especially at Venice and at Rome, the prophecies were as eagerly discussed as in Spain, but without the same unanimity as to the empire threatened. One anonymous correspondent of William Allen's (or perhaps of Father Parsons's?) had fresh light on the subject which seemed important enough for the little house on the Via di Monserrato to send the Vatican a fair copy for the attention of His Holiness. In the ruinous foundations of Glastonbury Abbey, wrote the informant, a mysterious upheaval of the earth had recently disclosed a marble slab which had been buried throughout the centuries beneath the crypt. Carved on the marble as if in letters of fire were the prophetical verses beginning 'Post mille exactos a partu virginis annos'. It was clear, therefore, that these terrible lines could not have been written by any modern German. However Regiomontanus had come by these verses, none other than Merlin himself could be their author, and his dark science, or God's inscrutable providence, had brought them to light in these latter days just in time to warn

Britons of the impending destruction of the empire of Uther Pendragon's seed. The prophecy was the more weighty since it was well known that Merlin had also prophesied the re-establishment of Arthur's line and other notable matters. No comment from the via di Monserrato indicates how seriously Cardinal Allen and his friends took this communication. No trace survives to show whether the story was really current in England. But opposite 'atque decresunt Imperia' a sceptical contemporary hand wrote in Italian: 'It doesn't say what empires or how many.'

'What empires were threatened and how many?' The same question troubled the Emperor Rudolph II. Often that winter, looking out from his tower in the Hradschin across the snowy roofs of Prague, the Emperor watched the three planets approaching their ominous conjunction. No prince in Europe believed more firmly in astrology than Rudolph II, and none was more aware how difficult it often was to interpret the stars correctly. He could read at least as much in them himself as many a professional, and he needed very little time to tell a charlatan from a serious practitioner, but for all his skill in the art he was never satisfied unless his own results tallied with those of the best living authorities. He generally kept one or two about the Court when he could find reliable ones, and he consulted by letter, sometimes by special courier, with others as far away as Catania in Sicily or the island of Hven in the Danish Straits. He was busier than ever with the stars as February 1588 approached, so busy that Philip II's ambassador, Guillén de San Clemente, could not get to talk to him for weeks, and the Venetian resident heard that important dispatches from Poland lay unopened on his table.

Consultation with the experts confirmed Rudolph's own forebodings. There was no sign in the heavens of any final destruction of the globe, or for that matter of the impending Last Judgment in which so many men of Rudolph's century implicitly believed. In common with most scientific astrologers Rudolph discounted such beliefs, just as he was sceptical of all scriptural numerology and suchlike superstitions. According to the stars there would certainly be unusually bad weather in 1588 and probably an abnormal number of locally destructive floods and earthquakes — but in the way of natural catastrophes, nothing more serious. On the other hand it seemed as certain as anything could be that there would be grave revolutions in human affairs, empires would wane and there would, indeed, be lamentations on every hand.

Which empires would wane was a question on which the other astrologers were as undecided as Rudolph himself. Whatever happened in

Poland, where Rudolph's brother, Maximilian, was contesting the crown with a candidate from Sweden and not doing very well, somebody's empire was bound to wane, but it hardly appeared likely that these fearsome signs presaged no more than another upset in the bumpy course of Polish politics. It was more likely that the crisis in the west was what was meant. Whether Philip triumphed and thereby overturned the Government in England, and probably in France as well, or whether Philip failed and found his own swollen empire waning, the warning of the stars would be justified. Rudolph, who was a Habsburg, of course, and officially, at least, a Catholic, but who found himself chafed by Spanish successes and Spanish pretensions whenever he allowed himself to think about them, could hardly tell which result in the west would please him less. The other possibility was even more distasteful. However many kings might call themselves emperors in these days, Rudolph himself was The Emperor. His dignity descended in uninterrupted succession, as Rudolph was fond of reminding people, from that emperor whose authority Christ by His death had acknowledged. It seemed alarmingly probable that such unusual portents threatened nothing less than the eternal empire of the Roman people. It would not disappear, of course. It was established in the nature of things, and could not disappear. But if it waned much more it would be almost invisible to the naked eye. Certainly Rudolph could only view the possibility of any further dwindling of his uncertain authority with the liveliest alarm. Rudolph decided that in the circumstances it would be safest to do nothing, to see as few people as possible, to stir as seldom as possible from the Hradschin, and to make no avoidable decisions until time should disclose which empires were in danger. It was a refuge from the terrible uncertainty of the stars to which Rudolph was to resort more and more often in the years to come.

Among the rabble-rousing preachers of Paris there was no uncertainty about the message of Scripture and the confirmatory message of the stars. They meant that the day of God's vengeance was finally at hand. The English Jezebel would be justly punished. The rebels in the Low Countries would be finally put down. And, as a matter of course, the French heretics would at last meet the fate they had so narrowly escaped in the year of St Bartholomew's. But all this was incidental to the overthrow of the wickedest of tyrants, Vilain Herodes. His private vices were only surpassed by his public derelictions. To crimes against nature he had added treason against the laws of God and therefore against the fundamental laws of France. He not only refused to exterminate the heretics as the law of God and of France required but he was actually conspiring with them to make their leader his successor to the throne. Now God was weary of his iniquities. He was to be cast down and humbled, and the painted mignons and treacherous politicians who ruled in his name would be put to the sword and the dogs would lick their blood. This overthrow and refounding of the realm of France was what Scriptures foretold and the stars predicted, and what the epidemic of monstrous births and horrendous visions in the provinces — to say nothing of unprecedented fogs, frosts and hailstorms and generally nasty weather — now clearly announced.

Shortly after his election some indiscreet friars had ventured to criticize the policies of Sixtus V and promptly found themselves in the galleys. In Elizabethan England disrespectful language about the sovereign would have cost the speakers their ears, if not their heads. In Spain use of Scripture to stir up sedition would have had the prompt attention of the Holy Office. Nor did Henry III of France fail to resent these attacks after his own fashion. As the old year drew to a close, sitting in state in the Louvre with the judges of his highest Court about him, he summoned the theologians of the Sorbonne and chief preachers of Paris before him and publicly accused them of calumnies and libels directed against his person and his throne. It was a bitter tongue-lashing, delivered with the high eloquence and royal dignity of which Henry III was a master, built upon irrefutable logic and adorned with mordant wit and genuine pathos. Among the stern legists who sat beneath the throne glowering at the frightened clerics huddled at their Bar, probably not one could have made a better speech for the prosecution. And probably not one would have been so weak and so foolish as to do what Henry did next. Having convicted the seditious preachers of deliberate lies told with treasonable intent he abruptly dismissed them with the warning that they must earn his pardon by their repentance, and that the next time his law-officers would punish them as they deserved. In the antechamber their courage came back. They swaggered out of the Louvre, sneering. If the King dared not punish them this time he never would. Within a fortnight the pulpits were more abusive than ever. Ironically enough, on one point the Huguenot preachers and pamphleteers agreed with their Leaguer enemies. About the fate of their common sovereign, Henry III of France, both parties shared the same hope.

Even more than the Leaguers and the Huguenots, one would have said the Dutch needed whatever encouragement could be found in the prophecies. It was a grim winter for them. After the fumbling loss of Sluys and what looked to the States General like a deliberate attempt on his part to disrupt their union and partition their territories, the Earl of Leicester had flounced back to England. When Dutch envoys followed him to complain to the Queen, Elizabeth had scorched them with a blast of reproaches and ended by promising contemptuously to include them in any peace she might make with Spain. The Dutch reply was that if the Queen made her peace with Spain at the price of their liberties they would fight on alone. As the year closed it almost looked as if they might have to, and with less unity and fewer resources than at any time since the siege of Leyden. Nevertheless the admiralties of Holland and Zeeland gave Justin of Nassau the means to patrol the western Scheldt and the coast of Flanders with a fleet strong enough to cope with any force Parma could muster by sea, thus securing England as well as Walcheren against surprise. Meanwhile, if any of the embattled burghers thought that the prophecies should be used to encourage their friends and frighten their enemies, no one recorded or heeded their opinion.

Instead, the enterprising printers of Amsterdam, remembering that their almanacs would sell in conquered Flanders and Brabant as well as in the free provinces, and in both areas to Catholics as well as to Protestants, took a splendidly impartial view of the impending catastrophe. They found it unnecessary to dwell on the horrors of war and the breaking down of authority. Their readers would have seen enough of that sort of thing. Anyway, the prophecies promised rarer terrors, enough to make men's hair stand on end and pry the pennies out of their pockets. So, citing strings of authorities from Regiomontanus to Rudolph Graff, honorary imperial astronomer at Deventer, and one Wilhelm de Vries of Maestricht, a Godfearing man given to remarkable visions, the Amsterdam printers expatiated on the natural catastrophes in store for everybody. There would be violent tempests, they promised, and terrible floods, hail and snow in midsummer, darkness at midday, bloody rain, monstrous births and strange convulsions of the earth, though after August things would quieten down and the later autumn would even be moderately lucky. Judging by the unusual number of their almanacs for 1588, still in existence, the Amsterdam printers hit the popular taste exactly.

Perhaps, if they had had the chance, the English printers could have done as well, but the chance seems to have been denied them. Very few English almanacs survive for 1588, and those that do are curiously non-committal.

Walter Gray's may be taken as typical. In the general prediction for winter he says: 'Here and in the quarters following might be noted, according to artificial skill, many strange events to happen which purposely are omitted in good consideration. God Almighty who only knoweth what shall come to pass, turn all evils away from us. Amen.' And later, of the two total eclipses of the moon: 'What the influence of these may be (within this year to happen) ... I purposely omit to lay down more than this, that there is likelihood of an earthquake with fear of the plague and pestilence.' Almanacs were not generally so sparing of the feelings of their readers, and to induce their vendors to suppress titillating horrors beside which earthquakes, plague and pestilence were trivial must have required strong pressure, the kind of pressure only the Privy Council could exert.

Did it come in the first instance from the Queen herself? How much Elizabeth believed in astrology we know as little as we do about most of her beliefs. Certainly she had had her horoscope cast by Dr Dee, and in the days before he had begun to listen to stranger voices than those of the stars she had consulted him on matters astrological as well as geographical. So, for that matter, had some of her most distinguished councillors. Surely Dr Dee had told her what her subjects all knew by instinct anyhow, that her fortunes were governed more than those of most princes by the moon, and she needed no astrologer to tell her that the second and more terrible of the moon's eclipses came at the beginning of her ruling sign, the Virgin, and just twelve days before her birthday. The awful conjunction must have been obvious to every dabbler in astrology in her kingdom, and most of the makers of almanacs would have needed no warning passed on by the Stationers' Company from the Privy Council that to prophesy, even by indirection, the sovereign's death was high treason.

How seriously Elizabeth herself would have taken these matters we cannot know, but we do know that she disapproved on principle of popular chatter about high affairs of State, and it would have been like her to want to keep discussion of these unfortunate prophecies to a minimum. Her people were nervous enough in any case that winter. In December a false rumour that the Spanish fleet was in the Channel sent some of the more timid inhabitants of the coastal towns flying inland, dismaying the Lord Lieutenants and their deputies and infuriating the Queen. Rome heard that the English, a superstitious race, were much preoccupied with signs and portents, and one of Mendoza's English correspondents wrote to him that in the eastern counties men were saying that the old prophecy about soldiers coming to conquer England with snow on their helmets would soon be fulfilled. In the circumstances the less talk there was about Regiomontanus's verses the better.

Of course, the prophecy could not be kept secret. It had been discussed at length in a popular pamphlet in 1576. The editor of the second edition of Holinshed's *Chronicles* (1587), who had probably gone to press before the Privy Council had alerted the Stationers' Company, had included a solemn reference to the ancient prophecy 'now so rife in every man's mouth' that in the year of wonders, supposed to be 1588, either a final dissolution or a horrible alteration of the world was to be expected. Copies of the prophecy and allusions to it turn up in the private correspondence of the period, and one would be tempted to guess that a rough English jingle embodying the gist of Regiomontanus was current in every alehouse. So the Privy Council having clapped the cat in the bag was constrained to let it out again. The makers of almanacs were forbidden to allude to the prophecy, but two pamphlets were permitted, probably encouraged, to argue against it. One, by Thomas Tymme, 'A preparation against the prognosticated dangers of 1588' was mostly pious exhortation, but the other was full-dress academic argument. Its title-page, somewhat abbreviated, runs: 'A discursive problem concerning prophecies, how far they are to be valued or credited ... devised especially in abatement of the terrible threatenings and menaces peremptorily denounced against the kingdoms and states of the world this present famous year 1588, supposed the Great-wonderful and Fatel Yeare of our Age. By I. H. Physition.' Its author was Dr John Harvey, the younger brother of Edmund Spenser's tutor Gabriel and a man of equally wide and curious learning, himself the author of several almanacs and, though no caster of horoscopes for pay, one of the leading students of astrology in the kingdom.

Harvey began by citing the Latin verses and translating them elegantly in the classical quantities his brother advocated for English verse. He went on to cast doubt on their authorship and scorn on their supporters, to pick holes in their astrological facts and conclusions and to point out other conjunctions in the past, just as ominous — or almost as ominous — which had occasioned no such alarms and had, in fact, entailed no notable catastrophes. No doubt it was as triumphant a refutation as learning and ingenuity could manage, but what strikes one now is the gingerly fashion in which certain aspects of the argument are skirted, almost as if Dr Harvey wanted to leave himself a loophole in case these calamities did actually befall. That a scholar like Harvey would have undertaken this polemic even if he felt more relish for it, without official invitation, seems unlikely. Was the invitation actually, if indirectly, from the Queen herself? Again, it would have been not unlike her to try at once to suppress an unpleasant argument and arrange to have it refuted.

Dr John Dee, astrologer.

XVI

THE COMPANY OF THESE NOBLE SHIPS

GREENWICH AND ENGLISH WATERS,
JANUARY TO MARCH 1588

To suppress an unpleasant argument and arrange to have it refuted, to hold out one hand in friendship and keep a sword in the other, to follow at the same time two apparently irreconcilable lines of policy and play two contradictory roles with such histrionic gusto that even old friends never quite knew earnest from acting, this was how, by choice or by what she thought necessity, Elizabeth I regularly played the game of high politics. Even in the thirtieth year of her reign, when the Queen's ambiguities cannot have been altogether unexpected, they continued to confuse not only her enemies but her servants and advisers. People were puzzled at the time, and many have been puzzled ever since by her behaviour in that anxious winter while England expected the shock of the great Armada.

The feverish preparations at Lisbon, the reinforcement of Parma's army, said plainly that the King of Spain meant war. But Elizabeth kept Drake straining at the leash at Plymouth, and refused to sanction Hawkins's plans for a blockade of the Spanish coast. Instead, protesting that she was not and hoped never would be at war with the King of Spain and wanted nothing more than to bring his subjects in the Netherlands back to their true obedience, the Queen kept her tall ships tied up at their docks throughout the autumn, unrigged and unprovisioned, their guns in the Tower, their crews no more than a few watchmen. If Santa Cruz had come to the Channel in October, Parma might have crossed practically unopposed and marched straight on London. Or so the duke said afterwards. English seamen and English statesmen, aware of the risk, bewailed to each other the royal guilelessness which left the country so exposed.

Then, in December, on the strength apparently of one ill-informed report, but perhaps from a knowledge of Philip's actual orders to his admiral, Walsingham warned his mistress that Santa Cruz might be coming out of Lisbon before Christmas. In less than a fortnight the fleet was mobilized and ready for action, all the Queen's ships and most of the auxiliary merchantmen armed, manned and in some sort provisioned for a campaign. Had Santa Cruz obeyed his king's orders he would have found a warm reception. England had not been left quite so naked to her enemies after all.

By the time the reception committee was ready, however, it was known at Greenwich that the visit would be postponed, and to the disgust of her captains who saw no use in having a fighting-force and not using it, Elizabeth straightway cut back the strength. Four galleons, the largest the *Antelope* of four hundred tons, and four pinnaces were sent to help the Dutch to patrol the coast of Flanders, but the rest were ordered to lie in the Medway or in Plymouth Harbour with only half their wartime complements aboard. We have a scribbled list of these dispositions in Burghley's hand and an accompanying paper showing that the economy in wages and victuals would save the Queen every month two thousand four hundred and thirty-three pounds, eighteen shillings and fourpence. As Elizabeth reckoned her budget that was a sum very well worth saving, but her captains and councillors, who shuddered at such nonchalance, for once did not even among themselves attribute the cut in strength to the Queen's thrift. She was duped, they felt sure, by the double-tongued Duke of Parma, and deluded into lowering her guard by a false hope of peace.

That Elizabeth did hope for peace, even so late as the spring of 1588, we can be fairly sure. In spite of the mounting war-fever among the Puritans a good many of her subjects shared her hope, mostly because of the state of the cloth trade. A Lancastrian Parliament once declared that 'the making of cloth in all parts of the realm is the greatest occupation and living of the poor commons of this land', and in the century and more that had passed since its importance had increased. Normally woollens amounted to four-fifths of English exports, and when exports diminished the clothiers promptly threw spinners and weavers out of work and the fleece from the squire's flock was scarcely worth selling. A bad market for woollens pinched more purses than any other kind of catastrophe, and of late the market for woollens had been very bad indeed. First Antwerp had been closed, then Seville. Thanks to Parma's captains and to Martin Schenck the Rhine, up which English cloth had travelled to the south German towns, was unsafe for shipping, and Spanish diplomacy and Hansa jealousy had cut the vent of English stuffs at Hamburg to a trickle. Even the plunder of a Spanish plate-fleet could scarcely repay the losses of another year as bad as 1587. From merchant clothiers in London to goodwives in the Cotswolds many would have been glad to see the quarrel in the Low Countries patched up on almost any terms, so the cloth trade might come back to what it once had been, though one should not forget that others in the cloth trade, ascribing all their ills to the Spaniards, clamoured the louder for war.

Elizabeth was more sensitive than most princes of her age to the economic woes of subjects, and more aware than most of the connection between general prosperity and royal revenues. She had, also, more immediate reasons for worrying about money. Though the Dutch complained of her parsimony and her own captains complained more loudly still, she had poured tens of thousands of pounds into the Low Country wars, and the money had vanished with scarcely more effect than if it had been shovelled on to quicksand. Ireland was quiet for the moment, but Ireland was never quiet long and open war with Spain was sure to raise new troubles there. Parliament had talked very big against the Spaniards when last it met, but the Queen knew her commons well enough to know that loud as they were against popery and Spain, a war in the Low Countries, another war in Ireland and another on the ocean and along the Spanish coast would come to more than they would want to pay for.

Even if she had felt she could afford it Elizabeth would still have shunned war. Not, Sir John Perrot to the contrary, because she was afraid. She liked to boast at times that she had as much courage as her father. She had more. She took deliberate risks of her person and in her policies at which Henry VIII would have blenched. But she preferred calculated risks, and war was dismayingly unpredictable. To embark on war was to launch oneself on an irresistible current, sweeping into darkness. If only she could win back to peace she could be again as she had always been, the mistress of her own and her country's fate.

To Elizabeth's common sense the way back to peace seemed simple. Philip had but to accept the terms which his lieutenant, Don Juan of Austria, had accepted eleven years before: the ancient liberties of the seventeen provinces to be respected, and Spanish troops to be withdrawn from the Netherlands. In return the States General would return to their allegiance to their hereditary lord and promise to uphold the Catholic faith. In fact, Philip would have to make two considerable concessions. He would have to abandon any notion of a centralized Government of the Netherlands with powers of arbitrary taxation. This he had already said he was willing to do. And he would be obliged, if not explicitly to tolerate heretical sects, at least tacitly to acquiesce in their toleration in some provinces, since their ancient liberties once restored and Spanish troops withdrawn there would be no means of enforcing a policy of persecution if the local authorities refused to persecute. But appearances could be saved. Officially there would be only one faith in the Netherlands, the Roman Catholic faith, as officially there was only one faith in England. That, Elizabeth thought, was how it should be: cujus regio, ejus religio. And though a clause in the treaty about liberty of conscience might conciliate the stubborn Dutch, who so far showed no disposition to take any part in the negotiations, it was scarcely necessary. A little reflection ought to convince them that under the terms proposed there would be just as much liberty of conscience, and for that matter of worship, as the local authorities chose to permit.

As for Philip's preference for ruling over a desert rather than over a land full of heretics, when he said that he had not tried the alternative. Flanders and Brabant were not much better than deserts these days, and Holland and Zeeland if he conquered them by the sword would be in worse case still. Elizabeth found it difficult to believe that Philip would insist on so barren a victory. In the past the King of Spain had shown himself a sensible man, ready to compromise, reluctant to press matters too far. Now by a little flexibility he could be rid of the endless, ruinous Dutch war and have the old Anglo-Burgundian alliance back again, insuring him at little cost against French invasion of the Netherlands. And his realms and hers, instead of being at each other's throats, would again be each other's best customers. If the Dutch stood out England would stand aside, but Elizabeth and Burghley were not alone in believing that when the position was clear Holland and Zeeland would not refuse so favourable an offer if they saw that otherwise they would have to fight on alone.

The English commissioners for peace, already instructed and on their way to Ostend, had some other claims to advance and questions to reserve. They were to ask for admission for English ships to the ports of the New World, and freedom for English sailors there and in Spain from molestation by the Inquisition. They were to be coy about including the dominions of the Crown of Portugal in the proposed mutual guarantees. But mostly these were just talking-points. There was only one small one on which Elizabeth was inflexible. In the revolted provinces the English held certain towns as security for moneys advanced to the rebels. Before the English evacuated these towns somebody was going to have to pay that money back — if not the estates of Holland and Zeeland, then the King of Spain.

How far the Queen was deceived by Parma into thinking that there was still a chance for peace in 1588 is more than we can know. Parma had been trying for a long time to make her think he wanted peace. Up to the spring of 1587, at least, he really did want it. Without Dutch shipping and Dutch deep-water ports he saw little chance of a successful invasion of England, and he preferred to deal with one enemy at a time. In the autumn of 1587, however, Parma had been instructed by Philip that the invasion of England was to go forward without fail, and no peace was to be made on any terms. But Elizabeth was to be lured into negotiations, and these were to be spun out interminably to confuse the English and keep them off-balance.

Parma acted accordingly. When the five English commissioners finally crossed from Dover to Ostend it was possible to prolong for weeks the preliminary conversations about where the conference should be held, and when Bourbourg was tentatively decided on to spend more weeks on what the conference would talk about when it did meet, and what powers its delegates held to treat and conclude about anything. With bland efficiency the veteran diplomats in Parma's service conducted their delaying action, fooling old Sir James Croft, puzzling the experienced Dr Dale and even arousing a momentary hope of success in the sceptical Earl of Derby. Lured forward by hints that the Spanish delegates were just on the point of yielding, the conference once it got started kept on talking, in spite of the mounting dismay of the Dutch and the English war party, until the guns of the fleets were heard in the Channel. In consequence Elizabeth was able to declare then and afterwards that she had never closed the door on peace, and had patiently and honestly pursued it to the last. And although statesmen like Walsingham and fighting-men like Hawkins cried out that England was like to be ruined by the Queen's blindness, and that the proper course was to attack and push the war to a quick conclusion, it is not clear that England was damaged or Spain helped by the long negotiations at Bourbourg.

In fact, England may not have been the chief loser. In September 1587, with the arrival of powerful reinforcements from Italy Parma's forces were at the peak of their strength. For once his magazines and his treasury were full; he had never commanded before, he was never to command again, so magnificent and formidable an army. Whether or not the English fleet could have profited by a bold offensive, Parma certainly could have. He had taken Antwerp with less power than he could now dispose of; Ostend should have proved an easy conquest. All Flanders could have been cleared of hostile posts, and even Walcheren might not have been beyond his grasp. But he was ordered to amuse the English with negotiations while he waited for the Armada and to avoid any movements that might alarm them. So his fine army rotted throughout the winter in their cold wet cantonments, provisions ran short, sickness set in and by the following July his effective strength was only seventeen thousand instead of the thirty thousand ready in September. The combat potential of a great and costly army had been wasted for almost a year and nothing at all accomplished. No wonder the Duke of Parma saw the whole enterprise of England with an increasingly jaundiced eye.

Nor did England drop its guard. Within the realm a system of beacons had already been set up, ready to flash along the coasts and inland to every county the warning of a Spanish fleet in sight. If the exhortations of the Privy Council were heeded, and apparently on this point, anyhow, they were, the system was extended and improved and kept in instant readiness. At the first sight of flame or smoke and the following clangour of bells, the members of the trained bands were to repair to their usual places of meeting, muster by companies and under their captains converge on the appointed rallying place whence they would be led by Lord Lieutenants or their deputies to meet the enemy.

Perhaps it was just as well that the trained bands did not have to try conclusions with Parma's veterans. But there seem to have been gentlemen of spirit among them and sturdy yeomen, not so ill-armed for the most part as is sometimes said, and not so untrained in handling their weapons, nor all of them unseasoned in war. Such as they were, they were what England had to meet an invasion by land, and during that winter of anxious waiting, as far as the orders of the Privy Council could reach or the exertions of the local authorities and of the captains home for the purpose from the Dutch wars could effect it, they grew better armed and better trained each month. Meanwhile, especially along the south coast and in the eastern counties, town ditches were cleaned and deepened, mossy breaches in town walls unregarded since Bosworth were hastily repaired, here and there stone curtain-walls were banked with earth against artillery, and the seaport towns competed with one another for every piece of ordnance they could add to their seaward batteries. By land, at least, England was better prepared for the chance of invasion by April 1588 than she had been the previous autumn.

Englishmen who knew most about it, however, never believed that it would come to a fight by land. Slowly, over the years, the English had become conscious that they were guarded by the sea and the sea was theirs to guard. The progress of the Hundred Years War and its end had heightened that consciousness. Henry VIII in spending more money on ships of war than any other king in Europe was building on a tradition already established. The loss of Calais and the growing enmity with Spain sharpened still further the sense of depending on the sea, and by 1588 Elizabeth I was the mistress of the most powerful navy Europe had ever seen. Its backbone was eighteen powerful galleons, the smallest of three hundred tons, built and armed in a new fashion and capable of out-sailing and outfighting any possible enemies afloat. There were also seven smaller galleons of one hundred tons or more, and an adequate number of seagoing pinnaces, light, fast, handy craft, useful for scouting, carrying dispatches and inshore work.

The fighting-ships, the 'galleons', were built for war not commerce, and so with a keel longer in proportion to their beam than was usual in merchant vessels. This type, wherever it was first developed (Portugal perhaps), by 1570 was the normal warship of Atlantic waters. But the Queen's galleons were different. For ten years her zealous servant John Hawkins had been in charge of building and repairing her fleet, and Hawkins was a man with advanced ideas about war at sea. He wanted his galleons even longer for their width, and so capable of mounting more guns and of sailing nearer the wind. He wanted the deep waist decked over. The sailors stationed there might feel naked and exposed when, instead of being sheltered behind a wooden wall which rose above their heads, they found the bulwark stopping at their middles, but the extra deck space made room for still more broadside guns. And because he believed in fighting with the big guns instead of boarding Hawkins wanted the towering castles, bow and stern, reduced so drastically in size that old-fashioned captains who valued the high-built castles 'for their majesty and terror' complained that he was abolishing them altogether. If he bothered to reply Hawkins might have answered that the upper decks of the castles could mount only light, secondary batteries, bases and slings and other such man-killing pieces, while the lofty superstructures impaired a ship's sailing qualities and caused excessive rolling. Whether he replied or not, Hawkins had his way. In the years of his administration all the Queen's new ships were built on the sleek clean lines he favoured, and almost all the older ships were rebuilt to match them. The result was a fighting-fleet

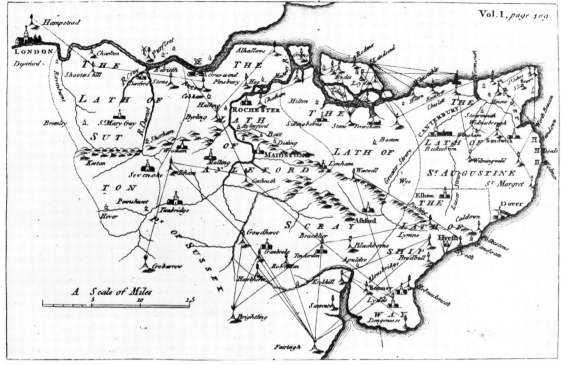

A map of the beacons in Kent, as they were appointed by the Lord Lieutenant of the county in 1588 when the Spanish invasion was expected.

A plan of Great Yarmouth, late sixteenth century.

Draught of a ship compared with a fish. Artist: Matthew Baker from *Fragments of Ancient Shipwrightry*.

Ship designer with assistant, 1586. Artist: as above.

faster and more weatherly than any that had ever been seen on the ocean before.

At the same time Hawkins's rival, enemy and collaborator Sir William Wynter was working to arm the ships in a fashion as revolutionary as Hawkins's design. The man-killing guns were reduced in number, the ship-killing guns were increased. Iron guns gave way to brass, and culverins and demi-culverins, long guns throwing an eighteen- or nine-pound shot with relatively high muzzle velocity and fair accuracy at ranges upwards of a thousand yards, more and more replaced the stubby barrelled smashers like the demi-cannon, a thirty-pounder with a short uncertain range. We cannot be quite sure how many of the Queen's ships were armed according to Wynter's proportions or better by 1587, but it is safe to say that through his efforts and Hawkins's the Queen possessed a fleet capable of outsailing and outmanœuvring any enemy in any weather and at its chosen range (the point-blank range of a demi-culverin, a long nine-pounder), of outgunning him decisively.

What Drake and Hawkins and others complained of, and what historians have complained of since, is that Elizabeth did not fling her splendid fleet boldly at the Spanish coast, to cut off trade with the Indies and hold Philip's warships helpless in port. Instead she kept most of her ships at anchor with only skeleton crews and in a secondary state of readiness, and in doing so she violated what became in the later days, when navies had time to develop such things, one of the basic strategic doctrines of the British navy. Perhaps she should have listened to Drake and Hawkins, though one remembers that they predicted a speedy victory if the fleet took the offensive, and that when later on it did so nothing of the sort occurred. Elizabeth might not have had a sound opinion about that, one way or the other. But she had ruled long enough over a sea-faring people to know that ships and crews were never the better for a long winter in the open Atlantic. Even if none were lost to tempest or to enemy action the ships would need fresh spars and caulking, cordage and canvas, and a thorough careening and rummaging before they could be useful again; while the crews, huddled together in insanitary squalor and fed perforce mostly on salt beef and stockfish, weevily biscuit and spoiling beer, would be weakened by bad diet and depleted by illness, even if typhus, the dreaded 'gaol fever' or 'ship fever', had not, as it too often did on long voyages, killed off half of them. Whether Elizabeth consciously counted over all these dangers, or just husbanded her precious ships as instinctively as she husbanded her money, one may doubt that she would have risked them in the winter on the coast of Spain even had there been no Bourbourg conference.

As she arranged it her crews kept themselves healthy on land on fresh food, a fair half of them at their own expense, thus sparing both the victuals packed and stored against the spring campaign and the Queen's purse. And the energies which her captains would have preferred to spend plundering Spanish merchantmen and daring the King of Spain under the guns of his forts they spent instead in bringing the Queen's ships to the last taut pitch of readiness. At Plymouth where Sir Francis Drake with the western squadron chafed to be gone and expected each courier from London to bring the wished-for orders, old William Hawkins, elder brother of great John, seventy that year and Lord Mayor of Plymouth, took charge of the state of the ships. In the January and February spring tides William had the great galleons careened on the foreshore, scraping and tallowing one side by day and the other by night, so that no ship was out of the water more than twenty-four hours. The night-work meant using the light of torches and cressets which in the great gales of wind was extremely chargeable, but old William rejoiced in the sight of his brother's ships sitting aground so strongly and so staunch 'as if each were made of a whole tree', and was in no mood to pinch pennies in so worthy a service.

John Hawkins himself was with the Lord Admiral and the eastern squadron where it lay in the Medway, strung out along Gillingham Reach past Chatham dockyard with the pinnaces within sight of Rochester bridge and the great ships as far down as Queenborough. In the same spring tides all these ships, too, were being careened and scraped and tallowed, but this was among the least of John Hawkins's cares. John was free at last of the contract by which he had built and rebuilt the Queen's navy and he had the promise of a command at sea, but he was still Treasurer and a member of the Navy Board and so busy with all the last-minute preparations, the accounts and other paper-work, that he had scarcely time to worry properly about the Queen's folly in negotiating with Parma and the malice of his enemies who were still charging that he had built the Queen's ships of rotten wood so that most of them were unfit for sea.

The Lord Admiral, Charles Lord Howard of Effingham, was as eager to be at sea as Francis Drake. He was a man well past fifty and had been Lord Admiral for less than three years, having been chosen less because of any demonstrated fitness for command at sea than because he came of an illustrious line — three of his house having served the Tudors as Lord

Lord Howard of Effingham, Earl of Nottingham, in his seventies. From a portrait by
D. Mytens in the Greenwich Hospital Collection.

Admirals — and because he was an ardent Protestant of unquestionable loyalty. But Charles Howard was not without some experience afloat and he was determined to learn his job and fill his post with credit. He clamoured so loudly for a strong force at sea, crediting every rumour that Parma was about to come out from Dunkirk or that a Spanish fleet was about to slip past Dover and bear away for Scotland, that finally he was allowed to put eight more ships in full commission and amuse himself by cruising between Dunkirk and Flushing. Meanwhile he was indefatigable, boarding every ship in the Medway and finding his way into every place aboard where any man might creep, looking and, to his joy, in vain for leaks or rotten timbers or any other sign that John Hawkins and his ship-wrights had scamped their work.

From the first Charles Howard was in love with the ships of his command. 'I protest it before God,' he wrote Walsingham, 'that were it not for Her Majesty's presence I had rather live in the company of these noble ships than in any place.' 'There is not one', he wrote after he had inspected them, 'but I durst go to the Río de la Plata in her.' And later he could scarcely contain his delight when the *Elizabeth Bonaventure*, having run aground at the entrance to Flushing, he and Sir William Wynter went aboard her and observed that though she stuck for two tides before she could be floated: 'in all this time there never came a spoonful of water into her well ... except a ship had been made of iron, it were to be thought impossible to do as she had done; and it may be well and truly said there never was nor is in the world a stronger ship than she is.' As for the galleon he had chosen as his flagship, he wrote Burghley: 'I pray you tell Her Majesty for me that her money was well given for the *Ark Ralegh* for I think her the odd ship in the world for all conditions ... We can see no sail, great or small but how far soever they be off we fetch them and speak with them.'

The *Ark* had won a special place in Howard's heart, but he was in love with all the royal ships and his subordinates were scarcely behind him in enthusiasm. His cousin Lord Henry Seymour, commanding the *Bona-venture*, boasted that she would prove as strong a ship in twelve hours' fight with the Spaniards as she had in twelve hours on the shoal; and even Sir William Wynter, who as long as he thought he could get the contract for the Queen's ships out of Hawkins's hands had bombarded the Council with charges that John Hawkins was cheating Her Majesty and betraying his country by building ships unfit for sea, now gave way to admiration. 'Our ships do show themselves like gallants here', he wrote. 'I assure you it would do a man's heart good to behold them.' 'The best ships in the world', more than one of their captains said of them, and there was a singular unanimity in their wishes that the Spaniards were at sea and in sight so they might try conclusions. However anxious and impatient and suspicious Elizabeth's sea-dogs might be while they were fretting on the beach, once they were afloat and in the company of their noble ships they grew, as far as the impending action was concerned, calm and confident. Whoever might doubt of victory, they did not.

Whether by spring they would have been equally confident if Elizabeth had let them spend their strength on the Spanish coast is something we can never know. As it fell out, when the spring campaign began their crews were full and healthy, their stores of powder and shot, victuals and drink, if not all they could have used, were more than current estimates called for, and their needs for new spars and cordage and canvas, new blocks and pulleys and boats ('these be the fruits these seas bring forth especially in this time of year', wrote Sir William Wynter frankly) were not more than the dockyards could conveniently supply. That the fleet which finally met the Spaniards in the Channel was still at something like its top efficiency was surely due in larger part than anyone has ever said to Queen Elizabeth's niggardly prudence.

The *Ark Royal*: Howard's flagship against the Armada.

XVII

'IN THE HOPE OF A MIRACLE'

LISBON, FEBRUARY 9TH–APRIL 25TH, 1588

DON ALVARO DE BAZAN, Marquis of Santa Cruz and Captain General for the Ocean Seas, hero of Lepanto, victor of Terceira and a score of other famous fights, designated Commander by Sea for the invasion of England ever since that enterprise began to be planned, died at Lisbon on February 9th, 1588. With him, people came to think later, died something of the glory of the Spanish navy and Spain's best hope of victory. If only the old marquis had lived to command in the Channel, people said, everything would have been different. But, worn out at sixty-two by his labours to put the fleet in readiness, he died, his heart broken by the harsh reproaches of his king. Or so the Spanish chroniclers of his time and a growing mass of legend and speculation ever since assert.

It is hard to believe that even Horatio Nelson could have led the Spanish Armada to victory in 1588, and the evidence that Santa Cruz was working himself to death in Lisbon, depending as it does on some twenty letters by the marquis explaining to the King why the fleet cannot sail just yet, and promising that it will sail soon, is inadequate. Nor were the King's letters to the marquis harshly phrased. But they were impatient, and so far they bear out the legend. Indeed, in the strange correspondence of that winter the prudent king and the daring sea-dog seem to have exchanged characters. The King who had once written 'In so great an enterprise as that of England, it is fitting to move with feet of lead', now wrote: 'Success depends mostly upon speed. Be quick!' And the captain who had once argued for a bold blow at the main enemy and against the folly of delay and defensive war now had to hear his own arguments turned against him, while he mumbled about the imprudence of leaving the Spanish coasts undefended, and the unwisdom of undertaking a campaign not thoroughly prepared.

No such considerations moved the King. Before Santa Cruz got back from the Azores in September Philip had sent orders that as soon as he was joined by the galleasses of Naples and the victuallers from Andalusia the marquis was to sail with whatever forces he could collect straight for 'the cape of Margate' and the mouth of the Thames. Speed and secrecy would supply the place of greater strength, and though the season was a dangerous one there was hope that God, whose cause theirs was, would give favourable winds. Only a detailed list of the damages the galleons had suffered on the Azores voyage prevailed on the King to grant some weeks' delay. Thereafter Santa Cruz won permission to stay in port and try to pull his fleet together by grudging extensions of a week or so at a time. In December Philip was insisting that some sort of fleet, even if it numbered no more than thirty-five ships, and whether commanded by Santa Cruz or not, should sail at once to support a cross-Channel jump by Parma's army, and Santa Cruz was glumly promising to get such a fleet to sea. It may have been news of this that caused the sudden English mobilization in December. It was certainly news of the formidable English power in the Channel that led Philip to agree that perhaps, after all, thirty-five ships might not be enough and that Santa Cruz might wait until he could muster greater strength. But the King stipulated for a sortie not later than February 15th, and as that date approached sent the Count of Fuentes to Lisbon to keep Santa Cruz up to the mark.

Philip had changed. He who had always been so slow, so patient, so prudent, who had liked to say 'Time and I are two', and whose favourite phrases had been 'to enjoy the benefits of time' and 'to wait until the time is ripe', had been for almost a year in the grip of some terrible urgency, like a man for whom time is running out. Without having found out whether Parma was ready he ordered Santa Cruz to set sail; he ordered Parma to cross to England at once, without waiting for Santa Cruz. And he fretted and fumed at every check as if he himself would be held accountable for the delay by the only Superior he recognized. Philip had always been a pious man, but never before had he referred grave difficulties and dangers to the will of God, as if executing that will relieved him of the need for human precautions. He had never been a ruthless egotist or shown a taste for illimitable power; he had never claimed a special destiny, only a special responsibility; but now he walked forward on the path he thought appointed for him as confidently, as unswervingly, as blindly as any saint or world-conqueror in history.

As for Santa Cruz, though he was constantly promising to get the fleet to sea in just a few more weeks, there is such a strong smell of pessimism and discouragement about his letters that the King may be forgiven for having suspected that he manufactured delays. The marquis did not need to be assured that he was fighting in God's cause, but he had seen too many campaigns against the Turks to be over-confident on that score. To be sure of beating the English he had wanted at least fifty galleons. He had thirteen, and one of those so old and rotten that he doubted whether he could get her to sea. He had wanted, besides, another hundred great ships, heavily armed, plus forty hulks for victuals and stores, six galleasses, forty galleys and some seven or eight score small craft. Instead he had by the end of January, besides his thirteen galleons, four galleasses and a motley collection of sixty or seventy other ships, hired or commandeered in every sea from the Baltic to the Adriatic, some of them leaky or cranky, many of them slow, clumsy sailers, and the best of them, Oquendo's Guipúzcoans and Recalde's Biscayans, undermanned and absurdly under-gunned. Even for such a fleet he had scarcely half the auxiliary small craft he needed.

Nevertheless Santa Cruz felt he would really have to get to sea this time, and he dragged himself about in fumbling haste, while stores and guns were hurled aboard anyhow, and the prisons, the hospitals, the merchant ships in the harbour and the fields about Lisbon were scoured for pressed men to make up the depleted crews. Then, when his sailing date was scarcely a week away, the old man took to his bed and died.

Philip II had already picked his successor. The day the news of Santa Cruz's death reached Madrid the King sent off, along with instructions prepared three days earlier, a commission appointing Don Alonso de Guzman el Bueno, Duke of Medina Sidonia and Captain General of Andalusia, his Captain General of the Ocean Sea.

The year before the Duke of Medina Sidonia's prompt arrival at the head of the local militia was credited with saving Cadiz from the horrors of a sack by the pirate Drake. Probably that was, so far, his most notable service to the Crown, though he had kept the king's peace in Andalusia with tact and dignity, overseen the defences against English, French and Barbaresque corsairs, expedited recruits, supplies and shipping to Lisbon and in general discharged conscientiously and efficiently all those tasks of justice and administration expected of his rank and place. Perhaps these facts may have had some slight influence on Philip's choice. It may have counted more that the duke was known to be a mild and affable gentle-man, not tetchy or ambitious, and so less likely to fall out with Parma; not proud or headstrong or arrogant, and so with a better chance of getting along with the prickly characters who would be his immediate subordi-nates. Probably it counted still more with Philip that the duke was (for a duke) of practically blameless life and a devout son of the Church. But what certainly counted most was that he was head of the house of Guzman el Bueno, one of the most ancient and illustrious in Castile, a grandee of such dazzling eminence that no officer in the fleet could feel insulted by his promotion, or find it beneath his dignity to obey him.

From portraits and letters we know something of Medina Sidonia's personal appearance: a man of middle height, small boned and neatly made, with a thoughtful mouth and forehead and eyes brooding rather than piercing. It is a sensitive face, unheroic perhaps, but certainly not unintelligent or unappealing, and marked, even in a portrait taken three years before the great catastrophe of his life, by unmistakable melancholy. He does not look like a lucky man.

From a letter he wrote to Idiáquez, the King's Secretary, on receipt of his new commission we get a remarkable insight into the duke's character. He can scarcely believe, he says, that the King means to appoint him to such a charge and begs to be relieved of it:

> My health is not equal to such a voyage, for I know by experience of the little I have been at sea that I am always seasick and always catch cold. My family is burdened with a debt of nine hundred thousand ducats, and I could not spend a real in the king's service. Since I have had no experience either of the sea, or of war, I cannot feel that I ought to command so important an enterprise. I know nothing of what the marquis of Santa Cruz has been doing, or of what intelligence he has of England, so that I feel I should give but a bad account of myself, commanding thus blindly, and being obliged to rely on the advice of others, without knowing good from bad, or which of my advisers might want to deceive or displace me. The Adelantado Major of Castile is much fitter for this post than I. He is a man of much experience in military and naval matters, and a good Christian, too.

This is not exactly the spirit that conquered Mexico and Peru and made the Spanish *tercios* the admiration and terror of Europe, but perhaps it does not deserve the easy scorn it has sometimes received. There is intellectual honesty in this self-appraisal, and courage in its exposition. There is no reason to believe that there was anything conventional or insincere in Medina Sidonia's protest. It was not the custom of Spanish noblemen to disqualify themselves for high office, especially for high military office. Nor is there any reason to suppose that the complete acquiescence with

The Duke of Medina Sidonia (after 1610). From among the family portraits at Sanlúcar de Barrameda.

which the duke took up his post when the King again pressed it upon him represents anything except a sense of fealty to the Crown and the courage to bear any burden imposed by duty. With a prayer that the King might be right in supposing that God would uphold his weakness and remedy his defects the duke said goodbye to his household at San Lucar and rode hard across-country for Lisbon.

What he found there was a kind of frozen chaos. In the mad week or so preceding the marquis's death, guns and supplies had been tumbled helter-skelter on the ships, and crews herded aboard with orders to stand by for instant departure and on no account to go ashore. There were soldiers and mariners on most of these ships without money or arms or proper clothing. There were crews, the commands of unlucky or incompetent masters, who had practically no food. Some ships were laden far too deeply for safety: some floated practically empty. In the wild scramble towards the end every captain had apparently grabbed whatever he could get his hands on, particularly in the way of additional ordnance. Some ships had more guns than they had room for; others had almost none. One galleon had several new bronze pieces stowed between decks amidst a hopeless clutter of kegs and barrels; one Biscayan scarcely bigger than a pinnace had a huge demi-cannon filling most of her waist. Some had guns but no cannon balls; some had round shot but no guns to fire them. Since the Captain General's death the fleet had been in a state of suspended animation. There were plenty of veteran officers who could see what was wrong, but no one with the authority to get things sorted out.

That was Medina Sidonia's first job. By a desperate appeal to the King he succeeded in preventing Santa Cruz's private secretary from making off with all the old Captain General's papers, with all the battle plans, intelligence reports and administrative files of the fleet, before the new Captain General could even see them. There was nothing irregular in the secretary's intention. The papers, all of them, were the personal property of the old marquis, just as if they were private letters, and Medina Sidonia did not ask, nor would the King have dreamed of ordering, that they be surrendered. But at least the new commander did manage to get a long look at what his predecessor had been up to.

Also the duke put himself together a sort of informal staff. Don Diego Flores de Valdés, the brilliant and ambitious officer on whom later the duke was to rely too much, was still with the galleons of the Indian guard at Cadiz, but the duke commandeered the services of Don Diego de Maldonado and Captain Marolín de Juan, both experienced seamen and

195

well recommended. From Don Alonso de Cespedes, commanding the heavy artillery, he borrowed an Italian expert in naval gunnery. And his three ablest squadron commanders, Pedro de Valdés, Miguel de Oquendo and Juan Martínez de Recalde, made the nucleus of a useful Council of War. However they may have come to feel about him afterwards, his three chief subordinates began by liking and respecting their new commander, while he in turn attended to their advice, deferred to their judgments and addressed them with a humane courtesy, quite unlike the salty old marquis's growls and grunts and barks. For the moment the staff-work of the fleet was more harmonious than it had ever been under Santa Cruz.

So, with one or another of his squadron commanders at his elbow, the new Captain General began to inspect his motley fleet. Clearly, what he found shocked him, but his letters to the King though plain enough when plain speaking was needed are usually carefully restrained. In particular they breathe no word of blame for the predecessor from whom the duke inherited his troubles. Probably the duke felt that, until illness and worry prostrated him, Santa Cruz had been doing the best he could with an almost impossible situation. The chief blame for the mess in Lisbon Harbour was Philip II's. Under the conditions of the time, keeping as many units of a fleet as possible in a state of constant readiness throughout the winter while other units were being slowly added insured the deterioration of the ready units, ships and crews. The semi-demobilization of the English ships was the better system. But of this Medina Sidonia failed to persuade his impatient master as completely as Santa Cruz had, though he did manage, at last, to get some of his men ashore.

The first task was redistributing guns and cargo. Necessarily both jobs went on together, with unpleasant surprises about both coming up from time to time, but the guns were uppermost in everybody's minds as they had been ever since Santa Cruz and his captains began to think seriously about what lay ahead. A legend has grown up that the Spaniards despised artillery and thought that cold steel was all that was needed to win a fight at sea. There may have been popinjays mincing about Madrid who regretted that ever this villainous saltpetre should be digged out of the bowels of the harmless earth, and protested that but for the vile guns they would themselves have gone to the wars, but the professionals did not talk so. Single ship actions — and in the Atlantic most of the fighting had been of this sort — did, it is true, often end with grappling and boarding, just as battles of galleys in the Mediterranean usually did, and so both kinds of actions were finally decided, or appeared to be decided, by hand-to-hand combat. But no one who had ever commanded a fighting-ship at sea despised the heavy guns. It was the first complaint of Santa Cruz's subordinates that they had not enough of them, and what they had were not big enough, and Santa Cruz forwarded their complaints to Madrid with a vigorous endorsement and the further reminder that, of course, the galleons ought to have first choice of the heavier pieces. The Council of War thoroughly understood the point and beseeched the King for funds; Philip understood too, and somehow the money was found.

So stimulated, the arsenal at Madrid promised to cast thirty-six new brass pieces, cannon and demi-cannon, culverins and demi-culverins by December 15th, and the works at Lisbon promised thirty. Between sixty and seventy guns were bought up from foreign ships in Spanish harbours, though it is a fair guess that these were mostly small, six-, four- and two-pounders, and mostly iron; and more large brass guns were expected from Italy and, via the Hansa ports, from Germany. But gun-founding was a difficult art. Casting a big brass gun was not as tricky an operation as casting a statue like Cellini's Perseus, but there were too few masters who could do it, and too many of those few lived in England. Moreover, good guns were enormously expensive, especially the long-range guns of the culverin family which used a huge amount of gun-metal in proportion to the weight of the ball they threw. Consequently there never were very many culverins and demi-culverins to be had, even for ready money, and the facilities for casting more were limited. We do not know how badly the deliveries of ordnance at Lisbon were behind schedule when Santa Cruz died, only that they were and continued to be disappointing. Even before he had finished seeing the supplementary guns which Santa Cruz had wangled properly redistributed the duke began to worry about how to get more — more big ones, ship-killers — to replace the little man-killers which still made, so his captains told him, too large a proportion of the fleet's batteries. Undoubtedly he did get some more, so that when the fleet finally sailed in May it must have been better armed than it was in February. But equally undoubtedly the total achievement was far below what the duke and his captains had hoped for. The best ships had been strengthened at the expense of the others, and yet even in the first line of battle the lack of long-range guns remained alarming.

By this time the number of ships in the fleet, especially of fighting-ships, had been considerably augmented. When Medina Sidonia took command Philip had finally agreed to detach the 'galleons of the Indian guard' from their regular duty and send them against England. Diego Flores de Valdés brought them round from Cadiz at the end of March — eight fine galleons, seven all alike, of about four hundred English tons each: smaller than the *Revenge*, that is, but about as big as the Queen's *Dreadnought*, the eighth only half that size but still counted fit for the first line.

The galleons of Portugal were a more heterogeneous lot than the galleons of Castile. The Portuguese navy had once been second only to the English and at times perhaps not second, but for many years before the extinction of the dynasty in 1580 the kings of the house of Aviz had spent less and less on their fleet. After Terceira there had been some repairing and rebuilding; and when he sailed to the Azores in the vain pursuit of Drake, Santa Cruz had been able to take out twelve Portuguese galleons, all that were left in European waters. Some of them proved ill-found, however. One had been lost on the way home, and another was so strained and leaky after a November storm that she had to be beached and broken up. Of the remaining ten Medina Sidonia's first inspection showed several in need of serious repairs, and one too small and too old to fight in the line and so rotten she could hardly carry sail. He favoured leaving her in port after distributing her heavier guns.

Fortunately, the foresight of the Marquis of Santa Cruz had provided a substitute which brought the Portuguese squadron well above its previous strength. This was the galleon called, in the Spanish order of battle, the *Florencia*, the newest and probably the most powerful warship that sailed with the Armada. Santa Cruz had intended her as the flagship of the Levantine, that is the Italian squadron, since she was an involuntary loan from Philip's reluctant ally the Grand Duke of Tuscany, the one galleon in the Tuscan navy and the apple of the Grand Duke's eye.

The last thing in the world the Grand Duke had wanted to do with her was to send her into northern seas to fight in the King of Spain's crusade. She had fallen into Santa Cruz's clutches in a curious way. Among its many results the siege and capture of Antwerp and the closing of the Scheldt disrupted the European spice market. Even during the revolt Antwerp had been a centre of distribution, and by 1585 pepper and cloves, nutmeg and mace and cinnamon were piling up in the warehouses of Lisbon. The Grand Duke of Tuscany had a brilliant idea. Why should not Florence become the new emporium of the spice trade, and why shouldn't he enrich himself in the process? He made diplomatic inquiries and found India House and the Council of Portugal cautiously favourable. Philip himself was encouraging, prices and terms of payment were agreed on, and the deal seemed so nearly closed that the Grand Duke sent his fine new galleon to bring back the spices. Nothing less would do, for the cargo would be of enormous value, calling for a ship like the *San Francesco*, capable at need of standing off a whole fleet of Barbary corsairs.

When Captain Bartoli got the *San Francesco* to Lisbon he found that, as so often happens in large commercial transactions, some sort of hitch had occurred. The King's factors were not prepared to deliver the spices. While he waited for the businessmen to finish their haggling he was delighted to show his ship to the famous Spanish admiral who commanded in Lisbon, and even more delighted when the great Santa Cruz showed himself most enthusiastic about the *San Francesco*. The Marquis praised her neat trim lines and her staunch construction, and particularly admired her fifty-two brass guns — a heavier armament, he admitted, than any of his own ships carried. In a word he had never seen a finer ship, and he thought whoever commanded her must be a happy man. In the weeks that followed other Spanish captains were rowed over to admire the *San Francesco*.

Weeks became months and still there were no spices, and from being delighted with Spanish attentions Captain Bartoli began to be suspicious. What he wrote on the subject so alarmed the Grand Duke that he decided to forgo any profits on spices, and ordered Captain Bartoli to bring the *San Francesco* back to Leghorn where he had immediate need of her. When after trying in vain to get the usual clearance Captain Bartoli weighed anchor and, in obedience to his sovereign's command started to take an informal departure, the admiral's barge brought him the curt word that the forts had orders to sink him if he entered the channel. That was in November 1586, and for the next eight months the chief business of the Tuscan ambassador at Madrid was to try to get the *San Francesco* out of Lisbon.

Then, when he was getting ready to pursue Drake, Santa Cruz sent Captain Gaspar da Sousa with a strong company of Portuguese infantry aboard the *San Francesco* and a message to Captain Bartoli that he was to sail with the Portuguese galleons and follow da Sousa's orders in case of contact with the enemy. The performance of the *San Francesco* on the Azores voyage, where she was the only ship which sprang no leak and lost no spar, made it less likely than ever, as Bartoli wrote his master with rueful pride, that the Spanish would ever let her go; but the Grand Duke Francis kept trying to get her back until the day he died, and his successor, Ferdinand I, was still trying when she sailed for England.

With the *Florencia*, as the Spaniards renamed the *San Francesco*, and the galleons of the Indian guard, Medina Sidonia had twenty galleons, a force almost equal in tonnage if not in gun-power to the Queen's twenty best ships, and these, supplemented by the four galleasses of Naples and by four large armed merchantmen kept with the galleons of Castile, made up his first line of battle. The second line was forty armed merchant ships, and though few of these were as formidably armed as the best merchantmen in the English second line many of them were a great deal larger — larger indeed than any ships in either fleet except the Queen's two biggest, the *Triumph* and the *White Bear*. Since February Medina Sidonia had got hold, besides the greater part of the Indian squadron, of a great Venetian carrack, another big Italian, probably Genoese, and six or seven more merchant ships from Biscayan ports. He had added some extra hulks and got together enough light craft to double February's list. By the end of April he had something like a hundred and thirty sail, great and small, more or less ready for sea.

Besides augmenting the number of the Armada he had strengthened it in other ways. As many ships as possible had been careened and tallowed and, by using the last of the seasoned wood in the Lisbon yards and all that could be scraped up along the coast, most of the rotten timber had been replaced and cracked spars changed for sound ones. Also, some of the galleons and a number of the merchantmen got new high bow and stern castles. Traditionally such castles turned a merchantman into a warship, but some at least of the galleons both of Spain and of Portugal seem to have been, normally, 'race-decked' (in Spanish, *rasa*) all on one level — that is to say with no raised forecastle and only a relatively low aftercastle and poop-deck. Race-decked ships were faster and more weatherly, but when it came to fighting most Spanish captains preferred lofty castles for the men to shelter within and fight from. So did some English captains, Martin Frobisher, among others. No radical innovator like John Hawkins had Medina Sidonia's ear, and, after he took over, those ships of the Armada which had not already mounted lofty superstructures had them added by carpenters in Lisbon Harbour.

In a good many ways the fleet benefited by the delay Medina Sidonia won for it, and the influence he was able to exert in every department of Spanish administration. The supplies of morions, corslets, pikes, half-pikes, muskets and arquebuses, all gravely deficient at the beginning of March, were up to what plans called for by the end of April. The allowance of powder was almost doubled and, perhaps on the advice of the Italian artillery expert, almost all the powder was 'musket powder', fine corned. Most important of all the supply of cannon balls for the great guns was increased, so that every piece could fire fifty rounds. This turned out to be nowhere near enough, but it was a great deal better than the thirty rounds per gun that Santa Cruz had been willing to settle for.

In some ways, however, all the duke's influence and unsparing exertions could not improve the condition of the fleet, could not even prevent its deterioration. There were more things wrong with many of the ships than it was humanly possible to put right. Every week in port with full crews meant the consumption of another week's victuals, so that stores had to be constantly replenished. What was worse, meat and fish and biscuits packed into casks when the sailing had been set for October turned out by May to be inedible by even the most tolerant standards. Worst of all was the human attrition. Though no real pestilence swept the fleet, every week the bills of mortality lengthened; and badly fed, ill-clothed, unpaid as they were, every week soldiers and mariners deserted. Medina Sidonia did get more money, and the rate of desertion which had been highest in December diminished somewhat in March and April. Peasants torn from the plough could, in appearance at any rate, fill up the ranks of the soldiers, but already in November Santa Cruz had been complaining that he could not find enough trained seamen. By April the shortage was much more grave. The shortage of trained gunners would have been equally disturbing, except that it was overshadowed by the shortage of great guns, especially culverins.

Nevertheless, whatever inner misgivings he may have felt, Medina Sidonia knew that he could not ignore the King's impatience much longer, and also that there was little he could do in any time that would be allowed him to remedy remaining weaknesses. On April 25th he went to the Cathedral of Lisbon to take from its altar the blessed standard of the expedition, as an announcement that it was about to sail and an advertisement of the holy nature of the mission. Every man who was to sail with it had confessed and communicated. They had all been warned severely against blasphemous swearing and other sins that soldiers and sailors are prone to. The ships had all been searched to make sure that no women had been secreted aboard. Now the Captain General went solemnly to the Cathedral, accompanied by His Most Catholic Majesty's Viceroy, the Cardinal Archduke. The Archbishop of Lisbon himself said mass and pronounced a general benediction on the Enterprise. The standard was lifted from the altar and borne across the Plaza Mayor to the Dominican

Convent where the duke himself laid it on that altar in token of his personal dedication. Then the banner was borne back between kneeling lines of soldiers and sailors to whom friars read the papal absolution, and indulgence granted to all partakers in this most holy crusade. On the blessed banner, on one side of the Arms of Spain was the image of Christ crucified, and on the other of His Holy Mother. Beneath was a scroll with the words of the psalmist: 'Exurge, domine et vindica causam tuam' — 'Arise, O Lord, and vindicate thy cause.'

Of the accounts of this touching ceremony the driest is by the papal representative in Lisbon, on whom the Pope chiefly relied for spot news of Philip's naval preparations. No one in Europe took an acuter interest in the Enterprise of England than His Holiness Pope Sixtus V. He had been urging it on Philip since the first year of his papacy, and for almost as long Philip had been trying to borrow money from him against it. But His Holiness had been far from sure that Philip meant to invade England at all. He refused to lend anything on a mere supposition. Instead he swore to Olivarez with a great oath that on the day the first Spanish soldier set foot on English soil he would not lend but give the King of Spain a million golden ducats. Until that day, however, though Philip might have permission to collect the special tax for a crusade from his own clergy (he would have done so, anyhow) and whatever papal blessings and indulgences he thought useful, he could not have a single *soldo* from the papal treasury. Naturally, now that Sixtus was at last convinced that Philip did mean to launch the Enterprise, he had a special interest in its chance of success.

To satisfy his curiosity he had not only alerted his nuncio at Madrid but sent a special emissary to Lisbon, ostensibly on church business. Just a few days before the ceremony of the standard this observer had reported to Cardinal Montalto an illuminating conversation.

He was talking privately, he said, to one of the highest and most experienced officers of the Spanish fleet (can it have been Juan Martínez de Recalde?) and found the courage to ask him bluntly: 'And if you meet the English Armada in the Channel, do you expect to win the battle?'

'Of course,' replied the Spaniard.

'How can you be sure?'

'It's very simple. It is well known that we fight in God's cause. So, when we meet the English, God will surely arrange matters so that we can grapple and board them, either by sending some strange freak of weather or, more likely, just by depriving the English of their wits. If we can come to close quarters, Spanish valour and Spanish steel (and the great masses of soldiers we shall have on board) will make our victory certain. But unless God helps us by a miracle the English, who have faster and handier ships than ours, and many more long-range guns, and who know their advantage just as well as we do, will never close with us at all, but stand aloof and knock us to pieces with their culverins, without our being able to do them any serious hurt. So,' concluded the captain, and one fancies a grim smile, 'we are sailing against England in the confident hope of a miracle.'

Spanish galleons.

XVIII

THE DAY OF THE BARRICADES: I

PARIS, MAY 12TH, 1588 AND BEFORE

AT five o'clock on the morning of Thursday, May 12th, from his bedroom on the corner of the Rue des Poullies, Don Bernardino de Mendoza heard the tramp of many armed men coming down the Rue Saint-Honoré. Even to the ambassador's purblind eyes there was no mistaking these burly figures, looking in their padded doublets and voluminous pantaloons even bigger than they were. They were the King's Swiss, the regiments from Lagny. They filled the Rue Saint-Honoré from side to side and for most of its length, marching as they might have marched entering a captured city, colours uncased, pikes and halberds at the ready, the slow matches of the arquebusiers and musketmen alight. Behind them the regiments of the French Guard were coming through the Porte Saint-Honoré, and the early sun was beginning to glint on morions and pike-heads, gold lace and gun barrels. Mendoza watched the column hold on past the narrow streets that led to the Louvre and angle left towards the Cemetery of the Holy Innocents. As they did so there came the rolling thunder of twenty tambours and the shrill squealing of a score of fifes. From the direction of the gate the music of the French Guard took up the defiant rhythm.

It looked as if the King of France were going to make one last try to be master in his own capital. Mendoza was not altogether surprised. Yesterday had been full of rumours — and the special measures of the evening, the strengthening of the garrisons at the Bastille and the Châtelet, the comings and goings at the Hôtel de Ville, the mustering of the city's militia from the more reliable quarters, and the patrols under loyal Parisian officials posted to guard for the night the principal squares and gates and bridges, all looked as if something unusual was afoot.

If Mendoza was not much surprised he must have been a little uneasy. The coup d'état now impending had been planned for three years and more. It was the mine whose perfectly timed explosion would at the very least paralyse the French monarchy on the eve of the Spanish invasion of England as Parma had demanded, and might do much more, even to blowing the ruins of France into the grasp of the King of Spain. In the past fortnight the Sixteen, the secret revolutionary committee of the League in Paris, had shown their hand openly as never before. That had been unavoidable. And it was necessary that the head of the League, Henry of Guise, and some scores of its minor chieftains and captains should now be in Paris, even though a grave risk was involved. The Parisian Leaguers did not expect to seize power without a fight, and had anticipated that the King might have to be prodded into some rash act of violence which would incite a popular uprising. But the massed column of Swiss swinging down the Rue Saint-Honoré while evidently promising violence scarcely suggested rashness. It looked as though the King, with unexpected courage and decision, intended to forestall by a coup d'état, the coup d'état planned against him. Unless Mendoza's Leaguer friends knew how to defend themselves the heads of the more illustrious and the pendent bodies of the commoners might be adorning the battlements of the Louvre before nightfall.

In the past three days things had gone so oddly that Mendoza had reasonable grounds for anxiety. Up to the time Henry of Guise had entered Paris, about noon on Monday, May 9th, and been by prearrangement 'accidentally' recognized by a throng of Parisians in the Rue Saint-Martin, everything had gone according to plan. If Mendoza's information was correct the Armada should have been dropping down past Cascaes just as the Duke of Guise rode through the Porte Saint-Martin — and indeed so it would have been, give or take a day or two, if the winds had been right. Thanks to Mendoza the duke's entry had been a miracle of perfect timing, and in the same style the ambassador had managed all the long complicated preparations with consummate skill and almost perfect secrecy.

If in May 1588 very few people suspected how closely Mendoza was connected with the Leaguer nobles headed by Guise, even fewer suspected his connection with the Leaguers of Paris, headed by the secret Committee of Sixteen. Shrewd Dr Cavriana who, from his vantage-point as Queen Catherine de Medici's physician, supplied the Grand Duke of Tuscany with political intelligence, guessed that the man who called the tune, and called it so confidently before the first notes were audible, must be paying the piper, and in the midst of the troubles in Paris referred casually to Mendoza as he 'who arranged this dance and leads it'. But though he was one of Mendoza's closest friends Cavriana was only guessing. Nicholas Poulain, the King's spy among the Sixteen, probably knew more of

Mendoza's connections than he and his master thought it tactful to publish — certainly he knew enough to justify Henry III's formal charge that Mendoza had given aid and comfort to his rebels and ought to be withdrawn, but Poulain seems not to have suspected how largely the supplies of arms secretly stored here and there in Paris, in the Hôtel de Guise, in friendly convents and the houses of good Catholics, had been paid for by the Spanish ambassador. Even today the means by which Mendoza communicated with the Sixteen are far from clear. He was too old a conspirator to write down more than he had to about conspiracies, even for the information of his king.

As far as we know the revolutionaries began to organize in January 1585, when Mendoza had been in Paris about three months and had just heard that the secret treaty of Joinville between King Philip and the princes of the house of Lorraine was ready to be signed. That treaty, with its promise of Spanish subsidies to revive the Holy League of the nobles, had been the occasion of Mendoza's being sent to France. At the last he stayed in Paris, leaving its negotiation to others — not, one supposes, because he preferred the social atmosphere of the Parisian conspiracy. There were no princes or nobles on the secret Committee of Sixteen, no gentlemen for that matter, and no bourgeois from the highest circles. There were several petty officials, a couple of lawyers, a curé, a process-server, an auctioneer, a tinsmith, a butcher and suchlike. But they were energetic and clever men, their violent partisan passions, their hatred of all kinds of innovation and of everybody with ideas different from their own, and their personal ambitions, combining to make them what we have come to recognize since as typical 'radicals of the right'. In time, Mendoza came to regard them as Spain's most valuable allies in France, and in the end they came to regard him as their natural chief.

Even in 1585 it was clear that they could be very useful. Whatever they believed themselves, they told their stupider neighbours that all good Catholics must arm to escape being massacred by the Huguenots with whom the King, led by unworthy favourites like Epernon, was secretly allied. They told each other and the committees in the provinces with whom they corresponded, that they were justified in going to any lengths to escape the yoke of a heretic king. They preferred Guise to Navarre and most of them did not want to wait even until the last Valois should die a natural death before bringing Guise to power. It was understood among them that the paramilitary force they were creating was meant to seize Paris. Of all this Mendoza heartily approved.

Now, of course, Mendoza may have been put in touch with the Sixteen by Maineville, the Duke of Guise's liaison agent in Paris, though it sometimes seems that Maineville was informed about the Paris committee by Mendoza. Or he could have learned about the revolutionaries from the Duchess de Montpensier, the sister of the Guises, on whom Mendoza had called almost as soon as he reached Paris, and at whose town house he soon became a familiar figure. That restless female politician, the patroness of all the most intemperate pulpit orators in Paris, who wore at her girdle a pair of golden scissors 'for the tonsure of Brother Henri' and liked to boast that her retinue of curés and monks and friars was more use to the League than any army, was inevitably as deep in the counsels of the Sixteen as she could penetrate. Or Mendoza may have communicated with the Sixteen through the Jesuits. His own confessor was a Jesuit, he himself had worked hand in glove with Father Claude Matthieu, the French Provincial of the Society, on more than one occasion, and the French Jesuits were nearly all ardent supporters of the League and welcome in Leaguer circles. Then we learn that from the first one of the commonest meeting-places of the Sixteen was the wine-shop of a Spaniard named Sanchez, said to have served under Alva in the Netherlands, a man who took messages and ran errands for Mendoza. But it is most likely, though we have no proof, that Mendoza worked with the Sixteen, or at least with their inner circle of five, directly and closely, with no intermediaries at all. Certainly, when later on he joined them openly, they welcomed him as an old and tried friend and collaborator. And before he had been six months at his post he was telling Philip with great confidence, and as far as the Leaguers were concerned considerable accuracy, how 'Paris' felt, and what 'Paris' would do in each political crisis.

We do not know how much Mendoza advised.the Sixteen about their elaborate military plans, from the first a major part of their activities. Each of them was captain of one of the sixteen 'quarters' of Paris, and in addition the five principal conspirators were 'Colonels' of the five arrondissements. Each quarter had its own command post, its own cachés of arms, and plans for its defence and for keeping in touch with the rest when the insurrection began. The committee could not recruit equally from all parts of Paris. In some streets they had no adherents at all, and in several quarters their followers were a small minority, so that for the backbone of their combat effectives they had to rely on the rowdies and the enthusiasts, on elements like the butchers, the watermen and the horse-copers, always ready for rioting and plunder, and on the students of the Sorbonne. Nevertheless, with the aid of organization, systematic terror and the loud voices of the friars, they counted on dominating the whole city.

To the tactics of street fighting they gave special study. They were delighted with the suggestion of some veteran of the Dutch wars (could it have been Mendoza?) that they supplement the iron chains, which since the fourteenth century had been used to close the streets of Paris, with barricades. Fairly satisfactory ones they were told could be improvised out of carts, barrows and household furniture, but the best contrivance, as experience had shown, was to use barrels and hogsheads filled with earth and stones. These could be rolled quickly to chosen spots and then heaved upright to form breastworks musket-proof and easily defensible. Considerable advance preparation was required, of course, but empty barrels could be stored in some friendly cellar until they were needed without arousing any more suspicion than would the piles of earth and cobblestones beside them. Any extra cobblestones would come in handy to throw down from roofs and upper windows. By the spring of 1587 the Sixteen were so confident that by their barricades they could isolate and reduce all the royalist strongpoints, the Châtelet, the Hôtel de Ville, the Bastille, the Arsénal and the Louvre itself, and their rank and file were so eager for something more exciting than conspiring, secret drilling and lugging cobblestones, that it was all Mendoza and Guise could do to prevent an uprising in April. They managed, but Mendoza was alarmed. April 1587 would have been too soon.

Now, though Mendoza might wonder whether the new model barricades would contain several thousand veteran infantrymen as easily as they would have done the few hundred guardsmen and the doubtfully loyal town militia he had expected to find on the King's side, he could congratulate himself on his timing. Paris would be ripe, he had written Parma, at any time after Martinmas, 1587, but he'd need a few weeks' notice. Then he had heard from Spain that Santa Cruz would surely sail by February 15th, and he arranged everything for that date. Early in February the Duke of Guise fired off a provocative manifesto, demanding the removal from around the King of persons suspected of heresy (he meant the reigning favourite, Epernon), unequivocal support for the League, Chambers of the Inquisition to be established in every province, all Huguenot property to be confiscated and all Huguenot prisoners of war who refused to recant to be put to death. There was more, enough to ensure war throughout France for years to come. Then Guise moved to

Soissons with a powerful following, Leaguer captains began to converge on Paris, and the Duke of Aumâle, Guise's firebrand cousin, renewed his attacks on the King's garrisons in Picardy. Meanwhile the Paris pulpits began to clamour for their Joshua, their David.

Henry of Valois was so stung that, encouraged by Epernon, he swore he would raise an army and sweep the Leaguers out of Picardy himself. At that moment Mendoza heard from Madrid that the Marquis of Santa Cruz had died, and, inevitably, the Armada would be delayed. The next morning (was it coincidence?) the Queen Mother persuaded Henry to try to subdue Guise by the gentle arts of negotiation instead of the harsh rod of war, and Guise at Soissons showed himself unexpectedly inclined to listen to persuasion. This, at least, was no coincidence. Mendoza had advised him of a hitch in the plans, and Guise had replied characteristically that if there was to be a delay he would need more money.

In April, in spite of all the other demands on King Philip's resources, Guise got the money. The League and its chieftain were more important than ever to the invasion plans. Since the death of Joyeuse the Duke of Epernon was all-powerful with the King, and Epernon, though a Catholic, was all for Coligny's plan of reuniting France by a war with Spain. He was getting ready to start for Normandy, of which province Henry had made him Governor, with an army strong enough to establish his authority in all the Channel ports. From there he planned to go to Picardy, throw the Leaguers out, and make sure of Calais and Boulogne. Then he would join the English in the Channel with all the ships he could muster, including the *Rochellais*; or, if the Spanish fleet had been victorious and Parma had crossed to England, he would invade Flanders and Artois and try to reconquer them for France before Parma could get back. So, at least, Philip heard from Parma, from Olivarez, from Mendoza, from the English exiles and from his own secret sources of intelligence. And by April 15th Philip could assure Mendoza that in less than four weeks Medina Sidonia would sail.

It had long been understood what must happen next. In the last week of April every pulpit on the left bank, almost every pulpit in Paris, rang with appeals and lamentations. The King and his vile favourites were conspiring with the heretics to massacre the good Catholics of Paris. If the Duke of Guise ever wished to enter Paris as a friend, let him come now and defend God's truth and God's people! Thoroughly alarmed, Henry III sent his councillor, Bellièvre, to exhort the duke to keep out of Paris until the people had calmed down, and so prevent bloodshed. When

Guise replied evasively Bellièvre was instructed to command the duke, on his allegiance, not to come to Paris.

Bellièvre delivered the royal command to Guise on Sunday morning, May 8th. He gathered that Guise intended to comply, and rode back to Paris. That evening the duke, too, started for Paris slightly attended. He rode through the night, breakfasted near Saint-Denis and went straight through the camp of the Swiss and into Paris by the Porte Saint-Martin. Guise had ridden with his hat pulled low over his brows and his cloak across his face. In the Rue Saint-Martin one of his companions, as if in jest, pulled off his hat and tossed back the cloak. There were few Parisians who did not know that proud, handsome, virile face, that scar worn like a decoration. 'M. de Guise!' the cry spread. 'M. de Guise, at last! We are saved! Long live M. de Guise! Long live the pillar of the Church!' Shops and churches emptied to provide a wildly excited, more than royal escort.

So far everything had gone according to plan. The neighbourhoods were all alerted. Some eight or nine hundred Leaguers, many of them experienced soldiers, all of them well armed, had already filtered into Paris and were being lodged at strategic points — the convent of the Jacobins, the bishop's palace, the Hôtel Montpensier, the Hôtel de Guise — enough seasoned fighting-men to balance the reinforcements the King had brought in a few days before. The Duke of Epernon, the one person Henry trusted who had courage enough to make a bold decision and influence enough to get the King to accept it, was by now deep in Normandy and with him some of the King's best troops. Epernon could not get back in time to affect the decision in Paris, but on the other hand he had not been in Normandy long enough to do much harm. Once Henry III was dead or a prisoner in the hands of the League, or merely their submissive puppet — Mendoza did not care much which — the Norman towns would put themselves at M. de Guise's disposal. Whatever happened, France would be in no condition to threaten Spain.

What happened next was not according to plan. Guise should have turned left off the Rue Saint-Martin and mounted the Rue Saint-Antoine to his own *hôtel*, where his captains and partisans awaited him and whence he could dictate terms to the King, with or without the use of the barricades, as circumstances should suggest. Instead he turned right, crossed the broad Rue Saint-Denis and plunged into the maze of little streets towards St Eustache where Queen Catherine de Medici and what was left of her famous flying squadron lodged, not inappropriately some thought, in the Home for Repentant Girls.

When her dwarf cried out from the window that the Duke of Guise was approaching the Queen told him he was mad to say so; and when her own eyes identified the affable man on horseback in the midst of his delirious admirers her lips were drained of colour and her voice choked and trembled. Whether her visible emotion was because she had not known that Guise would come to Paris, or because she knew that at this juncture he should not be coming to her, no one can say now. After he had been received and had made his obeisances Guise declared in a loud voice that he had come to clear himself of slanders and to offer his services to the King, trusting in the Queen Mother's aid and counsel. Then Catherine drew him into the embrasure of a window and for a few minutes their voices were inaudible, though one observer thought that the duke looked embarrassed and Catherine frightened. A messenger was sent to the Louvre and presently returned, and Catherine ordered her chair.

The first Mendoza knew of this turn of events was when he was drawn to his window by the sound of an uproarious ovation and saw the Queen's chair issue from the Filles Repenties and sway through the crowd in the direction of the Louvre, with, walking beside it, his hat in hand, bowing right and left to the ecstatic throng and continually pelted with flowers, the unmistakable figure of the Duke of Guise. Sixtus V on hearing that Guise had entered Paris exclaimed: 'The fool! He is going to his death!' Mendoza knew that Henry III did not rule Paris with the iron hand with which the great Pope ruled Rome, but the last of the Valois was still master of his own palace, and the ambassador must have felt a moment of dismay when he saw the man upon whom all his plans depended disappearing on his way to those grim portals.

In fact, at that moment Guise's death was being discussed at the Louvre. Closeted with the King was Alphonse d'Ornano, a Corsican of the Corsicans, and a devoted captain of the King's. When he heard his mother's message, Henry said to Ornano: 'M. de Guise has just arrived in Paris, contrary to my express command. In my place what would you do?'

'Sire,' said Ornano, 'do you hold the Duke of Guise for a friend or for an enemy?' And reading his answer in the King's face: 'Just give the order, Sire, and I will lay his head at your feet.'

La Guiche and Villequier and Bellièvre, temporizers and timid men, broke in with horrified expostulations, but the Abbé d'Elbène warmly approved Ornano's simple solution and quoted with obvious relish the exhortation transmitted by the prophet Zechariah: 'percutiam pastorem et dispergentur oves' — smite the shepherd and the sheep shall be scattered. There was a good deal to be said for the abbé's Biblical wisdom, and Henry III was still debating it when the shepherd in question, accompanied by his cheering sheep, reached the Louvre.

Inside the Louvre the atmosphere was different. Double ranks of stolid Swiss stood round the courtyard. The great staircase up which Guise mounted was lined with gentlemen guardsmen of the Forty-five with brave, stupid, honest Crillon at their head. The duke doffed his hat and made Crillon a deep bow; Crillon jammed his hat tighter on his head and stood stiff as a ramrod, glaring past the duke with the fixed stare of an executioner. As the duke climbed the staircase bowing right and left not one of the Forty-five returned his greeting.

At the bottom of the long room the King stood amidst a knot of gentlemen. Among them Guise may have seen Ornano looking from him to the King and back again with the look of a terrier trembling to be unleashed. As he made his reverence he heard the King's voice, as sharp and hostile as a thunderclap: 'What brings you here?' Guise began a speech about his loyalty, about the slanders against him, but Henry cut him off: 'I told you not to come.' And turning to Bellièvre: 'Did I not tell you to tell him not to come?' And Henry turned his back on the duke and walked a few paces towards the window, his shoulders hunched and his fingers clenching and unclenching. It may have been then that an un-friendly observer saw the duke sink down on a chest against the wall 'not deliberately failing in respect for the king, but simply because his knees would not support him'.

It was certainly then that Catherine de Medici, whose age and bulk made negotiating the staircase a slow process, appeared at the door of the apartment. 'I came to Paris,' said Guise, raising his voice, 'at the request of the queen, your mother.'

'That is right,' said Catherine, advancing on her son. 'I asked M. de Guise to come to Paris.' No one was ever able to think of Catherine de Medici as a royal or even a charming figure, yet she had dominated many scenes in the stormy decades since her husband died. She was to dominate this scene too. The unwieldy black-draped body had its own curious dignity, the dough-white face with its sloe-black buttons of eyes its own pervasive calm. She seemed wiser and steadier than all these excitable males and incalculably older, as if she had always been queen-dowager and the fountain-head of ultimate authority, as indeed for most of them she had.

As she walked down the room towards her son one wonders whether her glance crossed Guise's in an assurance of complicity, and whether either of them remembered that she had come forward just so in this Louvre, almost sixteen years before, between Henry of Guise, hardly more than a boy then, and the wrath of another king. At that time, too, the Paris mob had been ready to take arms. At that time, too, Guise had been playing a slippery double game between Court and mob, between ambitious political intrigue and religious fanaticism. If she and Guise remembered, they would have remembered also that then they had a third accomplice to endorse their counsels of political expedience and religious zeal and to help them drive the poor, weak, half-crazy young king into an act that would haunt him for the rest of his short life. Now the wheel had come full circle and their accomplice on that St Bartholomew's Eve stood apart from them, braced to meet their onset — Henry, once of Anjou, now of France, weaker than his brother Charles and stronger, madder and saner, penned for ever into his predestined role by the burden of his knowledge and his guilt, as his former accomplices, his mother and his cousin Guise, were penned in theirs.

We do not know what arguments Catherine used to keep Henry from giving the nod to Ornano, whether she pointed to the crowds in the street below and appealed to his fears, or told him that Guise could be out-manoeuvred and appealed to his vanity, or whether she assured him that Guise was guiltless (she knew better) and appealed to the strong sense of justice which, oddly enough, was a part of Henry's complex character. Nor do we know why Catherine, who was not squeamish about killing, deprived her son of his last chance to be master in his own capital. We can only be sure it was for some selfish personal reason.

Catherine did not inconvenience herself for the faith; as a Pope's niece she had long felt sure the Church could look after its own affairs. She had no more interest in the orthodoxy she sometimes invoked than she had in the principles of justice and toleration she also mouthed. In fact she had no interest in any abstractions at all — not in the French monarchy to which her son Henry was unselfishly devoted, not in France, not in Christendom, not even in a dynasty. She was interested in the comfort, safety and personal aggrandizement of herself and her immediate family; or now that her last and favourite son Henry and her wild brilliant daughter Marguerite had both turned against her, now that it seemed certain she would never have a grandchild who could inherit the crown of France, she was concerned chiefly about herself. She must have thought she was safer if she intervened in Guise's favour. She may have thought that she would be reasserting her influence over her son.

Whatever her arguments and whatever her motives, she triumphed. Her cynical selfish advice was taken for the last time, as it had been taken so often before, and as so often before it served in the end only to compound horror and confusion, proving fully as destructive as if it had been distilled from the highest principles. At her urging Henry sulkily relinquished his prey, and she swept her son and the duke off to visit her daughter-in-law, the Queen Regnant, in her bedchamber, whence by a private stairway Guise could regain the safety of the streets. When Mendoza heard of the episode at the Louvre he concluded that if Guise was more of a fool than he had taken him for, Henry was much more of a weakling and a coward. That judgment left him the less prepared for the sight of the Swiss infantry streaming down the Rue Saint-Honoré.

Queen Catherine de Medici, from a drawing attributed to François Clouet.

XIX

THE DAY OF THE BARRICADES: II

PARIS, MAY 12TH, 1588 AND AFTER

THE two days of mounting tension after Guise entered Paris proved that the King could come to no reasonable terms with the League, and that he had lost control of his capital. When Guise called again at the Louvre he came at the head of four hundred gentlemen with armour under their doublets and pistols in their sleeves, and what he presented was less like an explanation than an ultimatum. On the morning of the eleventh an attempt by the authorities to expel 'the foreigners' from Paris ended in farce. By the eleventh it was believed that the number of soldiers of the League who had infiltrated Paris had increased to fifteen hundred or two thousand. They trickled through every gate, they swaggered in groups in every street and square, even under the windows of the Louvre. But the town watch thought it prudent to report that they could find no 'foreigners' at all in Paris. And when the municipal authorities at the King's command set up a special watch and ward on the evening of the eleventh, although some companies were faithful to their posts until relieved, others had melted away by midnight, and several on hearing their orders had flatly declared that instead of standing guard in a strange part of the city they were going home to bar their doors and defend their goods and their families. All sorts of wild rumours were afloat, and there was a feeling in the air of imminent catastrophe. Before midnight Henry III ordered the Swiss and French Guards quartered in the suburbs to enter Paris at dawn.

In the early light they swung down the Rue Saint-Honoré and into the Cemetery of the Holy Innocents, Marshal Biron on horseback at the head of the column, Crillon on foot with drawn sword leading the French Guards, and Marshal Aumont with several troops of horse bringing up the rear. From the Cemetery of the Holy Innocents Biron sent off columns on their several missions: so many companies to the Place de Grève in front of the town hall where the chief magistrate of Paris, the Prévost des Marchands and the loyal town council expected them; so many each to the Petit Pont and its Petit Châtelet and to the Pont Saint-Michel, the

215

two bridges which joined the Île de la Cité to the left bank; so many to the Marché Neuf just between them and not far from Nôtre-Dame; and finally a detachment to the Place Maubert, the chief gathering-place of the monks and students of the Sorbonne. A strong reserve remained in the cemetery. By seven in the morning Biron was able to report to the King that all the troops were posted as His Majesty had commanded.

The tramp of feet at a street's end or under their windows, the shrill of fifes and thunder of drums, first awakened the Parisians to the realization that Paris was in the hands of the King's soldiers. Later on the citizen partisans of the League liked to remember with what prompt indignation Paris had sprung to arms: how the city had buzzed like an angry beehive, how the cobbler from his last, the merchant from his counting-house, the magistrate from his parlour, had boiled forth into the streets, each catching up whatever weapon was handiest — a sword, a pistol, a halberd, an arquebus, a club, a cleaver; how the chains had gone up in every quarter and the barricades had begun to rise like magic, men, women and children flinging themselves with fury into the work.

Actually it wasn't quite like that. Almost everywhere several hours elapsed before the first barricades rose. Although some of the Parisians had been preparing for a moment like this for several years the first reaction was a sort of stunned consternation, followed by frozen immobility. After all, no one had expected so many soldiers. The King had seized Paris by force. The least this could mean would be a series of prompt executions. It might mean worse — a selective massacre or a general sack. It was hard to say which was more alarming, the ribald mirth of the French Guards who shouted up at shuttered windows, 'Put clean sheets on your beds, bourgeois! We shall sleep with your wives tonight,' or the bland blankness of the huge Swiss. Paris shuddered.

What went up like lightning in those first hours were not barricades but shutters and bars on the shops and houses where they had been taken down. In the bright light of mid-morning the streets of Paris were empty, no figure to be seen in the open, no face at any window. The butchers around the Marché Neuf were no more eager to try conclusions with all those Swiss than were the peaceable burghers around the cemetery. Even the garrison of the Hôtel de Guise, though it was stuffed with men and munitions like a castle awaiting siege, did not venture out at first into the Rue Saint-Antoine, up and down which clattered casually a patrol of Aumont's horse.

Only one Parisian quarter prepared from the first to defend itself — the

Latin Quarter. When he heard that the King's guards were entering Paris Guise sent the comte de Brissac, the most violent and pugnacious of the Leaguer captains, with a band of Picard partisans to alert and reinforce the university. Brissac and his party crossed to the left bank well ahead of the royal troops and found Crucé, one of the Sixteen and colonel of his arrondissement, already issuing arms to a motley crowd of students, seminarians, monks, porters and watermen assembled in the Rue Saint-Jacques, most of them with white crosses on their hats in memory of St Bartholomew's, an affair in which their leader, Crucé, had played a great part.

When a mixed contingent of French Guards and Swiss under Crillon debouched from the Petit Pont and headed for the Place Maubert they found barricades already rising in the Rue Saint-Jacques — the nearest, under the protection of an armed party commanded by Brissac himself, almost across their path. Crillon would cheerfully have charged the unfinished barricade, swept the Rue Saint-Jacques from end to end and gone on to 'smoke the blackbirds of the Sorbonne out of their foul nests'. True, he had only a hundred pikemen and thirty arquebusiers, but they were professional soldiers and he was Crillon. He was not allowed to demonstrate what that meant. He had his orders, and could only glare angrily in answer to Brissac's taunts and lead his pikemen off to the left towards the Place Maubert.

They occupied it quietly enough; but before long, at either end of the barred and shuttered Carmelites, and at the mouth of every street opening into the great square, they saw other barricades going up. Brave Crillon, bound by specific orders, could only fume and exercise the vocabulary for which in an age of picturesque blasphemy he was famous, while he watched the barricades begin to block every exit from the Place Maubert. As for the Swiss, a number of the big good-natured fellows handed their pikes to their comrades and turned to to help the sweating civilians carry loads of cobblestones and heave the heavy barrels upright. As their captain explained later, they had been assured by Marshal Biron who had had it from His Majesty in person that their mission was to defend the people of Paris against armed foreigners. So far they had not seen any foreigners, but they were glad to see the Parisians willing to help in their own defence.

Later, the same scene was enacted wherever royal troops were posted. In most parts of the city the first barricades were erected at points prudently remote from any royal force, but as the apparatus of the Sixteen recovered from the shock of the morning and reassembled itself, and as the King's troops made no further hostile move — the mounted patrols even drawing rein courteously and turning back wherever they found people at work on a barricade — the courage of Paris quickened and presently the Parisians were boldly piling up their obstructions within a few yards of the peacefully lounging soldiers.

In the morning the King held Paris in the palm of his hand. By mid-afternoon it had been torn from his grasp. From his spy, Poulain, Henry had a list of all the chief Leaguers in Paris, knew where they lived, knew where they met, knew where their arms were stored. His strategically deployed troops could have controlled all the main lines of communication, keeping them open for loyal movements, denying them to the Leaguers and preventing any dangerous assembly except on the left bank — and there, if Crillon could not have handled the situation with the men he had, he could easily have been reinforced. A few files of pikemen would have sufficed to arrest the most dangerous pulpit demagogues, most of the Sixteen and their chief lieutenants. The three chief concentrations of Leaguer strength, the university, the Hôtel de Guise and the Hôtel de Montpensier, were isolated from one another by the royalist positions and could have been reduced one at a time or simply held under siege. The loyal judges of the Parlement of Paris would have been glad to deal with the rebel conspirators as they were brought in. But after he had assigned their stations Henry had only one further set of instructions to his men, repeating them emphatically to each unit as, sitting on his horse, he watched them pass through the Porte Saint-Honoré. They were to remember that they had been brought to Paris to protect it. On no account were they to injure in any way the person or the property of any citizen of Paris. If they did their lives should answer it. Henry thought a mere military demonstration would suffice to overawe his capital. He had forgotten that nothing is more dangerous than a show of force if no force may be used. One does not wave a pistol under the nose of an armed enemy and then let him know that it won't go off.

Only slowly did the Parisians make the exhilarating discovery that the King's troops wouldn't fight. By an hour past noon, except for the increasing number of barricades — most streets had them every thirty paces or so — there was no hostile gesture. What the troops noticed first was that the carts with their provisions had not come. They had been held up, of course, far off near the gates by the rising barricades, but there was no way of knowing that. Meanwhile the King's soldiers had no food, no wine, not even any water. Eventually this led to the only royalist act of indiscipline of the day. The Swiss and French Guards at the Marché Neuf began to gobble sausages and other edibles off the stalls.

Meantime the King was getting worried. All the morning he had been bland in the midst of excitement, obviously enormously pleased with his boldness and his cleverness. Then he began to hear about the barricades and to get increasingly anxious messages from his commanders. The streets were blocked in every direction, and though probably they could be cleared they couldn't be cleared now without serious fighting. The provisions had not come, and each detachment was cut off from the others. Finally Henry sent orders. There was to be an orderly withdrawal and retirement upon the Louvre, the most advanced units retiring first. Above all there was to be no bloodshed and no violence offered to the citizens of Paris. In spite of the barricades messengers were still getting back and forth from the Louvre, and all his commanders got their orders.

Probably the first shot was fired in the Place Maubert just as Crillon began to lead his detachment back to the Marché Neuf. By a Swiss, said the Leaguers; by a citizen, said the royalists. Whoever fired, he cannot have hit what he was aiming at. The bullet killed a non-combatant (a tailor? an upholsterer?) watching the scene from the doorway of his shop. Then the shooting began. Crillon's men cleared the first barricades easily enough, but in the tangle of narrow streets between the Place Maubert and the river they got into serious trouble; stones and tiles were hurled down on them, and the fire of small arms from upper windows and barricaded alleys became continuous. They emerged into the Rue Saint-Jacques only to find that the Petit Pont was barricaded against them and held by a mixed force of students and soldiers of the League, and to be fired upon from the Petit Châtelet. It must have been about this time that alarm bells were rung — first, perhaps, from St Julien-le-Pauvre with St Séverin and St André quickly following suit, and all the church towers of the left bank joining in and being answered by the sound of the tocsin from the city and from all the churches beyond the river.

What had happened at the carrefour Saint-Séverin was that Brissac had pushed another barricade right up against the Petit Châtelet, and at the first sound of firing from the Place Maubert had rushed the gatehouse, ejected its garrison, and from the little castle's platform had threatened the guards on the bridge with its wall-pieces. These troops, apparently leaderless except for a bewildered junior officer, had fallen back on the Marché Neuf.

Brissac's movement had at least left the carrefour Saint-Séverin empty for the moment of Leaguers, and Crillon led his column across the Rue Saint-Jacques and on towards the Pont Saint-Michel. Stones were still thrown and shots still fired from upper windows, and there may have been one or two barricades to cross — though they cannot have been stubbornly defended, for presently the contingent from the Place Maubert emerged on the river bank to find the Pont Saint-Michel empty of its friends but not yet held by its enemies, and, crossing it, were just in time to see the debacle of the main force.

At the Marché Neuf for the past several hours M. de Tinteville and others of the King's supporters, including apparently a municipal official or two, had been haranguing the surrounding citizens or arguing with them, assuring them the troops meant no harm to the city and trying to get them to pull down their barricades and disperse. They had enough success so that when Marshal Aumont came to order a general withdrawal (apparently he assumed, if he thought about it at all, that Crillon's contingent had joined the guard at the Petit Pont), the Swiss made the first few hundred yards of their retreat unharmed.

But the black-gowned orators of the League were screaming: 'Smite the Amalekites! Let none escape!' As they passed the Madeleine a cobblestone from a window stretched one Swiss on the pavement and at this success the stones fell faster. Then from the windows and roof-tops the arquebusiers opened fire. The clamour of alarm bells began to fill the air. The column blundered on, only to find after plunging into the Pont Nôtre-Dame that half-way across the passage was hopelessly blocked. From the tall houses that lined the bridge on both sides and overhung its passage 'they threw down on us', one Swiss captain wrote, 'great stones and blocks of wood and all manner of furniture. We found ourselves entangled among barricades while some gentlemen, accompanied by soldiers and an infinite number of people armed with arquebuses, fired on us as if we had been enemies of the king. All this time various strange monks cried out, inciting the people against us as if we had been Huguenots and desecrators of sacred objects.'

For a while the Swiss endured this bewildering onslaught of the people they had come to protect as if it were as senseless as a thunderstorm, as if it could not be true. Then, as they began to realize that it might easily go on until they were all killed, they threw down their arms and began to beg for mercy, crossing themselves, fishing out crucifixes, rosaries and scapulars to prove they were Catholics, calling out: 'Bon chrêtien! Bon

France! Bon Guise!' or any other scrap of conciliatory French they could think of. Presently Brissac came to rescue them from their assailants and to lead them, disarmed and prisoners, back to the Marché Neuf. There he took Crillon's surrender, too.

At the Place de Grève and at the Cemetery of the Holy Innocents the King's troops stood firm and returned the fire of their tormentors, so that they suffered almost no casualties, but as the crowds of citizens hemming them in grew in numbers and in fury it began to seem more and more doubtful whether they could cut their way back to the Louvre, and more and more likely that they would be butchered where they stood. At this point the chieftains of the Sixteen, beginning at last to feel themselves in control of the situation, sent an ironical message to the King to inform him of the plight of his troops, and Henry sent Biron to beg the Duke of Guise to save the lives of his men.

Guise had been in his *hôtel* all day. He had received two envoys there already. M. de Bellièvre had come in the morning to order him to quieten the people and withdraw with his partisans from Paris. The Queen Mother had come shortly after, perhaps from the King, more likely on her own initiative, hoping she might find him grateful for her intervention on Monday and so willing to negotiate some sort of peace. Guise shrugged off both embassies. He was sorry the people of Paris felt they had to defend themselves from their King, but what was going on in the streets was clearly no affair of his. One could see that he was not in arms, not leading an insurrection. He was resting peacefully in his own home. But to Henry's abject plea for an end to the killing, with its overtones of complete capitulation, Guise responded at once. Dressed just as he was, in white satin doublet and small-clothes and armed only with a riding-crop, he set off on his peaceful errand.

Once in the streets he was greeted like a conqueror. 'Vive Guise! Vive Guise!' And some cries of 'It's time to escort my lord to his coronation at Rheims! To Rheims!'

'Hush, friends,' said the duke, laughing, 'do you want to ruin me? Cry, rather "Vive le roi!"' And so with a growing crowd of adoring citizens around him he made his way first to the cemetery, then to the Place de Grève and finally to the Marché Neuf, ordering the barricades to be pulled down as he passed; and so, retracing his steps, brought the King's regiments back through the heart of the city, their arms restored but their colours cased, their matches extinguished, their weapons reversed and their music silent, like a surrendered garrison leaving a conquered town. Had anyone else tried to snatch their prey from under their noses now they had smelled blood the Parisians would have been furious. But Guise could do no wrong. The generous gesture only increased his popularity, and from the Marché Neuf all the way to the portals of the Louvre he moved in the midst of a storm of delirious cheering. If he had not been so before, from this day on Henry de Guise was King of Paris.

Paris slept little that night. Bonfires glowed in the streets and around them the armed citizenry sang Leaguer songs and recounted their recent prowess, or told each other of the great deeds they would do tomorrow. The Louvre slept less. In the courtyards and in the cavernous halls and kitchens of the ground floor weary soldiers dozed beside their arms; above, the rooms blazed with candles and cressets, and courtiers kept watch at windows and stairways with drawn swords. The King slept least of all. His mother had returned earlier in the evening from her second mission of the day to the Duke of Guise. Henry had been obliged to trust her; there was no one else he could trust, not even himself. But she who had returned so many times with some half-victory, snatched by patience and dexterity from the jaws of defeat, now brought back only a grim message. If Henry of Valois would dismiss his guards and his friends, alter the succession as the Catholics desired and surrender all the substance of his power into the hands of the Duke of Guise and the other great Leaguer lords, the duke would permit His Majesty to go on calling himself King of France. After he had heard his mother the King did not speak again for hours, but sat in the great audience chamber 'like the image of a dead man', tears trickling slowly down his cheeks, only now and then sighing to himself: 'Betrayed. Betrayed. So many treacheries.' So many indeed that Henry could not remember when they had begun, or how many of them had been his own. It was too late now to count or even to regret them.

No wonder Dr Cavriana, who observed from a respectful distance the King's misery, wrote that May 12th would be remembered as the saddest day in the history of France, and Estienne Pasquier who watched the growing crowds around the bonfires that night found that the day's events had changed his lifelong disbelief in astrologers, since Regiomontanus had so clearly predicted this unparalleled catastrophe. From whatever point of view one looked at it, May 12th was a historic occasion. In the first flush of his triumph, and with a generous disregard for pedantic accuracy, Guise wrote to one of his lieutenants: 'I have defeated the Swiss and a part of the royal guard, and am holding the Louvre so closely besieged that I expect to give a good account of all within it. This victory is so great that it will be remembered for ever.'

Some of his allies thought the victory less than complete. Throughout the night the iron-throated blackbirds of the League had been shouting to impromptu audiences that the time had come to finish with Vilain Herodes for ever. Brissac and Crucé and others of the Sixteen were of the same opinion, and before mid-morning the people of Paris, less drunken from the casks broached during the night than from the heady wine of victory, were pouring from every quarter towards the royal palace. The King watched the crowds increasing and judged their temper by their noise. He besought his mother to seek out Guise once more and beg him to quell the riot.

Guise was not sure what he could do. It was hard, he said, to pen in a herd of raging bulls. While Guise and Catherine talked barricades were already going up around the Louvre, eight hundred students from the Sorbonne under Brissac and four hundred armed monks were prepared to spearhead the assault. The cry began to go up: 'Come, let's fetch this bugger of a king from his Louvre.'

They were too late. Henry had learned one thing that Catherine did not know, that the noisy mob outside did not suspect, and that perhaps even Guise was not aware of. The Porte Neuve was unguarded. Not long after his mother had taken her departure the King with only a small group of his captains and councillors accompanying or following him, sauntered out of the unguarded New Gate at the end of the Louvre's gardens, cut rapidly across the gardens of the Tuileries to the stables, mounted and rode for Saint-Germain. His way wound up the Butte Montmartre and it was there he drew rein for a last look at his beloved city and an exercise of that pathetic eloquence which was one of his gifts. 'Farewell, Paris,' one of his attendants heard him say. 'I have honoured you above any place in my kingdom. I have done more for your wealth and glory than any ten of my predecessors, and I have loved you better than ever I loved wife or friend. Now you have repaid my love with treachery, insult and rebellion. But I shall be revenged on you'; and Henry swore a solemn oath: 'When next I enter you, it shall be through a breach in your walls.' Before dark the royal party crossed the Seine. They slept that night near Saint-Germain and the next day they were welcomed in Chartres.

Guise was still talking with the Queen Mother when he got word that the King had fled from the Louvre. 'Madame,' he cried, 'you gull me!

While you have kept me talking the King has quitted Paris and gone where he can stir up more trouble for me! I am a ruined man!' Perhaps Guise's consternation was genuine. But he may have thought that it would be too embarrassing to have the King on his hands, either as a prisoner or as a corpse, and equally embarrassing to have to protect him from his own Parisian allies who were determined to make him one or the other. Of the three Henrys, Henry of Guise had the fewest convictions, was the smoothest politician and the most likely to take a devious course to his goal. Also he was an experienced commander, and when he said he held a place straightly besieged he was unlikely to neglect a known means of entrance and egress. Yet somebody failed to order a guard on the Porte Neuve, or perhaps somebody ordered that it be left unguarded. Guise was confident that the King's power was broken, at any rate. From now on he was master of France.

Not everybody shared his confidence. When Alexander of Parma heard the first news of the revolt in Paris he ordered bonfires to be lit in celebration, but when he heard that Guise had rescued the Swiss from the people, failed to storm the Louvre and then, to cap it all, let the King escape, Parma shook his head. 'The Duke of Guise,' he said, 'has never heard our Italian proverb: "He who draws his sword against his prince should throw away the scabbard." '

If Bernardino Mendoza was worried about the King's escape from Paris he did not show it. Between the lines of his severely factual account of the Day of the Barricades one can read the pride of the craftsman in a difficult, complicated piece of work punctually and successfully accomplished. Whether Henry III knuckled under to Guise now or tried to oppose him scarcely mattered. Epernon could not hold Normandy now, and there was no longer the slightest danger that the French would molest the Low Countries in Parma's absence. Parma's flank was secured and so was Medina Sidonia's. As far as danger from France was concerned the Armada had sailed in perfect safety, just as Mendoza had promised that it should.

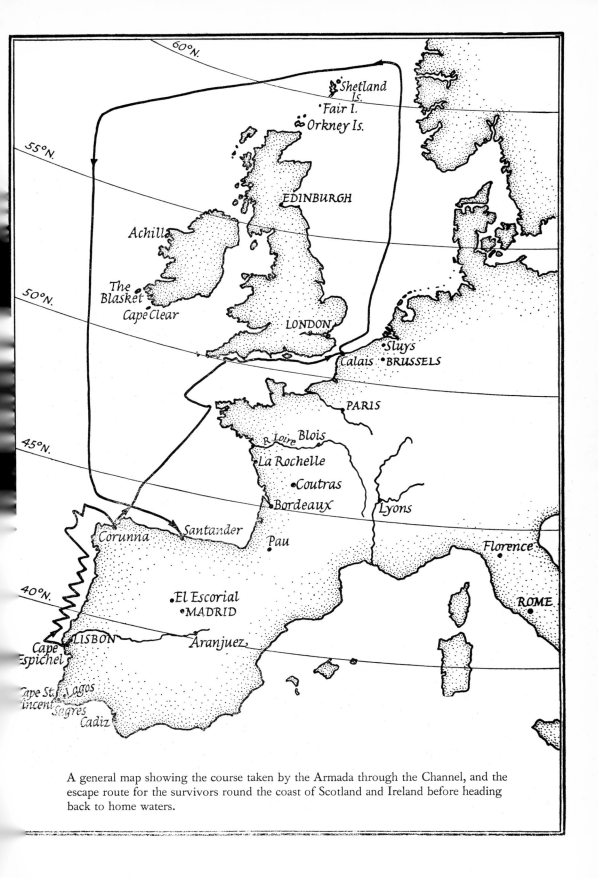

A general map showing the course taken by the Armada through the Channel, and the escape route for the survivors round the coast of Scotland and Ireland before heading back to home waters.

XX

THE INVINCIBLE SETS SAIL

LISBON TO CORUNNA, MAY 9TH – JULY 22ND, 1588

IN fact, when Mendoza wrote the Armada had not sailed at all. In spite of the expectant bustle ever since the duke had taken the blessed standard it was not until May 9th, the very day Guise entered Paris, that the last cask was stowed and the last conscript got aboard. That morning the ships began dropping down past Belem, but just inside the bar they had to cast anchor again and wait. The wind was blowing hard off the sea, right down the throat of the passage. It went on blowing, one gale following another — more like December, the harbour pilots told Medina Sidonia, than like May.

All along the Atlantic coast it was a strange May, almost as violent as the astrologers had promised. In Normandy, where Epernon drew back from assuming his government, unexampled hailstorms ravaged fields and orchards' and, so it was said, killed cattle in the fields. In Picardy, where Aumâle still knocked in vain at the gates of Boulogne, the rain turned roads to quagmires and brooks to impassable torrents. Off Flanders Howard and Seymour were jounced and shaken, and even the staunch Dutch warships, built for such waters and such work, were fain to run into Flushing and leave blockading Parma to the elements. Also blockaded by the elements, the Armada lay for almost three weeks anchored off Belem.

In the interval Philip had time to send his Captain General further news and instructions. The English fleet was said to be very weak. (That was Mendoza, relying on exaggerated reports of the charges against Hawkins.) Probably Drake would fortify himself in Plymouth (like almost everyone else on the Continent, Philip often spoke as if the English fleet were just an extension of Francis Drake) and either refuse battle altogether or sally out after the Armada had passed and take it in the rear when it was engaged with the other English fleet near Dunkirk. (Philip was well informed about the disposition of the English forces.) Perhaps Drake would wait to attack until the soldiers had been landed. The duke must be careful not to weaken his fleet too much before Drake was defeated. After he had made a junction with Parma he might at discretion attack the

English at sea or in their harbours, but before that, although he was not to avoid battle, he was not to seek it. Above all he was not to allow himself to be distracted from his appointed rendezvous, even if Drake threatened the coast of Spain.

Philip liked to anticipate every eventuality his subordinates might encounter, and give precise, specific instructions about dealing with each one. For instance, he several times informed his Captain General that the English ships would be faster than his and have more long-range guns, so they would prefer to keep their distances. (As if the duke hadn't been told this on every hand!) Therefore, the King went on firmly, the duke would have to recover the wind of the enemy, bear down on them and force them to fight at close quarters. What the King left out was any hint as to how to work this interesting trick. But if Philip's instructions were not always helpful his main intention was clear. The duke was to get on with it, meet Parma 'off the cape of Margate', cover his landing and protect his line of supply. The sooner the better.

By now Medina Sidonia was eager to be off. The Armada was as ready as it would ever be. Everything the experience of the most seasoned fighting-men in Europe suggested — everything, that is, within the realm of the possible — had been done. The fleet had been organized with professional expertness, primarily according to fighting and sailing capabilities, secondarily by region and language. The first line, the galleons, were in two strong squadrons — the galleons of Portugal, ten (counting the *Florencia*), and the galleons of Castile, also ten, somewhat smaller and less well armed than the Portuguese but reinforced by four great ships normally in the West India trade. These two squadrons were intended to act together, and before they reached the Channel the commander of the galleons of Castile, Diego Flores de Valdés, was aboard the *San Martín*, Medina Sidonia's flagship, acting as his Chief of Staff. Also rated in the first line were the four galleasses of Naples under Hugo de Moncada. They were a kind of hybrid warship, half galleon and half galley, fast, heavily gunned and capable of manœuvring with oars; great things were expected of them. The second line was composed of four squadrons of ten ships each, large merchantmen, some at least heavily armed — the Biscayans under Juan Martínez de Recalde, the Guipúzcoans under Miguel de Oquendo, the Andalusians under Pedro de Valdés, and the Levanters (from Venice, Ragusa, Genoa, Sicily, Barcelona) under Martin de Bertendona. There were also thirty-four light, fast ships, *zabras*, *fregatas* and *pataches* for scouting and dispatch-carrying, some of them attached to one or another of the fighting-squadrons; but one group kept together with a small galleon as its flagship, to act as a screen. Finally there was an unwieldy squadron of twenty-three *urcas*, 'hulks', freighters and supply ships, very few of which could be expected to look out for themselves in any kind of a fight, and four of the galleys of Portugal brought along at the last minute for reasons which remain to this day obscure. In all, one hundred and thirty ships, great and small.

We know a good deal about this Armada as it waited to sortie from Lisbon Harbour. Medina Sidonia had an elaborate report drawn up, not just the order of battle by squadrons but the name of each ship in every squadron, its estimated tonnage, the number of its guns, its sailors, its soldiers. For good measure he added the principal gentlemen-adventurers on each ship, listed by name with the number of their combatant servants, also the gunners, the medical corps, the friars and regular priests (one hundred and eighty of these), the organization of the *tercios* with a list of their officers and the strength of every company, the siege-train, the field-guns, the small-arms of all kinds, the total supply of powder (all fine-corned arquebus powder, he noted proudly), the number of cannon balls of all weights (123,790), the lead for bullets, the match. The report also listed provisions, biscuit, bacon, fish, cheese, rice, beans, wine, oil, vinegar, water, in so many thousands or tens of thousands of hundredweights, or in so many pipes and tuns and casks. Even if the figures are not all accurate (and they certainly were not), the quantity of detailed information is greater than we have about any other fleet of the sixteenth century; and even if the total strength adds up to less than half the fleet and army Santa Cruz had wanted for the Enterprise, it still looks in the pages of description like a very formidable force indeed. In the official publication embodying all these figures the fleet is called 'La felicissima armada', 'the most fortunate fleet', but popular parlance at once substituted 'invincible' in tribute to its awesome strength. Thanks to the Spanish taste for irony this armada has been known as 'La Invencible' ever since.

It seems odd that Medina Sidonia's detailed report should have been published. Today such a document would be classified 'Top Secret' until long after its last item was well known to the enemy, and even in those days Walsingham's agents had been working hard to collect some scraps of its wealth of information. But published it was, with relatively few changes, all exaggerations of its strength, at Lisbon only ten days after it was drawn up and while the invasion fleet still lay in the Tagus. Two weeks later there was another edition at Madrid with official 'corrections'.

Thence it spread to Rome, to Paris, to Delft, to Cologne, so rapidly that copies were for sale in Amsterdam before the *San Martín* had raised the Lizard. Protestant printers added to the dull lists of pikes and corslets, fish and biscuits, whatever whips and chains, gridirons and pincers, racks and thumbscrews they thought their public would demand, and enterprising publishers kept the whole thing standing in type to be used over again whenever a fresh rumour gave the excuse for another leaflet about the Spanish fleet. Naturally, along with the embellishments of fancy, some of the later editions contained misprints of figures and quaint errors of fact, but basically even the least accurate still gave a fair idea of the information supplied to the King and the Council of War and printed with official approval at Madrid. Howard and his captains, if they had wanted to take the trouble, could have carried with them into action reasonably accurate copies of the enemy's order of battle, based on information supplied by the enemy. Burghley did have a copy. We can only conclude that the Council of War at Madrid believed that the propaganda value of their show of strength would do more good than the disclosure of the information could do harm. Perhaps, at last, they had absorbed some of their master's sublime confidence.

For the moment the Duke of Medina Sidonia was as confident as anyone. He was impressed by the perfection of organization he and his staff had achieved. They had worked out the signals and other means of communication between squadrons, arranged their rendezvous points, and created a set of sailing orders and one of fighting instructions. They had divided the most experienced pilots so that every squadron commander had at least several, Spaniards and Bretons, Dutchmen and renegade Englishmen, who were familiar with the Channel and the North Sea. They had compiled, multiplied and distributed to every ship a set of sailing directions which, though silent about the east coast north of the Thames estuary and deceptive about Ireland, was, for the stretch from the Scilly Isles to Dover, about as good as anything going, with landmarks, harbour entrances, soundings, tides and notes of at least some of the principal reefs and dangers. And before they got the King's warning about Drake's probable tactics they had devised a special formation to meet just such a contingency. The duke proudly sent his master a diagram. Whether all this professional efficiency did more to increase Medina Sidonia's confidence than the assurance he received from a very holy friar that God would give Spain the victory, no one knows now. Perhaps what counted most was simply that this fleet he commanded, ready at last to meet the enemy, its new-built fighting castles glistening with fresh paint, its banners snapping from the mast-heads, its decks thronged with handsome cavaliers, looked gay and gallant and altogether invincible.

As soon as the weather moderated enough to make it feasible, therefore, the duke began to work out of Lisbon river. On May 28th, his flagship the *San Martín* in the lead, the royal galleons of Portugal passed Castle St Julian, replying in turn to the fort's salutes. By May 30th, in spite of fitful and contrary winds, the whole Armada was standing out to sea, close-hauled to a north-north-west breeze with the hulks making so much leeway that, if it kept together, the fleet would be south of Cape Espichel before it had sea room for a new tack.

The fleet did keep together, but that meant, as its commander soon realized, 'governing our progress by the speed of the most miserable tub among us'. A good many of the hulks proved to be crank and sluggish sailers, so that by June 1st, after being at sea for forty-eight hours, the flagship was still south-south-west of the Rock of Lisbon, total distance made good since clearing the bar, perhaps fifteen sea-miles. Thereafter, beating their way up the Spanish coast turned out to be weary work. The weather was unhelpful. Sometimes the winds boxed the compass in the course of a day, blowing from the east, the south, the west, the north and round to the east again. Sometimes there was no wind at all and the great fleet drifted idly, without steerage-way, its sails flapping, rolling helplessly with the long Atlantic swells. Sometimes there were sudden furious squalls, as likely as not from the least convenient quarter. With such weather and with such a heterogeneous fleet it took thirteen days from the Rock of Lisbon to Finisterre, a distance of a little more than one hundred and sixty sea-miles.

There was only one offset to the exasperation of this inchworm progress: it might give an opportunity to remedy the defect in his preparations that Medina Sidonia was now most worried about — provisions. Vast stores of foodstuffs, as sixteenth-century Spain reckoned such things, had been concentrated at Lisbon; but in the long winter's delay much had been consumed, and it was only human to eat first what had come in most recently. After he took over the duke had tried to enforce the rule that the barrels and bags longest aboard or longest in the water-front warehouses should be opened first. Whether or not his orders had been obeyed he could only guess, but as May grew warmer and the fleet still lay in the river more and more ships reported spoilage. The prospect was becoming alarming. Up to the last minute the duke was sweeping the Portuguese countryside, and appealing to Madrid for more food. When he weighed anchor he left orders that as further supplies came in they should be sent after him at once. He had already begged that whatever provisions could be got together in the northern ports should be put aboard victuallers who could meet him somewhere off Finisterre, so that the Armada could replenish its stores at sea.

For four days the fleet hung about in the neighbourhood of Finisterre looking for the tardy victuallers, and in this time another alarming situation developed. Practically every squadron reported some of its ships short of water. Even though the water-casks had been stowed over a month before there should still have been ample water for another three or four months, but many of the casks seemed defective and what water remained in them was too often already green and stinking. It was easy to guess that from now on every time another cask was broached the chances of its contents proving potable would be less. At a regular Council of War it was the unanimous opinion of the 'generals', the squadron commanders, that the whole fleet ought to put in to Corunna, to pick up what provisions it could — but, above all, to water.

That was on Sunday, June 19th, twenty days after the Armada had left Lisbon. By the time Medina Sidonia's flagship had found its anchorage the sun was already low, and it was agreed among the commanders that rather than try to complete the operation in darkness the part of the fleet farthest from the entrance should stand out to sea and cruise back and forth until daylight. Some fifty-odd ships, great and small, reached the harbour before dark; the slower sailers, nearly all the hulks and most of the Levanters with, to look after them, Recalde's squadron, plus six or seven galleons, the four galleasses and some light craft, turned away and stood out beyond the headlands. The evening was sultry, with fitful variable airs.

Sometime after midnight there came howling out of the south-west the worst tempest of that abominable season. Even in the sheltered harbour of Corunna one ship tore loose from its anchorage, and a pinnace dragged its anchor and collided with a galleon. Fortunately the ships still at sea had some hundreds of leagues of open water to leeward and could run before the storm. There was nothing else they could do. As they ran, they scattered.

On the afternoon of the twenty-first the weather had abated enough so that the duke could send out some of his pinnaces to look for the scattered ships. He had already sent couriers along the coast and presently got word that de Leiva with ten ships, hulks, Levanters and a pinnace, had straggled into the near-by port of Vivero, and two of the galleasses had found shelter in Gijon. The next day Juan Martínez de Recalde appeared with two galleons and eight other ships, but the situation remained pretty grim. On the twenty-fourth two galleasses and twenty-eight other major ships were still missing, including the Florentine galleon, one of the galleons of Castile, and the two best ships of Recalde's squadron. Six thousand soldiers and sailors were on them out of a total of only about twenty-two thousand effectives, and of the remaining sixteen thousand many were ill, some with ship's fever, more with scurvy and dysentery from the spoiled food. Most of the ships that had ridden out the storm were badly battered, many were leaking, with spars and masts carried away, anchors lost and other damages.

Since he had left Lisbon Medina Sidonia had become increasingly disillusioned with the force he commanded. In the slow climb up the coast every day had revealed fresh defects. The worst weakness was the food. New reports of spoilage came in daily. Obviously too many of the casks, both for food and water, had been dishonestly made of green wood. The duke was too angry to reflect that, like everybody else in that confused disorderly winter in which he had taken command, the contractors may have done the best they could. Probably they could get nothing better than green pipe-staves. Over the fleet lying at Corunna hung the pall of Drake's bonfires at Cape St Vincent the year before. The seasoned staves that should have guarded the Armada's food and drink had been cold ashes now for a twelvemonth.

Reviewing the situation the duke sat down to write a difficult letter. He reminded His Most Catholic Majesty of the misgivings he had expressed when he first took command at Lisbon, and even before. In part, these misgivings had arisen from the fact that even an optimist could reckon the force assembled at Lisbon as no more than barely equal to the task assigned, though it was axiomatic that the fate of kingdoms ought not to be risked on an evenly balanced trial of strength. Now that the storm had scattered the fleet the strength he could muster was much less, and there was grave reason to fear that some, at least, of the missing ships had succumbed to the elements or would fall prey to French and English corsairs. It seemed almost unbelievable, he added gently, that such a mishap should befall in the month of June, the best sailing month of the year, and to a fleet sailing in God's cause. (Mishaps and frustrations in the past six weeks seem to have lessened the duke's willingness to rely on miracles.)

Besides the number of ships missing, he went on, and the damage to those he had reassembled (itemized lists of both enclosed), his manpower was much depleted by illness, and the position in regard to food and water was worse than he had thought possible. In view of all these things, he wrote, and of Parma's report that his own effective strength was scarcely more than half what it had been the previous October, he besought His Majesty to consider whether it would not be better to reach terms of peace with England or at least to defer the Enterprise for another year.

Philip's reply was prompt and firm. The duke would do his best to remedy the defects he had mentioned. Some might prove beyond remedy, and he might be obliged to sail with a weaker force than he had expected. But in any event he was to sail at the first opportunity. There was no change in his instructions.

One does not know which to wonder at more, the courage and intelligence of the duke's letter or the blind confidence of the King's reply. For a Spanish gentleman of the golden age to suggest that he be relieved of leading an assault, however desperate, took moral courage of a kind as unusual in that century as the courage to lead such assaults was usual. And no one had ever given Philip, or was ever to give him again, so straightforward and sensible an estimate of the situation into which he was heading. But it was more than a year since the Prudent King had paid any attention to prudent advice. He seemed to hear nothing now but 'Forward, in God's name!', and his letter to his admiral was merely another repetition of the same command.

At least he did not make the mistake of some subsequent historians. He did not take the duke's letter as a proof that Medina Sidonia was either a fool or a coward, or in any way unfit for his command. Nor is there any evidence from the halt at Corunna to justify such an opinion, or to indicate that any of the admiral's subordinates held it. The duke did not share his misgivings with the Council of War which he summoned as soon as de Leiva rejoined. It was unnecessary to review the situation with these veterans. He merely asked them whether the fleet should go out to try to collect the missing ships or sail straight for England, or remain in Corunna and wait for the stragglers to rejoin. His officers replied as was the custom, in reverse order of seniority, soldiers and sailors speaking as their turn came. Almost unanimously they voted for the third course. It would be better to stay in Corunna, refit, take on what food and water they could, and hope that most of the missing might still come in. One squadron commander dissented. Pedro de Valdés, 'general' of the Andalusian squadron, wanted to sail at once because he thought there was little hope of replacing the spoiled provisions and held that the situation would only get worse the longer they waited. His opinion was duly recorded at length, and in addition he wrote a personal letter to the King (naval correspondence did not go 'through channels' in those days), reiterating his arguments and saying that he feared that his obstinacy had offended the admiral. But even he did not suggest that his commander was either incompetent or afraid.

It was a month after the storm before the fleet was finally ready, but on the whole the delay seems to have been worth it. All really necessary repairs were completed; as many ships as possible had been careened, caulked and tallowed. Some additional provisions, biscuits and salt fish had been found in the Biscay ports, and, if less than had been hoped for, at least the diet of fresh meat, vegetables and fresh bread on which the men were kept spared the remaining stores and did wonders for their health. One of the duke's first measures had been to set up a hospital ashore for his fever cases. The threatened epidemic was checked, and the complements of soldiers and mariners brought back to something like their full effective strength, with no more than the normal amount of cheating on the muster rolls.

Best of all, the last of the missing ships finally straggled in. Two groups had been as far as the Channel, one had cruised between the Scilly Isles and the Lizard, taken a couple of prizes and looked in at Mounts Bay, oddly enough without seeing an English ship of war. The other, just before it ran before a north wind back to Corunna, had caught glimpses of what may have been Drake's main body. Altogether the situation by July 21st had been restored to something like that of two months before, and though the duke was still worried — rightly worried as it proved — about those leaky casks, in some respects he felt better prepared than he had been at Lisbon. When, with a brisk south wind filling its sails, the Armada finally steered for England Medina Sidonia had recovered a mood of cautious optimism.

XXI

'THE ADVANTAGE OF TIME AND PLACE'

PLYMOUTH, THE SLEEVE AND BISCAY TO 45° N
APRIL 18TH – JULY 30TH, 1588

UNSEASONABLE weather and inadequate stores worried the English captains as much as they did the Spaniards. The Queen's ships, all in full commission by April, were provisioned by a hand-to-mouth system, or lack of system — a month's ration at a time and no more until the last supply had almost run out. From Margate the Lord Admiral wrote in desperation: 'We shall now be victualled beginning the 20th of this April unto the 18th of May ... [According to reports] the likeliest time for the coming out of the Spanish forces is the midst of May, being the 15th. Then we have three days' victual. If it be fit to be so, it passes my reason.' And he went on to say how much better things had been managed in the days of 'King Henry, her Majesty's father'.

Howard was wrong about his history but quite right about his logistics, and Lord Burghley, to whom he wrote, would have known that even if things had never been managed much differently they ought to be now. The difficulty was not a lack of goodwill on Burghley's part or on the Queen's. It was not, whatever Francis Drake sometimes darkly suspected, a matter of treachery, of a gullible sovereign and deceitful councillors. It was not even want of money, or reluctance to spend it. It was simply lack of the facilities and organization to provide very large quantities of food and drink fit to be kept for months aboard ship. The naval effort of 1588 was as unprecedented in England as it was in Spain, and the English had less experience than the Spanish in provisioning large expeditions. To keep a great fleet supplied with rations for two or three months ahead, when its crews go on eating up what you send them, requires an organization not to be improvised on the spur of the moment.

With the coming of spring Drake was impatient to be off again. He heard and apparently believed that in Lisbon Harbour the King of Spain had between four and five hundred ships, manned by eighty thousand mariners and soldiers. Nevertheless, with four more of the Queen's galleons of the middling sort and some London ships, enough to bring his

1. Augusti 1588

We whose names are hereunder written have determyned and agreede in counsaile to folowe and pursue the Spanishe flete untill wee have cleared oure owne coaste and broughte the Frithe weste of us And then to returne backe agayne aswell to revictuall oure shipps which stand in extreame scarsitie as alsoe to guard and defend oure owne coaste at home with further protestatione that if oure wantes of victualles and munitione were supplied we wold ~~suppl~~ pursue them to the furthest that they durst have gone.

C. Howard George Cumberland

Thomas Howard Edmond Sheffeylde

Fra: Drake Edw Hoby

John Hawkyns

Thomas Fenner

1° Augusti. Determyned by the counsaile to returne from the pursuite of the fleete

Resolution by a Council of War to pursue the Armada northwards, August 1st, 1588.

strength up to fifty sail, he was ready to try to stop the Spaniards in their own waters. Not that he thought he could repeat the exploit of Cadiz Bay at Lisbon, but as he later told an Italian journalist-historian he meant so to blockade the coast that the Spanish fleet could not come out of the river with any comfort, or if it did come out he would attack it and harass it so that it would never reach England. Somehow — still according to what he told Petruccio Ubaldini — the blockade was to be combined with 'attacking several different places along the coast', which would stimulate the courage of the English, since it is safer to fight far from home than near it, and what must be avoided above all was letting the Armada get into the Channel where it could be joined by Parma. His confidence that he could do all this with fifty ships, if Ubaldini quoted him correctly, was because 'he knew (without self-flattery) what great fear his name inspired all along the coast of Spain'.

The terror of his name probably was his chief reliance. He certainly believed, and he had some reason for believing, that with El Draque on their coasts the Spaniards would never dare sail for England, and that he could combine a profitable summer of freebooting a-sea and ashore with a game of hide-and-seek with the Spanish fleet, the sort of game he played to perfection. At best such a game might give him a chance to defeat the Spaniards in detail; at worst it should tire them out and keep them too busy to think of assailing England.

Or, at least, so we must conjecture his plan. He did not make it very clear to Ubaldini and, on the evidence of his surviving letters, he made it even less clear to Queen Elizabeth. When he thought that he was at last going to be allowed to sail he replied to her inquiry as to how he intended to distress the fleet in Lisbon that he could not tell. So far two things were uncertain, the strength of the enemy and 'the resolution of our own people which I shall better understand when I have them at sea, ... for one flying now as Borough did [at Cadiz] will put the whole in peril, for that the enemy's strength is now so greatly gathered together'. But if Drake did not clarify the details of his plan (probably he had no detailed plan, but relied on the luck and the inspiration which had never failed him), he did reveal another source of his confidence. 'Touching my poor opinion how strong your Majesty's fleet should be to encounter this great force of the enemy's, God increase your most excellent Majesty's forces both by sea and land daily; for this I surely think: there was never any force so strong as there is now ready or making ready against your Majesty and true religion; but ... the Lord of all strengths is stronger and will defend the truth of his word ... ' In some ways Drake and Philip were a good deal alike.

If Drake did not know just what he was going to do he was quite clear that he was the man to do it, and where and when. 'Your Majesty shall stand assured,' he says in the same letter, 'if the fleet come out of Lisbon, as long as we have victual to live upon that coast, with God's assistance, they shall be fought with ... The advantage of time and place in all martial actions is half a victory; which being lost is irrecoverable ... Wherefore, if your Majesty will command me away with those ships which are here already, and the rest to follow with all possible expedition, I hold it, in my poor opinion, the surest and best course; ... ' So far, Drake, the naval genius and religious enthusiast. Then follows, for the rest of what Drake thought was a sentence, Drake the practical commander: 'And that they [the rest who were to follow] bring with them victuals sufficient for themselves and us, to the intent the service be not utterly lost for the want thereof ... for an Englishman, being far from his country and seeing a present want of victuals to ensue, and perceiving no benefit to be looked for but only blows, will hardly be brought to stay.'

This was written just two days before Medina Sidonia took the standard from the altar of Lisbon Cathedral. But neither the victuals nor the reinforcements were forthcoming for more than a month, both prevented by the same kind of violent and unseasonable gales that held the Spanish immobile in the mouth of the Tagus. It seems unlikely that Drake could have got as far as Lisbon in such weather, unlikely that he could have cleared Land's End and Ushant even if he had managed to work out of Plymouth Sound, but he despised the opposition of the elements as much as he dreaded the devious human intrigues which in his view always beset his way, and he went on arguing for an immediate descent on the Spanish coast in urgent letters and in at least one personal appearance at Court while the Queen changed her mind and changed it back again.

For how much of this time he was preaching to the converted it is hard to say now. Hawkins had always been of his opinion, and most of the navy board and the senior commanders afloat had come round to it. At first Howard had preferred a defensive stance, but sometime in May — if not in April — he had adopted the view of the majority, and thereafter he argued for it as energetically as Drake did himself. Finally, reluctantly, the Queen herself began to consider that the fighting-men might after all be right, and that the advantage of time and place, in which was half a victory, might be found on the coast of Spain.

In the light of what we know now some doubt is permissible. In one thing Drake was quite wrong: Medina Sidonia had express orders not to be diverted by any English offensive, but to sail for the Channel and his rendezvous with Parma no matter what Drake did. If Drake had relied on the alarm caused by his appearance in person on the coast of Spain to keep the Spanish fleet at home he might have missed the Armada altogether. He seems, besides, to have been as mistaken about the nature of the unprecedented battle to come as were the rest of the veterans of both navies. Like Santa Cruz he was prepared to sail to meet the enemy with thirty rounds of ammunition per gun. In the actual encounter the English had spent more than that before they had done the Armada any real damage. Off Weymouth they were able to remedy their miscalculation; if they had been off Lisbon instead they would have been in serious trouble. English ships and English seamen being what they were, barring some appalling piece of bad luck it seems unlikely that Drake's squadron could have been badly hurt. On the other hand, unless he was favoured by some remarkable accident it seems equally unlikely that with fifty ships or even more Drake could have done much to delay the Armada's advance. If he had encountered the Spanish at sea Drake would, if we may judge by what happened later, simply have fired off all his ammunition without disturbing the Armada's formation, and then been obliged to run before them back to a home port. In the circumstances this would have been an English defeat, damaging to morale at the very least, and perhaps upsetting the favourable balance of forces in the Channel.

Wisdom after the event is easy, but in the spring of 1588 none of the naval experts on either side foresaw much of what was to come. The size of the forces involved and the nature of their armament were unprecedented. No naval campaign in previous history, and none afterward until the advent of the aircraft carrier, involved so many fresh and incalculable factors. At the time the best English naval opinion agreed with Drake, and it was more bad weather and tardy victualling than it was anybody's prudence that kept him from risking battle off the coast of Portugal instead of in the Channel.

In one way Drake's argument for an offensive had been too effective. He had asked for eight royal galleons and a total of fifty ships. That was about the largest independent command he could hope for. Instead, the Queen decided to commit the bulk of her forces, fourteen of her heaviest galleons and most of the armed merchantmen and volunteers. That automatically made the commander the Lord Admiral. Perhaps the Queen, much as she admired Drake, felt that with Howard in charge the operation would be less likely to turn into a buccaneering expedition. Or perhaps she merely took the sensible view that if everything was going to be risked on an offensive it ought to be as strong as possible. Drake accepted gracefully the post of Vice-Admiral which Howard bestowed on him, and during the next months there is no trace of any friction between them. But from what Drake said to Ubaldini afterwards it is clear that he was disappointed.

Howard's arrival at Plymouth and the ceremony of Drake's hoisting his flag as Vice-Admiral of the combined fleets did not take place until May 23rd (O.S.), June 2nd by the new calendar. On that day Medina Sidonia had beaten his way almost thirty sea-miles north of the Rock of Lisbon, his best day's run so far — though no one in England, of course, knew that he was yet at sea. Howard had been delayed by bad weather; he was to be delayed still further, just as Medina Sidonia was, by laggard victuallers, then by changes in his orders, then by bad weather again, by the alarm occasioned by the appearance of ships of the scattered Spanish fleet in the approaches of the Sleeve, by a real indecision as to what position to take up when the Spaniards might be aiming at any target from the west of Ireland to Dunkirk, and by the Queen's renewed reluctance to let her fleet go off to Spain when the Spanish might be, for all anyone knew, already on her doorstep.

Three weeks after he joined Drake, Howard, cooped up in Plymouth Sound by the same gale that had dispersed the Spaniards, was still appealing for a free hand and for more food. It was a dark plot of the Spaniards, he believed, to delay and keep them in uncertainty until their rations were all spent and they would be obliged to demobilize the fleet because they could not feed it. Had he realized how like his worries were to Medina Sidonia's, who that same day was writing his painful letter to King Philip advising the abandonment of the Enterprise, it might have been some comfort to him. But no one in England knew anything of the Spaniards except a mass of contradictory rumours. So Howard fretted away another three weeks, 'plying up and down' as the Queen directed him to do in some indifferent place from which he could cover all the approaches to England, Scotland and Ireland (Howard protested angrily that there was no such place), chasing phantom Spanish squadrons reported from off Ushant or from the Scilly Isles, fuming at the non-appearance of the expected victuallers, and growing more and more concerned about the health and morale of his crews.

Then, suddenly, everything brightened. Definite intelligence came in that the bulk of the Spanish fleet, after being scattered and badly mauled by the storm, had reunited at Corunna. From London came warrants and victuals and word from the Queen that the fleet might, if it seemed best, go and seek the Spaniards in their own ports. And a fair fresh wind sprang up from the north-east. Howard and Drake and Hawkins did not even finish loading stores. They spread their sails and were off for a quick run to the Spanish coast, some ninety-odd armed ships, great and small, a gallant and valorous armada.

Five days later they were back in Plymouth Sound. In the middle of the Bay of Biscay, some two-thirds of the way between Ushant and Corunna, the wind had perversely hauled round to the south, a fair wind for England but the foulest possible for Spain. If they tried to beat their way against it the Spanish fleet might be sighting Land's End before the English had rounded Finisterre. There was nothing for it but to turn and run back again. As they dropped their anchors in Plymouth Harbour, Medina Sidonia was weighing his at Corunna. That was on July 22nd.

In the next week at Plymouth, Drake and Howard were having the same troubles that the Spanish had been having. Though the Queen's ships, to Howard's delight and no doubt to Hawkins's less vocal satisfaction, had proved staunch enough, some of the merchantmen had strained themselves and sprung leaks in the rough weather of the past seven weeks, and some needed new spars and cordage. Although messes had been scanted six to four, six men being served four men's rations, some ships were short of food and a good many were short of water. And, surest sign of a fleet that had been too long at sea, some ships had much sickness. One of the first tasks was to get the men stricken with fever ashore and to appeal to the justices of the peace in Devonshire and the adjacent counties for fresh recruits. There was no time to clean and rummage the ships properly but what could be done was done, and the fresh stores, ammunition and provisions were got aboard with all convenient speed. There was talk that the Spaniards had given up the Enterprise for this year and that the fleet would soon be partially decommissioned, beginning with the four biggest and most expensive of the Queen's ships, but there is no sign that any of this affected the tempo of preparations at Plymouth.

Then on Friday, July 29th (July 19th, O.S.), after dinner, Captain Thomas Fleming, of the bark *Golden Hind*, one of the screen assigned to cruise in the mouth of the Channel, arrived to report that he had sighted a large group of Spanish ships near the Scilly Isles with sails struck, apparently waiting for the rest of the fleet to come up. According to the legend Drake was playing bowls on Plymouth Hoe when Fleming brought the news. Presumably Howard was there too, since Fleming although attached originally to Drake's western squadron would have reported to the Lord Admiral, not to Drake; but there is little room in the legend of the Armada for anyone but Drake. At any rate, in the legend it is Drake who replied (one fancies the leisurely bowler's stance as he hefts his wood and eyes the jack, one hears the echo of the west-country drawl): 'We have time enough to finish the game and beat the Spaniards, too.'

Of course, it need not have happened. There is no contemporary authority for it; the earliest record is more than forty years after the event. But forty years is within the limits of fairly reliable oral transmission. It could have happened. The words are like Drake; they have his touch of swagger and his flair for the homely jest to relieve a moment of tension. Also it would be quite like Drake to say the first word, even though his commander-in-chief stood at his elbow. And finally, it would be like Drake, too, to appreciate a second or two before any of the others and be amused by the fact that there was indeed time.

Fleming cannot have made his report much before three o'clock in the afternoon. He had sighted the Spaniards only that morning and can have come scarcely less than ninety sea-miles since. Now at about three o'clock that afternoon the tidal stream would begin flooding into Plymouth Sound, building up even with a neap-tide a current of well over a knot. No one was going to try to get out of Plymouth against a south-west breeze with that tide running, and in fact no one did. The fighting-fleet, the Queen's galleons in the lead, did not begin to warp out of the Sound until the freshening of the ebb after ten that night. There was plenty of time to finish a game of bowls.

The Spaniards had achieved a kind of tactical surprise. It would be possible to say that for the moment they had the advantage of time and place which should be half the victory. They had the weather-gauge and their enemy was trapped in harbour to leeward. But it would be easy to exaggerate the completeness of the surprise. Fleming's warning had come in good time, as given the position of the screen, the skill of its skippers and the speed and weatherliness of its ships, there was every reason to suppose it would. The English fleet was in as full a state of readiness as was compatible with the fact that some ships, mostly it would seem the smaller merchantmen, were still loading stores. Howard's words, 'The southerly wind that brought us back from the coast of Spain brought them out. God blessed us with turning us back', do not sound as if he had been very surprised, and indeed it would be odd if he and his Council of War had not foreseen the possibility of just this development, and expected it as confidently as one can expect anything in a naval war. No matter how quick and bold the Spaniards were, they could scarcely be quick and bold enough. This tide now running as the last bowl curved towards the jack would be the last on which the enemy could catch the Queen's fleet in Plymouth Harbour.

At nightfall, with scant wind and an ebb-tide, the royal galleons and the heaviest and best-armed of the merchant ships began warping out of Plymouth Sound and anchoring in the lee of Rame Head. The next day the wind freshened from the south-west; but Howard, when all the ships that would be coming out on the late morning ebb had joined, to avoid being caught by the enemy on a lee shore, began to beat out to sea and led fifty-four sail to leeward of the Eddystone. The whole thing was a considerable feat of seamanship, but Howard dismisses it in a sentence and nobody else found it worth mentioning. After all, the fleet had been going in and out of Plymouth under all sorts of conditions for the past two months. Probably they thought more of the promise that they would not have to go back in again until they had seen the Spaniards.

Weymouth
(Aug.3)

The Shambles
Portland Bill
(Aug. 2)

Fowey   Plymouth   Tor Bay

Dodman
Point
(July 30)
(July 31)

Scilly Is.   Start Point

Eddystone

The Lizard
(July 29, 4 p m)

E N G L I S H

The Sleeve

Ushant

An outline map showing the phases of the battle between the Spanish and English fleets.

NORTH

SEA

Harwich

LONDON
Tilbury
Greenwich
Richmond
Rochester
Margate (Aug.) Straits (Aug.9)
The Flushing
W. Scheldt
Dover
(Aug.6-7)
Ostend
Nieuport
Sluys
Calais
Dunkirk Dixmude
Gravelines
Boulogne

The Owers

CHANNEL

Dieppe

Le Havre
Rouen

PARIS

The Battle in The Narrow Seas
— July 29ᵗʰ to August 9ᵗʰ 1588 —

The bold line on the map shows the Armada's approximate course with the dates
on which it passed important points.

XXII

ENTRANCE TO THE ARENA

THE LIZARD TO THE EDDYSTONE, JULY 30TH–31ST, 1588

At daybreak on Saturday, July 30th, when all the English who could warp out of Plymouth before the next ebb were already anchored behind Rame Head, the greater part of the Spanish Armada was still hull down to the Lizard. Its voyage from Corunna had not been without incident. The first four days had been pleasant with a fair breeze, and the only vexation the necessity of plodding along with shortened sail so as not to walk away from the wretched hulks. Unencumbered by them the other divisions of the fleet — even the Levantine carracks — could probably, their commander thought, have been in the Channel by this time.

Even so, they were almost as high as Ushant when on the morning of the fifth day, Tuesday, July 26th, the wind dropped and the fleet drifted, becalmed, under a lowering sky. That lasted until noon; then it began to blow hard out of the north with blinding rain squalls, violent but short. The fleet, more spread out but keeping together, bore away westward to get sea room. Already the galleys, too long and low and narrow for the waves of Biscay, were having trouble. One of them, the *Diana*, soon sent word that she had strained her seams, was leaking badly and wanted permission to drop out and try to get back to a friendly port. In granting it Medina Sidonia extended the same permission to the other galley captains if in their opinion the heavy seas were overstraining their ships, but they hung doggedly on through the gathering darkness.

In the night the wind hauled round to west-north-west and increased in violence; by morning it was blowing a full gale with mountainous seas and poor visibility. Still the Armada kept together, under storm canvas, guiding on the *San Martín* and making what northing it could. All day the gale blew, and on until after midnight with unabated violence. Then it began to slacken, so that day broke bright and clear with no more than a stiff breeze and the seas going down. When the duke surveyed his fleet he found that not only had the galleys parted company but forty sailing-ships as well, all the Andalusians, a good many of the hulks and odd ships from several other squadrons.

The pilots heaved the lead and reported seventy-five fathoms and so — checking the sounding against the kind of sand and shell on the bottom — a position about seventy-five leagues south of the Scilly Isles. The duke resumed his northward course, still with shortened sail, sending off one pinnace to see how many ships had already reached the rendezvous, another to warn any laggards to catch up and a third for general reconnaissance. Presently the first came back to say that the missing sailing-ships were ahead, waiting off the Scillies under the command of Pedro de Valdés, and late in the afternoon of the next day, Friday, July 29th, the fleet that had sailed from Corunna was reunited.

All, that is, but five ships. Four were the galleys. Of these, three finally made different ports, battered but navigable. The fourth, the *Diana*, which had parted earliest, stranded trying to get into Bayonne. Her crew, even her galley slaves, and her guns were saved, but the hull had to be broken up. Among the galley slaves was an imaginative Welshman, David Gwynn, whose tale of how he freed his fellow slaves on the *Diana*, exterminated her Spanish crew and then successively captured the other three galleys, enjoys a celebrity which no amount of refutation has much dimmed.

One doubts whether the duke deeply regretted losing the galleys, but the fifth loss was more serious. That was the *Santa Ana, capitana* (flagship we would say) of Recalde's Biscayan squadron, usually called the 'Santa Ana de Juan Martínez' to distinguish her from the other three *Santa Anas* in the Armada. She was rated at 768 (Spanish) tons, carried over three hundred soldiers and sailors, and was armed with thirty guns, some of them brass pieces of great weight. She may have belonged to Recalde himself or been built to his specifications, but she was either an ill-found, a badly commanded or a very unlucky ship. After the storm off Corunna she was the last of the Biscayans to rejoin, and the one most in need of repairs. This time she did not rejoin at all. For some reason she ran before the storm eastward up the Channel to shelter in the bay of La Hogue, where she remained for the rest of the campaign. Had Recalde been aboard her, instead of on the royal galleon *San Juan de Portugal* as Medina Sidonia's vice-admiral, the loss would have been much greater. But then, if Recalde had been on her the *Santa Ana* probably would not have forsaken the fleet. The Armada waited vainly for her off the Lizard until the morning of Saturday the thirtieth. At least the delay gave the *capitana* of the galleasses, the *San Lorenzo*, Don Hugo de Moncada's flagship, time to repair her rudder. Weak ships, galleasses, the duke grumbled, for these rough seas. Perhaps they were. The *San Lorenzo* was to break her rudder again in less favourable circumstances.

Before the Armada began its march up the Channel on the morning of Saturday, July 30th, on board the *San Martín* within sight of the Lizard there was held a Council of War about which much has been written, little to the purpose. The duke communicated to His Most Catholic Majesty the same day the council's one positive decision: not to go farther than the Isle of Wight until a rendezvous with Parma had been definitely arranged, since they could count on no deep-water port beyond the straits and the first tempest would have them on the sands. Later on, Captain Alonso Vanegas, a generally reliable witness who was aboard the *San Martín*, reported that, when the squadron commanders met to discuss last-minute tactical dispositions, Don Alonso de Leiva urged an attack on Plymouth where, so Madrid had told them, lay Drake with the western wing of the English fleet, intelligence just confirmed by the crew of a fishing-boat picked up by one of the pinnaces. Some of the other officers present agreed. To this, Vanegas says, the duke replied that there were two reasons for not going into Plymouth. In the first place it was contrary to the King's instructions, and in the second place the entrance was reported to be narrow and difficult and thoroughly commanded by strong shore batteries. After some further discussion a unanimous decision was reached. This is all we know at first hand except that, when his English captors asked Pedro de Valdés if the Armada had intended to go into Plymouth, he replied that it might have done so had a favourable opportunity offered, but that he, personally, had been against it in any circumstances.

Later on, however, when the beaten ships had straggled back to Spain, when most of the captains present at the Council of War were dead or prisoners and popular feeling was looking for a scapegoat, the tale got about that all the squadron commanders had urged the attack on Plymouth, but that Medina Sidonia, falsely alleging that the King's orders left him no choice, had overruled them. Thus the duke's falsehood, arrogance and cowardice lost the Armada its best chance of a victory. An early spreader of this tale was a Dominican monk, Juan de Victoria, who left a manuscript history of the campaign, chiefly remarkable for its wild inaccuracy and its venomous libels of the duke, to whose pride, stupidity and cowardice it attributes every Spanish disaster. No one else goes as far as Victoria, but there are feebler echoes of his slanders in some of the better-known Spanish chroniclers. These, and the fact that Fernández

Duro chose to include a considerable excerpt from Victoria in his otherwise authentic collection of Armada documents, have given Victoria's version of the Council of War more credence than it deserves.

In fact there is no reason to doubt that the Council of War was unanimous. The idea that Medina Sidonia could or would have tried to browbeat his experienced lieutenants into a decision they disapproved of is absurd. The custom of the Spanish service was that when a Council of War was divided, even by a single dissent, its members had to be polled, their individual opinions recorded and the whole record transmitted to the King, as was done after the council at Corunna. Medina Sidonia was a great stickler for the customs and etiquette of the service, the kind of commander William Borough would have liked to serve with; he would never have omitted so serious a formality. Nor would he have ignored the consensus of his senior officers. After six months of command he was beginning to find his sea-legs and to feel more self-confidence, but to the end he spoke very modestly of his ignorance of naval and military matters and he always followed expert advice.

Just as there is no warrant for questioning the unanimity of the council's decision, so there are no strong grounds for condemning its soundness. There were so many unknown factors — the state of the channel into Plymouth, the strength of the shore batteries, the whereabouts of the English fleet — that it would have been a rash commander who would have risked cracking on sail, leaving his transports to look after themselves and gambling everything, the whole success of his mission, on the chance of catching the English vulnerable. The best intelligence available said that Drake was, or had been, in Plymouth, and Howard somewhere to the eastward. If Drake could be caught unprepared in Cattewater, or just emerging from the Sound, it might mean victory; but if the leading ships got jammed in the entrance to the harbour, hotly engaged with Drake and the shore batteries, and Howard swooped down on the rear, it would mean catastrophe. Given the various possibilities it is hard to think of a better decision than the one the council apparently reached — to proceed cautiously up the coast, try to find out where the enemy was and act accordingly.

Actually, of course, there was not the slightest chance of surprise, not the slightest chance of seizing Plymouth, even if Plymouth had been the port they most wanted to seize. As they sat debating off the Lizard almost fifty miles from the contemplated target Drake and Howard were already behind Rame Head with the strongest English ships, waiting for their approach. Of the many possible situations which the council must have considered, one of the least favourable was taking shape ahead of them.

When the council broke up the Armada began its careful advance up the Channel, Bertendona's Levant squadron and the galleasses in the van; then the main body led by the duke with a squadron of galleons, followed by the Guipúzcoans and the Andalusians on either wing with the hulks tucked neatly in the centre, then Recalde with his Biscayans and the rest of the galleons bringing up the rear. As they were sighted from the land the first beacons roared into flame, and presently from headland after headland the smoke towered skyward round the curve of the invisible shore carrying the warning past Plymouth, until, all the south coast alerted, the beacons glared redly above Dover to be seen by the ships off Dunkirk and signalled from the North Foreland to watchers on the Essex shore. At the same time, faster than any courier, other lines of beacons marching inland spread the alarm, until by morning not only London knew and Nottingham, but York and far-off Durham, that the Spaniards had come at last.

For a while the Armada's only sight of the enemy was an English pinnace which, as they passed the Lizard, suddenly skittered between the ships of the van almost under the lee of the towering carracks, and danced away, replying with an impudent toy cannon to the indignant thunder of *La Rata's* guns. In the late afternoon the fleet anchored in a long line, probably (the wind was west-south-west) in the lee of Dodman Point. As they did so look-outs saw sunlight glinting on topsails out beyond the Eddystone — hostile ships, no doubt, but how many and doing what it was too far away to see. Medina Sidonia sent off some pinnaces to find out what they could.

Squinting into the glare, Howard's topmen could just discern the long line of the Spanish fleet like a floating wall, black and menacing, crowned with a multitude of towers. They could not count them or distinguish separate ships, but the gentlemen who swung themselves up the shrouds to look could reflect that never since the beginning of the world had any eyes before theirs beheld so vast an array of hostile sailing-ships of war. They would learn their quality tomorrow. Then clouds obscured the sun, there was a squall of rain and in the gathering dusk each fleet disappeared from the other.

That night after midnight one of the Spanish pinnaces, commanded by an English-speaking officer, came back with a Falmouth fishing-smack it had picked up and her crew of four. From them the duke learned that

Howard and Drake had joined forces and been seen that afternoon, standing out to sea. A little later, before dawn, occurred the most decisive movement of the first week's fighting. The wind on the evening of the 30th was west-south-west, and the Spanish fleet was to windward of the English and so held the important advantage of the weather-gauge. By morning the wind had hauled round to west-north-west, blowing off the land, and the Spaniards' windward position, if they had stayed where they were or edged north-east towards Fowey, should have improved. When day broke they were still to windward of a squadron of English ships, which they sighted beating its way along the shore, trying to work around ahead of them to the west. Presently it was exchanging cannon shots with the Spanish van. But behind them, and directly to windward, the Spanish saw the main body of the English fleet. The Spanish had lost the weather-gauge, and, since the wind for the next nine days blew mostly from the west, they were never except for brief intervals to regain it.

We do not know how it was done. Howard must have stood out to sea and then back, close-hauled, around the Armada's seaward wing, and the Armada must have sailed or drifted some miles to the eastward to make the feat possible. All Howard says is: 'The next morning, being Sunday, all the English that were come out of Plymouth recovered the wind of the Spaniards two leagues to the westward of the Eddystone.' 'All the English that were come out of Plymouth' implies a second shock to the Spaniards almost as great as the first, for even as they watched the eleven landward ships weathered the Spanish vanguard and stood off on a new tack to join their admiral. This was the first intimation most of the Spaniards had that they were opposed by ships more weatherly than any they had ever sailed in. With ships like these holding the weather-gauge the range and the nature of the battle would be, as the wiser mariners like Recalde had long feared, at the enemy's choice.

Expecting the English to attack, Medina Sidonia fired a signal gun and the Armada formed in battle order, each unit making or slackening sail with military precision, and changing course with due regard to its neighbours until the whole fleet presented to the English for the first time the famous crescent formation which was to puzzle and awe them all the way up the Channel. It was not, of course, a perfect crescent, but with the extended wings pointing towards the enemy, and thickened centre, it was sufficiently like one to make any experienced seaman wonder how so heterogeneous a lot of ships could achieve so smoothly and maintain so firmly so complicated a formation.

The English could not have done it; they had no practice in that sort of thing. English seamen did not underestimate Iberian seamanship: nobody thought the Portuguese, who had led the rest of Europe into the farthest oceans, and the Basques, who won their daily living from some of the roughest and most treacherous waters in the world, fair-weather sailors; nor did those who had made the West Indian voyage despise the seamanship it required. But the manœuvre Howard's fleet was watching displayed a skill new to the watchers, a skill as surprising in its way as the Englishman's easy recovery of the weather-gauge had been to the Spaniards. And, in a way, as dismaying. For this was a formation of great defensive strength.

The daunting thing about the crescent formation was that ships bent on holding the weather-gauge could only attack its protruding wings where, of course, its strongest ships were placed, and whence any ship badly damaged could easily be 'recovered into the midst of the fleet'. On the other hand, woe to any English ships rash enough to penetrate between the backward extending horns. They would surely be enveloped and cut off by the powerful galleons on either wing, which would have the wind of them as soon as they entered the demilune and would catch them in such cramped quarters that all their speed and agility would not avail them. Then they could be forced to fight at close quarters and eventually to grapple, and their comrades could only rescue them by charging into a general mêlée and fighting hand to hand. This was the kind of action the Spanish hoped to precipitate and the English most wanted to avoid.

So as they dressed their chosen formations, the Spanish in their strange crescent, the English in line or perhaps double line ahead, the adversaries looked each other over, and neither side much liked what it saw. If the English were astonished by the size of the Armada — a weight of ships beneath which the ocean seemed to groan — and by its grim order, the Spanish, who knew how many of their own ships would be useless in the battle, were surprised not only by the speed and nimbleness of the enemy but by his numbers and by the size and apparent power of his first line. That morning, as they faced each other, the opposing admirals must each have been wondering with a certain numbness what he was going to do next.

There was cause enough for uncertainty. Fleets like these were a new thing in the world. Nobody had ever seen two such in combat. Nobody knew what the new weapons would do, or what tactics would make them most effective. This was the beginning of a new era in naval warfare, of the long day in which the ship-of-the-line, wooden-walled, sail-driven and armed with smooth-bore cannon, was to be queen of battles; a day for which the armour-plated, steam-powered battleship with rifled cannon merely marked the evening, so that antiquarians will probably lump the two together when they have thought of a name for the period which, until just now, we have called 'modern'. In the beginning there was no name for the ship-of-the-line, and no idea how to use it. That morning off the Eddystone nobody in either fleet knew how to fight a 'modern' battle. Nobody in the world knew how.

A crescent formation at the capture of San Salvador, a detail from John Pine's engraving of the 'House of Lords Tapestries'.

XXIII

FIRST BLOOD

THE EDDYSTONE TO START POINT, JULY 31ST, 1588

APPROPRIATELY enough, the first modern naval battle in history began with gestures out of the Middle Ages, out of romances of chivalry. The Captain-General of the Ocean Sea hoisted to his maintop his sacred banner as a signal to engage, as Castilian commanders at sea had always done since first they sighted the Moorish galleys. And the Lord Admiral of England sent his personal pinnace, the *Disdain*, to bear his challenge to the Spanish admiral, like King Arthur sending Sir Gawaine to defy the Emperor Lucius. Then, his defiance delivered, at about nine in the morning Howard led the English fleet in line ahead — 'en ala' the Spanish called it — single file, one ship behind another, against the northern shoreward tip of the Spanish crescent.

The wing attacked was de Leiva's, mainly the Levant squadron, which had been the vanguard as long as the Armada had been reaching north towards the shore in an effort to cut off the leeward detachment of English ships. In most accounts of the battle de Leiva's squadron is still called 'the vanguard', although in taking its new formation the Armada had changed front to flank, each ship turning east ninety degrees or more, so that de Leiva was on the left wing and his Levanters formed the horn of the crescent projecting towards the rear on that side.

The rearmost ship, in the post of honour and of danger, was de Leiva's own *Rata Coronada*; and as Howard's *Ark Royal* began to cross his stern Don Alonso put down his helm, meeting the English flagship broadside to broadside and steering a course parallel with it across the chord of the arc formed by the Spanish crescent as he tried to edge to windward to close the range. Behind him swung into action Bertendona's great carrack, *Regazona*, the biggest ship in the Armada, almost as big as the Queen's *Triumph*, and following Bertendona the rest of the Levant squadron. Howard, under the impression that the *Rata* was 'the admiral' — that is, the flagship, of the Spaniards — 'wherein the duke was supposed to be', exchanged broadsides with her for some time, 'until she was rescued by divers ships of the Spanish army'. Or that is how Howard tells it. In fact, the Levanters, not the most weatherly ships in the Armada, were quite unable to close the range and Howard had no intention of doing so, so the two lines kept well asunder. As far as we know nobody got hurt in that part of the action, or was in the least in need of rescue.

Meanwhile a group of English ships, led by Drake in the *Revenge* and including Hawkins in the *Victory* and Frobisher in the *Triumph*, assailed the other wing of the Armada, the 'rearguard', commanded by the vice-admiral, Juan Martínez de Recalde. They met a rather different reception. Recalde in the *San Juan de Portugal*, the largest of the galleons and a powerful ship, swung round to meet the attack, but the rest of the galleons sailed on. Later, when he discovered what was happening, Medina Sidonia seems to have been under the impression that Recalde either got separated from the rest of his squadron by accident or was deliberately deserted by them. His report to the King leaves both alternatives open. Neither seems at all probable. The galleons of Portugal were manned and commanded by veterans who would scarcely have panicked at the mere noise of a cannonade. Throughout all the rest of the fighting no squadron in either fleet behaved with greater gallantry. Nor can one easily imagine Recalde's own Biscayans deserting him. On the other hand, of all the squadron commanders Recalde was the least likely to get into trouble by accident. He was famous for the way he handled his ships and almost equally famous for the way he handled his men. If he left the duke with a choice between two improbabilities it must have been because he did not want to confirm the only likely conjecture, that he had disobeyed orders, parted from his squadron, ordering them not to follow him, and deliberately thrust himself into the midst of the enemy.

Recalde knew better than anyone that now the fleet had lost the weather-gauge its only chance of victory was to precipitate a general mêlée. He had seen enough of the action already to be sure that he had read the English admiral's intentions correctly, and that Howard meant to stand aloof and knock the Spanish ships to pieces with his culverins at a range at which his ships could not get hurt. But it was unheard of in the previous annals of war at sea for a single ship surrounded by enemies not to be boarded. Boarding was the only way a superior force could make sure of taking a valuable prize intact, and among the group bearing down on him Recalde saw one ship, surely larger than his and with bow and stern castles at least as high. It would be strange if her captain could not be tempted to close. Recalde knew that if he could once get his grappling-irons on one English galleon or, better still, on two, he could hold on until help came. Then, if the English in their turn should attempt a rescue, perhaps the general mêlée, on which everything depended, could begin. Even if he could lure the English close enough for him to use with full effect his big short-range ship-smashers, cannon and demi-cannon and periers, he might accomplish something. It was worth risking a single ship for, even worth disobeying a formal order.

Drake must have read Recalde's mind as clearly as Recalde had read Howard's. *Revenge*, *Victory*, *Triumph* and their companions closed the range, but only to a cautious three hundred yards or so, and proceeded to pound Recalde with the long guns which were their principal armament. He could not get at them and they would not come to him, though Martin Frobisher in the *Triumph* must have been, as Recalde hoped, sorely tempted. So for over an hour the *San Juan* alone withstood the battering of the English squadron, until the great *Grangrin* came up, followed by the rest of the Biscayans, drove the English away and guarded *San Juan* back into the midst of the fleet where she could patch her wounds.

The rescue of Recalde's ship seems to have been begun by the movement of the *San Martín*, which also led to the breaking off of the action. Recalde may have been willing to be bait in the trap a little longer, but whatever he had told his captains he could, of course, have told the Captain-General nothing. As soon as Medina Sidonia saw his vice-admiral in danger he spilled the wind from his sails and put his helm hard over. Immediately all the fighting-ships in the main body, the Andalusians, the Guipúzcoans and the rest of the galleons, imitated his action, waiting with their sails flapping until the slow drift of the rearguard fighting should come abreast of them or, if the English were completely preoccupied, perhaps even pass them, giving them the advantage of the weather-gauge. Instead, at the critical moment, the English sheered off out of range. That was the end of the first day's fight.

When the English broke off the action, about one in the afternoon, Medina Sidonia immediately went over to the offensive and tried to get to windward of them. Since the crescent was strictly a defensive formation which could only be maintained with a following wind the duke formed his fighting-ships for attack in squadron columns, each squadron in line ahead, leaving the sluggish hulks to pursue their course to leeward. No doubt the galleons made a pretty sight, heeling over, close-hauled in the fresh breeze, but the English easily kept whatever distance they pleased, now and then tossing in a derisive salvo of round shot, and the abrupt rushes of the Spanish fleet, first to port and then to starboard, had less chance than the brave blind rushes of the bull against his agile persecutors. For three hours the duke kept up his futile attempts; then he put up his helm and turned away, back towards the labouring hulks. 'The enemy having opened the range,' reads the official log, 'the duke collected the fleet, but found he could do nothing more, for they still kept the weather-gauge, and their ships are so fast and so nimble they can do anything they like with them.'

For both sides the first day's fighting had been a somewhat frustrating experience. The Spanish were exasperated rather than hurt. No ship in the fleet had taken as much mauling as Recalde's and its injuries amounted to no more than two cannon balls in its foremast, some stays and rigging shot away, and a handful of killed and wounded. But if the English long-range bombardment had inflicted so far only annoying jabs, they were jabs that had to be suffered, apparently, whenever the English chose and with little prospect of effective retaliation.

As for the English, if they were not hurt they were beginning to be alarmed. This was a bigger, tougher enemy than they had bargained for. Spanish seamanship and discipline all day had been impeccable, and the Spaniards had been as full of fight at the end as at the beginning. The Armada was more heavily gunned than they had looked for, with enough long guns to return their fire and, on its best ships, more short-range ship-smashers, cannon and periers than the Queen's galleons. If they could close the range sufficiently the Spaniards could do serious damage, even without boarding. And if the Spanish guns had done no damage that day, why, neither so far as anyone could see had the English. The Armada looked even more formidable at a nearer view than it had at a distance. At the end, as it stood away into the darkening afternoon, it was more than ever like an impregnable wooden wall, like a grim fortress bristling with towers.

The English were not proud of their performance. They had hunted the Spanish past Plymouth, and if the Armada had had any intention of looking in there (it had shown none), that at least was foiled. But now the Armada was proceeding with majestic deliberation in unbroken order up the Channel, towards its rendezvous with Parma. If that rendezvous were to be prevented they would have to do better. Howard, who had been willing to encounter the whole Spanish fleet with some sixty-five sail, now hesitated to join battle again until the rest of the ships in Plymouth had come up, and was writing everywhere for reinforcements, men and ships. His Council of War concurred. To Walsingham he wrote: 'We gave them fight [from nine o'clock until one and] made some of them to bear room to stop their leaks [this was rather what he hoped than what he knew]; notwithstanding we durst not adventure to put in among them, their fleet being so strong.' Drake, warning Seymour of the approach of the enemy, was even more laconic. 'The 21st we had them in chase, and so, coming up to them, there hath passed some cannon shot between some of our fleet and some of them, and as far as we perceive, they are determined to sell their lives with blows.'

The first serious Spanish losses came after the battle, two accidents, unrelated to enemy action but destined to cost the Armada two capital ships. The first seemed minor. Some time after four in the afternoon as the Spanish were re-forming their defensive crescent and the Andalusian squadron was closing up on the duke's right, its *capitana*, Pedro de Valdés's flagship, *Nuestra Señora del Rosario*, collided with another Andalusian and lost its bowsprit. Then, only a few minutes later on the duke's left there was a tremendous explosion. Oquendo's *almiranta*, the *San Salvador*, was seen to be ablaze; her poop and two decks of her stern castle had disappeared. Obviously the gunpowder stored astern had blown up.

The further we get from this event the more detailed and dramatic does its story become. In the diary or smooth log of his voyage sent to Philip on August 21st, Medina Sidonia says simply that aboard the *San Salvador* some barrels of gunpowder blew up. Presumably the duke had made some sort of inquiry and he had some of the survivors from the *San Salvador* aboard the *San Martín*, but if he found out no more than he reported it would scarcely be surprising. Everyone anywhere in the vicinity of the explosion seems to have been killed. Naturally, various conjectures were soon bruited in the fleet. Fray Bernardo de Gongora, who ended his voyage aboard the *San Martín*, heard that the explosion was due to some gunner's carelessness — a plausible guess. On another ship it was said that a gunner had set fire to a powder barrel, nobody knew why. Probably he was an Englishman. Some deserters, not from the *San Salvador*, picked up after Gravelines, had a much more definite tale. A Dutch master-gunner, rebuked for carelessness, laid a train to the magazine, lit it and jumped overboard; his subsequent whereabouts not stated. In Amsterdam an enterprising newsmonger had a better idea. The master-gunner (a Hollander, of course, and pressed for the service), reproved by Oquendo for smoking on the quarter-deck, calmly knocked out the dottle of his pipe into a powder barrel and so blew up the ship. Of course Oquendo was not aboard the *San Salvador*, but it is not only the Dutch who were confused by the fact that in a Spanish fleet it was not the *almiranta* but the *capitana* which was the flagship. What a barrel of powder was doing on the quarter-deck is another question. In Hamburg, some weeks later, the master-gunner was a German whom a Spanish officer struck with a stick.

By the time Petruccio Ubaldini took hold of it the story was ready for the full treatment. The master-gunner, a Fleming this time, was injured not only in his professional but his personal honour — the Spanish officer who reprimanded him had already cuckolded him and was now threatening the happiness and safety of his daughter, both wife and daughter being by some poetic licence aboard the *San Salvador*. The Fleming fired a powder train and sprang into the sea, destroying them all, and Ubaldini has a moving peroration on the folly of arousing in the human breast the savage passion of revenge. The baroque luxuriance of Ubaldini's version should have swept all before it, but it already had too many competitors and northerners may have found it, as they found some Italian baroque churches, a trifle too exuberant. In one form or another, however, the story of the liberty-loving or patriotic or revengeful Dutchman, or German, or Englishman, or Fleming, has become almost as firmly imbedded in the Armada legend as the story of David Gwynn.

The catastrophe it was invented to explain was real enough. Medina Sidonia acted promptly, fired a gun to call the attention of the fleet, and steered back towards the *San Salvador*, meanwhile sending off pinnaces and ships' boats with messages. Small craft converged on the burning ship to tow her stern around away from the wind so that the fire would not blow forward, to reinforce the depleted crew now desperately fighting the fire amidships (there was another great store of powder under the forecastle), to take off the maimed and burned and transfer them to one of the two hospital ships among the hulks. The *San Martín* stood by with the duke on the poop-deck, within easy hail, supervising and encouraging the operation, until two galleasses appeared to tow the *San Salvador*, her fires now under control, in among the hulks.

By this time it began to look like a squally evening, the sky lowering, the wind blowing in unpredictable gusts and a heavy choppy sea making up. Just as the ranks of the fleet opened to admit the two galleasses and their helpless charge Pedro de Valdés's ship, which was steering badly

259

without the balance of her head sails, was taken aback and lost her foremast, weakened, perhaps, by the collision and the breaking of the bowsprit. Again the duke acted promptly. Again he fired a gun to stop the fleet, and stood across to the *Rosario* where she wallowed in the rear. This time the *San Martín* was first at hand. There were few better seamen in the Armada than the flagship's sailing-master, Captain Marolín de Juan, and rough as the sea now was and wildly as the *Rosario* was behaving Captain Marolín succeeded in passing her a cable. The *San Martín* herself would take the crippled *Rosario* in tow. Scarcely had the cable been secured, however, when *Rosario* bucked like a bronco and it parted. The wind was increasing, the sea was getting rough, and it proved unexpectedly difficult to pass another line. The duke, on the poop-deck, stood watching the work with painful attention.

It had begun to grow dark, and a couple of pinnaces were standing by, when Diego Flores de Valdés came charging up to the poop-deck to protest. An experienced officer, commander of the galleons of Castile, he was serving on the flagship at the King's suggestion as the Captain-General's Chief of Staff and principal adviser on naval and military matters. The duke, he declared, absolutely must resume his station, and the fleet must resume its course eastward. Standing by like this in this increasing sea the ships might do each other mischief, and would certainly scatter so during the night that by morning the duke would not see half of them. It was impossible to continue this disorder in the face of the enemy, and to go on imperilling the success and safety of the whole fleet for the sake of a single ship.

There seems to have been a bitter excited argument. Diego Flores was, apparently, supported by another officer, perhaps Bobadilla, *maestre de campo general*. Finally the duke gave way, though he insisted on standing by until he saw Ojeda, in the small galleon that was the flagship of the screen, coming up with four pinnaces to take over, and received word that his orders to one of the galleasses and to the *almiranta* of the Andalusians to assist in the rescue had been received. Then at last he turned away, took up his station in the main body, and the fleet in close formation resumed its march. It was disturbing to hear, some time later, out of the darkness astern where the *Rosario* was drifting, the thud of heavy guns.

The duke had been on deck all day and had eaten nothing since breakfast. He did not go below now. He had a boy bring him a crust and some cheese to the poop-deck, and stood a long time, leaning on the taffrail watching the wake and the blackness beyond. Abandoning the *Rosario* was his first real failure, and he knew that whoever advised it and however wise had been the advice his would be the blame. Perhaps it was only then he remembered that Diego Flores de Valdés and Pedro de Valdés were not only cousins but inveterate and implacable enemies.

Elizabethan ships.

XXIV

'A TERRIBLE VALUE OF GREAT SHOT'

START POINT TO PORTLAND BILL,
JULY 31ST–AUGUST 2ND, 1588

THE English admiral, that same evening, was worried too. Somewhere along the south coast, his Council of War felt sure, the Spaniards meant to try to seize a port. Several possible ports and anchorages lay ahead and the question was whether, following his opponents, Howard could prevent their landing. By taking the weather-gauge, at the price of letting the enemy by the Lord Admiral had done a risky thing. Conservative military opinion expected him to meet the Spanish Armada head on, and hold the Channel against it as an army would hold a mountain pass. If the Spaniards now took advantage of his unorthodox behaviour to seize an anchorage and land, whatever the consequences to England, his own reputation would be gone and he could say farewell to fame and the big wars. Like Medina Sidonia Howard was advised by captains far more experienced than he, but like his adversary he could not share the final responsibility.

If he had to follow the Spaniards instead of blocking them, at least he could see to it that the pursuit was close and well co-ordinated. So when Medina Sidonia abandoned his efforts to recover the wind Howard hung out a flag for council, and while the Spaniards were struggling with the accidents to the *San Salvador* and the *Rosario* the English captains were debating the order of their pursuit. We know of that order only that it cannot have been in single line ahead, and that when it was understood by all, 'dismissing each man to go aboard his own ship, his Lordship appointed Sir Francis Drake to set the watch that night'. That is, Drake in the *Revenge* was to lead the fleet, and the rest, following, were to guide on the great poop-lantern at his stern. It was a graceful and, Howard must have thought, also a prudent gesture, to yield to his famous and experienced vice-admiral the honour and responsibility of leadership which would otherwise have been the Lord Admiral's own.

By this time evening was drawing in, and in the freshening breeze the English were hurrying after the Armada, which was nearing Start Point.

Somewhere to seaward cruised the *Margaret and John* of London, a privateer of two hundred tons and perhaps fourteen battery guns. The *Margaret and John* must have had a pretty turn of speed, for she was well in the van when she sighted (was, she says, the first to sight) a great Spanish ship in trouble, its bowsprit and foremast carried away, and standing by 'a great galleon', a galleass and a pinnace offering aid. According to the account of her own officers the *Margaret and John* came dashing down on the Spaniards, 'being accompanied neither with ship, pinnace or boat of all our fleet', whereupon the Spanish ships forsook their disabled companion and fled.

We need not believe quite all of *Margaret and John's* story. Since her officers were trying to establish a claim to a part of the loot of *Nuestra Señora del Rosario* they naturally did not understate their own role. We know that Ojeda's galleon (quite a small one, by the way, not much if any bigger than the *Margaret and John*) and one of the galleasses did forsake Don Pedro de Valdés at about nine in the evening, though it seems more likely that they did so on account of the approach of the English fleet than for fear of one ship, however venturesome. In the end the *Margaret and John* came up cautiously enough, kept to windward, and took her time looking over the situation. The *Rosario* seemed deserted, no sails drawing, no lights showing and not answering her helm. To test that conclusion the *Margaret and John* edged in closer and loosed off a volley of musketry. Presently a couple of great guns boomed in answer. The *Margaret and John* replied with a broadside and then prudently drew away, but stood by until some time around midnight when, by her account, seeing the Lord Admiral making sail after the enemy and fearing his displeasure she rejoined the fleet. More likely Howard heard the gunfire in his rear and sent a pinnace to order up the straggling marauder. Howard had marked the *Rosario's* plight and given orders that she be ignored and the fleet kept together. If the Spaniards tried to anchor in Tor Bay on the morrow he would need all the strength he had.

It would be helpful to know more about visibility that night. There should have been a moon just at its first quarter, but no contemporary account says anything about moonlight. After the gusty squall around five or six in the evening the wind seems to have dropped, until from Start Point on there was no more than a light breeze. Moon or no moon, visibility cannot have been very good. Perhaps the sky was heavily overcast, or perhaps there were those ghostly intermittent patches of fog one sometimes sees in the Channel. For one reason or another, though the

Ark was following directly behind Drake, her look-out lost sight of *Revenge's* lantern.

If the admiral had gone below this is when he would have been called, and all eyes would have strained forward. Presently they did see a lantern again, but farther away than they had expected. The *Ark* shook out more sail and hurried to catch up. Not even *Revenge* should show her heels to *Ark*. Had not the Lord Admiral sworn that for sailing qualities *Ark* was the odd ship of the world, matchless and unequalled? Steadily the guiding lantern was overhauled until *Ark* reached what seemed the proper interval. It was not until dawn was creeping over the water and leader and led were off the Berry, where if the Spaniards meant to try for Tor Bay, the whole fate of the campaign might be decided, that Howard realized he had been following the poop-lantern of the enemy's flagship and was almost inside the grim Spanish crescent. Only his two closest companions of the night, the *Bear* and the *Mary Rose*, were with him. The nearest of the rest of his fleet showed nothing but their top-masts above the horizon. Of Francis Drake and the *Revenge* there was no sign at all.

The exasperating thing about contemporary accounts of the Armada campaign is that they let us see what happened as if through a swirling fog. There are moments when the main outlines are discernible, but the details are obscured, there are scenes here and there, etched with perfect clarity, and there are times when one can see nothing at all. At this point the official English relation just says: 'Our own fleet, being disappointed of their light, by reason that Sir Francis Drake left the watch to pursue certain hulks ... lingered behind, not knowing whom to follow; only his Lordship with the *Bear* and the *Mary Rose* in his company ... pursued the enemy all night within culverin shot; his own fleet being as far behind as, the next morning, the nearest might scarce be seen half-mast high, and very many out of sight, which with a good sail recovered not his Lordship the next day before it was very late in the morning.' It is easy to forgive Howard for implying that his lonely pursuit of the Spanish fleet was an act of hare-brained recklessness instead of a simple mistake, particularly as he makes no charges against Drake, and does his best without emphasis to exculpate him. But it is hard to forgive him for not saying what happened next.

We must assume that the three English ships came about and clawed desperately away, and that the Spanish did not attempt to pursue. None of the contemporary Spanish narratives mentions the presence at dawn of three English galleons close in their wake, though the apparition must have been almost as astonishing to them as theirs was to the English. Meteren has a sentence which may have some bearing. Hakluyt renders it: 'At the same time [that is the same day that opened with Howard almost barging into the Spanish fleet] Hugo de Moncada, governor of the foure Galliasses, made humble sute unto the Duke of Medina that he might be licensed to encounter the Admirall of England, which libertie the duke thought not good to permit unto him.' This sounds like an echo of some complaint one of Don Hugo's companions brought back to Spain. It might or might not be true, but for the moment after dawn it is not implausible. The *Ark* and her companions were certainly observed, and probably the *Ark* was recognized. The galleasses were the only units of the Spanish fleet which had a real chance to overtake since they could row directly into the wind and for a dash of a few miles make very good speed. If the galleasses could head off the three English ships the galleons would have time to come up, envelop and smother them.

If Moncada made the request Medina Sidonia must have refused it, and one must ask why. Did he really think that his orders to proceed up the Channel were so peremptory that they would not brook the delay involved in crushing three of the enemy's capital ships? His behaviour next day makes this seem unlikely. Had the wind freshened with dawn, and hauled round enough so that it did not look as if the galleasses would have a chance? That is not at all impossible. Or did Medina Sidonia remember that in the old-fashioned etiquette of naval battle it is the admiral's duty and privilege to engage the enemy's admiral, and feel reluctant to grant to Don Hugo the opportunity he could not use himself? Did he, perhaps, feel further that it scarcely became a Spanish gentleman to fall upon his enemy with odds of twenty to one, and therefore prefer to postpone the hoped-for meeting? Since the duke's snap judgments tended to stem rather from romances of chivalry than from military common sense, that is not impossible either. If there was, in fact, the slightest chance of bringing the *Ark* and her companions to battle before the rest of the English came up this was Medina Sidonia's second mistake in less than twelve hours.

Somehow Howard scrambled out of danger and watched the Armada hold on its slow march up the Channel. It showed not the slightest interest in Tor Bay after all.

During the afternoon the straggling English ships rejoined, among them the *Revenge*. Drake told Howard a straight-faced tale. 'Late in the evening' he had discerned shadowy outlines passing to seaward. Fearing lest the enemy might be trying to slip round under cover of darkness and gain the weather-gauge Drake turned starboard to challenge them, putting out his poop-lantern so as not to mislead the fleet. He had with him only the *Roebuck*, a big Plymouth privateer, Captain Whiddon, and two of his own pinnaces — the first rank, presumably, of the pursuit. When overhauled by this little squadron the mysterious strangers proved to be harmless German merchantmen, and Drake had just started back to rejoin the Lord Admiral when as the sun rose, lo and behold, right there in his path, only a cable-length or so away lay the crippled flagship of Don Pedro de Valdés. At first Don Pedro had shown a disposition to bargain, but when he heard that his challenger was Drake himself he thought it no shame to yield on assurance of fair treatment. Drake had sent Captain Whiddon with the *Roebuck* to escort the prize into Torbay, but had kept his illustrious prisoner a guest on the *Revenge* and brought him now to present him to the Lord Admiral.

No one at the time seems to have blamed Drake's behaviour in this extraordinary episode. No one, so far as we know, spoke of it with the slightest disparagement except Martin Frobisher, and his quarrel was rather over the division of the *Rosario's* spoils than over the manner of their acquisition. Yet it is a very odd story indeed. Why did no one else see the mysterious German hulks? And if Drake could be excused for leaving his post to investigate them, what excuse can there have been for his putting out the lantern which was supposed to guide the whole fleet and not telling the Lord Admiral what he was doing? If Howard had been told he could have lighted his own poop-lantern and the fleet could have continued in good order. But no excuse was offered, and none seems to have been thought necessary.

Howard gravely accepted the story of the German hulks, but he must have chuckled at Drake's surprise on stumbling upon the crippled Spanish flagship. Francis Drake was famous all over the seven seas for the craft or instinct which led him to the exact spot in a vast expanse of water where he could find a specially desirable prize, and such *Nuestra Señora del Rosario* certainly was, by far the richest as it turned out to be taken in the entire campaign. This was exactly what made excuses unnecessary. No one was prepared to blame a feat which everyone frankly envied. Conduct which in any modern regular navy would have resulted in court martial and disgrace just brought Sir Francis added fame and a tidy packet of prize money. His contemporaries never blamed him; why should we?

By the same token perhaps we should not blame Don Pedro either. Nobody has. When they learned the story his fellow countrymen, though loud in their execrations of the duke and his adviser, Diego Flores, for abandoning *Nuestra Señora del Rosario*, had for its commander only sympathy — sympathy which subsequent historians have mostly continued to echo. Yet it is hard to feel that Don Pedro shows to advantage in this episode. The handling of the *Rosario* is the chief excuse for saying that the masters and crews of the Armada were indifferent seamen; the failure to defend her reflects seriously on Spanish courage. For both Don Pedro must be held responsible. The collision that cost the *Rosario* her bowsprit and the subsequent loss of her foremast may have been unavoidable. But a ship whose bowsprit and foremast have carried away need not remain helpless for more than ten hours. The *Rosario* was supposed to have one hundred and eighteen seamen, and carried in addition some three hundred soldiers. In an emergency soldiers had been known to haul ropes and handle axes even in the Spanish navy. With many hands, the winds calming and the sea going down it should have been possible to contrive some sort of jury-rig forward to help to balance the rudder, and with properly trimmed sails *Rosario*, though sluggish, need not have been out of control. But when *Margaret and John* came up, four hours approximately after the foremast went, *Rosario* was wallowing helplessly with no sign of activity on deck, so that she looked deserted. Wallowing helplessly she was still when Drake found her.

Just as Don Pedro failed to repair his ship, so he failed to fight her. He had about as many men aboard as the *Revenge* and the *Roebuck* combined, and so far they had scarcely fought at all. The *Rosario* was one of the biggest and stoutest ships in the Armada, and one of the most heavily gunned — not inferior in either respect to Recalde's galleon or the duke's, though probably clumsier. Her castles loomed so high over the English ships that she would have been perilous to board, and resolutely defended she should have been able to hold out for hours, keeping the two English ships out of at least one day's action and perhaps crippling one of them. Instead, with a graceful bow, her captain surrendered to the fame of Francis Drake, making the enemy a free gift of a strong forty-six gunship, with a great store of arms and munitions and fifty-five thousand gold ducats in the captain's cabin. Perhaps Don Pedro did not clearly deserve what such conduct would have risked at a later period — hanging — but even by sixteenth-century standards it seems odd that he should have become, as indeed he did both in England and in Spain, something of a minor popular hero.

Later on the same day that Pedro de Valdés surrendered, Monday, August 1st, the English picked up a second prize. About noon the master of the *San Salvador* sent word that she was slowly sinking. The explosion which had wrecked her after-decks had started too many seams, and water was rising in the well faster than the pumps could handle. Her crew were taken off and some of her stores, but oddly enough not the powder and great shot in her forward hold, and she was let drift astern. She should have been scuttled, but either somebody failed to get the word or the English came up too fast. Lord Howard himself went aboard her, but made a very brief inspection; the stench of burnt corpses was too much for him. Later Captain Fleming, commander of the pinnace which brought the first news of the Armada, managed to tow the waterlogged hulk into Weymouth. The news of the two prizes raised all spirits on shore. The first day's battle off the Eddystone had been clearly seen by crowds of watchers on the land, but it had been hard to tell whether things went well or ill.

Later on Monday afternoon, when the wind had fallen to a whisper, Medina Sidonia signalled for a council, chiefly to arrange a new tactical grouping. All the fighting-ships were divided between a powerful rear-guard to be under Don Alonso de Leiva until Recalde finished repairing the *San Juan*, and a smaller vanguard under the duke himself. The duke chose the van because he expected to find ahead of him at any moment the eastern wing of the English fleet under Hawkins, he thought, actually under Seymour. From the fresh sails constantly coming up it was easy to see that Howard was calling for reinforcements.

When the chance for battle came, however, it came in the opposite direction. On Tuesday morning the flat calm of the late night was broken by a dawn wind blowing fresh from the east. The Spaniards had the weather-gauge.

Howard grasped the situation at once. The Spaniards first saw him in the growing light leading his line close-hauled north-north-east towards the land, in an effort to get by the Spaniards' left wing and so recover the wind. At dawn the Armada had Portland Bill almost abeam and Howard seems to have been worried about Weymouth, as the day before he had been worried about Tor Bay. This time the Spaniards were too near in-shore and too quick off the mark to be outflanked. As soon as he saw the English movement Medina Sidonia led the galleons of the vanguard to

intercept, and Howard, seeing that he could scarcely weather Portland
Bill before the Spanish van would be upon him, came about on the opposite tack and the English line began reaching south-south-west in an
effort to weather the Armada's seaward wing. Promptly the Spanish
rear-guard, led by Bertendona, took an intercepting course, and the
distance between the leading ships of the two columns narrowed to
culverin range, to musket shot, to half-musket shot. As it became
clear that again the English were cut off, both lines erupted in flame
and smoke.

So began a curious battle which lasted the rest of the morning, managed,
as Camden remarked when he had reviewed the evidence, 'with confusion enough'. So perhaps it was; many of the details remain obscure.
But there is no doubt about the objectives of the two commanders, and
with more narratives than Camden could have used to guide us the main
outlines are fairly clear. The English tried repeatedly to weather the
Armada's seaward wing; the Spanish tried repeatedly to board or tempt
their more nimble enemies to do so. Both sides failed, but most of the time
the opposing lines were within gunshot of one another and sometimes at
close range. Both admirals were impressed with the fury of the action;
both singled out some ships for special praise. The roar of the cannon, we
are told, was like the continuous roll of musketry, and the smoke was
blinding. The oldest soldiers had never witnessed such a cannonade. As
long as the wind held from the south-east the whole seaward battle drifted
westward into Lyme Bay.

Meanwhile a smaller battle was going on under the lee of Portland Bill.
There, at anchor, lay Martin Frobisher in the *Triumph*, the biggest ship
in either fleet, more or less covering and being supported by five middle-
sized London merchantmen, and under attack by the four galleasses. It
may be that Frobisher and his companions, having failed to weather the
Bill, were unable to follow Howard's change of course in time and saw
nothing for it but to anchor and wait until the drift of the fight westward
gave them the wind and room to manœuvre. Or it may be that Frobisher
had a more cunning purpose. Just a couple of miles east of Portland Bill a
long shallow bank of broken shell, the Shambles, rises irregularly towards
the surface, and from the tip of the Bill a tidal race sets towards it, sometimes running almost four knots. Wise ships give that death-trap a wide
berth. To assail the *Triumph* by the nearest way a ship would have to
cross the race. To come up more cautiously a sailing-ship would have to
lose the weather-gauge and struggle with tricky currents. The *Triumph*

with her high-built castles would have handled a little less nimbly than most of the English, but was easier to defend against boarders. Perhaps Martin Frobisher was tired of playing at long bowls. If so he could hardly have chosen a stronger corner to get his back into.

When Howard changed his course Medina Sidonia saw the plight, or what looked to be the plight, of Frobisher's little squadron, and sent the four galleasses under Don Hugo de Moncada in to finish them off. When he had time to look again, an hour or so later, he saw the four galleasses manœuvring warily just within long culverin range of the *Triumph*, like experienced dogs who find themselves in the pit with an old, quick and cunning bear. The tide was now ebbing, the race boiling and the current thrusting the galleasses aside, but Medina Sidonia would not have been able to see that. He sent off a pinnace to put a flea in Don Hugo's ear.

A little later the wind veered round to the south, and Howard, who had disengaged and had been keeping half an eye on the *Triumph*, was able to lead a line of the Queen's galleons and the bigger volunteers down to 'rescue' Frobisher. We don't know whether Frobisher wanted to be rescued. Perhaps we should, if we knew whether Drake's *Revenge* was one of the rescue party, for some three weeks later at Harwich the irascible Yorkshireman was saying that Drake thinks to cozen us of our shares in the loot of the *Rosario* but we will have them, or 'I will make him spend the best blood in his belly', which does not sound as if he was labouring under any insupportable burden of gratitude.

Medina Sidonia saw Howard's rescue and promptly led his vanguard, sixteen ships, to intercept the English line. Before the squadrons came into contact, however, the duke looked back and saw that Juan Martínez de Recalde, who had taken his repaired *San Juan* out to join the fray, had been cut off and was beset by a dozen ships. The shift in the wind had left all the Armada except the duke's squadron to the leeward of Recalde. Immediately the duke sent word back along his line that they were to put about and go to the rescue of the vice-admiral. The *San Martín* alone held on to meet the English, and as the *Ark* began to pass her swung broadside on and struck her topsails in invitation to the Englishman to grapple and board. This was how battles at sea were settled in the books the duke had read, admiral against admiral, sword to sword on a sanded quarter-deck; this was the moment for which he had let pass yesterday's opportunity.

Instead of grappling and boarding, Howard poured in a broadside at close range and passed by. So did the next English galleon, and the next, and all the rest of Howard's line. Then they came about and poured in a second series of broadsides, and a third. Meanwhile the ships which had been pestering Recalde joined the ring about the Spanish admiral, so that it looked from the deck of Recalde's *San Juan* as if the *San Martín* were fighting single-handed against at least fifty heavy ships. She was blazing away from every gun-port, and, by the report of those aboard her, returning the English fire with such effect that the English kept farther away towards the end of this action than they had at the beginning. Since the Armada was far to leeward of its admiral the *San Martín* fought alone for a full hour. Then a line of galleons came up, Oquendo leading and, in Howard's phrase, the Spaniards 'flocked together' around their battered flagship.

At this point the English drew off. The galleasses had already stopped annoying the *Triumph*, and since the wind was again fair from the west and the English well to windward the Armada re-formed its defensive crescent and resumed its ponderous march. Some shots were exchanged at long range that afternoon, but the rescue of the Spanish admiral really ended the day's battle.

The bitter lesson for the Spanish was that even when they had the weather-gauge they could not grapple and board the English ships, which were fast enough and weatherly enough to keep whatever distance they chose. The Spanish all thought that the enemy seemed to be right, too, in trusting to their guns, for the English had more big guns and of longer range, and better gunners who could fire much faster. Everyone in both fleets said three times as fast, though it must have been hard to keep count.

The bitter lesson for the English was that, in the face of Spanish discipline, their chosen tactics were not working. They had not expected to sink many of the Spanish fleet at the first encounter, or the second, but they had expected to cripple the galleons one by one so that they would have to drop out of formation and be overwhelmed. So far they had taken only two Spanish ships, the *Rosario* and the sinking hulk of the *San Salvador*, and, although the English may have thought their gunfire a contributory cause, both of these had been crippled by accidents. Meanwhile, in the two days' fighting and especially in the furious battle off Portland Bill, they had expended, as Howard said, such 'a terrible value of great shot' that most ships had none left. The admiral could not fight again, he wrote desperately to those ashore, without more powder and ball.

Meanwhile he could not see that he had done the Spanish any harm. They had kept their formations better than their foes, and not abandoned a single ship in the course of battle. They had not taken Weymouth, but there was no sign they had ever meant to, and now their closed ranks moved majestically forward as before.

The track of the Spanish Armada, from an engraving by Augustine Ryther of a chart drawn by Robert Adams, c. 1590, from the Roxburghe Club reprint. (opposite, above)

The Spanish Armada approaching the English coast, off Lizard Point, July 29th. (opposite, below)

July 31st. The Spaniards formed a crescent, thereby threatening to draw any attacking English ships into the centre and enclose them, at the same time taking the wind from the English sails. (overleaf, above left)

August 2nd. Off Portland Bill the two fleets engaged at close range, but neither side could gain the upper hand. (overleaf, below left)

The Armada re-formed its crescent shape and continued in a south-easterly direction. Off the Isle of Wight the ships were almost becalmed. The English divided their ships into four squadrons and came within range but the engagement on August 4th was again inconclusive. (overleaf, above right)

By the time they were off Beachy Head on August 6th and 7th, both fleets were short of ammunition. There was nothing to stop the Spaniards reaching Calais, where their objective was to meet Parma and transport his army across to invade England. Parma failed to be ready in time. While the Armada waited, the English broke up the crescent formation using fire-ships, and with intermittent skirmishing the Spaniards retreated northwards. (overleaf, below right)

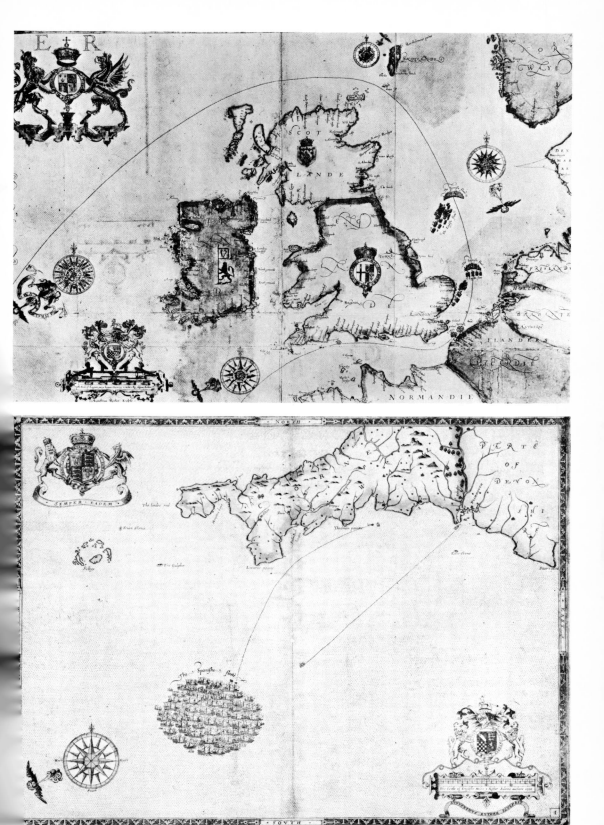

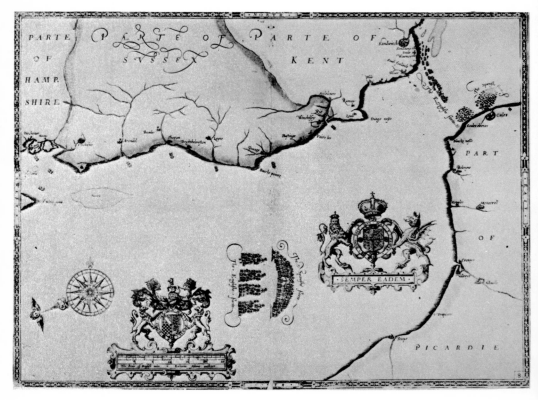

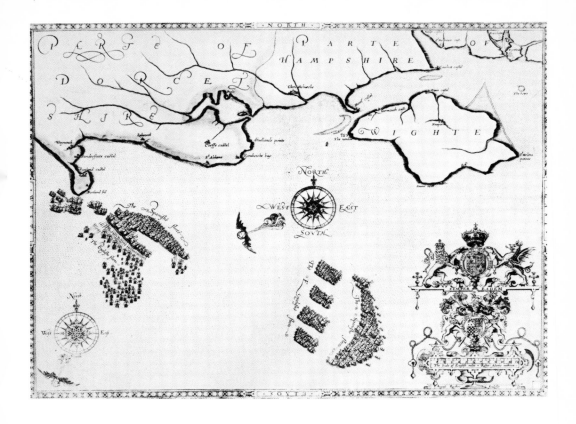

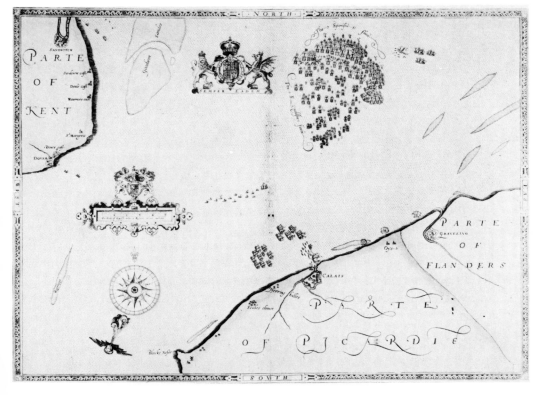

XXV

IN FORMIDABLE ORDER

PORTLAND BILL TO CALAIS ROADS,
TUESDAY, AUGUST 2ND TO SATURDAY, AUGUST 6TH, 1588

FROM Portland Bill to Calais Roads is rather less than a hundred and seventy miles. The Armada with the English in chase made the distance in about a hundred hours or a little more. Even deducting the time consumed by two sharp but indecisive engagements, that makes an average speed of less than two knots. The wind was to blame. After Tuesday morning's fight off Portland Bill there were recurrent periods of dead calm, some light variable airs, and the rest of the time a very gentle breeze breathing from some quarter of the west. The Spanish could scarcely have asked for better weather. It enabled them to keep their close formation with a minimum of risk and trouble, it deprived the English of part of the advantage of their superior agility, and it gave the Duke of Medina Sidonia time to send a stream of messages to Parma, warning him to be ready to embark his troops at a moment's notice, asking for additional supplies, inviting him to come out and join the Armada in an attack on the English.

Meanwhile the English followed warily, constantly reinforced by volunteers from the Channel ports, always able to bring the Spaniards to battle when they liked, but quite unable to disrupt their order. So these two brisk actions proved, although both times the English seized what looked like favourable opportunities.

On Wednesday, August 3rd, dawn showed a great Spanish ship straggling behind the seaward horn of the crescent, and immediately the English crowded on sail to try to cut her off. We have no English account of this action, but the *capitana* which the Spaniards identified as foremost in the fray can only have been Drake's *Revenge*. His regular post seems to have been on the seaward wing, and Howard would certainly have included the fight in his relation if he had been in it himself. On the Spanish right, Recalde in the *San Juan* had resumed his post. He promptly led a group of first-line ships to help their straggling comrade.

The straggler was the *Gran Grifon*, the flagship of the *urcas*, commanded by Juan Gomez de Medina. In asking for her to strengthen his seaward wing Recalde had shown less than his usual judgment, for though she was a solidly built great-ship of six hundred and fifty (Spanish) tons and thirty-eight guns she was an awkward, clumsy sailer, just about fit to keep up with the hulks she was in charge of. As soon as she saw her predicament she began to flounder back towards the safety of the crescent, but before long the English *capitana* glided abreast of her, gave her a broadside, came about and gave her another, then crossed her stern and raked her at half-musket shot. Other English ships came up and presently the *Gran Grifon* was beset on all sides. No one offered to board her, however, and she was able to stagger on, shrouded in smoke, her guns roaring defiance, until she reached Recalde's column.

The whole Spanish right rear was now hotly engaged; Recalde, Oquendo, de Leiva, Bertendona and the great galleon of Florence bore the brunt of the battle, while Drake persistently hammered away at the *Gran Grifon* which, by this time, from we do not know what damage to masts, rigging or rudder, was out of control and in serious distress. Medina Sidonia sent the galleasses to get her out of danger, and one of them managed to take her in tow and snake her back into the midst of the fleet, while the others traded shots with the *Revenge* and brought down her mainyard, or thought they had. Still the fight on the right wing waxed hotter, until the duke and the vanguard came astern and struck their topsails as a signal for a general engagement. At this the English drew off to long culverin range, but continued to fire occasional shots and manœuvre threateningly, until the duke decided that they did not mean to accept battle but were only trying to delay him, whereat he resumed his station and the Armada once more took up its march.

Although much less than half of either fleet was engaged that Wednesday morning, and the whole action was probably over in a couple of hours, Spanish casualties were officially reported as sixty killed and seventy wounded, ten more killed than in the battle of the day before off Portland Bill, and the heaviest losses of any day in the Channel. Probably the terrible punishment taken by the *Gran Grifon* accounts for most of the casualties, but one gets the impression that the English were closing the range more often, and that, consequently, both sides were suffering and inflicting heavier damage.

On Wednesday afternoon the wind dropped altogether and the two fleets drifted within sight of one another, a scant mile or so apart and a few miles south-west of the Needles. Now and then a gentle puff would fill the sails of one fleet or both, and urge forward the ships coming up to join Howard with reinforcements, negligible fighting-ships for the most part, pinnaces and coasters and harbour craft, but crowded with eager young gentlemen volunteers and laden with still more welcome stores of round shot and powder.

Howard took the occasion for another council. He and his captains must have been as dissatisfied as their opponents with the way things had gone so far. During the fight off Portland Bill the English battle line had broken up into three unco-ordinated groups, and only the nimbleness of the seaward ships and Frobisher's sturdy defence had kept them from being more roughly handled. The Spanish, on the other hand, in every action had preserved their formations and, in spite of their slower ships and the handicap of their non-combatant hulks, had manœuvred with a unanimity and precision which had repeatedly saved them from serious loss.

The answer, the English Council of War decided, was an organization by squadrons. They had had four days to watch the Spanish system in action, and Drake and Howard may have learned more about it from their talkative guest Don Pedro. Accordingly, they divided their present forces, about a hundred sail, great and small, into four roughly equal squadrons. Of course, Howard would command one and Drake another; of the other two, one was entrusted to John Hawkins, veteran seaman and creator of the Queen's new navy, and the other, somewhat surprisingly, to Martin Frobisher, the recent hero of Portland Bill.

Armies and navies have often remodelled their tactics or their organization in imitation of some admired antagonist, but not often in the face of the enemy and within sight of the crisis of a decisive campaign. The new organization does seem to have worked better than the old one. Its adoption was a credit to the intelligence of the English Council of War, and a tribute to the efficiency of their adversaries.

It got its first trial by battle next morning. Since midnight there had been a dead calm, and again the dawn showed Spanish stragglers — two of them this time, the royal galleon *San Luis de Portugal* and a West India merchantman of the Andalusian squadron, a *Santa Ana*, drifting not far apart and far enough from their proper places in the formation to offer attractive targets. But this time there was no wind at all. John Hawkins, who was nearest, ordered out his boats, and the fighting-ships of his squadron were towed towards the enemy, the *Victory* in the lead, until musket balls began to whistle about the ears of the rowers.

This was the proper weather for galleasses, and Medina Sidonia sent them to rescue the two stragglers. Three of them came up promptly, towing with them for additional fire power Don Alonso de Leiva's great carrack, *La Rata Coronada*, and for a while the part of Hawkins's squadron that had managed to tow into range looked like being outgunned. But the Lord Admiral's *Ark* was coming up on Hawkins's left, his boats' crews straining at their oars, and just beyond, Howard's kinsman Lord Thomas in the *Golden Lion*.

For a while the two groups banged away at each other while the rest of the fleet looked on. There was no breath of air to fill the sails and so no manœuvring except by the galleasses. 'There were many good shots', noted the Lord Admiral proudly, 'made by the *Ark* and the *Lion* at the galleasses in the sight of both armies.' And in the end the galleasses were damaged so that 'one of them was fain to be carried away upon the career [that is, listing] and another, by a shot from the *Ark* lost her lantern which came swimming by, and the third his nose.' Howard adds complacently that thereafter they never appeared in battle again.

The Spanish accounts just say that two of the galleasses took the *San Luis* and the *Santa Ana* in tow, and thereupon the six ships withdrew out of the midst of the enemy fleet. Like other commanders since, Howard seems to have overestimated a little the damage he had done. The loss of a poop-lantern and a figurehead would scarcely disable two ships. If the third was listing from being hulled the leak must have been repaired promptly, for the galleasses were all in action again a half hour or so later and kept their usual stations all the way to Calais and beyond.

At this point a breeze sprang up and, as at Portland Bill, there were two simultaneous but for a time unconnected actions. The Spanish rearguard was attacked by three English squadrons while Medina Sidonia led his vanguard in an offensive against the fourth. To understand we must look at the shoreline. The two fleets had sailed or drifted during the night far enough east so that dawn found them off the southern tip of the Isle of Wight and perhaps a league or less off-shore. They were approaching, therefore, the eastern entrance to the Solent, which King Philip had recommended to his admiral as an emergency anchorage should he have to wait for Parma, and beyond which that innocent Council of War off the Lizard had decided not to proceed without firm word that Parma was ready to come out. To secure themselves there, the Spanish believed, it would suffice to 'seize the Isle of Wight', and this according to intelligence received would not be too difficult, as perhaps it might not have been had it not been for the awkward presence of the English fleet. Medina Sidonia still had no firm word from Parma, and we do not know whether he still contemplated trying for a beach-head on the Isle of Wight and an anchorage at Spithead or whether more sensible counsels had prevailed, but Howard seems to have been afraid that this was what he would try and so wanted to keep inshore.

At any rate the landward English squadron, Frobisher's, was at dawn nearer inshore than any Spanish ships, completely overlapping the Armada's left wing. On this day, at this time, the tidal current set strongly eastward, so that during the battle in the dead calm both fleets would have drifted eastward at something better than a sea-mile in an hour. Moreover, the nearer inshore the stronger the current, so that it is not surprising that Frobisher in the leading ship on the extreme left should have found himself, when the breeze sprang up, north and east of the Spanish van. If the first morning breeze had come from the same quarter on Thursday that it had on Tuesday, that would have given Frobisher the weather-gauge. Instead it came from the south-west, and Frobisher and the leading ships of his squadron were caught, somewhere off Dunnose, to leeward of the Spanish van.

At the moment that the wind sprang up a half dozen of Frobisher's squadron, including the *Triumph*, were already engaged with the *San Martín*, which for the first half-hour or so had been getting somewhat the worst of the argument. As the wind got up a dozen or more heavy Spanish ships bore down to support their Captain-General, and the English, seeing their danger, turned away. Most of Frobisher's squadron managed to slip back round the Spanish left wing, but the *Triumph*, which had been the leading easternmost ship, was cut off. Medina Sidonia promptly led his reinforcements to slice through the retreating line, and it looked as though the *Triumph* was caught to leeward. In a desperate manœuvre Frobisher got out his boats and began to tow away. Other English ships, when they saw what he was doing, sent him their launches until presently eleven had him in tow, while two of Howard's biggest galleons, the *Bear* and the *Elizabeth Jonas*, came round the flank to delay the Spanish attack. Medina Sidonia, however, kept on his intercepting course, still hopeful of boarding a big English ship at last, 'the only way we can win a victory', when the wind freshened and veered, the *Triumph* shook out her sails, cast off her boats and stood away to rejoin her squadron.

At this moment Medina Sidonia's attention was caught by what was happening on his seaward wing. There Drake had concentrated his attack on the extreme right tip of the Spanish crescent. Normally that would have been the post of Recalde in the *San Juan*, but Recalde was off with the vanguard trading broadsides with the *Bear*, and the tip of the horn was defended by the *San Mateo*, one of the royal galleons of Portugal — a stout ship with a gallant captain, but three hundred tons smaller than the *San Juan* and with only thirty-four guns instead of fifty. Finally the *San Mateo* fell back within the crescent to be replaced by the *Florencia*, a much stronger ship; but the movement, though it did not break up the formation, somewhat jostled it, and as Drake redoubled his attack on the outer edge of the crescent and the wind freshened the whole southern wing seemed to edge eastward and northward.

Normally that should not have worried the duke much. But from the poop-deck of his flagship the pilot who stood beside him could see something that would, the look and colour of very shoal water too close under his lee, stretching north-eastward as far as the eye could see, with here and there the black tooth of a rock showing. Francis Drake and John Hawkins would have known all about the Owers, and if they could have held the Spaniards' interest and kept nudging them northward they would have had the whole Armada on the rocks in another twenty minutes. The admiral fired a gun to collect his fleet's attention, shook out fresh canvas, and stood away south-south-east. The fleet conformed, the distance from the deadly reef gradually widened, and the Isle of Wight and the English fleet fell farther and farther astern. It had been a near thing, and the anonymous witness who wrote that the admiral, after seeing victory snatched from him by a hair's breadth (the escape of the *Triumph*), had saved his whole fleet from disaster by no greater margin, was not exaggerating much.

The English followed without trying for another chance to engage. For one thing they were almost out of powder and shot. Howard had sent desperate appeals all up and down the coast and the local authorities had responded nobly, but cannon balls are not articles the ordinary justice of the peace keeps about him in any quantity, and plough chains and leather bags full of scrap-iron are not really adequate substitutes. For another thing Howard had a rendezvous with Seymour and the eastern squadron off Dover, a powerful reinforcement; and for the next trial of strength, probably the decisive one, he felt he needed all the reinforcements he could get.

Sure at last that the Spaniards would not land on the south coast, Howard celebrated Thursday's battle as if it had been a victory. In the calm of Friday morning he knighted Hawkins and Frobisher and several of his own kinsmen on the deck of the *Ark*, as on a victorious field. If we may judge by what he said afterwards, however, and how he behaved, he was not easy in his mind. So far, neither his ships nor his men had suffered severely, and he felt sure he had inflicted heavy damage in both on the enemy. But this was a stronger, tougher, more pugnacious opponent than anyone among his captains — except, perhaps, Drake — had bargained for. After four battles — any of them, in ships engaged and shot expended, easily the greatest that had ever been fought at sea — there was no slackening of Spanish discipline, no breach in their formidable order, and the Spanish were as eager to shorten the range and come to hand-strokes as they had been that first morning off the Eddystone.

Medina Sidonia was even less in the mood for celebration. He had pursued his way successfully towards his goal, and if he had not been able to crush his English tormentors they had not hindered his march. But now that he approached it, he liked his destination less than ever. Soon he would be entering a strait beyond which lay a stormy treacherous sea with not a single friendly haven where his ships could anchor. So far he had had no firm word about when Parma would be ready to embark, or how and where they would meet. Nor had he found any way to deal with the English fleet. He could not lay them aboard, and though he was sure that he had done them serious damage by his gunfire, crippled some of them and perhaps sunk a few, and killed a lot of their men, they were constantly reinforced from along the coast, grew more numerous every day and were wearing down his strength with their long-range fire.

Besides, he knew that from now on he was likely to do them little damage by gunfire. The enormous, the incredible stocks of ammunition brought from Lisbon were almost spent. There was still enough powder. After all, he had brought enough powder, he thought, for a considerable campaign ashore. But in some ships there were no more cannon balls at all of the more useful sizes, and in the whole fleet there were too few. Howard, in a similar predicament, could expect fresh supplies from every English port, but there was only one source to which Medina Sidonia could apply. He sent off an urgent appeal to Parma for cannon balls at once, as many as possible, of all sizes, but especially ten-, eight- and six-pounders. Meanwhile, in the calm of Friday, while Howard was bestowing knighthoods on his relatives, the duke was reading the results of inventories and extracting from the *urcas* and the weaker ships what cannon balls they had or would admit to having, in order to replenish the exhausted lockers of the galleons.

Martin Frobisher, from a portrait by Cornelius Ketel.

From a set of playing cards engraved in the seventeenth century.

Both commanders seem to have overrated the effect of their fire on the enemy, a not unusual mistake. Captain Vanegas estimated the total Spanish casualties in the four battles in the Channel at one hundred and sixty-seven killed and two hundred and forty-one wounded. This does not count, of course, perhaps a hundred and fifty killed and wounded by the explosion on the *San Salvador*, or the four hundred, more or less, captured on the *Rosario*. Even adding these in the rate of attrition, on a force of more than twenty thousand effectives, is not particularly severe. Captain Vanegas seems to have been charged with keeping the official casualty figures for the fleet, and to have performed his duties conscientiously, but his estimate is certainly too low for two reasons. In the first place wounded were only so reported when they were disabled. In the second place Spanish captains, like all captains in the sixteenth century, were reluctant to report men killed, because as long as their names were on the muster rolls the captains drew the dead men's pay. 'The men are dead, but not the pay', Burghley noted wearily of the English forces in the same campaign.

If Vanegas, with the advantages of Spanish discipline and experience, was unable to get accurate casualty lists, none of the casualty estimates from the English fleet for this period are credible at all. If the Spanish shot was spent as harmlessly as most accounts declare, then there is scarcely any excuse for Howard's failure to close the range. But it seems certain that English casualties in the first four battles were much fewer than Spanish, perhaps by a half or more. Similarly, though ships in both fleets lost yards and minor rigging, none in either lost a mast through gunfire or was badly enough damaged to force it to drop out of the line for more than a day.

Two factors unite to account for the small results of all this cannonading. For one thing there was too little experience with the use of great guns in fleet actions. No one knew what they would do. The English believed, and so did the Spanish, that a fleet with a marked advantage in long-range weapons, culverins and demi culverins, could lie off at extreme range or nearly, and knock the enemy fleet to pieces without danger to itself. It turned out not to be so. At ranges of three to seven hundred yards a sixteenth-century culverin or demi-culverin might fail altogether to pierce the thick hull of a galleon or stout greatship, and when it did would only make a small hole quickly caulked by an alert crew. Sinking even a single ship in this fashion could prove a tedious business. Later on, tacticians learned that the heaviest possible broadsides of big ship-smashing guns at the shortest possible range were what were decisive in fleet actions.

Besides, the gunnery on both sides must have been dismally bad. Sixteenth-century ships' guns were hard to aim and uncertain to fire and, of course, errors that would have made no difference at fifty yards meant a complete miss at five hundred, but with decent training the gun-crews on both sides should have been able to do a great deal better. Most of the trained gunners in the Armada had never fired a gun from a ship's deck, and though the English had some skilled naval gunners they had not enough. The Spanish admired the speed with which the English served their pieces; they had nothing to say about their accuracy. Among the English an amateur like Howard might applaud the performance of the English gun-crews, a seasoned professional like William Thomas was merely appalled. 'What can be said but our sins was the cause', he wrote to Burghley after the battle, 'that so much powder and shot spent, and so long time in fight, and, in comparison thereof, so little harm?' At that, English gunnery was better than Spanish. Of the two fleets, after a week in the Channel the Spanish was the more sorely punished.

It was not the punishment of his fleet that was worrying the duke, but the approaching debouchment into the North Sea with no appointment with Parma. There seemed to be only one thing to do. As the Armada drew towards Calais Roads late Saturday afternoon it struck its sails and its anchors thundered down. It was a smartly executed manœuvre, and there was a good chance that the English, taken by surprise and carried forward by wind and tide, would be obliged to stand on past the road-stead and so lose the weather-gauge. But the English might have been waiting for the duke's signal. Before the Spanish cables had stopped running out the English were dropping their anchors, and the two anchored fleets stood at gaze by Calais Cliffs, just a long culverin-shot apart.

XXVI

THE HELLBURNERS

THE NEIGHBOURHOOD OF CALAIS, AUGUST 6TH AND 7TH, 1588

As Howard dropped anchor in Whitsand Bay, Seymour's squadron, summoned from its blockading station, was tacking in from the north-west. When it dropped anchor beside him some hours later the English fleet was the stronger by thirty-five sail, five of them Queen's galleons, and of those, two—the *Rainbow* and the *Vanguard*—the newest and finest of the lot. All the time that Howard had been slogging up the Channel this useful force had been cruising back and forth between Dunkirk and Dover on the off-chance that Parma would try to come out.

It had been a waste of strength, but neither Seymour nor the Queen's councillors thoroughly trusted the Dutch, partly because of the sulky attitude of the Dutch Estates over the long drawn out negotiations at Bourbourg, partly because, although Justin of Nassau protested that he could take care of Parma, all Seymour had seen of the Dutch for months had been a couple of shallow-draught sloops patrolling the coast farther inshore than the English cared to venture. News came swiftly across the hostile lines from Bruges to Flushing, and Justin of Nassau had felt sure that he would be warned in time if Parma should decide to try a sortie. He had earnestly hoped that Parma would. There was nothing he would have liked better than to find all that formidable infantry and their invincible commander afloat in flat-boats on blue water. The farther offshore he caught them the farther they would have to swim.

So Justin kept his fleet snug in Flushing or cruising in the Western Scheldt, and hoped that Parma would believe the reports that the Dutch were unprepared by sea. Instead it was Seymour who believed them and, to Justin's vexation, paraded up and down the Flanders coast enough naval strength to sink a dozen flotillas like Parma's. Since the directors of Dutch policy thought it would be tactless to let Queen Elizabeth suspect that the loot of London was bait in a Dutch mousetrap, Seymour got no inkling of what Justin was up to and Justin was reduced to hoping that Seymour would be blown off-station, or get tired and go away. Deadlocked in misunderstanding throughout weary months, while the peace commissioners wrangled at Bourbourg and no word came of the Armada, the Dutch and English grumbled about each other with increasing irritation and suspicion, as allies so often do.

The approach of real danger silenced grumbling. Justin heard that the Armada was off the Lizard and that Parma's camps, lethargic for months, were buzzing with activity; then, a little later, that though the fleets had clashed and clashed again the Armada was keeping on up the Channel. However tempting it might be to try to catch Parma so far off-shore that not a single barge could escape, it was not to be thought of while an unbeaten Spanish fleet might appear at any time in the same waters. Until the Armada was driven off any sortie must be stopped at once. This was the kind of task Dutch warships were built for, and, with a minimum of fuss, Justin of Nassau led down past Dunkirk all the ships he needed for the job. Before Seymour set sail to join Howard, the Dutch had already taken over. No one told Howard.

When the admiral hung out a flag for council that Sunday morning there were more urgent things to talk about. Calais is less than thirty miles from Dunkirk. Parma and Medina Sidonia were already, or would soon be, in touch. Obviously the Armada meant to ride here at anchor until Parma was ready, and wind and weather served. The English captains had no clear notion of Parma's strength by sea; they did not know whether he could get his flotilla out, or how much it would complicate their task if he did, but it was not a risk they wanted to run. If the present Spanish anchorage was unsafe theirs was no safer, and they felt sure that the lee shore on which they might be driven was an unfriendly one. So far, M. Gourdan, the Governor of Calais, had taken no official notice of the presence of the Lord Admiral of England, but boats had been seen going back and forth between his castle and the *San Martín*. Gourdan was believed to sympathize with the Holy League, and in any case, since the *V*ing had knuckled under to Guise, all Frenchmen except the Huguenots must be counted as potential enemies, little better than vassals of Spain. All that going and coming of boats between the Armada and the shore could only mean that some sort of mischief was afoot, and it seemed clear that the Armada had better be shifted before Medina Sidonia could concert his plans, either with the French Governor or with Parma. There was only one way to do it: fire-ships.

Wynter had seen that when he cast anchor the night before. Probably every experienced officer in the fleet had seen it. The newcomers, Lord

287

Seymour and Sir William Wynter and Sir Henry Palmer, were as impressed by the menacing strength anchored under Calais Cliffs as were the captains who had tried it. Nobody wanted to come to close quarters with the Spaniards, or thought it would do much good to bombard them, so the council must have been mostly about ways and means of getting fireships. Its first decision was to send Sir Henry Palmer in a pinnace to Dover for ships and combustibles, and it was not until after Sir Henry had left on his mission that bolder and more sensible views prevailed. To wait for ships from Dover would mean deferring the attack until some time on Monday at the earliest, and missing the favourable conjunction of a tide near the top of the springs and a freshening wind from the south-south-east. The proper moment would be that night, Sunday night. Drake offered a ship of his own, the *Thomas* of Plymouth, of two hundred tons, and Hawkins one of his; and with the mounting enthusiasm six more were recruited, the smallest of ninety tons, all the rest from a hundred and fifty to two hundred. This would be a fleet of fire-ships worthy of the great Armada, and the captains scattered to the work of getting them ready and stuffing them with everything available that would make a blaze. Crews saved their own gear, of course, and no doubt the water-barrels and stores were mostly taken out, though one of the owners later billed the Treasury for quite a remarkable amount of butter, beef and biscuits left aboard and burned. But not only were spars and sails and rigging left, since the ships would bear down on the anchorage, it was hoped, under full sail, but all the ships' guns were left double-shotted to go off when the fire made them hot enough, to add to the terror if not to the destruction of the enemy. These fire-ships were hastily improvised weapons. Oddly enough there were none prepared in advance anywhere on the coast. But though the work had to be done at top speed, nothing that ingenuity could suggest or the resources of the fleet supply seems to have been spared.

It would have heartened Howard if he could have known what all that going and coming of small craft around the *San Martín* was about. M. Gourdan's boat was sent only in reply to one from the duke, and it bore chiefly the cold warning that the Armada lay in an exposed and dangerous anchorage — something the duke's pilots had already told him — and it would be better if it did not stay there too long. The chill was scarcely taken off this welcome by a small present of fruit and other refreshment for the duke himself. Calais is a long way from Chartres, and, like a good many place-holders in France that summer, M. Gourdan may have been wondering how much there was to this reconciliation between the King and the Duke of Guise, and waiting to see which way after all the cat would jump. At any rate, he seems to have decided on an attitude of correct neutrality. He did give permission for the stewards of the Armada to buy what fresh food they could ashore, a permission which would account for most of the movements of small boats which the English saw, but there is no reason to suppose that he would not have extended similar courtesies to Howard on request. Howard and his council assumed that the French were hostile; as far as the Governor of Calais is concerned, there is no confirming evidence.

Howard would have been heartened, too, if he could have known the contents of Medina Sidonia's messages to Parma. The duke had got one off almost as soon as he dropped anchor, reminding Parma that although he had sent to him often, keeping him informed daily, he had heard nothing in reply for weeks. He continued: 'I am anchored here, two leagues from Calais with the enemy's fleet on my flank. They can cannonade me whenever they like, and I shall be unable to do them much harm in return. If you can send me forty or fifty flyboats of your fleet I can, with their help, defend myself here until you are ready to come out.'

Flyboats were those fast shallow-draught little ships-of-war with which, in the early days of the revolt of the Netherlands, the Sea Beggars had terrorized the Channel, and with which ever since the rebellious Dutch had commanded their coastal waters. Flyboats were just what Parma lacked. So far from being able to send forty or fifty to reinforce the Armada he could scarcely have sent a dozen, even if no one had tried to prevent him. The 'fleet' he had assembled at Dunkirk and Nieuport consisted almost entirely of canal boats, without masts or sails or guns. They were, for the most part, the kind of flat-bottomed, double-ended, open-decked barges used for transporting cattle, and of these Parma had just about enough to pass his infantry across to Margate in the most favourable weather if he packed the men in like cattle. As for the flyboats, they were where Parma knew they would be, standing off and on between Dunkirk and Ostend — the tough little ships of Justin of Nassau, treating the treacherous banks and shoals of Flanders with the contemptuous familiarity of children on their own playground.

That Medina Sidonia should have had no notion, even as late as Saturday evening, August 6th, that Parma was helpless to help him, seems so strange that most people who have written about it since have assumed that a principal element in 'the fatal misunderstanding which wrecked the campaign' was Medina Sidonia's refusal, through panic or stupidity, to recognize the obvious. Nothing could be more unlikely. Medina Sidonia may have made mistakes in the conduct of his campaign but he was not a stupid man, and whatever influenced his decisions, those we know about show no sign of panic. Parma had outlined his position clearly enough, but not to Medina Sidonia. Parma had written to Philip often in 1587, and repeated with emphasis in January 1588 that his barges could not venture to sea unless the Armada were able to protect them from enemy warships. In April he sent two emissaries to Madrid to urge that because of the difficulties of the Enterprise as it was planned it should be deferred, and a truce concluded to give him a chance to seize Walcheren and the deep-water port of Flushing. When Philip refused to change his plan one of Parma's emissaries, the future historian Luis Cabrera de Córdoba, revealed, according to his own account, the crux of the difficulty. As he remembered it, he said to the King: 'Look, your majesty, it's going to be impossible for the duke of Parma's ships ever to meet the Armada. The Spanish galleons draw twenty-five or thirty feet, and around Dunkirk they won't find that much water for several leagues. The enemy's ships draw so much less that they can safely place themselves to prevent anything coming out of Dunkirk. So, since the junction of the barges from Flanders with the Armada is the whole point of the enterprise, and it is impossible, why not give it up now and save much time and money?'

Of course, Cabrera de Córdoba wrote some time after the event, and he may not have spoken quite so bluntly or so presciently. But it would be odd if someone had not told Philip substantially the same thing, not once but several times. There is one thing even more odd. In the few and formal communications they exchanged it is perhaps natural that the Duke of Parma did not reveal to the Duke of Medina Sidonia all his difficulties, and that he should have alluded to his own naval forces with a grandiose vagueness which allowed the Spanish duke and his staff to draw quite false conclusions. But Philip must have had a fairly accurate picture of Parma's weakness by sea. Why, in all the long and elaborate instructions and advice with which he pursued Medina Sidonia, from the time the duke first took command in Lisbon until long after it was too late to instruct or advise him further, did Philip never mention the central crucial difficulty? He did warn his Captain-General to keep well off the treacherous banks around Dunkirk. But he repeatedly told him to rendezvous with Parma at sea, or to meet him 'off the cape of Margate'. The clear implication was that it was only the English galleons that Parma could not cope with, that

he could deal with the Dutch flyboats without help. No wonder that the
Spanish duke's successive messengers as they arrived at Nieuport or
Dunkirk were shocked and appalled by what they saw.

Medina Sidonia got his first intimation of catastrophe on Sunday
morning. Bearing up to the fleet a little after daybreak came Don Rodrigo
Tello's pinnace, which the duke had sent off two weeks before to announce
to Parma that the Armada had reached the height of Ushant. Don Rodrigo
had found Parma at Bruges, and was the bearer of letters acknowledging
all the duke's messages. Parma wrote that he was delighted by the safe
arrival of the Armada and he promised that in another six days everything
would be ready for his sortie at the first favourable opportunity. But when
Don Rodrigo left Dunkirk the night before there was no sign of Parma's
arrival there, and the ships he had seen at Nieuport and Dunkirk were
miserable things — mere empty bottoms without masts or spars or guns,
and no stores loaded. Don Rodrigo did not see how they could possibly
be ready in less than a fortnight.

There is something strange in Parma's behaviour in this whole episode.
Apparently he had found the preparation of the barges a frustrating business, and the building of flyboats at Dunkirk even worse. The carpenters
and shipwrights worked with exasperating slowness, and whenever their
pay was in arrears they downed tools and refused to work at all. Rotten
timbers and green planks were always getting mixed with the sound ones,
so that many barges had to be torn apart and rebuilt, several flyboats
proved useless, and during the embarkation exercise one set of barges
went down to the bottom of the canal leaving the men up to their necks
in the water. It was hard to find cannon for the flyboats, even when money
was in hand, and impossible to find enough experienced seamen. But
Parma had encountered difficulties of this sort before, and by threats and
rewards and cajolery, by ingenuity and tireless industry and the inspiration of his presence and example, they had been overcome. This time he
let the tempo slacken. Discipline and inspections grew lax; the snail's pace
of shipbuilding slowed down further. The froth of activity stirred up by
the news that the Armada was in the Channel seemed mostly aimless.
Parma gave the necessary orders, but he did not stir from Bruges until
the afternoon of Monday, the 8th, and then on Monday and Tuesday he
hustled his embarkation with a useless show of speed.

There is something unreal about the whole scene that stormy Tuesday
evening at Dunkirk; one flyboat with no guns and its mast unstepped,
another with no running rigging, another waterlogged and on its beam

ends in the mud of the canal; some barges left uncaulked and already beginning to leak; others whose seams started the minute they were loaded; and the soldiers being tumbled into the sound barges like sacks of wheat, laughing incredulously when they saw the bare coffin-shaped boxes in which they were expected to put to sea. Dark fell and the embarkation went on by torchlight, Parma standing by white-faced and impassive, and more and more men being crowded into the barges, though Dunkirk bar was a fury of white water and the beaten Armada was running before the wind (it would be strange if Parma did not know this) already many leagues to leeward.

All through this scene one gets the feeling that the great captain was playing some sort of charade, that he was making a series of gestures purely for record. 'He acted', says Cabrera de Córdoba of the week before, 'as if he did not believe that the news of the Armada's coming could be true.' Perhaps, instead, he simply believed what Cabrera de Córdoba had told Philip months before. Even if the Armada destroyed the English fleet it could not hurt the Dutch as long as they stayed behind the banks. And even if he had had a hundred armed flyboats, instead of a pitiful dozen fit for service, they could come out only one at a time and Justin of Nassau's fleet could sink them as they came out until their passage was blocked by wrecks. If Parma was able to face the failure of the Enterprise with stony calm it may have been because he had foreseen long ago that it was doomed to failure.

That curious scene at Dunkirk was on Tuesday night. On the previous Sunday morning, even after he heard Rodrigo Tello's news, Medina Sidonia still refused to believe that the Enterprise was hopeless. He urged all ships that could to fill their water-casks, tried in vain to borrow some round shot from M. Gourdan, and sent off a string of messengers to Parma, all armed with arguments and pleas and exhortations. Ever since he had found, off Portland Bill, that even when he had the weather-gauge he could not close with the English, Medina Sidonia had been persuading himself that all he needed for victory was a force of light fast ships, such as he believed Parma had, to supplement his heavy ones. If only Parma could be convinced of this, surely he would come out and together they would sweep the English from the seas.

Meanwhile he had other anxieties. If the English began to cannonade him he had so few rounds left for the galleons' great guns that he would scarcely dare to return their fire, and before long they would realize his helplessness and come in to ship-killing range. But this was not his gravest danger. With the English to windward of him and a strong current running towards the strait his tight-packed anchorage was in the classic position for an attack by fire-ships. Of all the dangers to a fleet of wooden sailing-ships, fire was the gravest; their sails, their tarry cordage, their sun-dried decks and spars could catch fire in a minute, and there was almost nothing about them that would not burn. But the duke had reason to fear worse than ordinary fire-ships. If King Philip had warned him once he had warned him a dozen times that the English were preparing many strange fireworks and diabolical inventions. In part, this warning was the result of the war of nerves which Sir Edward Stafford waged through his contacts with Mendoza in Paris. But it had at least one solid fact to back it, a fact known to Medina Sidonia alone, he thought, but actually a common item of gossip in the fleet. It concerned the inventor of the hellburners of Antwerp, the most terrible weapons ever used by men in war, fire-ships which were actually enormous bombs capable of killing more men in one blast than might fall in a great battle, and of strewing a circle more than a mile across with a litter of flaming wreckage. The designer of these infernal machines, the Italian engineer Giambelli, was said to be now in England, working for Queen Elizabeth. And so he was indeed. At the moment he was harmlessly occupied with a somewhat impractical boom, meant to close the Thames at Gravesend. The only effective weapon he lent the English for the Armada campaign was the terror of his name. It was enough.

Worrying about strange fireworks made Medina Sidonia see, with some alarm, a number of ships joining Howard on Sunday afternoon. They were harmless supply ships, actually, but the duke thought it probable that Giambelli's infernal machines had arrived at last. There was not much he could do. He ordered out a screen of pinnaces and ships' boats equipped with grapnels to catch and tow the fire-ships ashore. And he sent word round the fleet that an attack by fire-ships was to be expected but would be dealt with by the screen. Ships were not to shift their ground as long as the screen was doing its work. If some fire-ships got through, however, they were to slip and buoy their cables and stand out to sea, letting the fire-ships drift by inshore on the current. Then they were to anchor again as soon as possible so as to have some chance, at daybreak, of picking up the buoys at their former anchorage. That was the beginning of an anxious night.

Until nearly midnight nothing happened except that the freshening of the south wind and the flying scud across the moon gave promise of a blustery morning. Then lights appeared at the edge of the English fleet. Not lights, fires; two, six, eight of them moving forward rapidly and growing in brilliance until the watchers at the Spanish anchorage could see plainly eight tall ships with all sails set and lines of fire beginning to run up their rigging, driving straight towards them with wind and tide. The fire-ships seemed to maintain a perfect line, and to keep so close together that two pikemen on adjacent ships, if men could have lived on those blazing decks, could have leaned out and clashed their pike-heads above the intervening water. The watchers could see also, black against the glare, the pinnaces of the screen closing in.

This was the critical moment. The two fleets had anchored so close together that the pinnaces would have to work within gunshot of the enemy, and the line of the fire-ships was so tightly serried that the only way the pinnaces could get at them was to snatch them off a pair at a time from the ends. These flaming monsters were no mere fishing-smacks, stuffed with brush and straw, to be fended off with oars. Getting a grapnel to hold on them, swinging them around and towing them on to the beach would be a feat of seamanship requiring nerve and brawn and split-second timing, for the line was driving along so fast, pushed by a strong wind, a spring tide and the set of the Channel current all working together, that it would cover its whole course in a few minutes. Apparently the first pair of pinnaces executed their manœuvre smartly enough, for the next morning the charred ribs of two fire-ships lay smouldering well short of the Spanish anchorage; but, a few seconds later, just as the next pair of pinnaces came into position and when, one must assume, the men standing in their bows were ready to throw their grapnels, the double-shotted guns heated now almost white-hot began to go off, spraying their shot at random over the water and by the force of their recoil sending up a fountain of sparks to be blown down among the boats. Startled, the pinnaces sheered off, there was a moment of tangled confusion; and in that moment the six remaining ships swept past and bore down on the anchored fleet, the sound of their exploding guns heard above the roar of the flames and the fountains of sparks shooting skyward. There could be no doubt. Here, once more, were the deadly hellburners of Antwerp.

XXVII

THE ORDER BROKEN

CALAIS ROADS TO GRAVELINES, AUGUST 8TH, 1588

WHEN he saw that his screen had lost the fire-ships Medina Sidonia fired a gun, slipped his cables and stood out to sea close-hauled. This time, however, the fleet did not conform. Instead, something like a panic swept the crowded anchorage. Perhaps there had been too many lurid stories of hellburners spread by too many veterans of the Flanders wars. Perhaps, though this is less likely, Medina Sidonia's orders had got twisted in oral transmission. Whatever the reason, most captains simply cut their cables and ran before the wind, scattering, some here, some there, as if they were as much afraid of one another as they were of the fire-ships. The strong set of the current and the rising gale swept the whole disorderly mob out through the straits and on towards the sands of the Flemish coast. The formidable Spanish order was broken at last.

The *San Martín* made one short leg out to sea and another back again, and dropped her sheet anchor a mile or so north of her first anchorage. Just beyond her, four of her closest companions of the night also anchored. Recalde's *San Juan*, the *San Marcos* and two more — perhaps the *San Felipe* and the *San Mateo*, all royal galleons of Portugal, at any rate — as usual in the post of danger and of honour. When the blustery dawn came these five were all of the great Armada in sight, except Don Hugo de Moncada's *San Lorenzo*, the *capitana* of the galleasses, rudderless and with something wrong with her mainmast, crawling along inshore like a wounded beetle. She had fouled her unlucky rudder ('Frail ships for these rough seas!') on a neighbour's cable, and got involved in some complicated collision in the night's panic. Nearer Calais jetty the ribs of six fire-ships smouldered. After the last loaded gun had gone off there had been no more explosions. They were not hellburners after all.

Southward, the English still lay at their last night's anchorage, but a gun was fired from Howard's *Ark* and trumpets called across the water. Anchors were coming up, sails being shaken out, banners hoisted. The whole naval force of England, a hundred and fifty sail, all the Queen's

The engagement between the fleets off 'Dunne Nose' near the Isle of Wight. The Spanish fleet is on the left.

galleons, as many more tall heavy-armed merchant ships and private men-of-war, and some five score smaller craft, the Grand Fleet in fact if not in name was moving to the attack.

Medina Sidonia had to decide at once what to do, but fortunately it was the kind of decision which came easily to him. He was the commander. It was his duty to face the enemy, alone if need be, until his scattered command could be rallied. He weighed anchor and stood out defiantly into the straits. Behind him came Recalde's *San Juan* and the other three royal galleons, close-hauled under light canvas. As they made the open strait their pinnaces scudded away from them before the wind, sent to rally the scattered ships and order them back to support their admiral.

Until day broke Howard was not sure of the success of his fire-ships. Obviously two had been towed ashore, and perhaps all the rest had been similarly diverted, for except for their dying glow there was no sign of any conflagration. The Spaniards might have moved out and then returned to re-anchor, or they might not have shifted at all. In either case there would be nothing for it but to try to dislodge them by gunfire, and Howard himself meant to lead the first assault. This time there would be no cautious long-range bombardment. The emphasis all the English accounts put on shortening the range in this Monday's battle shows that everyone realized they had been keeping too far off.

The scene at dawn changed Howard's plans. The Spanish had scattered. Howard sent his other four squadrons to deal with the only Spanish galleons in sight, yielding the honour of giving the first charge to Sir Francis Drake, and led his own squadron to capture or destroy the great galleass. That crippled monster, seeing the English line bearing down, scrambled desperately towards the shelter of Calais Harbour. A fast-ebbing tide, a heavy surf, no rudder and no knowledge of the contour of the beach, made escape unlikely, and at the last moment the straining exertions of the galley slaves tugging at the great sweeps only drove the galleass that much more firmly aground. There she lay, quickly heeling over more and more towards her beam ends as the water ebbed from beneath her, her deck canting inshore and her port batteries pointing foolishly skyward, stuck fast under the walls of Calais Castle.

For the English there was one exasperating circumstance about this incident. English galleons drew, on the whole, more water than Spanish ones, and galleasses far less than any galleon. The *San Lorenzo* had grounded too far inshore to be smashed up by gunfire. Howard ordered off a flotilla of ships' boats to carry her by boarding, and these for a while had hot work. The *San Lorenzo* was canted over so far that none of her guns could be brought to bear, but that very fact helped to shelter her crew and made her sides harder to climb. For a time the boats wheeled warily past the galleass to seaward — it was too shoal for them to get round to the more vulnerable landward rail — keeping up a brisk fire of small-arms and being briskly answered. Such indecisive attempts at boarding as they made were beaten back, and there began to be wounded and some dead in the boats. Then Don Hugo de Moncada was shot through the head by a musket ball, and the defenders he had been holding at their posts, seeing very little future probably in this kind of fighting, broke and, jumping from the low landward rail, waded and scrambled ashore. Already the English sailors were clambering over the seaward rail and through the gun-ports beneath it.

By conquest and the laws of war the loot of the galleass was theirs, as M. Gourdan the Governor of Calais acknowledged, and they soon stripped her clean of everything of value a man could lift and carry. But the Governor reminded them that the vessel, with her guns and rigging, was his; and when it looked to him as if they were going not only to disregard his warning but to plunder, as well, the burghers of Calais who had gathered on the beach to watch the fight, he opened fire from the castle on their boats. It needed that to persuade the boats' crews to pull back to their ships where Howard was impatient to join the now distant battle.

The looting of one stranded ship seems a strange reason for keeping a powerful squadron for hours out of a major battle. But it is to be remembered that the *San Lorenzo* was the strongest ship of a formidable class which had given a lot of trouble in the Channel, and it was worth some delay, in Howard's cautious but sensible view of his mission, to make sure before leaving her unwatched that she was permanently out of action. His returning boats were able to assure him that she was, that no one would ever get her afloat again. That proved so; the *San Lorenzo* rotted to pieces under Calais Castle. Meanwhile Howard steered for the sound of the guns.

Of the last fight of the Armada, off Gravelines, as of the battles coming up the Channel, we can catch only partial glimpses. Nobody on either side left a satisfactory record of the movements of even a single ship. The ordinary fog of war at sea, the noise, the smoke, the danger, the confusion, the too many things to do in too little time and the difficulty of making out what anybody else is doing, was compounded, as before, by the fact that in this campaign nobody understood the new weapons employed or the tactics they required, and compounded afresh by Monday's fight having been the first in heavy weather, high winds, rough seas and limited visibility.

Some things seem clear. The wind must have been about south-south-west, perhaps no more than a strong breeze in the morning, perhaps a moderate gale. The *San Martín* and her consorts must have moved before it, though under small canvas, through the straits and into the North Sea, with the *San Martín* the rearmost, and the *San Juan* with one or two of the others getting well to leeward. Even at this point Medina Sidonia was concerned to lead his straggling fleet away from the dangerous Dunkirk banks and into deep water. Perhaps he meant the more leeward of the scattered ships to form on Recalde's *San Juan* and the nearer ones on the *San Martín*. Nobody says. At any rate, his northern movement gave the English something of a stern chase and delayed the beginning of the action.

Sir Francis Drake in the *Revenge* gave the first charge, as the Lord Admiral had appointed him to do. The Spanish flagship, as the English approached, wore round farther to present her broadside to the enemy and lay to, and for some time, while the distance between the *Revenge* and the *San Martín* lessened, both ships held their fire. This time the English were determined to make every shot tell and the Spanish, since they had so few left, were obliged to. Not until the ships were at about 'half-musket shot' (a hundred yards?) did the *Revenge* fire first her bow guns, then her broadside, to be answered in thunder from the *San Martín*. It may have been in this exchange that the *Revenge* was 'pierced through by cannon balls of all sizes', as Ubaldini says. Fenner in the *Nonpareil* came close after Drake, followed by the rest of Drake's squadron, each ship as she came up loosing off her broadside and risking the *San Martín's* reply. Then the whole squadron followed its commander on a course to the north-east, out of the ken for a while of any of the surviving narratives.

That is not to say they may not have been doing good work somewhere. Corbett's guess that Drake saw that the proper tactical target was farther to leeward where the stronger galleons were hauling off the shoals and re-forming in deep water, is very plausible. That does seem to have been the critical point; and to have prevented and broken up this rally would have been a tremendous gain, far more decisive than the capture or sinking of the *San Martín*. It is no reflection on Drake's tactical insight that Sir Martin Frobisher, who came up next, did not appreciate it. Later on, at Harwich in the presence of Lord Sheffield and others, Frobisher was to say of this action: 'He [Drake] came bragging up at the first indeed, and gave them his prow and his broadside; and then kept his luff, and was glad that he was gone again like a cowardly knave or traitor — I rest doubtful, but the one I will swear.' Frobisher was angry at Drake over another matter, and he was always a hot-headed man, likely to say more than he meant. But certainly he did not fathom the purpose of Drake's movement or try to support it. If he had it might have succeeded.

Instead, Frobisher stayed and fought the *San Martín*. The *Triumph's* castles were higher and its bulk greater, and Frobisher lay close to the Spanish flagship, though he did not offer to board, beating her with his great guns, while the rest of his squadron swarmed across her bow and stern and under her lee, riddling her upper works with shot. When Hawkins came up in the *Victory* and way was made for him, it almost seemed that Medina Sidonia was fighting alone against the whole English fleet. Or nearly alone. The *San Marcos de Portugal* in which the Marquis of Peñafiel and a number of other persons of illustrious lineage served as gentlemen adventurers, had never been far off from the admiral. She had been able to close some of Drake's squadron and since had stood by, taking her share of the fighting and like the *San Martín* replying to the fire of the enemy, not just with her woefully stinted great guns but, the range was so close, with muskets and arquebuses.

By the time all Hawkins's squadron had come up other Spanish ships were beginning to join the fight. They were the familiar names, the same ships that had borne the brunt all the way up the Channel — the galleons of Portugal, the galleons of Castile, de Leiva's carrack and Bertendona's, the Florentine galleon, Oquendo's flagship, two or three of the biggest and best-armed Biscayans like the *Grangrin*. At first there were only seven or eight of them, then fifteen, then twenty-five, not the familiar crescent but its tough outer rim, a shield behind which the slower and weaker ships could form. Seymour and Wynter, when they joined the battle, found the Spaniards back in something like regular formation. 'They went', says Wynter, 'into the proportion of a half moon, their admiral and vice-admiral in the midst and the greatest number of them; and there went on each side, in the wings, their galleasses, armados of Portugal and other good ships, in the whole to the number of sixteen in a wing which did seem to be of their principal shipping.' The recovery of that formidable but tricky order in the first blustery hours of Monday morning was one of the more remarkable feats of Spanish discipline and seamanship. It was made possible, of course, by the leadership of the Duke of Medina Sidonia and the stubborn courage of his rearguard action.

With high courage and bold leadership on both sides, the victory goes to the best ships and the best guns. The superiority of English ships had been demonstrated already, time and again. They could outflank and worry the enemy at will, keep the weather-gauge, choose their own range and always be sure of disengaging when they liked. The superiority of English guns and gunnery the Spanish were inclined to concede, but the chief superiority of the English off Gravelines lay in the fact that they still had ammunition. When they decided to close the range, as must have been agreed Sunday morning, they cannot have known how short the Spanish were; but in the second phase of Monday's battle, when all five English squadrons were harrying and jostling the Spanish crescent and trying to worry it into bits, they found they could close to easy hailing distance and not take too much punishment.

The English were still overestimating the most effective range. 'How much the nearer, so much the better,' said Sir Richard Hawkins later. He had commanded the *Swallow* in his father's squadron, and learned by the campaign's experience. But at Monday's usual range the English guns could do real damage. The tough layers of Spanish oak guarding the lower hulls of the galleons were not smashed, but they were pierced repeatedly. Before the battle was over most of the Armada's first-line ships were leaking, and some were mortally hurt. Their upper works were only musket-proof at best, and by evening they had been beaten to bloody flinders. The slaughter on the upper decks must have been terrible.

The Spanish fought gallantly. Again and again one galleon or another struggled desperately to board. It was, after all, the only chance of fighting on even terms. Badly mangled as the *San Martín* had been in the first phase of the action, afterwards, twice at least, she thrust herself into the midst of the mêlée to rescue a ship in trouble. The crew of one of the *urcas* saw Bertendona's great carrack drive past, her decks a shambles, her battery guns silent and blood spilling out of her scuppers as she heeled to the wind, but musketeers still ready in tops and on her quarter-deck, as she came back stubbornly to take her place in the line. The *San Mateo*, which twice had found herself surrounded and fighting a ring of enemies, was in even worse case. More than half her men, soldiers and sailors, were killed or disabled, her great guns were useless, she was leaking like a sieve and wallowing low in the water, but when the *San Martín* bore up to cover her and the admiral offered to take off her officers and crew, Don

Diego de Pimentel proudly refused to abandon ship. Later an English galleon — probably Seymour's *Rainbow* — impressed by such heroic and useless sacrifice, steered close enough for an officer to hail, offering good terms. For answer a musketeer shot him through the body, and the *San Mateo* went on suffering broadside after broadside, and replying with a futile sputter of small-arms.

By this time Medina Sidonia could see his painfully re-established formation breaking up again before his eyes, ships being isolated, group being cut off from group, and the whole increasingly helpless mob of shipping being crowded inexorably on to the Flanders sands. The Lord Admiral had long since come up and, whether following Drake's example or not, the main pressure of the English attack was on the Armada's weather wing. It was four o'clock. The battle had gone on since an hour or two after sunrise and there looked like being time enough before sunset to finish off the Spanish fleet.

Then, just when it seemed that in another hour the Armada would be broken up and most of its ships driven on the sands, there came a violent squall with blinding torrents of rain. For fifteen minutes or so the English were too busy keeping out of each other's way to pay much attention to the enemy. When they had time to look they saw the Spaniards standing away northwards, already out of range and re-forming, even as the English watched, their old tough half-moon. Presently the *San Martín* defiantly shortened sail, and the reordered fleet conformed. The battered Spaniards were offering to renew the battle.

XXVIII

THE TARDY MIRACLE

THE BANKS OF ZEELAND AND THE NORTH SEA, AUGUST 9TH–12TH, 1588

THE English did not renew the attack. Not, one assumes, because they were dismayed by the re-formed Spanish order. They had broken it once and knew they could break it again. More likely, the moment of disengagement had given commanders time to find out that most ships had spent all or nearly all their ammunition, powder as well as shot. There was scarcely enough left for an hour's fighting like the last four. For the time, therefore, it seemed enough to keep the Armada in view while appealing for means to finish the job. In fact, from this point on neither fleet could have fought much of a gun battle, but neither knew the extent of the other's weakness.

That night Howard wrote to Walsingham: 'I have received your letter wherein you desire a proportion of powder and shot to be set down by me and sent to you,' (these hidebound bureaucrats!) 'which by the uncertainty of the service no man can do; therefore I pray you to send me with all speed as much as you can.' He would need victuals too, he said, and after a brief report of the events of the day: 'ever since [morning] we have chased them in fight until this evening late and distressed them much; but their fleet consisteth of mighty ships and great strength.' And he added in a postscript: 'Their force is wonderful great and strong; and yet we pluck their feathers little and little' — a modest enough appraisal of the campaign so far, and not even a pious hope that it might be nearly over.

Drake expressed more satisfaction with the results of the fight. 'God hath given us so good a day in forcing the enemy so far to leeward as I hope to God the Prince of Parma and the Duke of Medina Sidonia shall not shake hands this few days, and whensoever they shall meet, I believe neither of them will greatly rejoice of this day's service.' But this postscript is even more emphatic than Howard's. 'There must be great care taken to send us munition and victual withersoever the enemy goeth.' No more than Howard did Drake foresee that they would not fight with this Armada again.

The Spanish fleet, in fact, was in evil case. As far as the duke could find out, there was some powder left but no great shot at all, or almost none. For the first time the Armada had taken a real beating. Most of the first-class ships were leaking; most had lost spars and rigging and had their decks littered with wreckage; all had sustained heavy casualties. Some were more badly hurt still. During the squall a great Biscayan, the *María Juan*, which had been isolated and severely mauled earlier in the day, went to the bottom, though not before most of the men aboard her had been taken off. In the early part of the night the *San Mateo* and the *San Felipe*, both leaking so badly they could not live many hours more, turned aside and staggered towards the banks between Nieuport and Ostend where they went aground. In the morning they were both snapped up by Justin of Nassau's flyboats. Next morning an armed merchantman of Diego Flores's squadron, lagging hopelessly behind, went down in the sight of both fleets.

During the night the wind blew harder and the Armada ran on blindly east-north-east up the coast, the English in chase. The moment of greatest danger came early on Tuesday, August 9th. Medina Sidonia was keeping the rearguard, supported by Recalde in the *San Juan*, de Leiva's carrack, the faithful *San Marcos*, a Castilian galleon and the three remaining galleasses. All the rest of the Armada was some distance to leeward, and on the rearguard's weather quarter — a long-culverin shot away — followed the power of the English fleet. The wind had moderated some-what but it had hauled round to the north-west, and, sailing as close-hauled as they could, the Spanish could win no more sea room. What was terrifying was the change in the run and slope of the seas and the changed colour of the water ahead and out to seaward on the port bow. At its present course the whole Armada would be on the Zeeland Sands in less than half an hour.

Better to die in battle than to be drowned without a fight. Medina Sidonia lay to, and his little rearguard conformed. He sent pinnaces to order the ships ahead to lie to and await the enemy or, if they could, to beat their way back towards him. Some of them tried to obey. Meanwhile officers and men confessed and communicated, preparing to receive the enemy with the few rounds left for their small-arms and cold steel. But the English kept aloof, standing off and on with short tacks. It scarcely needed the pilots to tell the duke why. Even lying to, wind and current were shoving the rearguard to leeward. Anchors could not be expected to hold in this loose shifting sand. For the fleet ahead no course was possible except the one they were on, and that, in a few minutes more, would mean certain catastrophe. The English were standing by to watch the destruction of their enemies by the hand of God.

The pilots persuaded the duke that there was nothing to do but keep his previous course, trying to edge to seaward. From the chains of the *San Martín* the leadsman called seven fathoms, then six. She drew five. At any moment now the ships ahead would begin to strike; it seemed amazing that some had not struck already. Thereafter the waves would pound them to pieces more thoroughly than English broadsides. In those minutes every man in the Armada with eyes in his head must have tasted death. We do not know what prayers were offered, what vows were made. Then, as they braced themselves for the shock of stranding, the wind backed. Right round the compass to the south-east, one ecstatic witness says. More likely to west-south-west as the duke reported, but far enough and suddenly enough so that even the leading ships could weather the deadly sands and the whole Armada could stand away into deep water. Both the duke and his chaplain felt sure that the fleet had been aided by a miracle of God.

Of course, it was not quite the miracle King Philip and his admiral had counted on. If the Armada was saved the English were as far from defeat as ever. And Recalde, in his mood of grim irony, may have reflected that divine intervention — if a change in the wind at the tail end of a storm could be called that — had come rather late in the campaign. But Recalde was enough of a seaman to recognize that, in the matter of weather, ever since they had entered the Channel the Armada had been luckier than anyone had a right to expect.

The English must have thought so too. They were so disappointed by the Armada's inexplicable escape that they never mentioned it, and if it did not shake Drake's confidence in his alliance with the Deity, or his eagerness to wrestle another pull with the army of Spain, it made him and Hawkins and the Lord Admiral and everyone else more anxious than ever for further supplies of powder and shot. Meanwhile, 'putting on a brag countenance', the English held on after the enemy as if they lacked for nothing.

Councils of War were held on both the flagships that evening. That on the *Ark Royal* was anxious but brief. The ships were all sound, casualties had not been serious, everything was well except for the shortage of ammunition and an approaching shortage of food. In the hope that supplies would be sent after them presently it was determined that the main fleet would follow the Spaniards as long as there was a present danger that they might try to land in England or Scotland. Seymour, however, was to take his squadron back to the Downs to keep watch on Parma. Seymour exploded in anguished, outraged protests; the service he had done at Gravelines had earned him the right to be in at the death; he wanted to fight the Spaniards again, even if it had to be foot to foot with cold steel; he denounced Howard's evident intention to hog all the glory. But the Lord Admiral was firm. Somebody had to be there to stop Parma if he tried to cross, and Howard apparently never considered trusting that part of the operation to the Dutch. On the same day that Justin of Nassau's flyboats had taken two enemy galleons and prevented so much as a pinnace from peeping out of Dunkirk or Nieuport, Howard had written: 'There is not a Hollander or Zeelander at sea.' He knew less of the doings of his allies than he did of the enemy's. But there is no sign that he was thinking of his own glory or of anything except the safety of England. Patiently, doggedly, he meant to keep his ships between his country's enemies and her shores.

The council on the *San Martin* was longer and more painful. Almost all the first-class fighting-ships had major damage to report. All had taken heavy casualties, on some so heavy as to make it hard to work or fight the ships. Ammunition was very short. It scarcely looked as if in the next action the Armada would have much chance. Nevertheless the council voted unanimously, for reasons not stated, that if the wind changed in the next few days they would return to the attack and try to seize an English port or fight their way back through the straits. One of the unstated reasons was certainly an approaching shortage of food and water which made any long voyage hazardous. But the chief reason was probably the same one that kept Howard doggedly in their wake; as long as there was the least chance they must try to accomplish their mission. Anything was better than going home to Spain in acknowledged defeat. Nevertheless they sullenly agreed that if the wind held in its present quarter four more days so that they would have run into the Sea of Norway, they would have to try to get home to the westward around the British islands. They could not cut their margin of safety any finer than that, and if they could do nothing else, the duke summed up, it was their duty to save as many as they could of the King's ships.

The wind held. The two fleets sailed northward, past the height of Hull, past the height of Berwick. On the afternoon of the fourth day, Friday, 12th (O.S. 2nd) August in about latitude 56° N, the English turned away and headed for the Firth of Forth. Howard was satisfied that the Spanish did not mean to try for a landing, and food and water on his ships was running out.

From the poop-deck of the *San Martín* Medina Sidonia watched the English haul into the wind and drop farther and farther astern. He had hardly quitted his post there since the first nightmarish battle off Plymouth almost two weeks ago. Men had been killed all about him, a gromet, a musketeer, a boatswain and some of the greatest gentlemen of Spain, but except for a stiff leg from a gash in the thigh last Monday morning he had remained unscathed. Now and then he had gone below to snatch a little food or a few hours' sleep, but mostly he had eaten or neglected to eat whatever was brought him on deck, and he had stayed leaning on the taffrail through most of the short nights. He leaned there now, watching the wretchedly familiar topsails vanish into the west. He wore only doublet and hose and short cape. He had given his great boat-cloak to Fray Bernardo de Gongora, who had brought nothing from the *Rosario*, and his other cloak covered a wounded boy in his cabin below. It was cold. Yet he stayed leaning on the taffrail long after the last topsail had sunk from sight. If he had wondered sometimes, coming up the Channel, whether the Armada was advancing in triumph or fleeing from the enemy, there was no doubt now. This was flight, even though the English no longer pursued. This was defeat. He had done his best, and his best had not been good enough. Perhaps an abler, more experienced man? Francis Drake had said he would make the Duke of Sidonia wish himself back at St Mary's Port among his orange trees. We do not know where the duke wished himself that night.

XXIX

MYSELF YOUR GENERAL

TILBURY, AUGUST 18TH–19TH, 1588

O N Thursday morning, August 18th (8 August O.S.) the ships of the Grand Fleet came scudding before the tail of a north-easter into Harwich and Margate Roads and other havens around the mouth of the Thames. Six days before, at about the height of the Firth, they had broken off their chase and watched the Armada running north-north-east into the sea of Norway. The English fleet had seen no supply ships since those that had come over to Calais on Sunday week, so there was very little ammunition left, very little food, and what was worst — almost no beer.

That same morning the Queen's Majesty entered her royal barge at Saint James's and set off past London, preceded by her music blowing loudly on silver trumpets. In other barges were the gentlemen pensioners of her household — or all of them who had not slipped off to join the war at sea — turned out in half-armour with plumed morions, and the full strength of her yeomen of the guard; so that the procession of barges made quite a military show, comforting to the citizens who lined the foreshore to cheer, and, from the windows above London Bridge, watched the barges sweep grandly through on the ebb tide. Her Majesty was on her way to inspect her army at Tilbury.

Her Lieutenant and Captain-General, the Earl of Leicester, had received with delight the news of her impending visit and begged her to hasten it. A fortnight earlier he would have been less eager. On the afternoon of Thursday, two weeks before, when the Hampshire trained bands broke up their camp, after having watched the ding-dong battle off the Isle of Wight and seen both fleets vanish up the Channel, there was still no camp at Tilbury and nothing that looked like a military force except Leicester's own retinue. Even the men of Essex had not reported, though they had been ordered to do so the previous Monday. 'If it be five days to gather the very countrymen,' Leicester was to exclaim in exasperation when they finally did come in, 'what will it be, and must be to look for those who are forty, fifty and sixty miles off?' Since this was the army which must meet

Parma's landing if the fleet failed, it was going to need contingents from farther away than that. Not even the victuallers, to whom Leicester had been appealing by town criers in every market square, had put in an appearance — perhaps because they knew there was no profit to be made from a non-existent army. The arrangements for brewing were in utter confusion, and Leicester was sorely puzzled to know what to do for beer. Finally, the earl's own commission had not come (it had not, in fact, been signed), and until he received it the Captain-General designate had no power to remove an incompetent subordinate or to reorganize his battalions.

Four days later, when the Armada was off Dunkirk and Parma had a spring tide for his sortie, matters were still not much better. Four thousand Essex foot and a few hundred horse of the county had at last arrived, and a thousand foot, all armed with firearms, from London; but Black Jack Norris was still running errands for the council, and Sir Roger Williams had only just come back from Dover. In the absence of enough experienced officers the camp was sorting itself out with what Leicester regarded as exasperating slowness, and the earl himself still had to be, as he put it, 'cook, cater, and hunt' for his entire army. The bridge of boats to connect Tilbury Fort with Gravesend so that Leicester's army could cross to defend the south bank if Parma chose to land there (as indeed he planned to) needed a lot more work before it would be usable, and Giambelli's boom for closing the Thames had broken of its own weight with the first flood-tide. Yet Tilbury, where Leicester was working with that furious if sometimes misdirected energy characteristic of him, was still the kingdom's most developed centre of defence. The secondary camp in Kent was scarcely more than a potential replacement depot for the navy, and the great reserve army near Westminster, intended as a bodyguard for the Queen in case of invasion, existed mainly on paper.

Only London, after Tilbury, was in something like a state of readiness on the day when Parma should have landed if he was going to land at all. In spite of the thousand men spared to Leicester the trained bands had been recruited back to ten thousand; and although the ditch was foul, and the wall in places ruinous, internal perimeters of defence had been laid out, and behind them the Londoners, with the old chains last used against Wyatt's rebels again in place, were prepared to defend their city street by street. They had heard of Antwerp. They meant to make Parma's army pay even dearer for a richer spoil. Meanwhile armed patrols tramped about night and day, and the rigid surveillance by the city authorities of foreigners of all faiths was aggravated by the volunteer activities of the prentices, 'natural haters of strangers'. Petruccio Ubaldini, enthusiastic Protestant and loyal foe of Spain, was particularly harassed. 'It is easier', he wrote in resigned exasperation, 'to find flocks of white crows than one Englishman (and let him believe what he will about religion) who loves a foreigner.'

Everyone about the Queen hoped that this would turn out to be so, and that English patriotism, firmly based on xenophobia, would prove stronger than any religious bond. But no one could be sure. It was not true for the exiles. There were English pilots with the Spanish fleet, and companies of English soldiers commanded by English Lords and gentlemen in Parma's army. The most distinguished exile, Dr William Allen, now a cardinal, had published at Antwerp the book which for years he had been itching to write and publish: *An Admonition to the Nobility and People of England concerning the present wars*. Its main point was to tell his fellow country-men that the present Pope 'confirmeth ... the sentence declaratory of Pius V [against Elizabeth] ... as well concerning her illegitimation and usurpation and inability to the Crown of England, as for her excommuni-cation and deprivation in respect of her heresy, sacrilege and abominable life.' His Holiness further commands, Allen went on, that no man must obey or defend Elizabeth, but that all must be ready 'at the arrival of his Catholic Majesty's forces ... to join the said army ... to help towards the restoring of the Catholic faith and deposing the usurper in such sort ... as by ... the General of this holy war shall be appointed.' The rest of the pamphlet was devoted to a proof that the deposition of Elizabeth was right by natural law because she was a tyrant, and by divine law because she was a heretic, that it was the duty of all Englishmen to help to purge their country of the iniquity of her reign, and that by doing so they would help to save their own and their children's souls, as by any other course they would surely damn them. The flow of vituperative billings-gate with which these arguments were accompanied would seem to a modern reader somewhat to weaken their force, but William Allen's contemporaries rightly feared his pen. Elizabeth's government did their best to confiscate and destroy these pamphlets, but nobody knew how many of them passed covertly from hand to hand, just as nobody knew how many of Allen's seminary priests passed from country house to country house in disguise, advising the nobility and gentry of the old faith what their duty would be when the day of Divine Execution should arrive.

It was the common gossip of the Flanders taverns that a third of the English — half, some said, and some two-thirds, but a third, at any rate — were Catholics, and that Parma's landing would be the signal for a widespread rising. In the circumstances the Privy Council were taking no chances that English patriotism (and hatred of foreigners) would prove stronger than the bonds of religion. Leading recusants were placed in protective custody. Others were deprived of their arms and horses if they had any, and confined to their parishes or even to their houses. But the open, avowed Catholics in England, the known recusants, were a mere handful. The crypto-Catholics and conforming Anglicans with strong Catholic leanings were certainly much more numerous. How much more, and how far disaffected, no one knew, but there were not wanting privy councillors and county magnates to urge that strong measures be taken against all persons in any way suspected. 'It were hard for any man to face the enemy with a stout heart', wrote one of them, 'if he thought his house like at any time to be burned behind his back.' The dread of a great secret Catholic conspiracy of unknown strength was in many men's minds. It was one of the chief sources of tension in that uneasy summer of '88. In the circumstances the Government deserves full marks for refusing to yield to the pressure of alarmists, or to act during the emergency against any but known recusants. It was the wisest course, but it took courage.

Probably the main credit, if all were known, should go to the Queen. Walsingham always saw dangers larger than they were, and even wise Burghley was alarmed. But it was hard for Elizabeth to believe in religion as an overmastering motive, except for a few crack-brained fanatics who might be annoying, but not dangerous. Somewhat reluctantly she had consented to let the Crown act against Jesuits and seminary priests and their accomplices and abetters, as against the spies and agents of a foreign power, but further than that she would not go. Though Burghley warned of 'the secret treasons of the mind and heart' which required new means to combat them, Elizabeth refused to be stampeded by the Puritans into prying further than need be into her subjects' beliefs, or into suspecting popery and treason wherever one found a sentimental attachment to old ways.

Elizabeth was easy to upset but hard to frighten. She might chop and change and draw back a dozen times before an unwelcome step. She might ignore an ugly fact until she drove her ministers nearly mad. But the pressure of real danger braced her. 'It is a comfort', wrote Robert

Queen Elizabeth I, in a portrait by Marc Gheeraedts.

Anon. Design for a tapestry panel entitled 'Launch of the Fireships'.

Queen Elizabeth at Tilbury in 1588. Elizabeth is shown on her way to address the troops.

Cecil in those days when the fleets were at grips, 'to see how great magnanimity Her Majesty shows, who is not a whit dismayed.' Undismayed,
she led the martial procession of barges down the river, regaining on the
way a sense of participating in great events such as she had not known
since the initiative passed from the diplomats to the fighting-men. It may
have been on the river, or it may not have been until she landed at Tilbury
Fort and saw the encampment, that she took her next decision.

Tilbury was ready for the Queen to see. We do not know how great a
force Leicester had managed to assemble; surely less than plans called for,
or than the twenty-three thousand Camden speaks of so confidently, but
surely more than the 'between five and six thousand' which is all sceptics
will allow. This army might not have stopped Parma but it would have
given him trouble, and now it made a brave show lined up by regiments of
foot, with coats all (or nearly all) alike, and troops of horsemen in armour
with nodding plumes. The camp, too, was gay and clean, its ditches dug
and palisades emplaced at last, the particoloured pavilions of the nobles
and gentlemen bright and unfaded, the green booths where the rank and
file slept not yet bedraggled and foul. For the moment Tilbury combined
the glamour of a military spectacle with the innocent cheerfulness of a
country fair.

When her Captain-General came to welcome her and take her orders
for the inspection and review, the Queen told him her pleasure. She had
come to see the army (and to let them see her). She did not intend that
they should look at each other across the broad shoulders of her yeomen
of the guard or through the thicket of her gentlemen's plumes. She
needed no guards among fellow countrymen in arms for her service. And
so, whoever may have protested, the inspecting party was arranged. The
Earl of Ormonde went first, on foot, carrying ceremoniously the Sword
of State; behind him walked two pages in white velvet, one with the
Queen's elaborate silver casque on a white velvet cushion, the other leading her horse; then three mounted figures, the Queen herself, riding between her Captain-General and her Master of the Horse; and behind them,
on foot, Sir John Norris. That was the whole escort — four men and two
boys. The yeomen and the gentlemen of the household stayed lined before
Tilbury Fort, and the little party advanced into the ranks of the militia,
which exploded in a roar of cheers.

At a slow foot pace the Queen quartered through every corner of the
camp. In the burly figure on her right, unhelmeted, his red face surrounded
by an aureole of white hair and beard, few eyes could have detected any

more the bold gipsy charm and insolent grace of the Robin Dudley with whom Elizabeth Tudor had flirted thirty summers past, but perhaps Elizabeth still could. Many eyes besides the Queen's had observed the almost excessive beauty of the young man on her left — tall, strongly built, graceful, with a high pure forehead, dark dreaming eyes and a sensitive tender mouth, Robert Devereux, Earl of Essex, at twenty-three already Knight of the Garter and Master of the Horse, a soldier of note and bound to go far since he was Leicester's stepson and the Queen's own cousin.

That day, one doubts whether any except Elizabeth noted the two men. All eyes were on the Queen. She rode a white gelding with a back like a barn-door, and, if one may trust a portrait, a benignant rather simpering expression. She was clad all in white velvet with a silver cuirass embossed with a mythological design, and bore in her right hand a silver truncheon chased in gold. Like the cavaliers on either side of her she rode bare-headed, and there was a tuft of plumes, the sheen of pearls and the glitter of diamonds in her hair.

Perhaps an objective observer would have seen no more than a battered, rather scraggy spinster in her middle fifties perched on a fat white horse, her teeth black, her red wig slightly askew, dangling a toy sword and wearing an absurd little piece of parade-armour like something out of a theatrical property-box. But that was not what her subjects saw, dazzled as they were by more than the sun on the silver breastplate or the moisture in their eyes. They saw Judith and Esther, Gloriana and Belphoebe, Diana the virgin huntress, and Minerva the wise protectress, and best of all their own beloved Queen and Mistress, come in this hour of danger in all simplicity to trust herself among them. The touching rightness of the gesture whipped them to a pitch of enthusiasm which could find expression only in a wild babel of shouted blessings, endearments and protests of devotion. It must have been a long time since Elizabeth had enjoyed herself so much.

The day was so successful that she decided it would bear repetition. She passed the night at a manor house some four miles off, and came back the next day. This time there was a review and march past, followed by cavalry exercises which amounted to an impromptu tournament, and then the Queen went to dine in state in the general's pavilion and all the captains of her army came to kiss her hand. But before that, perhaps at the end of the review, she had spoken to her people words they would cherish:

'My loving people, we have been persuaded by some that are careful for our safety, to take heed how we commit ourselves to armed multitudes, for fear of treachery. But I assure you, I do not desire to live to distrust my faithful and loving people. Let tyrants fear. I have always so behaved myself that, under God, I have placed my chiefest strength and safeguard in the loyal hearts and good will of my subjects; and therefore I am come amongst you as you see, at this time, not for my recreation and disport, but being resolved, in the midst and heat of the battle, to live or die amongst you all, and to lay down for my God and for my kingdom and for my people, my honour and my blood, even in the dust. I know I have the body of a weak and feeble woman, but I have the heart and stomach of a king, and of a king of England too, and think foul scorn that Parma or Spain, or any prince of Europe should dare to invade the borders of my realm; to which, rather than any dishonour shall grow by me, I myself will take up arms, I myself will be your general, judge, and rewarder of every one of your virtues in the field. I know already for your forwardness you deserve rewards and crowns; and we do assure you, in the word of a prince, they shall be duly paid you.' The shout of applause was tremendous.

Meanwhile, during these two days, word was coming in of how the fleet had fared and what it had accomplished. On the whole the estimate was unenthusiastic. Of the Queen's ships not one had been lost or seriously damaged, and it seemed fairly certain that at least seven or eight Spanish greatships had in one way or another been put out of action; but powder and shot had been lacking for that last battle which might have finished off the Armada, and it remained a great and terrible fleet. 'All the world never saw such a force as theirs was', wrote Howard with a touch of awe, and he reminded Walsingham most unnecessarily that 'a kingdom is a great wager'. Even Drake, who, correctly, estimated the damage done to the Armada higher than anybody else, was not sure the Spaniards would not try to come back, and the general weight of opinion was much more pessimistic. The captains spoke not of a great victory won but of a great opportunity missed. Henry Whyte concluded his narrative to Walsingham: 'your Honour may see how our parsimony at home hath bereaved us of the famousest victory that ever our navy might have had at sea.' Walsingham got a whole batch of reports on Thursday at Tilbury and wrote gloomily to Hatton that night: 'So our half-doing doth breed dishonour and leaves the disease uncured.' He could hardly have been more downcast if the English fleet had been defeated.

The next day, as the Queen sat at dinner with her captains in Leicester's tent, word came that Parma was ready to come out on the spring tides, any time in the next few days. Elizabeth was more excited than alarmed. She declared roundly that she would not desert her army on the approach of the enemy but would stay and look the Spaniards in the face, and her captains and councillors had a great to-do to change her mind. They managed it finally by persuading her of what none of them believed, though it was perfectly true, that Parma would not come out until he had had favourable news of the Spanish fleet. So, somewhat disappointed, on Friday evening the Queen allowed herself to be escorted back to Saint James's.

It was clear, however, that there could be no demobilization at present, either by land or by sea. The camp at Tilbury would have to be kept up, and so would the one around London, now forming at last, no matter how expensive they both were. And all the Queen's ships would have to be kept in commission, even though there were grave difficulties about victualling, particularly about the beer, and on some ships like the *Elizabeth Jonas* an alarming sick-list. England dared not drop its guard until it was seen what the formidable Duke of Parma would do, and what ships might be coming, even now, out of the northern mist.

From a set of playing cards engraved in the seventeenth century.

XXX

DRAKE IS CAPTURED!

WESTERN EUROPE, AUGUST AND SEPTEMBER, 1588

I F, by the latter part of August, the English and the Dutch still knew too little to be sure whether the Armada had been beaten, everybody else ashore knew a great deal less. From Plymouth to the Isle of Wight the Spaniards had been in sight of the English coast, following the usual track of east-bound ships. Thousands of eyes had been on them, and throngs had crowded the headlands and downs to watch the four great naval battles which punctuated their progress. Daily, ships from the English fleet had come into one port or another with messages and requests, and some of the vessels that went out to join Howard with supplies and volunteers had been more like sightseeing excursions than reinforcements. Finally, the Queen's ships and their auxiliaries had come back to port and told their story.

By contrast the only view that anybody on the Continent, except the Dutch, had got of the campaign was at Calais; and at Calais, except for the fate of the *San Lorenzo*, it was by no means clear what had happened. Of course, Parma had had daily bulletins ever since the Armada had reached the Lizard. He must have known a good deal more about the Armada up to Sunday, August 7th than he gave any indication of knowing; but even he, unless he was playing a particularly pointless charade, must have believed as late as August 10th and perhaps later, that the Spanish fleet might return at any moment, and somehow miraculously drive away the Dutch. Meanwhile neither of the dukes, neither Parma nor Medina Sidonia, bothered to inform the one person after themselves most concerned — Don Bernardino de Mendoza.

Mendoza heard, fairly promptly, that Medina Sidonia had reached the Lizard, and a day or two later that a big unidentified Spanish ship (the *Santa Ana de Recalde* as it proved) had anchored in the Bay of La Hogue. But there was no indication of what this might mean, and then for six anxious days nothing but vague rumours of gunfire heard in the Channel, and contradictory reports that Spaniards had landed, that the Armada was beaten and fleeing up the Channel with Drake in pursuit, that it had won a

great victory and was advancing triumphantly towards its rendezvous
Mendoza added each item to his budgets of news for his master and foi
Count Olivarez at Rome, and to each he appended the notation that the
source was unreliable and the story unconfirmed; it would be wise to
suspend judgment.

Then, on Sunday, August 7th, Mendoza's agent at Rouen reported
something more substantial. Word had just come from Le Havre that
several Newfoundland fishing-barks there had passed through the
hostile fleets. They reported that the Armada had encountered Drake on
Tuesday, off the Isle of Wight. The English had drawn towards the land
so that the Spanish recovered the weather-gauge and pressed them hard.
The battle raged for twenty-four hours and the Spanish had the upper
hand. They sank fifteen English galleons and captured several others,
which they scuttled after removing their guns. In addition, they picked
up and made prisoner a number of Englishmen who had taken to the
boats or were struggling in the water. In all the battle the galleasses had
done exceptionally good work. These reports were confirmed, the Rouen
correspondent hastened to add, by letters from Dieppe where more of the
Newfoundland fishing-fleet had arrived. A Breton skipper said he had
been very near Drake's flagship during the battle. It was attacked by one
of the galleasses, which brought down all its masts at its first fire and sank
it at its second. The Breton (perhaps a distant cousin of David Gwynn's)
saw Drake flee in a small boat without waiting for the end of the battle.
Rouen was buzzing with news of the Spanish victory and a broadside was
being printed to celebrate it.

All this sounds as if it might be the gleanings of what the Newfound-
landers had managed to see of the fights off Portland Bill on Tuesday and
on the following Wednesday morning, with nothing thoroughly implausible about it except the wealth of specific information. No fishing-skipper
would have been likely to hang about in the middle of the greatest naval
battle men had ever seen to observe the effects on the *Revenge* of a galleass's fire or count the English ships sunk; but on the other hand sailors
have never been famous for their reluctance to supply corroborative detail,
adding verisimilitude to a bald and otherwise unconvincing narrative.
From a distance and through dense clouds of smoke the Newfound-
landers may have thought they saw something like the Rouen account.
Mendoza must have had confidence in the judgment of his Rouen agent,
for this time he transmitted the news without the customary cautions and
with expressions of rejoicing.

He did more. He spoke openly of a victory, and had a great bonfire piled in the courtyard of his embassy, opposite the main gate, ready to light as soon as the report from Rouen should be confirmed. Two days later, with more reports in hand, he set off for the royal Court at Chartres, meaning to demand a Te Deum in the cathedral for the Catholic victory, and to browbeat Henry III into further submission to the League.

As the Armada came closer to England, the King of France had come more and more to heel. His former favourite, the Duke of Epernon, had given up his government of Normandy and his place as admiral, been cold-shouldered at Court and hustled out of his town of Loches. Finally the King had been bullied into signing the Edict of Alençon, in which he yielded to the League's extreme demands, including a clause ordaining that no heretic or abetter of heresy should ever be received as King of France, a pusillanimous surrender of that principle of monarchical succession to which Henry III had always been most devoted.

So far, however, the King's concessions had been mostly on paper. Epernon still lorded it, for the moment at least, in Angoulême. Royal towns in Picardy, including Boulogne, still held out against the League. And though Navarre was active in arms south of the Loire, no royal banner stirred. It was rumoured that the Estates General, called for Blois in September and sure to be dominated by Catholic extremists, would be prorogued before they could assemble. Henry still seemed to hope that some event, perhaps an English victory at sea, would restore the balance of factions which was all his government now had to rest on. He was evading his final capitulation with every subterfuge. Mendoza, on the other hand, was determined to force a surrender so abject that Henry could never recover his freedom. The ambassador knew that just as the Day of the Barricades had been necessary for the Armada to sail in safety, so a victory over England was necessary if Henry was to be enslaved to the League and Guise, and France in consequence reduced to a Spanish vassal state. Mendoza had come to Chartres to force the next step in that process.

On the road he received another message. The Armada had reached Calais and the rendezvous with Parma had been effected. He could take it as certain that by the time he received this letter Spanish troops would have landed in England. With grim satisfaction Mendoza added that item to his packet for Rome, commenting that it chimed perfectly with the rest of his intelligence. He knew all about the promised million ducats. At last His Holiness would have to pay up.

His audience with the King was on the morning of Friday, August 12th. As soon as he decently could, Mendoza recounted the gist of his news. He was sure the King would wish to command a special service of thanksgiving throughout the realm in celebration of this great Catholic victory. He intimated that the King might now care to show his solidarity with the Catholic cause by deed as well as by word, and that he could best begin by returning to his faithful city of Paris. Henry heard him out with impassive courtesy, and replied: 'Your news, if it were certain, would be most welcome. But we, too, have news from Calais which you may wish to see.' And, at a gesture, Bellièvre handed the ambassador a letter from M. Gourdan, the Governor of Calais, dated August 8th.

Mendoza withdrew into an embrasure while his secretary perused the sheet and mumbled its contents in his ear. The Spanish fleet had come into Calais Roads with the English in pursuit. Rigging and upper works showed that it had been hotly engaged. Its admiral had asked permission to buy food, which had been granted, and powder and round shot, which had been refused. On Sunday night the Armada had been dislodged by fire-ships and fled into the North Sea, all except one galleass which was aground under the guns of the castle. In the morning the English, in good order, had taken up the chase.

Mendoza thanked the King and returned the letter, commenting only that 'Obviously, our reports differ.' He rode back to Paris and in another twenty-four hours was writing to his master that his earlier letter had been too optimistic. The bonfire in front of his embassy was not lighted after all. But for all that he did not abandon hope of delivering Henry III, bound hand and foot, to Guise, and Guise, bound hand and foot, to Spain; nor did he give up his dream of riding back into London a conqueror, with his old comrades of the Low Country wars behind him, just as he said he would.

Another week passed with vague and contradictory rumours, of which the most mysterious and disturbing was that a Hansa skipper reported sailing through an otherwise empty sea which was alive with swimming mules and horses. The only things Mendoza learned for certain that week were the identity of the ship at La Hogue (the *Santa Ana*), the willingness of the French to turn over to Spain the ordnance of the *San Lorenzo* at Calais, and the fact that at least four first-class ships had fallen into enemy hands — two to the English, two to the Dutch.

Then all at once a spate of reports. A Dansker had seen men abandoning ship and taking to the boats. Since Spaniards would have no friendly shore a small boat could reach, he concluded that the sinking ship was English. One of Parma's pinnaces sent to find the Armada had sighted a small group of English ships in much disorder fleeing towards England. Antwerp heard that Drake had had his leg shot off, and that the *Ark Royal* was taken. Dieppe learned that there had been a great battle off the Scottish coast and that all but some twenty-odd of the English fleet had been sunk or captured. But the most definite news came from England. Twenty-five ships, all that were left of the English fleet, had taken refuge in the mouth of the Thames. On August 13th there had been a battle off Scotland. Drake had attempted to board the *San Martín* and been captured. At least fifteen English galleons had been sunk and others taken, while many of the rest had been so damaged that it was likely that they had gone down in the ensuing storm. The storm had prevented the pursuit and destruction of the surviving remnant, and the duke had put into a Scottish haven to refit and take on water and stores while he waited for a fair wind to take him back to the straits. Meanwhile the English were stricken with panic. It was forbidden to write or say anything about the fate of the fleet. There was widespread fear of an uprising by the English Catholics, and the Queen had betaken herself for safety to the army.

It is not hard to see how these stories arose. The English fleet had been scattered by a north-easter on the Tuesday after it broke off the pursuit, and taken shelter on August 17th and 18th in various havens in and around the mouth of the Thames. The men were kept aboard, only high-ranking officers and official couriers being allowed ashore, and it was natural for Catholic sympathizers or survivors from Mendoza's spy system — by this time sadly disrupted — to jump to the conclusion that what they were seeing at a single port was what was left of England's beaten navy, and easy to believe that the tightened censorship and the Queen's visit to Tilbury were signs of panic. Meanwhile the earlier reports from Dieppe and Havre de Grâce had set up a kind of echo — the repetition that in the battle fifteen ships had been sunk can hardly be pure coincidence — just as the English rumours of August 16th to 19th, quickly carried to Bruges and Dieppe and Le Havre, reverberated in Paris and seemed to Mendoza to provide independent confirmation of what he had already heard directly.

All sorts of stories circulated during that next fortnight and were scooped up by enterprising printers for broadsides or for final paragraphs to a new edition of their reprint of the description of the Armada, usually, after August 20th, with a short account of the actions in the

Channel. Catholic or Protestant, these news pamphlets vary little in their narrative as far as Calais, except for pious or bellicose interjections which the printers thought appropriate to the taste of their readers, and optimistic overestimates by both sides of the damage inflicted on the enemy. But in the accounts which many of them include of the last (quite imaginary) battle in the North Sea they vary wildly, and some of the Protestant narratives are as fantastic in their tales of the havoc wrought by Drake — it is always Drake — as anything Mendoza believed.

On the Catholic side there were also various stories. Sometimes Drake was killed. Sometimes he was wounded. Sometimes he fled from the battle in a small boat and was never seen again. But the favourite version was the one Mendoza adopted, forwarded to Philip in Spain, publicly announced in Paris and finally lit his bonfire to celebrate. Drake was captured, trying to board the *San Martín*. He was now a prisoner in the hands of the Duke of Medina Sidonia. It seemed the most fitting end for the terrible pirate.

Drake is captured! The news winged its way from Cologne to Mainz and so to Munich, Linz and Vienna. Drake is captured! Paris told Lyons and Lyons told Turin and Turin told all Italy, though Venice had already had the same story, among others, in its own diplomatic pouches. 'Drake is captured', Mendoza wrote to his master. 'As yet the story wants confirmation from the duke, himself, but it is widely believed and seems highly probable', and he enclosed a bundle of reports. These formed the basis of a broadside published in Madrid on the authorization of Secretary Idiáquez, and also in Seville where it was accompanied by a spirited ballad, the work of a blind poet of Córdoba. For a moment the long strain of waiting was eased. Scarcely a noble house in Spain but had a son, a brother or a father in the Armada, and many had had no certain news since the end of May. The silence had seemed to bode ill; but now, although there was no official celebration and prayers continued to be offered for the Armada's success, it looked as though it was going to be victory after all.

At Prague Don Guillén de San Clemente, the Spanish ambassador, was sure it was victory. Hard on the heels of Mendoza's first report had come confirmation from the Rhenish towns, actually echoes of the same tales, and even though the Fugger agent had a quite different story Don Guillén ordered, on his own authority, a Te Deum mass at the cathedral. Don Guillén was beginning to give himself in the emperor's capital some of the airs of a viceroy; after all, he represented the senior, more powerful and more orthodox branch of the Habsburgs. To ambassadors the Emperor Rudolph denied having ordered the mass or having heard anything about a Spanish victory, but ambassadors were used to discounting what Rudolph said.

As soon as he had received Mendoza's first claim of victory Count Olivarez had gone straight to the Vatican, demanded and got a special audience, and, by his own account, told Pope Sixtus in no uncertain terms where his duty lay. He should celebrate a special Te Deum at St Peter's and order one in all the Roman churches. There should be festal illumination. The Cardinal of England should be given his legatine bulls at once, so that he could leave for the Netherlands with no further delay. And the first instalment of the million gold ducats might as well be paid over immediately. By this time Parma would already have landed in England.

Sixtus agreed that if Mendoza's report was correct all these things should be done. But it would be well, he said, to wait a few days for confirmation. So far he had heard this news from no other source. It was too soon to rejoice.

For Cardinal Allen it was not too soon. When one has hoped long it is easy to believe, and the word which Olivarez sent round to the via di Monserrato before he started for the Vatican had been expected so long that there was scarcely a thrill of joy in it, only the reminder of the immediate need for further action. Allen had wanted to go to Antwerp to see his *Admonition* through the press himself, but he had had to hand over the task to Father Cresswell because his bulls were not ready and it was important that he should reach the Netherlands fully accredited as legate *a latere* in England. Ever since the beginning of May he had been in a fever to be off, and Count Olivarez in the audience chamber and Father Parsons on the backstairs had been working in his cause as if they shared his sense of urgency. It was hard to make Italians understand how important it was that an Englishman, someone with the proper authority, should be on the scene as soon as possible after the first landing. Allen was not very well that summer, but it would be strange if his saddle-bags had not always been packed so that he could mount and ride as soon as the bulls were in his hands. That evening, August 28th, he was waiting at the Spanish embassy when Count Olivarez returned from his audience. It was hard to be told that one must wait, even a few days longer, though an exile should grow accustomed to waiting.

Then came Mendoza's second word of victory, but this time, though Allen was again impatient to be off, Olivarez was more wary. He gave his news at the Vatican with a touch of reserve, and His Holiness was frankly sceptical. This was not what he heard from the Bishop of Brescia, nor what he heard from Flanders, nor what had been heard at Venice from the Duke of Parma. It was true that at Turin they said that Drake was captured, and at other places that he was killed or wounded or missing; but there were also stories that Drake had won a great victory and the Spanish fleet had fled. The truth about matters like this could not be hidden. It would be better to wait and be certain. Then the news began to come in from England.

First came, as an enclosure in Morosini's dispatch from Paris of August 17th, a manuscript 'Journal of all that passed between the armies of Spain and England from July 28th to August 11th, 1588, according to news from divers places'. The dates are New Style and the language is French but the news is all from one place — the Privy Council in London, where the dispatches from the fleet were received — and in the chronological arrangement and selection of incidents it closely resembled the 'Abstract of Accidents between the two fleets' which Howard sent the Council. It also resembles the 'Discours véritable', without place or date of publication, which is one of the earliest printed accounts of the Armada campaign. From Morosini's warning that the source was English and therefore suspect one may guess that Stafford sent him the document straight from the embassy, just as it is also a fair guess that Stafford was simultaneously arranging the publication of the 'Discours véritable' by a Paris press. In the 'Discours' the only departures from the truth, as the Privy Council knew it, are the gross overestimate of the Queen's land forces, and the assertion that all the principal Catholics in the realm had rallied to them in arms. No known English Catholic had arms in his hands that summer. The loyalty of the English Catholics to the Protestant heroine was also the main point of the next propaganda pamphlet, 'Copy of a letter ... to Don Bernardino de Mendoza', which describes the Queen's visit to Tilbury, and refers briefly to England's victory at sea as notorious. The reference to naval affairs had to be brief, for the author of the letter — could it have been Burghley himself? — writing at about the end of August, obviously had no notion of what had happened to the Spanish fleet after Howard broke off his chase.

The first French edition had scarcely come off the press, however, and the English version was still in the print-shop when reports began to come in from Ireland. They can be read in excerpts in the next English pamphlet 'Certain Advertisements' or in more detail in the Public Record Office and elsewhere, and today their chronicle of shipwreck, starvation and massacre makes grim reading, but to Protestant Europe they were the most welcome news of 1588. Everyone that year had been expecting some dreadful catastrophe, some fulfilment of the prophecy in the ominous verses of Regiomontanus. Now it was known to whom catastrophe had been allotted. There was no doubt now about the extent of the English victory.

While the 'Advertisements out of Ireland' were still coming off the press the Privy Council got a copy of the Seville edition of Mendoza's second false report, complete with the blind poet's ballad, and immediately arranged for a reply. The pamphlet was printed in two columns, the Spanish claims paragraph by paragraph on one side of the page, and over against them a detailed and scornful refutation usually several times as long. The booklet was entitled 'A Pack of Spanish Lies' and was trans-lated into every major language in Europe. There were editions in Low and High Dutch, French, Italian, and a very special one in Spanish com-plete with a satirical reply in verse — the work, one supposes, of some Spanish Protestant refugee — to the *romanʒe* of the blind poet.

That last propaganda pamphlet was scarcely needed. The English had hung up their captured Spanish banners in St Paul's, the Dutch had published the interrogation of Don Diego de Pimentel and other prisoners from the stranded galleons, the Duke of Parma had broken up his camp at Dunkirk, and the reports from Ireland had a horrid ring of authenticity. Only Don Bernardino de Mendoza refused to give up hope that the Invincible Armada would reappear out of the northern seas and descend on the English coast. As late as September 29th Mendoza was still writing optimistic dispatches. The one of that date assures the King that according to reliable reports the Armada had finished making repairs and taking on fresh supplies in the Shetlands and Orkneys, and was steering southward once more towards the Flanders coast, bringing with it many Dutch and English prizes including twelve English ships of war. For weeks Philip had had Medina Sidonia's gloomy *diario* and the discouraging report of its bearer, Don Balthazar de Zuñiga on the state of the beaten fleet. Long before Mendoza's courier reached the Escurial Philip had heard that his Captain-General of the Ocean Sea, with a scanty battered squadron had straggled into Santander. In the margin of Mendoza's letter the King's weary pen scrawled: 'Nothing of this is true. It will be well to tell him so.'

XXXI

THE LONG ROAD HOME

FROM THE NORTH SEA, ABOUT 56° N, AROUND IRELAND TO SPANISH PORTS, AUGUST 13TH – OCTOBER 15TH, 1588

SATURDAY morning, August 13th, was the first time for a fortnight that the Duke of Medina Sidonia had not been able to see, beyond his splintered taffrail, the English fleet following doggedly in his wake. The Armada ran before a south-west wind. The time for turning back towards the Channel had passed, and however much the duke might have preferred going down with his flagship to going home in defeat he had made up his mind that the only way he could still serve his master was to bring as many ships as possible home.

The judgment of battle was irreversible. Since entering the Channel he had lost at least seven first-line ships, including a galleass, and the rest of his first-raters were so sorely beaten with great-shot as to be barely sea-worthy; a fifth of their men were killed or disabled, and their munitions were almost exhausted. Even morale, which had been high in the Channel, showed signs of cracking. On the morning of the ninth more than half the fleet had ignored the signal to lie to and await the enemy. The duke did what he could about that. He held a summary court-martial aboard the *San Martín* and, on evidence that his order had been received and deliberately disobeyed, sentenced twenty delinquent captains to be hanged. One of the culprits, a gentleman and a neighbour of his at San Lucar, he did have hanged at the yard-arm of a pinnace which paraded through the fleet with its grisly burden. The remaining nineteen were removed from their commands and committed to the custody of the Judge Advocate General, Martin de Aranda. But it would take more than judges and hangmen to give the fleet back the fighting spirit it had had off the Eddystone.

If there was no chance now of leading the Armada to victory, there scarcely seemed more of bringing it home. The *San Martín* was shot through and through by culverins and demi-culverins and had one great hole just above the water-line, the work of a fifty-pounder. In spite of expert patching she leaked like a sieve. Recalde's *San Juan* was in no better case below decks, and in addition had a mainmast too weak to carry sail. The *San Marcos*, which had fought beside the *San Martín* at Gravelines, was so knocked about that her captain had tied her up like a bundle, with cables passed under her keel, for fear she might fall apart. And these three Portuguese galleons seemed less damaged than three of the great Levantines which wallowed every day a little deeper in the water and tended to fall a little farther astern. Indeed, all the fighting-ships were badly battered, and some of the hulks, too, were in a bad way. One of them, known only as 'the bark of Hamburg', later went down so suddenly that though her crew were saved her stores were all lost.

Stores were the most serious problem. There was no more fresh food, of course. Most of the biscuit was mouldy or putrescent; much of the salt fish and meat was inedible. It was not likely that salt provision would be in demand, in any case, for the worst shortage was water. Every available cask and butt had been filled at Corunna; there should have been enough for three months. But again casks leaked, and some when opened held no more than a few inches of green slime. It was now seen how deadly was the blow that Drake had struck at Cape St Vincent. With a long hard voyage ahead squadron after squadron reported only enough water to last, with the severest rationing, for a month or less.

De Leiva was for making for Norway, Diego Flores for Ireland; but this time the duke, supported apparently by the rest of his 'generals', but without Recalde, who had taken to his bunk and was slowly dying, talked down the opposition and the council agreed unanimously. The fleet would go round Scotland and Ireland to the north and then, when they had sea room enough, bear away on a long starboard tack to Corunna. In the sailing orders issued to all ships that day the duke emphasized that Ireland must be given a wide berth 'for fear of the harm that may happen to you upon that coast'. He took what other precautions he could. He had all the horses and mules thrown overboard to save water, and he ordered every man in the fleet, without distinction of persons, on a daily ration of eight ounces of biscuit, a pint of water and half a pint of wine, nothing more. In the *San Martín*, at least, the order was strictly observed, the duke setting the example. It was not in his case much sacrifice. Ever since they had cleared the Tagus, food had appealed to him only when in calm water. 'At sea', he had once protested to Philip, 'I am always seasick and always catch cold.' His gloomier prognostications for this voyage had a way of coming true.

So the Armada held on 'into the Norway Channel', running easily north-north-east before the wind under moderate canvas until the pilots thought they had reached 61° 30' N, far enough so that a course west-south-west would miss the Shetlands. Already some ships had parted company. On the morning of the 14th the three great Levant carracks which had wallowed so low in the water were seen to turn away eastward, as if making in despair for the coast. They must have waited too long: they were never heard of again. After a squall on the night of the 17th the *Gran Grifon, capitana* of the hulks, and several of its squadron were missing. That day the fleet turned, and since it was now close-hauled on the port tack, the clumsier sailers tended to fall away northwards. It was misty with frequent showers, and the ill-clad men, especially the Andalusians and the blacks, suffered severely from the cold.

On the 21st the pilots judged that the fleet had reached about 58° N, at a point some ninety leagues north-west of Achill Head on the Galway coast, a landmark which for some reason, perhaps the proximity of Clare Island, the Spanish had got thoroughly confused with Cape Clear. This was the place to alter course, and the duke sent round the fleet to take a final muster. He was alarmed to learn that there were now three thousand sick, besides the wounded — a frightening increase in the past eight days. The water shortage, too, was worse than he had expected. Either some butts which had seemed sound had begun to leak or some captains were not enforcing rationing. The duke reaffirmed his sailing orders and took up his new course, meanwhile sending off Don Balthazar de Zuñiga in a fast pinnace to report his position to the King and deliver to him the melancholy narrative of the campaign.

Then the trouble began. For the next two weeks there were nothing but storms from the worst possible quarter, the south-west, and baffling head winds. On Saturday, September 3rd the duke found himself, according to the pilots, still in about 58° N and perhaps farther east than he had been two weeks before. Meanwhile seventeen ships more had parted company, including the *San Juan* with Recalde aboard, de Leiva's great carrack, the *Rata Coronada* and four other Levanters, four more greatships, one Andalusian, one Castilian, and two from Oquendo's Guipúzcoan squadron, several hulks and two of the remaining galleasses. But the wind had veered for the moment to the north-east. Medina Sidonia sent off another pinnace to the King, and once more led the remnant of his fleet on the long voyage home.

Nineteen days later the *San Martín* was signalling for a pilot off Santander. In the next few days sixty-six of the ships that had sailed for

England in July were reported as arrived in Spanish harbours. Only one more got back that year.

Later on it was learned, first from the English Press, then by confirmation from survivors, that the worst losses had been in Ireland. Five Levanters, led by *Rata Coronada* with Alonso de Leiva under whom the flower of the Spanish nobility had competed to serve, a great Biscayan, a Guipúzcoan, a Portuguese galleon and three hulks whose names we know, made for the western coast of Ireland in hope of food, water and a chance to repair their shot-torn hulls and rigging. Only two got away. The Portuguese galleon, Recalde's *San Juan*, managed to anchor in the lee of Great Blasket Island at the mouth of Dingle Bay, take on fresh water and get to sea again. She finally limped into Corunna in great distress on October 7th, one of the last survivors to be reported. One of the hulks, a hospital ship, left Dingle Bay with Recalde, but despairing of getting back to Spain with any of her patients still alive ran up the Channel in the hope of reaching a French, or perhaps just an English port. Instead, she piled herself up on Bolt Tail on the Devon coast. Her stores and some of her people were saved. All the rest of the ships that sought Ireland (the Lord Deputy reported seventeen, and there may have been enough unidentified hulks and pinnaces to make up that number) perished. They came in without charts or pilots, often without anchors, in ships so crippled as to be barely seaworthy and with crews so weakened by privation and disease they could barely work them, and split themselves on rocks, or wedged themselves on reefs, or were torn from insecure anchorages by sudden squalls and dashed against cliffs. The last to survive, the galleass *Girona*, fleeing the inhospitable island with such rescued castaways as she could collect, including de Leiva and the remnants of his company, was wrecked near the Giant's Causeway with the loss of all hands.

Thousands of Spaniards must have drowned on the Irish coast. The fate of those who got ashore was not less miserable. Many had their brains knocked out as they lay stretched exhausted on the beaches where they had come ashore. Others wandered for a while in the desolate parts of the west until they were hunted down and slaughtered like wild beasts by parties of soldiers, or reluctantly handed over by their Irish hosts to English executioners. One considerable group of gentlemen, presumably worth ransoming, surrendered on the promise that their lives would be spared, but were later killed, over the protest of their captor, by explicit order of the Lord Deputy. The Deputy, Sir William Fitzwilliam, had less than two thousand English soldiers, badly trained and badly armed, to hold down a nation quiet for the moment but rarely quiet long. He could not risk the presence on Irish soil of so many Spanish soldiers, even as prisoners. His simple policy was to kill them all as soon as they could be found. In the main, that was done.

Two myths should, perhaps, be dealt with here: the story, spread by the English almost from the Armada year, that the Spaniards who came ashore were spontaneously murdered by the Irish for their clothes and arms and jewellery; and the legend, persistent in the west, that black eyes and hair, aquiline profiles and swarthy cheeks show the blood of the Spaniards who came ashore from the Armada ships and stayed. Not infrequently the wild Irish did relieve their unbidden guests of their valuables. Perhaps, now and then, a throat was cut. But there is only one recorded instance of the killing of Spanish castaways by Irish not directly in English pay, and it aroused general reprobation. Usually the Irish sheltered the Spaniards, supplied their necessities, and, whenever they could, helped them out of the realm. Several hundred Spaniards did so escape, mostly to Scotland. They thought they had left few if any of their countrymen behind. Perhaps here and there some castaway found a roof and a wife in a friendly village, but not enough, surely, to have any effect on the look of the people as a whole. If one sees, time and again, the same physical types in Connaught and in Galicia, it must be for some other reason.

The wrecks in Ireland and around Scotland account for all the fighting-ships of the Armada lost, except to enemy action. At the Lizard on July 30th there were sixty-eight. On September 3rd, Medina Sidonia could still count forty-four. These had obeyed his orders and followed the course he set. They all got home, including all ten of the galleons of the Indian Guard, seven of the ten galleons of Portugal, eight of the Andalusians, seven of Oquendo's squadron, six of Recalde's. Only the Levanters were reduced to a skeleton, just two greatships left out of ten. It was a beaten, shattered fleet, but many a more experienced admiral has brought back fewer ships against less formidable odds, and whoever advised him (and at the crucial moment it was neither Diego Flores nor Recalde), these ships were saved by the leadership and will-power of their commander.

No one remembered the feat at the time, and few enough have ever remarked it since. The duke himself did not make a point of it. When after Gravelines he had tasted the full bitterness of defeat, he had assumed that it was his duty to salvage whatever he could. That he had saved, in ships and guns, anyhow, nearly two-thirds of his fighting strength, must have seemed to him small mitigation of the national disaster, and none at all of his personal disgrace. He blamed himself for what had happened. The English had better ships, better guns, more homogeneous and better-trained crews, and enjoyed besides what proved to be the decisive advantage of fighting close to their home base. The Armada had been sent, too weak and too scantily supplied, on an impossible mission. But when his contemporaries laid its failure to the incompetence of its commander, and said that if only Santa Cruz or Recalde or Oquendo or that odd hero, Pedro de Valdés, had been in command everything would have turned out differently, Medina Sidonia agreed with them. Perhaps that is why the judgment has so seldom been questioned since.

Who actually led the broken fleet on the last leg of its voyage, we shall never know. Captain Marolín de Juan should have done so, but that veteran seaman and skilled navigator had been unintentionally left behind at Dunkirk. There were four pilots aboard the *San Martín*, one of them an Englishman. Three died at sea. It must have been the fourth who brought the flagship staggering past Corunna before a westerly gale, and conned her to her landfall off Santander. We do not know his name.

As for the duke, on September 3rd, when the last decision had been made and the prows were at last turned homeward, he took to his bunk and stayed there. For days he had been burning with fever, and racked with the pangs dysentery can inflict on an empty retching stomach. For the rest of that nightmare voyage he tumbled in and out of consciousness, only vaguely aware of the contrary winds, the sudden storms, the missed landfalls. When he was lowered into the pilot boat at Santander he was too weak to sit upright, almost too weak to sign his name, though he sent off at once to the King, to the Governor of the province, to the Archbishop of Santiago, a series of pitiful pleas for help.

Help was needed. On the *San Martín* alone, besides those killed in battle or dead of wounds, one hundred and eighty were dead by September 23rd, the day she made port, of scurvy or typhus or influenza aggravated by hunger and thirst. More died daily, in the *San Martín* and all the other ships, while the unprepared countryside tried to assemble the food, the clothes, the beds and bedding that might keep them alive. Of the higher officers who came back scarcely one was fit for duty, and the two most famous, Recalde and Oquendo, were both dead by the middle of October. Many ships' companies were in even worse case than the *San Martín*. Several had no food at all and went on dying of sheer starvation, though anchored in a Spanish port. One had had no water for the last twelve days at sea, save what its rain-drenched crew could wring from

X ♠

The Spaniards Consulting
and at laſt reſolving to return
into Spain by the north Ocean
many of their Shipps being diſabled

IX ♠

Spaniſh Comanders taken priſo=
ners & brought into England.

VIII ♠

The Spaniſh Ships loſt
on the Coaſt of Scotland
and 700 Souldiers and
Marriners caſt a Shoare.

V ♠

The Prince of Parma
coming to Dunkerk with his
Army but too late is received
by the Spaniads with reproach

From a set of playing cards engraved in the seventeenth century.

their rags of shirts. One ran aground in Laredo Harbour because there were not enough men left able to lower the sails and drop the anchor. For weeks officers and men kept on dying, while food and money were scraped together and emergency hospitals fitted up.

The ships were in almost as evil case as the men. One sank shortly after she cast anchor. And some of the finest, like the *San Marcos*, were fit only to be broken up for the sake of their timber and their guns — among these, the Duke of Florence's fine new galleon. Captain Bartoli died the day after his ship made port. His first officer had been killed at Gravelines. The ranking soldier aboard, Captain Gaspar da Sousa, declared that no ship in the Armada had done better service or been more often in the thick of the fighting, and this the Duke of Medina Sidonia later confirmed in a formal letter to the Florentine ambassador. But such praise can scarcely have compensated the Grand Duke of Tuscany for the news that it was hopeless to try to get the *San Francesco* to Corunna for repairs, and that the only galleon in his navy would never carry his flag again. As far as we can tell, almost half the surviving fleet turned out to be unfit for further service. Only a miracle, one observer thought, had kept these shattered wrecks afloat so long.

From his sick-bed, surrounded by a makeshift staff mostly recruited ashore, Medina Sidonia continued to try to cope with the fleet's troubles and, whenever he felt able, to dictate letters and memoranda to Secretary Idiáquez and the King, most of them querulous, some of them almost incoherent. He fretted about the state of the ships and even more about the plight of their crews, unpaid, half clothed, ill-fed, still dying in the squalor of their stinking hulks because there was no place to house them ashore and no money to pay them off. Someone should be sent, he kept insisting, who could deal with these affairs, someone of experience and ability. He seems to have blamed his failure to take more energetic action not on his extreme illness — though there were days when he was out of his head with fever and others when though conscious he was too weak to sign his name — and not, as the fact really was, on circumstances beyond anyone's control, but on his own inexperience and incompetence. In one note to Idiáquez he wandered from the subject to protest that the King had been wrong ever to place him in command of the Armada. He knew nothing, he said, echoing his first response to the appointment and forgetting the grim lesson of the summer past, of the sea or of war. He had warned the King that he would be ill-served by a general who had no judgment of his own in these affairs, and did not even know whom to trust. And now see how things had turned out! He would never command at sea again — no, not if his head should pay for it!

All the duke wanted was to go home to the orange groves of San Lucar and the sun of his own country. King Philip, fairer and more generous to his defeated admiral than the rest of his contemporaries or most subsequent historians, after hearing Don Francisco de Bobadilla's report and reading a letter from the Bishop of Burgos and another from the duke's attendant physician, relieved Medina Sidonia of his command, excused him from coming to kiss hands at Court and gave him leave to go home.

In October a curtained horse-litter, escorted by the meagre remnant of the duke's servants, set out southward across the mountains. It did not stop at noblemen's houses. There were few in Spain that were not mourning. It avoided cities where insults might have been shouted and stones thrown. Martinmas had passed before it brought the duke back to San Lucar, and it was spring before he could walk and ride about his estates and seem himself again. If, in fact, he was ever quite the same. He lived to serve Philip II for another decade and Philip's son for twelve years more, in high and honourable posts, but his countrymen did not forget or forgive, and a French diplomat who saw him fifteen years later thought he could perceive in the melancholy duke's bearing and countenance the unhealed wound of the old defeat.

In England things were less different than one would think. The English fleet had no long and perilous voyage home, but when, Parma having missed the spring tide and nothing more being heard of the Armada, the Queen was impatient to begin laying up ships and dismissing crews, her captains and councillors were horrified at her recklessness. They persuaded her to wait, and the ships were kept fully manned and vigilant until the news began to come in from Ireland. In consequence men sickened and died at Harwich and Margate, at Dover and in the Downs, almost as fast as the Spaniards died at sea. One assumes that the same deadly killer was at work: ship's fever, typhus. In the best tradition of the Tudor services, however, officers and men blamed everything on bad beer. It was axiomatic that as long as there was plenty of good beer English soldiers and sailors were never unhealthy.

Then, when at last the Queen had her way, and demobilization began, there were the usual troubles about money, about clothes and food, and about lodging for men too weak to get home. Helpless, emaciated, half-naked seamen lay dying in the streets of Dover and Rochester as they did at Laredo and Santander. Nerves got taut, Frobisher offered to fight Drake in his shirt, and that old hero John Hawkins, the architect of English victory if any man was, began a letter to Lord Burghley: 'I am sorry I do live so long to receive so sharp a letter from your lordship'; and later wrote querulously to Walsingham: 'I would to God I were delivered of the dealing for money … My pain and misery in this service is infinite … God, I trust, will deliver me of it ere long, for there is no other hell.' He sounds like a Spanish paymaster, as Howard, in his helpless anger at the lengthening death roll in his fleet, sounds like Medina Sidonia.

And in England, too, men muttered that the high command had bungled their business. Why had not the Spanish been utterly destroyed? Why had the Lord Admiral been afraid to come to close quarters? (In Spain the same question was being asked, absurdly enough, about Medina Sidonia.) And the popular voice said with assurance that if Drake had been in command there would have been none of this stand-off fighting and nothing settled, while at the same time it spoke as if Drake had won whatever victory there was. Howard did not suffer as Medina Sidonia suffered — he was, after all, the winner. In his last years, when the defeat of the Spanish Armada had receded into that golden haze through which Jacobeans saw the reign of Good Queen Bess, and like most of the events of that reign, grown larger and more glorious the further it receded, there was fame enough for Howard, too. But for most people it was Drake's victory.

In the past twenty years or so historians have done Howard more justice. The most recent narrative says roundly: 'It was Howard's battle and he won it.' It has even been argued that Howard fought the battle the only way it could have been fought without too much risk, and that no admiral could have done better. There is a tendency of late to speak more kindly of Medina Sidonia, too, to recognize his courage and his administrative ability, but no one has yet said he could not have done better. It is at least arguable, however, that no one could. Unless he could have cut off the *Ark Royal* and her two companions that Monday morning off Tor Bay it is hard to point out a mistake he made which affected the outcome of the campaign. It can be argued that all his other decisions, including the decision to anchor at Calais and the choice of the route home, were as sound as his personal conduct was courageous. Not that such a judgment would have been much comfort to Medina Sidonia. Whatever he did, it was not enough. Nor does it matter at all to the dead whether they receive justice at the hands of succeeding generations. But to the living, to do justice — however belatedly — should matter.

335

'A Thankfull
Remembrance', 1588.

XXXII

END OF A TALL MAN

BLOIS, DECEMBER 23RD, 1588

BY late autumn, 1588 the affairs of Catholic France had come to deadlock. As the Armada advanced towards its rendezvous Henry of Valois had yielded more and more to Henry of Guise, but never quite the essentials. In August, when the rumours of a Spanish victory were thickest, he made Guise his Lieutenant-General, but he would not go back to Paris with him; and as the likelihood of a Spanish victory faded, slowly, slyly, the King's resistance stiffened. Slowly he began a cautious, indirect campaign to recover what he had lost.

Early in September, while the 'Discours Véritable' was being printed and Parma was breaking up his camp at Dunkirk, the King dismissed his ministers. They all went — his Chancellor, Cheverny; his *surintendant des finances*, Pomponne de Bellièvre; his Secretaries of State, Brûlart and Villeroy and Pinart; all the wheel-horses of administration, men who had governed France in his name ever since he was crowned, men who had been with him in Poland, men who were seasoned in the royal service while he was still in the nursery, dismissed without reproaches but without reason given, just 'granted leave to retire to their estates', to exile and political death. With the Estates General about to meet at Blois and the affairs of the kingdom in chaos this palace revolution seemed so senseless, so destructive of what was left of royal government, that most men assumed that the dismissals had been forced by the faction which had clamoured loudest for them, the radicals of the League.

Cheverny knew better, and so one suspects did his colleagues. The trouble was, these ministers had served Catherine de Medici long before they served her son. By force of habit they showed her the latest dispatches, accepted her corrections of the papers; they drafted, incorporated her views in their memoranda. When Bellièvre was dealing with Guise at Soissons he reported to the Queen Mother daily, and followed her advice. Later, after the barricades, Villeroy wrote to Angoulême on her instructions and without the King's knowledge, a letter which was meant to result in Epernon's death. Cheverny argued for a return to Paris because

337

that was what Queen Catherine wanted. Catherine knew why the ministers had been dismissed, and resented the dismissals as a rejection of herself.

It was, of course. Her son knew, if she did not, that she had already rejected him, that she had turned naturally, instinctively, from the failure to the success, from Henry of Valois to Henry of Guise. That was why, for more than a year now, she had always been able to persuade herself that whatever Guise wanted was really the best, the safest course for her son. That was why, after that day in the Louvre when she had saved the Duke's life, her son had never trusted her again. He could not follow the devious path he saw ahead of him with the eyes of her servants upon him.

The King was very much alone at Blois. His new ministers — honest, industrious nonentities — would do their work, but they were not men to talk to. Joyeuse and Epernon had been the last of the mignons — of the mignons who mattered, that is, boon companions and not playthings. Now Joyeuse was dead, and Epernon was sulking in Angoulême in the belief that his friend and master had tried to have him murdered. The King's wife was as much too dull and soft to share his thoughts as his mother was too sharp and hard. He had only tools around him, pens and daggers. What he had to do, he had to do alone.

Sometimes it was too much for him, and he would remain hours and days together shut in his chamber, speaking to no one, sunk in black lethargy. But mostly he played his part with his usual grace. As they arrived he received the members of the Estates with affability and charm. When they finally convened he addressed them with such eloquence and pathos as brought the hostile, suspicious assembly cheering to its feet. He spent much time with his cousin the Duke of Guise, the Lieutenant-General of his kingdom and Grand Master of his household, easily matching him in ironic banter and thrusts of double-edged wit. His mother felt the cold more than usual as winter approached and kept much in bed, so daily he hovered at her bedside, telling her the latest news of France and Europe, listening patiently to her advice. And always he was watchful, as a man must be when he is alone in a ring of enemies.

It was all slow, uphill work. His parliamentary tactics could scarcely have been shrewder if the whole team of his old ministers had been advising him, but he could make no headway with the Estates. He had hoped to use them not only to relieve his chronic poverty but to take the leadership of the League away from the Duke of Guise, but there were very few moderates in this assembly, and the radicals, drunk with a sip of power, were demanding many contradictory things. They wanted a more efficient central government. They wanted it under their constant supervision. They wanted peace and prosperity, economy and reform, lower and more equitable taxes and an immediate all-out crusade for the extermination of the heretics. They were so intent on all this that they refused to notice when the Duke of Savoy overran the last French outpost beyond the Alps. They would not vote any fresh taxes at all. The cry was reform before supply, and every concession the King made became the basis for new demands. It was a frustrating deadlock, but Henry did not perceive that the Estates were unmanageable because a new revolutionary wind was blowing. Instead, he blamed everything on the machinations of the Guises. Once the Duke of Guise was disposed of the King felt confident of handling the Estates.

Guise felt equally frustrated. The Estates, full as they were of ardent Leaguers, had got entirely out of hand. His plans called for a big army. Where was it to come from, if no money was voted? Meanwhile the King, and he, too, of course, would have to stay in Blois as long as the Estates were in session, and he did not feel altogether easy about being so far from Paris. He was King of Paris, but he was not yet King of France, and he did not need Mendoza's warning that for the moment he could count on very little in the way of Spanish support. Had he foreseen the Armada's ignominious failure he might have stayed away from Blois. Here, at the King's Court, he was in constant danger. As soon as the Estates were over he would get the King back to Paris, if he had to drag him there by force.

Meanwhile he took his precautions. Blois was full of armed Leaguers, and his own followers lodged in the castle itself outnumbered the royal guards. As Grand Master of the Household he held all the keys, and he could go anywhere in the castle day or night, even to the door of the King's bedchamber with armed men at his heels, and no one would question him. But what made him feel safest was his certainty that his sovereign was a poor spiritless creature who would never retaliate. When the Archbishop of Lyons begged him to use the King with more outward respect and not push him too far, Guise only laughed. 'I know him better than you do,' he said. 'To master him, one must defy him. This is a king who needs to be frightened.'

On the morning of December 19th one of his spies in the castle reported that the King had consulted several persons about how to rid himself of his persecutor, and that Alphonse d'Ornano had returned emphatically to his idea of the previous May: 'Kill him out of hand.' Guise shrugged off the report. There had been dozens of these meaningless alarms. At supper on December 22nd he found an anonymous note folded into his napkin with another urgent warning. He read it aloud to the company, reached to a near-by desk for a pen, scrawled across the paper 'He would not dare', and dropped it on the floor. He had outfaced his Valois cousin so many times, he was sure he could always do so.

The King had, indeed, put his problem to an informal group of advisers, just as Guise had heard. He had proof, he told them, of a conspiracy against his Crown and life. At the Cardinal of Guise's table a toast had been drunk to the duke as the next King of France. A man applying to the duke's secretary for a safe conduct had been told: 'If you can, wait a little. We shall soon be changing our title and estate.' He had received many warnings, the King went on, that before long he would be kidnapped and carried off to Paris, unless worse should befall him. Even Guise's brother, the Duke of Mayenne, had sent warnings. 'It is my life or his,' the King ended. 'What do you advise?'

Probably Montholon, the new Chancellor, answered first. There was no doubt that Guise was guilty of treason. There would be ample proof. Let him be promptly charged, tried and executed. The King smiled sadly. And where would one find the Court to try and convict a peer of France and the Captain-General of the League? In Paris, perhaps?

Marshal Aumont proposed a more direct expedient, and Alphonse Ornano seconded him bluntly: 'Kill him.' Ornano was ready, but Henry knew that there was no one whom the Guisards feared and distrusted more. Ornano would never get within a hundred feet of the duke with a weapon in his hand. The King looked at Crillon. The captain of the French Guards blushed and stammered. Somehow it had never happened to him to have to stab a man without warning. He didn't think he could manage it. A duel, now. He would be delighted to challenge the duke to a duel. And he felt sure he could kill him. Henry shook his head. It was no use trying to explain to Crillon what Guise would do with such a challenge. He thanked them all. He would think of something.

Before four days had passed, he had. There was one time when the royal apartments were not exposed to unannounced intrusions of Guisards. The Royal Council met in the ante-chamber which opened directly from the great circular staircase giving access to the royal suite. During its meetings all unauthorized persons were excluded; councillors were expected to enter unattended; the ushers of the Council kept the doors. And there was one body of men whose loyalty the King could count on

340

absolutely — the Forty-five. Epernon had recruited them four years ago. They were all noblemen, but petit-noblesse of Gascony, whose whole wealth each was a horse, a sword, a ragged cloak and a few rocky acres to starve on. They had no friends or connections at Court, and no one to rely on except the King. Fifteen of them were expected to be on duty night and day at the King's call. In return they were paid at a rate that seemed to them princely. Guise had spoken of them as an idle, useless, expensive gang of ruffians, and one of the reforms proposed by his friends in the Estates General was that they should be dismissed. The Forty-five knew this.

There were still some complicated arrangements to make. The François 1er wing of the castle, where the King slept, was a rabbit warren of twisty little stairways and unexpected passages. Two doorways usually open had to be blocked, and one door always locked had to be opened, so that some of the necessary actors could arrive on the scene unobserved. The King saw to everything himself.

On the afternoon of December 22nd he had a long talk with Guise, the only account of which is rather too pat to be true. But in it the King certainly mentioned that he and the Queen would be leaving the castle the next day to keep their Christmas in a pavilion in the park, and that before he left there would be a Council. Later he sent word that he needed the keys of the castle — something to do with tomorrow's moving. Guise tossed them to the messenger. That was before the last anonymous warning.

At seven in the morning Guise was roused in the bedchamber of his current mistress by word that there would be a meeting of the Council at eight, an unusually early hour. (The King had been up since four, making his final dispositions, telling the actors in his drama at the last possible moment, so that no word should leak out, just what they must do.) It was a miserable morning, a thin sleety rain outside and in the old castle a chill that struck to the bone, but Guise could only dress in what he had worn the night before — a satin doublet and small-clothes with a short cape — and hurry to the meeting.

On the great stairway Guise was surprised to find a throng of the archers of the guard. They were presenting a petition, their captain told him politely, asking for at least some part of their back pay. Some of the archers followed him up the stairs, begging his voice on their behalf, telling him how long it was since they had been paid and what miserable straits they were in. Then as the door of the council chamber closed behind him they swung about, shoulder to shoulder in solid ranks, blocking the grand staircase from side to side.

Guise was the last to arrive. His brother the cardinal, and the Archbishop of Lyons, the only two others of his faction attending, had preceded him just a moment before; the rest seemed to have come somewhat earlier. Guise was uneasy. He complained of the cold, and ordered a fire to be lit. He sent for some sugared fruits (the great stairway was blocked, and the fruits came from the King's cupboard). His eye began to water, the eye above his old scar, and he found he had no handkerchief. A page brought him one of the King's. The fire warmed him and he took off his cape. The Council was droning through some routine business about money when a gentleman brought him word that the King would like to see him in his cabinet. Excusing himself Guise pushed through the door to the King's apartments, his cape slung negligently over his left arm.

In the corridor lounged eight of the Forty-five. As he passed they fell in behind him like an escort. Almost at the door of the King's cabinet Guise suddenly whirled to face them, and the foremost struck him with a dagger. He tried to draw his sword but the hilt had become entangled with the cape, and before he could clear it his arms were seized by more of the Forty-five who emerged from a door behind him. He was a powerful man and, hampered as he was, he dragged his assailants this way and that about the lobby, struggling to free his arms and crying out as the daggers struck him: 'Ah! My friends! Ah! Gentlemen! Ah! Treachery!' Then for a moment he shook the pack loose and stood alone, swaying, took one step forward and fell headlong. Later, when they searched him, they found the draft of an unfinished letter beginning: 'To keep up the civil war in France will cost 700,000 livres a month.' It sums up his career, and may stand as his epitaph.

In her bedroom on the floor below the Queen Mother heard the strange scuffling and stamping overhead, and trembled. In the council chamber the Cardinal of Guise heard his brother's voice raised in anguish, and sprang to his feet crying: 'Treachery!' But Aumont's sword was drawn and his hand on the cardinal's shoulder, and a moment later the archers of the guard came in and led the cardinal and the Archbishop of Lyons away, prisoners. Before the morning was over a handful of noble Guisard intriguers were in custody, including the aged Cardinal of Bourbon who was to have been the puppet king of the transition, and the King's guards had invaded the session of the Estates and arrested its leaders, including those two heroes of the barricades the comte de Brissac, president of the nobility, and La Chapelle-Marteau, now head of the Revolutionary Government of Paris and president of the Third Estate.

There were protests, but no resistance. For the moment the party of the League in Blois was cowed and broken, and, since Henry III was not a bloodthirsty man, at a total cost of only two lives. The Cardinal of Guise died on the pikes of his guards, but none of the other persons arrested suffered worse than temporary imprisonment. Technically it was the most successful political operation Henry III had ever conducted, and Dr Cavriana noted as an interesting medical fact that the King's eye was brighter, his colour better and his step more springy than for months past.

We have no trustworthy account of what Henry III said when he came to the door of his cabinet to see his enemy dead at his feet, but memoirists and chroniclers who had read Plutarch and noted how often he was able to report the words of his heroes on important occasions could not all resist the temptation to have him say something. Mostly they gave him such lines as: 'At last I am king! No longer a prisoner and a slave!' Henry may, indeed, have said something of the kind. He was always a man of ready and appropriate eloquence, accustomed to remembering that people were likely to notice what he said and write it down, and according to Dr Cavriana he used very similar words in the jaunty account with which he horrified his mother next day. But there is another version, of slender authority but marked by that inconsequence which is so often the stamp of the authentic event. According to it, Henry stopped on the threshold of his cabinet to look down at the sprawled body, and said after a pause: 'How tall he is! I had not thought he was so tall. He is even taller dead than alive.'

The only trouble with taking this apparent irrelevance as genuine is that it is so relevant to what came afterwards, and that it was set down long enough afterwards for the point to have been clear to the writer. For Henry was not more King of France than he had been before he killed the King of Paris, but — as with shrill fury his mother told him he would be — less king than ever. On the news of Guise's death Paris revolted, city after city fell from its allegiance, and, before the King took the field against the rebel league in the spring, he had accepted in place of the tutelage of Guise the scarcely less embarrassing alliance of the King of Navarre, with the implied complicity of the Queen of England.

Not that Henry of Valois would have counted the murder at Blois, as most people did, among his many failures. When he told his mother that he was again the only King of France there is reason to believe that he was speaking not of the external trappings of royalty, the safety and authority and power she valued, but of its mystical essence, of the idea of a crown handed down legitimately from generation to generation in accordance with the fundamental law, of the King as a vessel of God's grace and mysterious agent of God's will. There was nothing meanly selfish in Henry's clinging to his crown. Even had he escaped assassination he would have had few enough years of life, and those not very pleasant. He would never have a son to follow him. If all he wanted was comfort and outward deference and the appearances of kingship, he could have had them in return for surrendering the reins to Guise, and promising the reversion of his crown to the house of Lorraine, the same bargain that the old Cardinal of Bourbon was willing enough to strike. But the King, who had betrayed so many friends and so many principles, could not betray the idea of kingship, and when he saw that no other course would prevent Guise's ultimate usurpation of the throne he struck him down with something as much like a public execution as he could manage.

And so, when Jacques Clement's dagger ended his life at Saint-Cloud some seven months later, Henry of Valois was able to hand on to Henry of Navarre his inheritance intact. The Grand Prior of France reports him speaking to Navarre from his deathbed: 'My brother, now it is for you to possess the God-given rights I have laboured to preserve for you. It is that labour which has brought me to the state you see. I do not repent myself of it, for justice, of which I have always been the protector, requires that you succeed after me in this kingdom.' Whether or not that is what he said it expresses well enough what he did, and the final meaning of his life. For a man with Henry III's many weaknesses, trapped in his unlucky position, it was a considerable achievement.

As for his persecutor and victim, there is no mystery about Guise except how so shallow an egotist attracted so many people. He was the type of the adventurer relying on a bold front and a calloused conscience, of the gambler playing for stakes beyond his means. Sooner or later his luck was bound to run out, and though Sixtus V and Philip II made the customary gestures of disapproval at the manner of his passing there is no sign that either was much disturbed. Guise was too greedy and too care-less of details to leave anyone with the impression that he served either the Church or Spain for any but his own ends. Spain probably regretted him more than Rome, but mercenaries are always expendable. He had been employed for a diversion on one flank of a vast operation, and when the main attack had failed he had been left for the moment exposed and without adequate support. In a way he was as much a casualty of the Armada as Hugo de Moncada or Alonso de Leiva; but whereas those captains had died in the performance of their duty Guise, so Mendoza implied, had chiefly his own rashness to thank. Mendoza had appreciated Guise's usefulness, but it had not been an easy partnership. Mendoza did not need to tell his master that there would be other claimants forthcoming for the Crown of France, and other exalted personages willing to pocket Spanish gold. According to ambassadors Philip II, when he heard of Guise's death, reflected for a moment, then said: 'This is a matter for the Pope.' Pope Sixtus, when he heard of it, nodded as if he had been expecting the news and said: 'So, the King of Spain has lost another captain.'

Assassination of the Duke of Guise at Blois, December 23rd, 1588, from a contemporary engraving.

XXXIII

THE WINDS OF GOD

THE ESCURIAL, NEW YEAR'S DAY, 1589

IMPERTURBABILITY in the face of triumph or disaster was a part of the public character of Philip II, a part of his legend in his lifetime. As a small boy he must have heard many times how his father, the emperor, had received the news of the great victory at Pavia with a self-restraint which had aroused universal admiration. Probably he resolved to emulate such behaviour, and found it the easier to do so because his temperament was naturally something less than effervescent. At any rate, by the thirty-third year of his reign Philip had become, for his many admirers, the typical Christian stoic, and a hundred popular stories illustrated his admirable self-control under trying circumstances. Some were like the comic classic about the newly appointed secretary who was so nervous in his unfamiliar duties that when he took a freshly written sheet from the King's hand, instead of sanding it he poured the ink-horn over it. He cringed in expectation of the royal wrath, only to be told gently: '*That* is the *ink*. *This* is the sand.' Some were like the pathetic anecdotes of the King's long-suffering patience with the growing eccentricity of his first-born son and heir, Don Carlos. There were so many such stories current within a decade of Philip's death that naturally some of his more sympathetic chroniclers found some to illustrate his iron self-control at the moment of his greatest disappointment.

Father Famiano Strada's apologue has the highest literary polish. As he tells it, the King was still nourishing the belief that the Armada was victorious when a courier from Santander (Maestre de campo Bobadilla?) reached the Escurial with the news of disaster. The royal Secretaries, Moura and Idiaquez, were aghast, and each tried to persuade the other to break the evil tidings. Finally Moura entered the royal cabinet, and when the King laid down his pen and looked up the Secretary stammered something about bad news of the Armada and thrust the courier forward. The King listened to the dismal tale without a change of countenance, and when it was ended, said: 'I give thanks to God by whose hand I have been so endowed that I can put to sea another fleet as great as this we have lost whenever I choose. It does not matter if a stream is sometimes choked, as long as the source flows freely.' And without a sigh or a change of expression the King picked up his pen and went on with his letters.

But Strada was, after all, Roman born and bred, and Spanish eloquence at its best is less ornate and has a deeper more iron-throated clang. Perhaps that is why, from the later seventeenth century on, Spanish historians preferred a variant version. The build-up, the frightened Secretaries, the serenely toiling King, the courier's grim news, all these are the same, but before he takes up his pen again the King says only: 'I sent my ships to fight against men, and not against the winds and waves of God.'

None of these stories, of course, could possibly be true. Philip had no opportunity to display his famous constancy in the face of unexpected disaster, because the full extent of the defeat was broken to him by slow degrees. Some time before the duke reached Santander, Philip had read Medina Sidonia's letter of August 21st with its accompanying *Diario* and listened to Captain Balthazar de Zuñiga's depressing report. He had heard both Parma's account of the missed rendezvous and, later, rumours of wrecks on the Irish coast. Nor is it believable that Philip would so instantaneously have blamed the winds and waves of the God his fleet had sailed to serve, especially since he had learned from Medina Sidonia's *Diario* that, up to August 21st, at least, the Armada had had all the best of it in the way of weather.

That Philip faced the bad news, as it came in, with dignity and constancy one can well believe, though there are limits to the constancy that can be expected of any human frame. He was seriously ill that autumn — an illness in the opinion of the diplomatic corps brought on, or at least aggravated, by anxiety and disappointment. The new papal nuncio thought that the King's eyes were red from weeping as well as from study, though if Philip wept no one saw him. And there were those to say that the events of the past ten months had aged the King as many years. It is after 1588 that his skin begins to have that curious mushroom pallor and to hang on his face in pouches. The beard loses the last hint of yellow in its white, is longer, and in some portraits looks curiously neglected. After 1588 the King went out of doors less often, saw fewer and fewer people, worked longer and longer in his solitary study.

But if Philip felt the blow of Fate, and showed that he felt it, he was not crushed by it. Almost as soon as he learned the extent of his losses he was assuring ambassadors that he would build another fleet stronger than the last, if he had to melt down every piece of plate on his table and every silver candlestick in the Escurial. It did not quite come to that, but American bullion had to be supplemented by scraping the cupboards of Castile and striking new bargains with Genoese bankers. After talking to some of his captains Philip saw more clearly that it was not just a question of hiring ships. He would have to build his own if he wanted sound ones. And he would have to expand Spanish production of cannon. Recruiting, gun-founding, shipbuilding, financing, the King's industrious pen put them all in train before the new year; and though things moved slowly, as they do in Spain, and there was much lost time to make up and many omissions to repair, so that few believed Philip would get his new fleet by the spring, nobody doubted that he would get it.

Meanwhile Philip had to come to terms with what had happened. The first step was his letter to the Spanish bishops of October 13th. After telling them briefly the news they already knew, and reminding them of the uncertainty of war at sea, he went on: 'We are bound to give praise to God for all things which He is pleased to do. Now I give thanks to Him for the mercy He has shown. In the storms through which the Armada sailed, it might have suffered a worse fate, and that its ill-fortune was no greater must be credited to the prayers for its good success, so devoutly and continuously offered.' And he tells the bishops gently that the prayers may be discontinued. No more ships were likely to come home. As early as this, then, the defeat of the Armada began to be ascribed in Spain to the winds of God.

It is easy enough to see why the English and Dutch should so ascribe it. 'God breathed and they were scattered', runs the legend on one of Queen Elizabeth's Armada medals. A Dutch medal records a similar sentiment, and the learned poets who celebrated in Latin verse the triumphant preservation of the Virgin Queen and the Protestant faith were so busy extolling the divine partisanship which drowned some thousands of Spaniards by a specially provided tempest that they scarcely had time to mention the English fleet.

Of course, better ships and better guns had won the battle before the Spaniards had any trouble with the weather, and even the losses off Ireland were due more to those barrel staves Drake burned at Cape St Vincent than they were to storms; but the more the destruction of the enemy could be seen as a direct act of God the clearer it would be that God was Protestant and that the common cause was, as it claimed to be, God's cause. So the great storm which destroyed the Spanish Armada joined the other legends — the massacres by the wild Irish, the vast Spanish ships and the tiny English ones, the cowardly Spanish commander skulking in a specially constructed shelter below decks, and the insulted gunner blowing up a galleon and leaping into the sea.

The odd thing is that all these legends are as familiar in Spain as in England, even the one about the Duke of Medina Sidonia 'lodged in the bottom of his ship for safety', which the author of *A Copy of a Letter ... found in the chamber of Richard Leigh* made up out of whole cloth to amuse his fellow countrymen; and the one about the tiny English ships and the vast Spanish ones, which must have begun when some literary landlubber, watching perhaps from the Isle of Wight, compared the swarm of English pinnaces with the ponderous *urcas* and neglected to notice the fighting-ships. At first thought, the hardest to understand is why the Spanish should have adopted the myth about the storm. Naturally the English welcomed a material proof that God was with them, but why should the Spanish accept the view that God was against them, that their fleet had contended in vain not against men but against the winds and waves of God? It is only at first thought that it is hard to understand. It is always easier to accept defeat at the hands of God than at the hands of men, and the Judaeo-Christian tradition is rich in resources for explaining apparently irrational behaviour on the part of the Deity. That this time God had let them be defeated did not mean that the Spaniards were not fighting in His cause or that He would not uphold them in the end.

Another seeker for the way of Christian stoicism, Don Bernardino de Mendoza, after he had absorbed the bitter fact of the Armada's defeat, put the point to his master with considerable eloquence and subtlety. Even the noblest crusaders, even St Louis himself, he observed with pardonable understatement, had not always been victorious. Our sins are so many and so heavy that no punishment God inflicts could be unreasonable; but God punishes those who truly love Him for their good, sometimes in this world as well as in the next. It may be that He chooses to humble those who fight in His cause so that through humility they may learn the way to victory. Philip underlined this sentence and scrawled an emphatic agreement in the margin.

Through humility to learn the way to victory. All that winter Philip's pen probed at the mistakes he had allowed himself to make: the heterogeneous fleet — next time the ships must be better, and up to some uniform standard; the lack of long-range guns — more culverins and demi-culverins, next time; the divided command, the bad co-ordination, the lack of a deep-water port, even the question of how to dominate Dutch coastal waters, the crucial question which somehow Parma had neglected and allowed everyone else to neglect. Philip reached no brilliant solutions, but at least he faced the problem and began to see how much there was still to be done. The shock of defeat had awakened him from the somnambulistic trance into which he had been plunged after the death of Mary Stuart. For the rest of his reign he was again the Prudent King, cautious even to the point of what looked like timidity, hesitant, watchful, given to second thoughts, providing against every possible contingency as far as he could before leaving anything to Providence.

There is one more anecdote which sounds authentic and relevant. We have no date for it, but it would be odd if it were not at least a year or two after 1588. Philip was walking in the inner garden of San Lorenzo when he heard the gardener declaring that after so much work done to train the pear trees on the south wall, God simply could not allow the promised fruit to be blighted. Philip called to him in a sterner tone than he commonly used among his monks. 'Brother Nicholas! Brother Nicholas, mind what you say! It is impiety, and almost blasphemy, to presume to know the will of God. It comes from the sin of pride. Even kings, brother Nicholas,' he went on more gently, 'must submit to being used by God's will without knowing what it is. They must never seek to use it.'

XXXIV

NOT A WHIT DISMAYED

RICHMOND, NEW YEAR'S DAY, 1589

HER Majesty kept Christmas that year at Richmond. It was a foul
season, with rain and sleet, and on New Year's Day a tempest
which toppled chimney-pots and carried away roofs in all the
Home Counties; but on the hearths of Richmond Palace fires blazed high,
and there was feasting and dancing and fooling, and stage-plays performed
by the children of Paul's, and merry games in which even the Queen took
part, and the usual giving on New Year's Day of expensive gifts. The
Queen's present to the Lord Admiral was magnificent, considering Elizabeth's usual scale, and Seymour and other noblemen received handsome
tokens in recognition of their services. Burghley gave the Queen a massive
piece of gold plate stamped with a symbolic memorial of her victory,
Warwick an elaborate sarcenet, bespangled with rubies and diamonds and
pearls and heavy with gold, and Howard another — not so costly as
Warwick's but probably as expensive as the silver-gilt plate he received.

Amidst the usual festivities, it was hard not to notice that the Queen's
Court was changing. Her cousin Lord Hunsdon, the Lord Chamberlain,
whom she had been accustomed to think of as not so much older than
herself, had suddenly gone stiff in the joints and snow-white in the poll.
Her Controller, Sir James Croft, only a few years older than Hunsdon,
seemed positively senile. Perhaps it was the whisper of treason which had
aged him since his return from Flanders; perhaps it was just that the folly
of his dealings with Parma drew attention to his advancing years. Croft's
enemy Walsingham, too, looked aged, though he was really a young man,
scarcely older than the Queen. The illness that kept him to his bed while
Mary Stuart's fate hung in the balance had not been mere policy after all.
Burghley rarely sat up late any more; he was thankful enough when his
gout let him get through a morning's work at the council table. And old
age, illness and death had torn other gaps in the familiar ranks. The
hardest not to notice was that long filled by a tall self-confident figure
which had grown more portly as the face had grown redder and the beard
whiter, but which still claimed and by a certain magnificence deserved the

place of jeune premier in the production in which the Queen figured as the star. Early in September, on his way to take the waters at Buxton, Leicester had written the Queen a line of gay greeting and tender solicitude. A few days later they told her he was dead. She wrote across his note 'His Last Letter', and put it by. If Elizabeth Tudor ever loved any man it was Robert Dudley. If she missed any face that New Year's Day at Richmond it was his.

Elizabeth was loyal to old friends. For a queen so notoriously fickle and changeable she changed her servants very seldom. But she was stimulated by new faces, and there were new faces to fill the gaps. There was, for instance, her handsome young Master of the Horse, the Earl of Essex. At the moment he and Walter Raleigh were glowering at each other like rival schoolboys, which was silly of the earl and reminded one how young he was. But with proper schooling he might be broken to the intricate ballet of the Court and learn to tread its difficult measures as gracefully and surely as his stepfather, Leicester, had done, and perhaps in time to come to fill something like Leicester's role. A prima ballerina needs a hand now and then to lean on, if ever so lightly.

As for Elizabeth, whoever might drop out from age or ill-health or weariness, she had no intention of doing so. She had already danced the first steps of this new dance, and found that she could lead its figures as well as she could the old. Last September 7th had been her fifty-fifth birthday, but she felt as well and as capable, as young almost, as ever she had. At least she could keep pace with the young, and would go on doing so while there was breath in her body. Almost a dozen years later, in her sixty-seventh year, she told courtiers who grumbled at a long progress she was planning: 'Let the old stay behind, and the young and able come with me.'

The plans for next summer's campaign, already well in train by Christmas, were plans for the young and able, for the adventurous youths and professional fighting-men who favoured a bold offensive. Drake would command the fleet this time. Perhaps Howard had been too cautious. Black Jack Norris would command the army, and together he and Drake would undertake nothing less than a full-scale invasion of Portugal, with Lisbon the major target. Don Antonio of Crato, the pretender to the Portuguese throne, would go with them, and there would be a chance to test his repeated assurances that once he set foot in Portugal his loyal subjects would rise as one man and chase the Spanish intruders back across the frontier. With luck the expedition might touch off a war on King Philip's doorstep that would keep him busy enough at home to make him harmless abroad.

The Queen hoped so. The preparations for the Armada, the long wait for the enemy to come, and especially the prolonged mobilization by land and sea after the Spaniards had fled from Gravelines, had all cost a deal of money. There was nothing for it but a new Parliament, and the opening session had been postponed until February only because it seemed more tactful not to ask for new subsidies until the last of the old had been collected. If Elizabeth knew her commons they would not be so eager to pay for this war as they had been to bring it on; and unless Drake and Norris and Don Antonio succeeded where Medina Sidonia and Parma and William Allen had failed, whatever was voted this session would be only a first instalment. Philip was a stubborn man. The war might go on for years.

Elizabeth had never been much given to vain regrets; if the war did go on and on, as prudence suggested it might, she would have to learn to make the best of it. In the past she had at times waged peace so that it was almost indistinguishable from war. For the future it would have to be her care to wage war so that it would be as much as possible like peace. As long as there was no fighting on English soil, and taxes did not eat up men's substance, life on the embattled island would seem peaceful enough compared to life in France or in the Netherlands. That it should stay so was always more important to Elizabeth I than winning victories.

Not that she did not enjoy the victories. Since Tilbury she had felt closer to her people than ever before. They walked for miles now with their children on their shoulders, and stood patiently for hours, to catch a glimpse of her setting out for a hunt, or moving — perhaps by torch-light — from one palace to another. When she went abroad there was always a press around her horse or her carriage through which her escort could hardly thrust a way, and the air was always full of shouted blessings and endearments. Going in triumphant state to St Paul's on the Sunday after the thirtieth anniversary of her coming to the throne, through streets gay with banners and garlands and packed with kneeling, cheering people, had been almost like a second coronation — in a way more satis-fying, as a promise fulfilled is more satisfying than a promise spoken. If she had ever had any doubts about her ability to rule England at war, she had none now.

EPILOGUE

NEW YORK, NEW YEAR'S DAY, 1959

HISTORIANS agree that the defeat of the Spanish Armada was a decisive battle, in fact one of the decisive battles of the world, but there is much less agreement as to what it decided. It certainly did not decide the issue of the war between England and Spain. Though no fleet opposed Drake, and only local defence forces opposed Norris, the English enterprise of Portugal in 1589 ended in failure, almost as disastrous as the Spanish failure of 1588. Thereafter the war dragged itself out for nearly fourteen years more — as long, in fact, as Queen Elizabeth lived. It ended in no better than a draw. Some historians say that the defeat of the Armada 'marked the decline of the Spanish colonial empire and the rise of the British'. It is hard to see why they think so. By 1603 Spain had not lost to the English a single overseas outpost, while the English colonization of Virginia had been postponed for the duration. Nor did the Armada campaign 'transfer the command of the sea from Spain to England'. English sea power in the Atlantic had usually been superior to the combined strengths of Castile and Portugal, and so it continued to be, but after 1588 the margin of superiority diminished. The defeat of the Armada was not so much the end as the beginning of the Spanish navy. The English could raid the Spanish coast but they were not able to blockade it. Drake and Hawkins had dreamed of bringing Philip to his knees by cutting off his revenues from the New World, but, in fact, more American treasure reached Spain in the years between 1588 and 1603 than in any other fifteen years in Spanish history. In the War of Elizabeth nobody commanded the seas.

It is sometimes said that the defeat of the Armada produced the mood of buoyant optimism which characterized the Elizabethan temper, and led to the great explosion of literary genius which marked the last fifteen years of Elizabeth's reign. 'Come the three corners of the world in arms and we shall shock them' from *King John* is usually quoted by way of illustration. Some doubt is cast on the validity of the first part of this assertion, even for those who have no doubts about characterizing with a phrase the whole mood and temper of a people, by the difficulty of demonstrating that 'buoyant optimism' was any more prevalent in England in the decade and a half after 1588 than in the decade and a half before. The second part, the assertion of a causal connection between the defeat of the Armada and the flowering of Elizabethan drama, is hard to refute; even harder, except by the method of post hoc, propter hoc, to prove. There is no link in England between the Armada campaign and any literary work as clear as one we can find in Spain. According to the accepted story a maimed veteran of Lepanto, a minor poet, in the confusing weeks before the Armada sailed from Lisbon, got his accounts of collections he was making for the fleet so embroiled that nobody could tell whether he was trying to cheat the Crown or not, and in due time he was sent to prison until somebody could straighten out his books. In his enforced leisure he found time to begin to write *Don Quixote*. Perhaps this proves that defeat may be just as stimulating to genius as victory, a proposition for which history can furnish considerable support. Or perhaps Cervantes and Shakespeare would have written much as they did whether the Armada had sailed or not.

The older historians, Froude and Motley, Ranke and Michelet, who said that the defeat of the Armada decided that the Counter-Reformation was not to triumph throughout Europe, have a much better case. Perhaps there was nothing that Medina Sidonia could have done to win the naval battle, but Howard could certainly have lost it. Had he done so, perhaps some way could have been found to get Parma's army across to England. Had Parma landed and taken Rochester, as he meant to do, and then marched on London supported by a victorious Spanish fleet in the Thames, the course of history in England and on the Continent might have been altered in any one of a number of ways. Even had Parma failed to conquer England, or to dethrone the Queen, just a limited Spanish success might have dealt the cause of Protestantism a serious, possibly even a fatal blow.

It seems more likely, however, that even had the Spaniards snatched a victory at sea the final picture of Europe, when peace came, would not have been much different. Philip and his militant advisers dreamed of a great crusade which should wipe out heresy and impose on Christendom the King of Spain's Catholic peace. Drake and his fellow Puritans dreamed of spreading the religious revolution throughout Europe until Anti-Christ was hurled from his throne. Both dreams were wide of reality. Neither the Catholic nor the Protestant coalition had the necessary unity, or could dispose of the necessary force. Systems of ideas, though usually self-limiting in their spread, are harder to kill than men, or even than nations. Of all the kinds of war a crusade, a total war against a system of ideas, is the hardest to win. By its very nature the war between Spain and England was likely to be indecisive, and men being what they are even its object lesson proved to be in vain. Most of Europe had to fight another war, thirty years long, before deciding that crusades were a poor way of settling differences of opinion, and that two or more systems of ideas could live side by side without mortal danger to either.

Nevertheless, the defeat of the Spanish Armada was in one sense a decisive event. Less for the combatants than for the onlookers. For the experts on both sides the outcome at Gravelines was surprising chiefly because the Armada had done as well as it had. But the landsmen, English and Spanish, were less certain which way the scales of victory would incline, and other peoples were less certain still. France and Germany and Italy had seen the Spanish colossus advance from victory to victory. Providence, God's increasingly obvious design, the wave of the future, seemed to be on the side of Spain; and, as Catholics, French and German and Italian Catholics rejoiced that Spain was clearly the elected champion of God's Church, little as they relished the prospect of Spanish dominance, while Protestants everywhere were correspondingly alarmed and dismayed. When the Spanish Armada challenged the ancient lords of the English Channel on their own grounds the impending conflict took on the aspect of a judicial duel in which, as was expected in such duels, God would defend the right. The solemnity of the occasion was heightened by the portentous prophecies about the year of the conflict, prophecies so ancient and respectable that even the most enlightened and sceptical could not ignore them. So, when the two fleets approached their appointed battle-ground, all Europe watched.

For the spectators of both parties the outcome, reinforced as everyone believed by an extraordinary tempest, was indeed decisive. The Protestants of France and the Netherlands, Germany and Scandinavia saw with relief that God was in truth, as they had always supposed, on their side. The Catholics of France and Italy and Germany saw with almost equal relief that Spain was not, after all, God's chosen champion. From that time forward, though Spain's preponderance was to last for more than another generation, the peak of her prestige had passed. France, in particular, after Henry III's coup d'état at Blois began to come back to her role of balance against the house of Austria, and so to being the chief guarantor of the liberties of Europe as long as those liberties were threatened by the Habsburgs. Without the English victory at Gravelines and its ratification by the news from Ireland Henry III might never have summoned the courage to throw off the Leaguer yoke, and the subsequent history of Europe might have been incalculably different.

So, in spite of the long indecisive war which followed, the defeat of the Spanish Armada really was decisive. It decided that religious unity was not to be reimposed by force on the heirs of medieval Christendom, and if in doing so it only validated what was already by far the most probable outcome — why, perhaps that is all that any of the battles we call decisive have ever done. Whether or not Parma could have reconquered Holland and Zeeland for Spain as he had reconquered the southern provinces, we shall never know. After 1588 he never had a chance; too much of his slender force had to go to sustaining the League against Henry of Navarre. The pattern of territorial, ultimately 'national' States which was to characterize modern Europe was beginning to emerge, and after 1588 each major State was not only to be free, but increasingly to feel free, to develop its own individual potentialities without conforming to any externally imposed system of beliefs. Since the Powers of Europe were not strong enough, and would not be strong enough for centuries, to inflict irreparable harm on one another, the problem of how to combine freedom to differ with safety from utter destruction could be left to the century in which it would arise.

Meanwhile, as the episode of the Armada receded into the past it influenced history in another way. Its story, magnified and distorted by a golden mist, became a heroic apologue of the defence of freedom against tyranny, an eternal myth of the victory of the weak over the strong, of the triumph of David over Goliath. It raised men's hearts in dark hours, and led them to say to one another: 'What we have done once, we can do again.' In so far as it did this the legend of the defeat of the Spanish Armada became as important as the actual event — perhaps more important.

A GENERAL NOTE ON SOURCES

ARCHIVES AND MANUSCRIPT COLLECTIONS

England

Public Record Office (*P.R.O.*) contains the originals of documents published by Bruce, Laughton & Corbett (see below) and unpublished documents about home defence.

British Museum (*B.M.*). In addition to the Yelverton MSS. and other collections acquired since 1945 the older collections yielded useful items.

Besides two 'newsletter' accounts of the death of Mary Stuart and other contemporary matter the Bodleian Library, Oxford (*Bod.*), possesses an unpublished 'Commentary on Certain Aspects of the Spanish Armada' by James P. R. Lyell, with numerous transcripts of Spanish documents, some from usually inaccessible private collections. Such transcripts as I have been able to check have proved reliable. There is another typescript copy of Lyell's essay at Harvard.

Spain

The Archivo General de Simancas (*Sim.*) contains not only many papers bearing directly on the naval and military aspects of the Armada campaign, these mostly published, but a large number of related diplomatic and administrative papers, especially the correspondence of Alexander Farnese and Bernardino de Mendoza, not published in full or much used for the years in question. In the major collections in Madrid I found no unpublished papers important for the Armada campaign.

France

All three major public collections in Paris proved helpful. In the Archives Nationales (*Arch. Nat.*) besides microfilm of Mendoza's correspondence there are miscellaneous papers relating to the League and to the War of the Three Henrys. The archives of the Ministère des Affaires Etrangères (*Aff. Et.*) contains reports from London, Rome and the Hague. In the manuscripts of the Bibliothèque Nationale (*Bib. Nat. MSS.*), besides Longlée's dispatches from Spain, adequately published, I found letters from Bellièvre and Châteauneuf in England and from Pisany in Rome, supplementing those in *Aff. Et.*, and a considerable bundle relating to Guise and the Day of the Barricades. I was unable to obtain access to other papers of Châteauneuf's, now in private hands.

The Netherlands

The Rijksarchief at the Hague is rich in papers from the Amsterdam and Zeeland admiralties, and there is additional material in provincial archives, much more than I have been able to utilize.

Italy

All the major State archives contain relevant materials. Papers at Genoa, Milan, Naples and Palermo bear mostly on Mediterranean defence, recruiting and supply, subjects necessarily no more than touched on in this book. The Archivio di Stato di Venezia (*Ven.*) is rich in political observations. Because he had involuntarily lent a galleon to the Armada the Grand Duke of Tuscany was keenly interested in its progress and his successor not less so. The Archivio di Stato di Firenze (*Flor.*) contains, therefore, a wide variety of reports and relations on Spanish naval affairs, mostly quite unused.

The Vatican Archives (*Vat.*) have been, however, the chief source of new material. Sixtus V probably received more copious and detailed reports from every part of Europe than any other sovereign among his contemporaries. He kept a specially sharp eye on his yoke-fellow in the Enterprise of England, Philip of Spain. Since all the useful documents on this subject turned out to be in *Lettere delle Nunziature* I have cited them simply by section and volume number, e.g. *Spagna*, 34.

PUBLISHED SOURCES

The only complete publications of diplomatic correspondence relevant for this study are *Dépêches diplomatiques de M. de Longlée, Résident de France en Espagne (1582-90)*, ed. A. Mousset (1912); *Négociations diplomatiques de la France avec la Toscane*, ed. G. Canestrini and A. Desjardins, VOL. IV (1872); and *Relations politiques de la France et de l'Espagne avec l'Ecosse*, ed. A. Teulet, VOLS. IV and V (1862), this last somewhat arbitrarily selective. The *Calendar of State Papers, Foreign*, XXI (4 parts) and XXII gives complete and usable summaries, only slightly abbreviated for the most part, of all documents within its purview in the Public Record Office. The *Calendar of State Papers, Venetian* skilfully excerpts relevant documents in the Venice archives, and the *Calendar of State Papers, Spanish, Elizabeth*, VOL. IV (1899) does the same, somewhat less reliably, for the archives at Simancas.

The naval documents for the Armada campaign have been published, for England, with discriminating competence by J. K. Laughton, *State papers relating to the defeat of the Spanish Armada*, 2 vols. (Navy Records Society, 1895), and J. S. Corbett, *The Spanish War, 1585-1587* (Navy Records Society, 1898), for Spain by C. Fernández Duro, *La Armada Invencible*, 2 vols. (Madrid, 1885) (F.D.) and E. Herrera Oria, *La Armada Invencible* (Valladolid, 1929) (H.O.). In VOL. IV of *The Naval Miscellany* (Navy Records Society, 1952) G. P. B. Naish has edited a small collection of Spanish documents from the National Maritime Museum, Greenwich and a translation of Ubaldini's second narrative from the MS. in the British Museum, supplementing both the Spanish and the English publications. The Duke of Maura has published with an introduction a hitherto unused group of documents from the family archives of the dukes of Medina Sidonia which throw some fresh light on Medina Sidonia's relations with Philip II, Gabriel Maura Gamazo, duque de Maura, *El designio de Felipe II* (Madrid, 1957).

For home defence and domestic repercussions of the Armada campaign the *Calendar of State Papers, Domestic*, II (1581-90) offers a guide to relevant materials in the Public Record Office and Dasent's *Acts of the Privy Council* and H. MSS. C. *Salisbury MSS*, VOL. III (1899) are also useful.

CONTEMPORARY NARRATIVE

I have seen between seventy and eighty contemporary pamphlets, broadsides, etc., directly connected with the Armada, printed in the years 1587-90. That is more than any bibliography I know of lists, but I have no doubt that search would disclose still others. A few are mere reprints or translations, but most contain some independent variations. Some combine items from two or more earlier pamphlets. Some are pure fantasy. Some are pure propaganda. But though the standards of this kind of journalism were no higher in the sixteenth century than they have generally been since, these pamphlets do not seem to me quite as negligible as Sir Julian Corbett found them. Sometimes they contain details also to be found in the reports and relations of the fighting-men, and sometimes they amplify and explain those reports or reflect them from a different angle. At the least these pamphlets tell us what people thought was happening or might happen, or what someone wanted them to think was happening. I have used them gladly, and cited them individually whenever it seemed important to do so.

In the same spirit I have used other broadsides, newsletters and political pamphlets whenever I could find them, and the contemporary chroniclers and proto-historians, especially William Camden, *Annales ... regnante Elizabetha*, ed. Hearne, 3 vols. (1717); L. Cabrera de Córdoba, *Felipe II, Rey de España* (1877); A. de Herrera, *Historia general* (1602); B. Porreño, *Dichos y hechos dei señor rey Don Felipe segundo* (Cuenca, 1628); E. Van Meteren, *Histoire des Pays Bas* (La Haye, 1618); C. Coloma, *Las guerras de los estados Baxos* (1625); F. Strada, *De bello Belgico* (1647); J-A de Thou, *Histoire Universelle* (Basle, 1742).

MODERN AUTHORITIES

The account of the Armada campaign in VOL. II of Sir Julian Corbett's *Drake and the Tudor Navy* (1899) remains a classic of naval history even though much of it must be accepted only with grave reservations. Corbett relied excessively on Ubaldini's second narrative (B.M. Reg. 14, A, xi. In Italian. A translation has been recently edited by G. P. B. Naish in *The Naval Miscellany*, IV) and tended to solve every difficulty of interpretation by assuming that Drake on every occasion must have acted and advised as if he were a combination of Horatio Nelson and A. T. Mahan. J. A. Williamson's chapter on the Armada in *The Age of Drake* (1938) supplies a balanced corrective of Corbett, and since then Michael Lewis's 'Armada Guns' in *The Mariner's Mirror*, XXVIII (1942), XXIX (1943) has cast fresh light on the tactics of both fleets. The most recent treatments of the first phase of the Anglo-Spanish naval war I have seen are D. W. Waters, 'The Elizabethan Navy and the Armada Campaign' in *The Mariner's Mirror*, XXXV (1949) which makes good use of the effect of the tides, A. L. Rowse, *The Expansion of Elizabethan England* (1955), and Thomas Woodrooffe, *The Enterprise of England* (1958).

In general, the absence in the following notes of reference to such standard works as J. B. Black's *The Reign of Queen Elizabeth* or to A. L. Rowse's Elizabethan studies is not meant to indicate that I have failed to use them, but that I have assumed that anyone who turned to the notes would be familiar with them and that it was unnecessary to document facts which could be verified within history's public domain.

Some debts, however, are too pervasive and long-standing not to be acknowledged. All students of Tudor naval history owe much to the work of J. A. Williamson. In particular his studies of the career of John Hawkins, culminating in *Hawkins of Plymouth* (1949), have been most useful to this book.

Similarly I have turned repeatedly to Conyers Read's *Mr Secretary Walsingham*, 3 vols. (1925) and always with enlightenment and profit.

Leon van der Essen's *Alexandre Farnese*, 5 vols. (1937) supersedes all previous scholarship about Parma's campaigns in the Netherlands, and though I have not followed it blindly I have never departed from it without trepidation.

I first began the study of Philip II's letters and state papers under the guidance of R. B. Merriman while he was still at work on his *Philip the Prudent* (1934). My view of that monarch's complex character, though not the same as my master's, was certainly influenced not only by Roger Merriman's published writings but by his correspondence and conversation during more than twenty years.

In much the same way, and in common with most students of Tudor history during the past quarter-century, my ideas of Elizabeth I, her character, techniques and policies, have been profoundly influenced by Sir John Neale, by his biography of the Queen, by his three magnificent volumes on her Parliaments, by his special studies of her finances and diplomacy, and by his personal advice. Let this general acknowledgment stand in lieu of the specific ones which ought to appear among the notes to every chapter where the Queen's name is mentioned.

A NOTE ABOUT SHIPS AND THEIR GUNS

Although the Armada campaign involved, on one side or the other, practically every kind of ship known to Europe, a confusing variety of types with an even more confusing variety of names, it is possible to describe them by reasonably simple categories.

The galleon was the standard fighting ship of Atlantic waters. It was likely to have two decks from stem to stern with its main batteries in broadside and castles fore and aft bristling with lighter quick-firing pieces. Galleons were longer, narrower and lower in the water than merchantmen of the same tonnage, though still stubby and high built by later standards.

Armed merchant ships supplemented galleons in the battle line; those of around three hundred (English) tons and over and so capable of mounting culverins and demi-cannon were commonly styled greatships. The most formidable English greatships, those of the Levant Company, were built for speed and ease of manœuvre and carried heavy batteries to repel corsairs so that they were sometimes mistaken by their peninsular foes for galleons. The biggest Mediterranean merchant ships, carracks, had lofty, overhanging bow and stern castles and deep holds; some were three deckers like those used by the Portuguese for the East India trade. Baltic hulks, *urcas*, were not often as big as carracks or as high built. Their butter-tub shape made them seaworthy and capacious but slower and clumsier even than carracks.

Small craft meant for reconnaisance, dispatch service and inshore work, the English generally called 'pinnaces' no matter what their rig. I have used that term for such craft in both fleets. The Spanish distinguished 'zabras', 'fregatas' and 'patajes' or 'patches' in descending order of size. All, like English pinnaces, were low in the water, faster and handier than bigger ships, and capable of using oars at need. Besides pinnaces separately commissioned, both fleets called their larger ships' boats pinnaces. These were either towed astern or carried on deck and so do not appear in rosters since they had no separately assigned crews.

Hoys and caravels, crumsters and galliots were other types of small coasters, sometimes used in war. They were usually fore and aft rigged; crumsters and galliots were frequently rowed.

Galleys and galleasses were warships purely; they usually cruised under sail, but used oars in battle. The galley was long, narrow, low in the water, and lightly gunned. The galleass was an attempt to combine the speed of the galley with the fire power and sea-keeping qualities of the galleon. The attempt was not altogether successful, but they were formidable ships. The galleasses of Naples with the Armada mounted fifty guns apiece, some quite large, and were manned by three hundred soldiers and sailors and another three hundred rowers.

Sixteenth-century guns are even more various than the ships. Both the heavy, muzzle-loading ship-killers of the main batteries and the small, breech-loading man-killers were divided into three general types: pot guns, very short and stubby, like the perier, the ancestors of the mortar which was one name for some of them; the cannon family, chunky, medium-length pieces, chief of which was the demi-cannon, a squat monster with a nine foot barrel and a six-inch bore throwing a thirty-two pound round shot point blank, perhaps five hundred yards, the ancestor of the eighteenth-century carronade; and the culverin family, the ancestors of eighteenth-century long guns.

Theorists often said that a culverin could throw an eighteen-pound ball and a demi-culverin one half that weight point blank for seven hundred yards, and at random (extreme range) for about two miles. So, ships 'a long culverin shot' apart were within a little less than two miles of one another, and those distant 'a half culverin shot' were separated by roughly three hundred and fifty yards. In fact, this is modified by the great differences in bore, calibre, weight and performance of guns called culverins and demi-culverins, and further modified by the fantastic variety of sixteenth-century weights and measures and by the cheerful disregard of accuracy on the part of most writers. So a ballistics expert might say that a culverin of such and such dimensions would throw a nine-pound ball twenty-five hundred paces without having an exact idea of what he meant by a pace or a pound, and without knowing whether the foreigner whose statement he was copying (theorists all copied from one another) was using values like his or quite different ones. Professor Michael Lewis sums it up by saying that our information about the guns of the Armada campaign is mainly relative.

NOTES TO CHAPTERS

Chapter I

There are a large number of 'relations' of the execution of Mary Queen of Scots which have some claim to credibility; but except for the official report signed by Shrewsbury and his associates (Bod. Ashmole 830 f. 18) and Bourgoing's *Journal* printed in R. Chantelauze, *Marie Stuart* (Paris, 1876), their provenance and authenticity and their relationship to one another and to the two earliest printed accounts, *Mariae Stuartae ... supplicium et mors* (Cologne, 1587) and *La Mort de la Royne d'Ecosse* [n.p.n.d. Paris? 1587?] (See Jebb, *De Vita ... Mariae*, VOL. II, London, 1925), pose many problems. Besides the official report and Bourgoing one seems to discern at least four eye-witnesses who concur in most details but differ in some. Some extant accounts depend on only one source, others are mixed. E.g. Bod. Ashmole 830 f. 13; Tanner 78; B. M. Lansdowne 51 f. 46; Yelverton 31 f. 545; *Aff. Et. Corresp. pol. Angleterre*, XXII f. 471 (Châteauneuf); xx f. 454 (Bellièvre); (Both printed in Teulet, *Relations*, IV); *Bib. Nat. MSS. Fds. Fr.* 15890 f. 27; *Vat. Francia* 21. Cf. Ellis *Orig. Letters* 2nd ser. III, 113, and M. M. Maxwell-Scott, *The Tragedy of Fotheringhay*, Appendices. One would say that two of the witnesses were Protestant in sympathy, two Catholic, but the small visual details in which they differ do not seem to be related to their sympathies. For instance, the colour of Mary's under-garments is variously described as 'crimson' or 'cramoisie', 'poupre' and 'a black bodice and brown petticoat', sometimes with, sometimes without 'scarlet ribbons'. Doubtless the light in the great hall was bad, but the last witness must have been colour-blind.

I have opted for crimson, not so much because it is in more early MSS. than any other but because if Mary had crimson under-garments (and we know she had) I think she would have worn them.

Chapter II

Châteauneuf and Bellièvre, as above. Mendoza to Philip February 28th, 1587 (Sim.); *Fugger News Letters* and see A General Note on Sources, p.

Chapter III

As above. Also *Calendar of State Papers ... Scotland*, IX, *1586–1588* (1915); *The Warrender Papers*, I (1931); R. S. Rait and A. I. Cameron, *King James's Secret* (1927); *Bagot Papers* (HMSSC. IV); N. H. Nicolas, *Life of William Davison* (1823), especially the appendices.

Chapter IV

Mendoza's correspondence, 1584–87, at Simancas; De Lamar Jensen's unpublished dissertation, *Bernardino de Mendoza and the League* (Columbia University, 1957); *Journal d'un curé liguer*, ed. Barthelemy (1866); Dolfin to the Senate, March 13th, 1587 (Ven.); Stafford's correspondence in *Cal. State Papers, Foreign, Eliz.*; P. de l'Estoile, *Journal du regne de Henri III*, ed. L. R. Lefèvre (1945); G. Ascoli, *La Grande-Bretagne devant l'opinion française* (1927).

Chapter V

Mendoza to Parma, February 28th, 1587 (Sim.); L. Van der Essen, *Alexandre Farnese*; Parma's correspondence, 1584–87 (Sim.), especially Parma to Philip II, February 14th, 1587 and March 22nd, 1587; *C.S.P.F.* (Holland & Flanders, 1586–87).

Chapter VI

Mendoza to Olivarez, February 28th, 1587; Olivarez to Philip II, March 25th and 30th, 1587, and William Allen to Philip II, March 25th, all at Simancas and calendared in *Cal. Span.*, IV. The whole file of Olivarez's correspondence (*Sim. Estado, Roma*, 950), very inadequately calendared, is of great value for the English exiles and for many political aspects of the Enterprise.

For the English Catholic exiles, A. O. Meyer, *England and the Catholic Church under Elizabeth* (London, 1916) is still indispensable. So, though less completely satisfactory, is Robert Lechat, *Les refugiés anglais dans le pays bas* (Louvain, 1914). Most, but not all, of William Allen's letters are published in *Letters and Memorials of William Allen* (1882) with a biographical introduction by T. F. Knox. For Parsons, 'The Memoirs of Father Robert Parsons' by J. H. Pollen in *Cath. Rec. Soc. Misc.*, II (1905) and IV (1907). There is a large and growing bibliography of special studies of English Catholics under Elizabeth. Besides browsing in it I have been fortunate enough to be able to use two so far unpublished dissertations, 'Spain and the English Catholic Exiles' by the Rev. Albert J. Loomie, S. J. (Univ. of London) and 'Robert Parsons, English Jesuit' by John Edward Parish (Columbia Univ.).

The Folger Shakespeare Library in Washington, D.C. has a bound set of letters, formerly in the collection of Sir Thomas Phillipps, apparently once in the files of the Spanish embassy at Rome, and all relating to the affairs of English Catholics. Many of these documents are not now to be found either at Rome or Simancas, and Phillipps's privately printed *De conquestu angliae per Hispanos* (Middlehill, 1869) published only the more legible of them. Allen's daydream of the rising of the English Catholics simply paraphrases his letter (of September 1585?) to Pope Sixtus V in Folger MSS. G.b.5. See my article in *Aspects de la propagande religieuse* (Travaux d'Humanisme et Renaissance, XXVIII. Geneva, 1957), pp. 325–39.

I am grateful to Sister Joseph Damien, of Saint Joseph's College, Brooklyn, N.Y. for details about the English College at Rome and adjacent buildings.

Chapter VII

Mendoza to Philip II, February 28th, 1587 (Sim.). Also at Simancas under the dates March 31st, April 1st and April 2nd in the divisions *Estado* (*Francia, Flandes, Roma, Estados Pequeños de Italia, Guerra Antigua, Mar y Tierra*, etc.) the sudden spate of orders, some published in Hume, Fernández Duro and Herrera Oria. R. Altamira, *Felipe II, Hombre de Estado* (Mexico City, 1950) is balanced and has a useful bibliography. For the Escurial, José de Sigüenza, *Fundación ... de Escorial* (Madrid, 1927); Lorenzo Niño Azcona, *Felipe II y la villa de Escorial* (Madrid, 1934); Louis Bertrand, *Philippe II à l'Escorial* (Paris, 1929).

Chapter VIII

For this and the next three chapters the English documents are mostly in *The Spanish War*, ed. J. S. Corbett (Navy Rec. Soc., 1897) and the classic narrative, here and there in need of correction, in Corbett's *Drake and the Tudor Navy*. There are many biographies of Drake. Among recent ones, I liked A. E. W. Mason's. In writing about Drake the hard thing is to separate the man from the legend.

Chapter IX

For the English view of the descent on Cadiz, as above, plus *News out of the coast of Spain* (London, 1587); 'A briefe relation of ... Drake ... in the Road of Cadiz' in R. Hakluyt, *Voyages*, IV and Robert Leng's narrative in *Camden Misc.*, V (1863).

For the Spanish view the documents printed by Fernández Duro and the Duke of Maura are supplemented by Novara's report to Sixtus V (Vat. *Spagna* 34) and a cluster of documents forwarded to the Grand Duke of Tuscany by his ambassador, Alamanni (Flor. *Arch. Med.* 4919 ff. 313–33). Besides a relation and a list of Spanish losses resembling Fernández Duro's there is 'A copy of a letter written by the chamberlain of the Bishop of Cadiz, 1 May, 1587' (Spanish) 3 pp. and an anonymous *Relatione sopra le cose de Drac* (Italian) 5 pp., quite independent of any other narrative, and certainly by an eye-witness, perhaps the Florentine consul.

The most illuminating document, however, is William Borough's chart of the operations at Cadiz, in the Public Record Office (S.P. 12 Eliz. 202 f. 20), but it should be studied in its original size, $17\frac{1}{2} \times 13\frac{1}{2}$ inches. In a plate like that in Corbett's *Drake*, II, it is quite useless. It is conclusive, among other things, about the number of the galleys, agreeing exactly with the narrative from Cadiz.

Theoretically, galleys could mount as bow-chasers full culverins (18 to 24 lb.) and by the eighteenth century Mediterranean war-galleys usually did; but I have seen no record of anything bigger than a demi-culverin (9 lb.) on any of Philip II's galleys, and sakers (6 lb.) were much more usual. I am assuming that this is what Acuña's galleys mounted. It seems a reasonably safe assumption.

Chapter X

As above. Again additional newsletters in the Florentine archives.

Chapter XI

As above, mostly from Corbett's *The Spanish War*.

Chapter XII

Van der Essen, *Farnese* and references there cited, especially F. Strada and *C.S.P.F.*, XXXI. Also Capt. Alonso Vasquez 'Los sucesos de Flandes' in C.D.I.E., VOL. 75. In Parma's correspondence at Simancas there is an anonymous and undated report on 'Juan Visaguerde flamenco' filed at the end of June 1591, and by internal evidence of about that date. Parma's letters for July 1587 contain military details, so does the report by Colonel Groenevelt 'De ce qui s'est passé durant le siège de l'Ecluse', in Yelverton MSS. XIV f. 502 ff. Roger Williams's letters are in the P.R.O., very full in *C.S.P.F.*, XXXI.

Chapter XIII

Political background, see notes to Chapter IV and add Joseph de Croze, *Les Guises, les Valois et Philippe II*, 2 vols. (1866); Comte Henri de L'Epinois, *La Ligue et les Papes* (1886); V. de Chalambert, *Histoire de la Ligue* (1898); M. Wilkinson, *A history of the League* (Glasgow, 1929); Van der Essen, *A. Farnese*, III, 236 ff. Jensen, *Mendoza* (ut. supra) throws new light on the Treaty of Joinville.

For the battle: François Racine, Sgnr. de Villegomblain, *Memoires* (1668) in VOL. II, 'Voyage de M. le duc de Joyeuse ... 1587'; Agrippa d'Aubigné, *Histoire Universelle*, bk. xi; Sully, *Memoires*, bk. ii. All three eye-witnesses—Villegomblain with Lavardin's horse, d'Aubigné near Navarre, Sully with the guns—and, as usual, because of the lapse of time not very reliable. De Thou, bk. lxxxvii; Père Matthieu, bk. viii; and du Plessis Mornay, bk. i, have more or less contemporary accounts of some value. Good modern narrative in Sir Charles Oman, *Art of War in the Sixteenth Century* (1937) and Pierre de Vaissière, *Henri IV* (1928).

Chapter XIV

As above. In addition, for the campaign of the *reiters*, diplomatic sources are of more use, especially Stafford in *C.S.P.F.*, Cavriana in Canestrini, *Négociations*, IV, Mocenigo

(Ven.), Morosini (Vat. *Francia*, 20) and, of course, Mendoza. Davila, *Guerre Civile de Francia*, bk. viii, gives a clear quasi-contemporary account of the campaign. Louis Maimbourg, *Histoire de la Ligue* (Paris, 1686) draws on documents no longer available, and is both suggestive and usually reliable.

Chapter XV

Leslie Hotson, *Shakespeare's sonnets dated* (N.Y., 1949) has a good summary of the impact of Regiomontanus's prophecy in England. The best extended contemporary discussion is Harvey's *Discoursive Problem*.

For Spain, besides Fernández Duro, I, passim, Novara, December 11th, 1587, and January 8th, 1588 (Vat. *Spagna*, 33) and Canciano to the Duke of Mantua, January 17th, 1588 (Mant. *Esterni*, 601).

Rome: 'Merlin' prophecy in Vat. *Francia*, 20 f. 379.

Prague: San Clemente to Philip II, October 1587–February 1588, passim. Letter from Germany to Cardinal Montalto, Vat. *Germània*, 108, 109, and Archbishop of Bari, 111.

Paris: Diplomatic correspondence of Mendoza, Stafford, Cavriana and Morosini. Also l'Estoile, Pasquier, De Thou and Curé Liguer.

Holland: *Corte Prophetie van tgene int Jaer MDLXXXVIII dragen ende gesekieden.* Amsterdam: Cornelis Claezoon; *Praedictis Astrologica: Die Grote Prognostication ... van dat wonderlijke jaer ... 1588.* Amsterdam: A. Barentz [1587]; *Een wonderlycke nieu profecije op dit wonderlyck Schuckeljaer ... 1588.* [n.p.] all three in Knüttel Collection.

England: W. Gray, *An almanacke and a prognostication for Dorchester.* 1588 (STC, 451); Thos. Tymme, *A preparation against the prognosticated dangers of 1588* (STC, 24420).

Chapter XVI

J. K. Laughton, *The Defeat of the Spanish Armada*, 2 vols. (Navy Record Soc.) 1894, begins December 21st, 1587, and prints the major naval documents for the war at sea. Other sources as above, especially Van der Essen, *Farnese* and *C.S.P.F.*

Chapter XVII

For this period Herrera Oria and duque de Maura, *El Designio* are specially valuable supplements to Fernández Duro. There are still some unpublished letters and other relevant documents at Simancas (see *Guerra Antigua*, 197, 199), mostly about ordnance and supplies.

The story of the *San Francesco* in Flor. Arch. Med., 4918, Alamanni to the Grand Duke and 5042, the Grand Duke to Alamanni and to Philip II. Also in 4918 sidelights on the situation at Lisbon, mostly apparently from Captain Bartoli. Conditions at Lisbon in much greater detail in Vat. *Spagna*, 34, 38, and especially Monsig. Mutio Buongiovanni to Cardinal Montalto, from Lisbon, January to May 1588 in *Spagna*, 36.

C. Ibáñez de Ibero, *Santa Cruz: Primer Marino de España* (Madrid, 1946) supplements A. de Altolaguirre, *Don Alonso de Bazán* (Madrid, 1888).

The documents I have seen amply bear out Professor Michael Lewis's contention that the chief officers in the Armada were trying to increase the armament of their ships in the winter of 1587–88, but they cast some doubt on whether they were as successful as Commander Walter's ingenious extrapolations suggest (*MM*, XXXV, 126 ff.). On the whole, I think *La felicissima Armada* (see note on Chapter XX below) represents with rough accuracy the *number* of guns actually in place about the end of April. After all, it is based on an official report. There is no evidence that any were added afterwards. Perhaps a few could have been borrowed from the shore batteries at Corunna, but this seems unlikely. I think Professor Lewis's statement that the Armada had more short-range heavy guns (cannons and perier types) than the English and many fewer long-range culverin types is almost certainly correct, but I am very dubious about the number of whole culverins he assigns to the Spanish fleet (*MM*, XXIX. Table 12, facing p. 104), and I am inclined to think that the final armament, whatever it was, was the result more of what guns could be obtained than of any settled policy.

Chapter XVIII

Mendoza's correspondence (Sim.). Also Ven. *Amb. Francia*, 1588; Jensen, *Mendoza*; Nicolas Poulain, 'Histoire de la Ligue' in Cimber and Danou, *Archives curieuses de l'histoire de France*, 1er ser. XI (1836), 289–323; Canestrini, *Negociations*; *C.S.P.F.*; and Vat., *Francia*, 1584–88, passim. See also above, Chapters IV, XIII and XIV.

Chapter XIX

As for Chapter XVIII, especially Mendoza's narrative of May 9th–13th (Simancas, *Estado*, K 1568 f. 31) and *Bib. Nat. Mss français*, 15909. In addition, the customary printed narratives of 'the Day of the Barricades', especially l'Etoile, *Journal* and *Archives curieuses* (ut supra) XI, 324–448. As one would expect the contemporary accounts do not always agree, and I have been obliged to resolve the contradictions as best I could. In the main I have tried to follow the narrator best situated to observe, especially when no motive to distort is discernible. E.g., for events within the purview of the Queen Mother's household, Dr Cavriana (in Canestrini, IV) and A. C. Davila (*Guerra Civile de Francia*); for the conditions of the streets, especially around the Place de Grève and the Rue Saint-Anthoine c. 9 a.m., J-A de Thou (*Memoires*, and *Histoire Universelle*, bk. XC) because he visited Guise at about that time; for occurrences in the Place Maubert and in the neighbourhood of Nôtre-Dame, the captains of the Swiss who were there ('Lettres des Capitaines des Suisses à la Reine Mère' in *Bib. Nat. Mss français*, 15909, f° 98 ff.), and for the circumstances of Henry III's flight from Paris, Cheverny and Bellièvre who accompanied him. Guise's letter of May 13th to d'Entragues is printed in *Memoires de la Ligue*, II, 313.

Chapter XX

As for Chapter XVII above, mostly Fernández Duro, Herrera Oria and duque de Maura. Detailed official report of the strength of the Armada in Herrera Oria, pp. 384–435 from the printed copy (Lisbon, May 9th, 1588 by Antonio Alvarez) in the Simancas archives is more accurate than that in Fernández Duro, reprinted by Laughton. The latter omits two small pinnaces from the list of Oquendo's squadron so that it has only 128 names, though it gives the correct total of 130 ships, a stumbling-block to historians since. Other editions: P. de Paz Salas, *La felicissima Armada*, etc. (also Lisbon: Alvarez); *Relacion verdadera del Armada … juntar en Lisbon … salir … 29 de mayo* (Madrid: viuda de Alonzo Gomez 1588), the source of most subsequent editions. *Le vray discours de l'armée*, etc. (Paris: G. Chaudière, 1588); *Warhaftige Zeytung und Beschreibung* (Cölln, 1588); *Relatione vera dell'armata*, etc. (Roma: Vicenzo Accolti, 1588). *Die wonderlijcke groote Armada … van Spaengien* (Gent, 1588); also early, is an independent text but its summary of the Spanish forces appears to be based on the Madrid edition above.

Chapter XXI

Mostly Laughton, with, when consistent, Ubaldini's second narrative.

Chapter XXII

For this chapter and the rest of the naval campaign the useful English documents are in Laughton. 'Howard's Relation', 1, 1–18 is the only continuous, strictly contemporary narrative. It is incomplete, but appears reliable as far as it goes.

So, from the Spanish point of view, does Medina Sidonia's *Diario*, F.D., II, No. 165; it is supplemented by Captain Vanegas, *ibid.*, No. 185, and Fray Bernardo de Gongora in J. P. Lyell, *A Commentary* (MSS. Bod. and Harvard), both from the flagship. F.D. has at least six other reasonably complete 'relations' from other ships, besides letters which describe particular episodes, and H.O. a seventh. M. Oppenheim published another from the Calthorpe MSS. (Navy Record Soc., XXIII), and *Cal. Span.*, IV, has two more, Calderon, pp. 439–50, and one from the galleass *Zuñiga*, 459–62, besides some but not all of Mendoza's reports on particular episodes. Most of the 'relations' and newsletters from Spain to be found in European archives seem to be based on one of the above, oftenest the duke's *Diario*, see CDIE, XIV, 449–61 and XLIII, 417 ff., or on contemporary pamphlets (see below), e.g. Paris, *Aff. Etr. Espagne*, 237, f. 76 ff. In Florence, however, there is a cluster of documents (Flor. *Arch. Med.*, 4919, ff. 477–521) which includes, besides the usual variants, two letters from Medina Sidonia and an independent narrative in Italian, apparently from the Grand Duke's *San Francesco*.

For the movements of Recalde's *Santa Ana*, see F.D., I, 170–1, II, 229, 371; *Cal. Span.*, IV, 425, 431, 457, 498. There are other references in Mendoza's correspondence not calendared, but even from published documents it is abundantly clear that the *Santa Ana* which was the flagship of Recalde's squadron was first at the Bay of La Hogue and then at Le Havre and never in any part of the fighting. Throughout the campaign Recalde was always on the *San Juan de Portugal*, the *almiranta general*. Besides the *Santa Ana*, Captain Vanegas, who kept the muster, says that 'one of the *urcas*' (no name) failed to rendezvous on Friday and presumably never rejoined. This may have been the *David* which never left Spain, or it may have been another cargo-ship. Nobody else mentions the delinquent, but then, officers in the Armada tried to think of the *urcas* as seldom as possible.

Fray Juan Victoria's story about the Council of War, which he says he got from one of Oquendo's captains, was first printed in *Colección de Documentos Ineditos*, LXXXI, p. 179 ff., later, from another MS. by F.D., II, No. 186. Victoria says he got the story from one Julian Fernández de la Piedra, one of Oquendo's captains, not identifiable. How such a person would have known what went on at a Council of War is not clear, and whatever the source of the story it is absurd on the face of it, and its account of the subsequent action off Plymouth differs enough from all other accounts to cast doubt on the presence of the witness aboard the Armada at all.

Several Italian ambassadors got copies of a sketch for a 'crescent' formation for the Armada (Flor. *Arch. Med.* 4919, f. 340); Novara to Montalto, June 4th, 1588 (Vat. *Spagna*, 38); Canciano to the duke (Arch. di Stato, Mantova, Esterni, 601). One of these must have formed the basis of Filippo Pigafetta, *Discorso sopra l'ordinanza dell'armata catolica* (Rome, 1588), see Corbett, II, 220 ff. Pigafetta's rather pedantic description is more elaborate and impractical than the sketches, but it is clear from the Spanish narratives, as well as from English references, that the Armada did normally proceed in a sort of crescent formation not unlike that shown in Adams's charts, but with the horns projecting much farther to the rear.

Chapter XXIII

Don Alonso Martinez de Leiva, Captain-General of the Cavalry of Milan is listed in the printed order of battle simply as a gentleman volunteer. He sailed in the *Rata Santa María Encoronada*, one of the ships of the Levant squadron, commanded by Martin de Bertendona. But his distinguished birth and military record gave him from the first a prominence in the councils of the Armada equal to that of the squadron commanders; the duke seems to have put him in general command of the van on the way to Plymouth, and thereafter the Levant squadron seems to have conformed to his movements, and the narratives often speak as if he commanded it.

About the loss of *Nuestra Señora del Rosario* there are two contradictory accounts. One is that in the duke's *Diario* which is corroborated and amplified in detail by three independent eye-witnesses on the flagship, Vanegas, Miranda and Gongora, and borne out by all the other narratives which mention the incident. The other is that of Don Pedro de Valdés himself (Laughton, II, 133–136), which gained considerable currency in Spain because Don Pedro's letters got there long before the Armada's return (cf. F.D., II, 427–8, 445, 448) and was taken up after their return by some of those who had served in the Armada (H.O., p. 352). I have followed the first, less because of the greater weight of testimony in favour of it than because of the discrepancies in Don Pedro's story.

Don Pedro says that he collided with a Biscayan ship when he was going to the rescue of Recalde. No other account associated Don Pedro with Recalde's rescue. All say that he collided with the *Santa Catalina* of his own squadron several hours after Recalde's rescue. None of the Andalusian squadron were even near Recalde during the battle.

Don Pedro says that the duke paid no attention to his distress. But in the next sentence he indicates that the duke's galleon wsa near him for some time and that he sent to it twice.

Don Pedro clearly implies that the duke not only refused him the help of the *San Martín* but refused to order help for him by any other ships of the fleet. But the officers of the *Margaret and John*, when they came up to him some time later, saw a galleass, a galleon and at least one pinnace standing by him trying to get him in tow, and are impartial witnesses to that part of the duke's story. There are some other odd points in Don Pedro's story, the bit about the mainmast, for instance, and the way the *Rosario* was defended 'all that night' against the attacks of numerous enemies, but what is clearest is its animus against the duke. Unless Don Pedro anticipated, as in fact happened, that any charges he made against the duke would recoil against his cousin and enemy, Diego Flores.

Chapter XXIV

Mainly Laughton and Fernández Duro. See also J. A. Williamson, *Age of Drake*, p. 325.

Chapter XXV

Wednesday's action in F.D., II, 235, 249, 258, 268, 275, 334–86. It is unnecessary to assume that Howard was silent about it because he was jealous of Drake. On the Spanish left, opposite Howard, observers who mention the fight at all speak only of 'a cannonade at long range'. Howard may have thought it no more. He does not seem to have kept as well informed about his subordinates as Medina Sidonia did, a matter of slacker discipline.

Corbett's reconstruction of the battle off the Isle of Wight, *Drake and the Tudor Navy*, II, 232–42 strikes me as convincing.

Chapter XXVI

For Dutch naval activity, English reports in Laughton and *C.S.P.F.* have been compared with relevant documents from the Dutch archives. Especially Rijksarchief, the Hague, Admiraliteitsarchief: Resolutiën Admiraliteit Zeeland, Port. 2447 (1584–90); Admiraliteitscolleges, Inkomende brieven admiraliteit Zeeland, Port. 2667 (1587); Rijksarchief in Zeeland te Middelburg: Ingekomen stukken, Port 1201 (1587) and Port. 1202 (1588); Register van Acten en brieven, Port, 1625 (1586–8). In spite of lacunae due to the ravages of time, the records of the admiralties give a fairly complete picture of Dutch naval strength and movements, 1587–8, and throw some light on Justin of Nassau's intentions. Ortel, from London, advised the Zeeland commissioners of the bad effect the misunderstanding over the Dunkirk blockade had had on English public opinion (Port. 1202, August 22nd, 1588) but it was, by then, too late. These papers also contain full intelligence reports on Parma's forces, and reasonably accurate news of the progress of the Armada. See also J. B. van Overeem, 'Justinus van Nassau en de Armada (1588)', in *Marineblad*, LIII, 821–31 (October, 1938).

For Parma's activities, mainly Van der Essen checked by reports of Medina Sidonia's messengers in Fernández Duro and Herrera Oria, but some additional details in Middelburg Ad., Port. 1202 (see above) corroborated by Cabrera de Córdoba and Coloma, both of whom should be reliable witnesses.

For the fire-ships, in addition to the published sources, 'Una carta sobre l'Armada enviada al Cardinal de Sevilla' (not related to HMC, *Salisbury*, *MSS.*, III, 351), Flor. *Arch. Med.*, 4919 f. 487 and 'Relazione ... de Cales', *ibid.*, ff. 532–3. Both anon. Also Gourdan to Bellièvre, August 10th, 1588, with anonymous newsletter from Calais, *Bib. Nat.* MSS. fr. 15809, f. 111; also Mendoza's correspondence (Sim.) and Morosini's (Vat.).

Chapter XXVII

As above, mainly Laughton and Fernández Duro, supplemented by Dutch admiralty records, as in notes to Chapter XXVI.

Chapter XXVIII

As above, mostly the four accounts from the *San Martín*.

Chapter XXIX

The seamen mostly in Laughton; the landsmen mostly in P.R.O. State Papers, CCXIII and CCXIV, as calendared in *C.S.P.D.*, II. Some of these printed in full by Laughton or by John Bruce, *Report on the arrangements ... for defence* (1798). Both the Morgan Library, N.Y. and the Folger Shakespeare Library have unpublished papers of interest for August 1588. Also for recusants, Folger MS. G. a 1, 'The advice of Lord Grey, etc.'

For Tilbury, 'Richard Leigh', *The copie of a letter*, etc.; Thomas Deloney, 'The Queen ... at Tilsburie' in Ed. Arber, *An English Garland*, VII; James Aske, *Elizabetha Triumphans* (London, 1588) (See Miller Christy, 'Queen Elizabeth's visit to Tilbury' in *E.H.R.*, XXXIV (1919), 43–61); Nichols, *Progresses*, II, 536 ff. contains Aske's poem. Also Ubaldini, and *Copije van een Brief uit Engelandt vande groote Victorie die Godt almachtich de Conuncklijcke Majestat ven Enghelant vorleent heeft* (Delft, 1588, 36 pp.) (Longer than and partly independent of 'The copie of a letter'. No relation to the Middleburgh *Cort verhael* with the examination of Don Diego Pimentel.) This pamphlet and the accounts forwarded by Morosini and Mendoza lead me to believe that at least one, perhaps several, newsletter accounts of the Queen's visit to Tilbury were circulating on the Continent before September 15th (N. S.). As usual, there are discrepancies which have had to be rather arbitrarily resolved. Perhaps Aske was, as Christy believes, an eye-witness, but he was also a poet and I am not prepared to follow him blindly.

For the authenticity of the Queen's Tilbury speech, J. E. Neale, *Essays in Elizabethan History* (London, 1958), pp. 104–6.

Chapter XXX

Diplomatic reports as above, plus Flor. *Arch. Med.*, 4344, letters from Prague.

Copie d'un lettre envoyée de Dieppe ([Rouen?] le Goux, 1588). Another ed. (Paris: G. Chaudière, 1588). *Les regrets de la Royne d'Angleterre sur le defaitte de son armée navale* [verse] (Rouen, 1588). *Relacion de lo que hasta hoy a los cinco de Septiembre de 1588 ... se ha sabido ... de la Felice Armada.* A broadside (n.p. [Madrid]), Copy in Real Acad. de Hist., Madrid (cf. F.D., No. 166, 172); *Relacion de lo sucedido a la Armada ... treze de Agosto* (Seville: Cosme de Lara, n.d.), 4 pp. Another edition with a ballad (see F.D.). Numerous echoes in French, Italian and German, including: *Warhafte Relation Uberschlag und Inhalt*, etc. (Nürnberg, 1588). Reprint with additional news to August 13th resembling F.D. 166. Also, *Spanischer Armada oder Kriegrüstung warhafte Relation* (Cölln: Gottfried von Kempen [Sept.?] 1588). Reprint as above of Etzinger translation of Lisbon ed., plus reports from both sides to August 22nd with reference to an Antwerp newsletter and summary indicating probable Spanish victory. Not based on Mendoza.

Gewisse und warhaftige Zeitung von der Engelendischen und Spanischen Armada (Amsterdam, August 20th, 1588). Drake's exploits in the Channel, at Calais and in the North Sea. Partly actual, partly imaginary. Influenced other pamphlets.

Discours veritable de ce qui s'est passé entre les deux armées ... depuis 29 juillet 1588 jusques à 11 Aoust ([Paris?] n.p. 1588). Cf. Morosini, August 17th, in Vat. Francia, xxxvii.

Obviously from the same press: *La copie d'une lettre ... à Don Bernardin de Mendoza* ([n.p.] 1588). English version: *The copie of a letter ... found in the chamber of Richard Leigh* (London: I. Vautrollier for R. Field, 1588). Italian translation. London: J. Wolfe. Dutch, Amsterdam: Cornelis Claeszoon, October 1588.

Certain advertisements out of Ireland (London: R. Field, 1588), often, both in French and English, printed with '*A copie of a letter*'.

A Pack of Spanish Lyes (London, 1588). Also in Harleian Misc., II.

Chapter XXXI

Archival and printed sources as above.

For the episode in Ireland, besides the documents calendared in *C.S.P.* Ireland, iv, and those printed by Laughton, I found William Spotswood Green, 'The Wrecks of the Spanish Armada on the Coast of Ireland' in *The Geographical Journal*, xxvii (1906), 429–51 a useful guide, and Cyril Fall's *Elizabeth's Irish Wars*, pp. 160 ff. a sensible summary.

The losses of the Armada on its campaign are usually said to have been 65 ships out of 130, or 64 out of 128. They were certainly less. The whole subject is beclouded by faulty arithmetic, beginning with contemporary documents and editions of *La felicissima armada*, and further embroiled by the fact that not only did many of the ships in the Armada have the same name—there are six *San Juans*, besides two *San Juan Bautistas* and eight *Concepcións*, mostly pinnaces—but some of them are known sometimes by one name, sometimes by another. In Recalde's squadron, for instance, there were two *Concepcións*, both great ships, and they are known sometimes as *Concepción Mayor* and *Menor*, and sometimes as *Concepción* de Zubelzu and *Concepción* de Juanes del Cano. F.D., No. 180 reports *Mayor* and *Menor* both home (II, 329). In No. 181 on the next page the *Concepcións* of Zubelzu and of Juanes del Cano are reported lost.

Document No. 181, on which Fernández Duro based his estimate of Spanish losses is itself a major source of confusion. It must have been prepared by someone with faulty information and probably at an earlier date than No. 180 since it lists as 'lost' seven ships reported safe, fails to list one which we know was lost, and ends: 'Lost: 41 ships, 20 pinnaces (*patajes*), 3 galleasses, and 1 galley, total 65', although the list shows only sixty-three names. In his introduction (VOL. 1, 140) Fernández Duro adopts this estimate, merely deducting two ships known to have been lost some time after reaching port (one burned, one sank). This gives him a total of 63 lost, 35 of them 'fate unknown', which Laughton says is 'probably as fair an approximation as can be arrived at'.

Everyone seems to accept this estimate, although a better approximation can be arrived at simply by subtracting the ships listed in No. 180 as having reached port from the known strength of the Armada that left Lisbon. Further documents printed by Fernández Duro, Herrera Oria and Hume (*Cal. Span.*, IV) suggest further deductions.

A more correct list would be—missing, circa October 10th:

Three galleasses, one stranded at Calais, guns saved, one wrecked on the Irish coast, one under repair at Le Havre, later returned safely.

One galley wrecked at Bayonne.

Twenty (F.D. says twenty-six) galleons and greatships as follows: one stranded at Le Havre, guns and stores saved; two captured by the English in the Channel; two by the Dutch on the sands; five sunk in the North Sea after Gravelines, including three Levanters; ten lost around Ireland, including five Levanters, the only uncertainty being which Levanters were lost where, and even here only two names are doubtful, one of this pair lost in the North Sea, the other in Ireland.

Eleven hulks. (F.D. says thirteen, but one of his list, the *David*, was reported unfit for service on July 13th and did not sail, and another, the *Falcon Mayor*, was captured in the Channel by the English in January 1589 on her way back to Hamburg, Laughton, II, 386.)

Eleven hulks, then. Of these, one sank in the North Sea from the effects of gunfire, two were lost around Scotland, Fair Isle and Mull, and two, known by name, on the Irish coast; one on the coast of Devon; one in Brittany. That leaves four whose fate is genuinely unknown, and they may all, or any of them, have been wrecked on the Irish coast or gone down at sea. But on the other hand they may, like the *Falcon*, have got back but not been reported. Two of them were probably in the company of Juan Gomez de Medina, when his *capitana*, *El Gran Grifon*, was wrecked on Fair Isle. Since he was running eastward, and the two other hulks were Germans, they may just have gone on home. No one has ever made a real search for records concerning these four ships, but even if no record survives that would not prove their loss.

Twenty small craft (*zabras* and *patajes*) which sailed with the Armada from Lisbon are not listed as having returned with it between September 22nd and October 10th, so F.D. calls them all 'lost, fate unknown'. This is absurd. Several, we know, got back to Spain carrying dispatches; several were sent to Dunkirk with dispatches for Parma and stayed there; five, including two which towed the fire-ships ashore, were still at Calais in November, *teste* Mendoza. Pinnaces were constantly going back and forth, and once detached from a squadron and their mission accomplished were either paid off or employed on another job. There is no reason why many of them should have been sunk or cast away on the Armada campaign. Except for the two *zabras* of Portugal, which got back, they were too little to do any fighting, and they were faster and handier than the bigger ships and equally seaworthy. If we cut F.D.'s 'twenty lost, fate unknown' to ten we shall still have a gross overestimate.

So, lost, at most, 31 ships (not 41), 10 pinnaces at most (not 20), 2 galleasses (not 3), 1 galley. Total, not more than 44 (not 65), probably five or six and perhaps a dozen less.

To balance this one should remember the sorry state of the ships that got back. Many of them had suffered so badly by English gunfire that they were unfit for future service.

The judgments of Howard and Medina Sidonia in this chapter are supported by the authority of J. A. Williamson, *The Age of Drake* (1938), pp. 304–34 passim. The quoted judgment of Howard is from T. Woodrooffe. *The Enterprise of England* (1958). Woodrooffe also speaks with justice of Medina Sidonia.

Until Williamson's correction, Medina Sidonia's reputation had suffered chiefly from the curious aberration about him of the first Spanish editor of Armada papers, Cesáreo Fernández Duro. Not entirely an ideal editor, Fernández Duro nevertheless produced an admirable and indispensable compilation, and supplied it with a commentary usually of great value. But in his discussion of the commander of the Armada he repeats baseless slanders, some of them quaintly enough of English origin, although they are completely refuted by the authentic documents he himself prints. Modern Spanish scholarship also tends to do greater justice to Medina Sidonia. See especially duque de Maura, *El designio de Felipe II*, which is based on the duke's private papers.

Chapter XXXII

Among the diplomats, mainly Dr Cavriana in Canestrini, *Négociations*, IV, 842–53

(Blois, December 24th and 31st) and Morosini (Vat. *Francia*, XXXVII, also 'Relazione di quel ch'è successo in Bles' in Francia II f° 153 ff.). Mendoza is briefer and vaguer.

Among the memoirists and chroniclers, mainly l'Estoile, d'Aubigné, De Thou and Palma Cayet; also documents in *Archives curieuses*, XII. Wilkinson lists a number of contemporary pamphlets about the murder of Guise, most of them in the *Bib. Nat.* and none of them very reliable.

Chapter XXXIII

Diplomats as above; historians as in notes to Chapter VII.

Chapter XXXIV

Mostly Nichols, Dasent and papers calendared in *C.S.P.D.* The most informative and best-balanced, if by no means the most readable, account of the attack on Lisbon and the subsequent progress of the war with Spain is still Edward P. Cheyney, *England from the defeat of the Armada to the death of Elizabeth*, 2 vols. (London, 1926).

And see A General Note on Sources.

PICTURE CREDITS